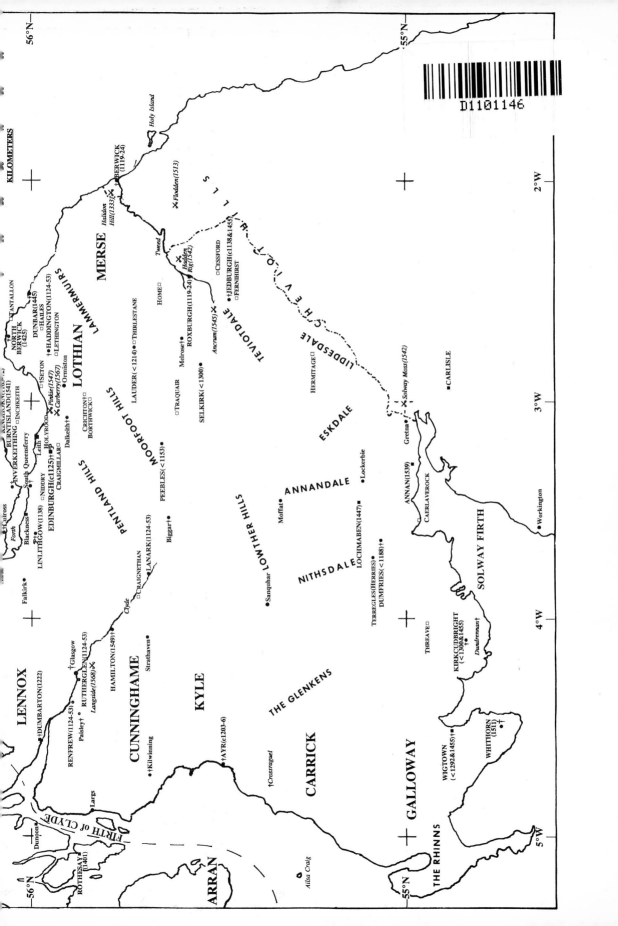

KILOMETERS

56°N

55°N

2°W

3°W

4°W

5°W

LENNOX

MERSE

LOTHIAN

LAMMERMUIRS

TEVIOTDALE

LIDDESDALE

C H E V I O T S

ESKDALE

ANNANDALE

NITHSDALE

MOORFOOT HILLS

PENTLAND HILLS

LOWTHER HILLS

THE GLENKENS

CUNNINGHAME

KYLE

CARRICK

GALLOWAY

THE RHINNS

ARRAN

FIRTH of CLYDE

SOLWAY FIRTH

Holy Island

BERWICK (1119-24)

Halidon Hill(1333)✕

✕Flodden(1513)

Tweed

HALES

✕Hadden Rig(1542)
ROXBURGH(1119-24)†

†JEDBURGH(c1138&1455)
□FERNHIRST

□CESSFORD

HOME□

✕Ancrum(1545)

□THIRLESTANE
LAUDER(<1214)●

Melrose†●
□TRAQUAIR

SELKIRK(<1300)●

HERMITAGE□

DUNBAR(1445)
NORTH BERWICK
TANTALLON
HADDINGTON(1124-53)
LETHINGTON
□SETON
Ormiston●
†Pinkie(1547)
✕Carberry(1567)
□DALKEITH†
CRICHTON□
BORTHWICK□

HOLYROOD
EDINBURGH(c1125)†
CRAIGMILLAR□
Leith●
NIDDRY□

INVERKEITHING
BURNTISLAND(1541)
INCHKEITH□
KINGHORN(...)
South Queensferry●

Kinross●

Falkirk●

Forth

Blackness●
LINLITHGOW(1138)†

PEEBLES(<1153)□

Biggar●

LANARK(1124-53)†
□CRAIGNETHAN

†DUMBARTON(1222)

†Glasgow
RUTHERGLEN(1124-53)
Langside(1568)✕
Paisley†●
RENFREW(1124-53)†

Strathaven●

HAMILTON(1549)†

●Kilwinning

†AYR(c1203-6)

†Crossraguel

Largs●

Dunoon●

ROTHESAY
(1401)†

Ailsa Craig◦

Sanquhar●

●Moffat

CARLISLE■

✕Solway Moss(1542)

Gretna●

ANNAN(1539)■
□CAERLAVEROCK

●Workington

●Lockerbie

LOCHMABEN(1447)■

TERREGLES(HERRIES)□
DUMFRIES(<1188)†●

THREAVE□

KIRKCUDBRIGHT
(<1300&1455)†■
Dundrennan†

WIGTOWN
(<1292&1455)†■

WHITHORN
(1511)†

MARIA Ř

MARY QUEEN OF SCOTS
The Crucial Years
By THE DUKE OF HAMILTON

Foreword by Professor Gordon Donaldson

MAINSTREAM
PUBLISHING

EDINBURGH AND LONDON

First published in Great Britain 1991 by
MAINSTREAM PUBLISHING COMPANY (EDINBURGH) LTD
7 Albany Street Edinburgh EH1 3UG

British Library Cataloguing in Publication Data

Hamilton, Duke of 1936–
    1. Scotland. Queens. Mary, Queen of Scots 1542–1587
    Maria R: Mary Queen of Scots – The Crucial Years
    I. Title
    941.105092

    ISBN 1-85158-363-7

Design by James Hutcheson, Wide Art, Edinburgh
Typeset in Palacio by Blackpool Typesetting Services Ltd, Blackpool
Printed in Great Britain by Butler and Tanner Ltd, Frome, Somerset

For Elly, Annie, Alex and Johnnie

There are three voices which cry

for eternal vengeance against England:

Joan of Arc from her funeral pyre;

Mary Stewart from her scaffold;

and Napoleon from his rock.

ALEXANDRE DUMAS, JEHANNE LA PUCELLE, 1842

Contents

Acknowledgments

SHORTLY BEFORE I FINISHED WRITING THIS BOOK, IT WAS SUGGESTED THAT some of the things I had written – especially about the English – might be thought immoderately provocative and annoying. After due reflection, I concluded that provoking and annoying the English is an honourable and in every way laudable exercise. Moreover, there is considerable historical precedent for it. It is also generally true that, for all their failings, the English have a more highly developed sense of the ridiculous, and a greater ability to laugh at themselves, than any other national group (even the Scots). So the book has not been watered down by any last minute 'out-takes', and appears exactly as written.

Now for those 'without whom this book would not have been possible': my thanks are due to Jillian Robertson, who suggested that I might write it; Eleo Carson, who persuaded me that I could; Professor Gordon Donaldson, who gave me confidence by saying, not only that I could, but that I should; and Professor Ken Cable, my co-author, recently retired Head of History at Sydney University who explained how to do so and – perhaps most important – what to leave out. Professor Cable's collaboration has been invaluable; an expert in European Reformation history, he wrote many of the biographical sketches, particularly those of ecclesiastical figures. He also correlated many of the events that occurred in Scotland with what was happening in England and on the Continent at the same time.

I am most grateful to the Rev. Charles Robertson, the minister of the Canongate for his advice on many Scottish religious figures of the period, especially John Knox. I should also like to express my gratitude to Nigel

Tranter and Marie Muir – both celebrated popular authors – for their guidance. I am also indebted to Dr Tony Goodwin and Kay Carmichael for putting me in touch with the Wellcome Institute for the History of Medicine and Lyndsay Wilson of the Institute for her assistance in helping me to try to identify the diseases and ailments suffered by various characters of the period.

I must also thank Dr Rosalind Marshall and Dr David Caldwell for contributing almost all the material in the appendices on Queen Mary's costume and jewellery and Scotland's military potential. I should also like to thank Elizabeth Steele, for her help with many of the biographies; Susan Rose-Smith, for carrying out invaluable research on the illustrations; the staff of the Scottish National Portrait Gallery, for their patient assistance in supplying many of them, and helping me to find others; and the staff of the Scottish Record Office for their invaluable help and advice. Thanks are also due to Edith Bouchard who, astutely recognising the fact that, although I can use a computer, I am almost totally incapable of typing, transferred a lot of the information I gathered directly on to disc.

Finally, another word of thanks to Professor Donaldson. He was kind enough to check the typescript before it went to the publishers. He made it clear that he saw his job as trying to help me avoid making any glaring historical mistakes, and that his assistance did not necessarily mean that he shared the views, political or otherwise. I am pleased to put this on record: the views are mine; the mistakes are mine, and I look forward to hearing about them, in case I ever have the opportunity to put them right; much of any credit that may emerge belongs to the people who helped me. I hope that I will be forgiven for not mentioning them all by name.

Angus Hamilton
January 1991

Foreword

'AGE CANNOT WITHER HER, NOR CUSTOM STALE HER INFINITE VARIETY.' IT IS very likely that the latter part of the phrase which Shakespeare put into the mouth of Enobarbus in *Antony and Cleopatra* would be true of Mary in the flesh, though as her life ended when she was only forty-four there was little time for age to wither her. However, in the years that have passed since her death the variety of writings about her has continued and there is no sign that the passage of time is doing anything to abridge interest in her. It is as apt now as it was ninety years ago to refer, as F. W. Maitland did, to 'the books that year by year men still are writing about Q. M. and her surroundings'.

Writers who have attempted to deal with the whole span of Mary's life, short as it was, have sometimes found themselves in a difficulty. Her life falls into two, if not three, parts – the Franco–Scottish (if they may be taken as one) of twenty-five years and the English of nineteen years. Not many writers have been able to maintain their interest all through and some have been little better than perfunctory in their treatment of that part of her life where they felt less at home. The Duke of Hamilton got round this difficulty by making no attempt to cover the whole of her life. He noted – which others no doubt had merely noticed and had dismissed – that what can be considered the two most critical years of her life began and ended on the same calendar day – 29 July: Mary's marriage to Darnley in 1565 and the coronation of her son and supplanter in 1567. His Grace concentrates on these two years and therefore produces a book of a novel type.

He has not discovered – who could discover? – any startling new facts among the crowded events which have so often been examined microscopically but he does bring something of a fresh approach.

Some people, learning that the premier peer of Scotland has written a book about Mary, and curious about its quality, may recall one of the most famous incidents in Mary's own life-story. When in 1564 Queen Elizabeth was torturing Sir James Melville by attempting to entice him into comparisons between her and Mary, and he was agonised between being polite to the woman before whom he stood and being loyal to his own queen, reference was made to Mary's playing upon the lute and virginals; Elizabeth (who was ready enough to display her own skill on the virginals) asked if Mary 'played well' and Melville's very guarded answer was 'reasonably for a queen'. So some may be tempted to say that this book has been written 'reasonably for a duke'.

But that would be less than fair, and the author himself makes no plea to be judged by other than professional standards. The fact that he is a duke has nothing to do with it; the fact that he is not a trained historian has much to do with it. Trained historians are apt to run if not quite in blinkers at any rate to some extent along rails of their own making or according to certain professional habits which impose constraints from which Angus Hamilton is quite free. He sees things that others have not seen and he is especially strong on characterisation; one feels that he is viewing his *dramatis personae* as men and women of flesh and blood and not as the embodiments of certain principles and policies. His estimates of personalities have a certain shrewdness and frankness.

There is no question of claiming that the author has a kind of 'private line' to the subject of his book. Yet he has very special reasons to be conscious of Queen Mary. His ancestor was her heir presumptive and for a time her regent; he is her descendant through Charles II; his apartments as hereditary keeper of the palace of Holyrood are immediately adjacent to 'Queen Mary's Apartments' (with which a private door communicates). His family home is Lennoxlove, which was once the home of Maitland of Lethington and which now houses the Hamilton collection of portraits and artefacts of Mary's time, including the famous Casket.

Angus Hamilton differs from most writers on Mary in not losing sight of the minor actors in the drama. In most books there are many men and women who make a brief appearance – perhaps worthy of no more than a passing mention – and then vanish without a word of their subsequent fortunes. Even some of Mary's many suitors – Austrian archdukes and Scandinavian kings – are little more than names. The Duke remedies this by compiling over a hundred biographical notes, for which many will bless him.

Gordon Donaldson
February 1991

PROLOGUE

The Scots

IN JUNE 1503, MARY QUEEN OF SCOTS' GRANDMOTHER, MARGARET TUDOR, LEFT London with her father, King Henry VII of England, on the long road north to Scotland. The king accompanied his thirteen-year-old daughter as far as Collieweston in Northamptonshire, on the first stage of her journey to marry James IV King of Scots. The marriage was designed to end centuries of warfare between the two nations and cement the 'Treaty of Perpetual Peace', sealed the previous year. 'Perpetuity' was to last just eleven years and end with the battle of Flodden.

A hundred years later, there was another royal journey – this time in the opposite direction. In May 1603, Queen Mary's son, James VI, King of Scots since 1567, left his wife and children (including his two-year-old second son, later to become Charles I) to continue their education in Scotland. He made a leisurely progress south with a huge entourage of his Scottish household and courtiers, was received by Sir Robert Cecil at Theobalds near Royston, and arrived in London as James I of England. He had succeeded to the Scottish throne at the age of thirteen months, when his mother was forced to abdicate, and was the first monarch to rule both countries. It had taken exactly a century for Henry VII's vision to become a reality. Scotland, having fought for its independence for so long, was on the way to becoming an English satellite.

The hundred years between the two journeys had been highly eventful. Scots and English had met in three major battles, all of which had been won by the English, and at least as many minor ones, mostly won by the Scots. It had been a time punctuated by feverish diplomatic activity with

Henry VII, *artist unknown,*
mid-16th century
(Lennoxlove)

periodic renewals of the 'Auld Alliance' between Scotland and France, which the English found alternately infuriating and alarming. It had also been the century of the Reformation which left the two countries irreversibly changed and the Protestant Church firmly installed in both. For more than half the period, the English scene had been dominated by the Cecils: Sir Robert, later Lord Salisbury, and his father William, later Lord Burghley. Sir Robert, the arch-courtier, had masterminded James's accession, sending him coded letters of subtle flattery while Queen Elizabeth was still alive, and arranging his journey south immediately after her death.

Union came because Henry VIII, despite all his matrimonial adventures and the frantic efforts of his three fertile wives, had not produced heirs who outlived those of Mary Queen of Scots. It was also a triumph of spinsterhood. Queen Elizabeth's cleverest conquest was gained by her steadfast refusal to take a husband, making the Union of the Crowns virtually inevitable on her death. One of the reasons for this may well have been that she suspected she was barren. At the very least, however, her determination not to put her fertility to the test made the succession of James VI a probability rather than a possibility.

After James went south, he was to return to the land of his birth only once in his remaining twenty-two years. Scotland lost its resident monarch for all time. There was nothing unusual, in this period of European history, for one person to rule more than one kingdom; other examples were: Castile and Aragon, France and Navarre from 1589, Spain and Portugal from 1580 and, perhaps best known, Denmark and Norway. The land of non-residence, however, tended to suffer from the ruler's absence. At the moment of James's accession to the English throne, the long sporadic process of the transfer of power from Edinburgh to London began. With the Act of Union of 1707, the Scottish Parliament disappeared, an example of the extinction of local assemblies that was taking place all over Europe. Since then, no significant body of Scotsmen, other than the General Assembly of the Church of Scotland, has deliberated in Scotland over Scottish affairs.

The Act of Union had two very different effects. It opened up the rapidly growing empire to full Scottish participation. Scots agreed with Dr Samuel Johnson (who had a Scottish biographer but was no respecter of the race) that their finest prospect was the highroad to England. They were better educated, more motivated and more able than most Englishmen. It is

Portrait of a Lady, *said to be Margaret Tudor, daughter of Henry VII, wife of James IV and grandmother of Queen Mary. Recent research, however, suggests that this may be Elizabeth of York, Henry VII's wife and therefore Margaret Tudor's mother (Lennoxlove)*

hard to imagine an English-born Moderator of the General Assembly of the Church of Scotland; yet Archibald Crawford Tait, Randall Thomas Davidson and Cosmo Gordon Lang were all Archbishops of Canterbury. Scotland, over the last century, has contributed Rosebery, Balfour, Campbell-Bannerman, Bonar Law (albeit a colonial Scot), Macdonald, Macmillan and Douglas-Home to the list of British prime ministers. Even in cricket (a game not usually associated with Scotland), three of England's captains have been Archie McLaren, Douglas Jardine and Mike Denness. Australia could have done without Jardine and his 'bodyline bowlers' but not without the Scottish contribution to local life. Three of the first six governors of New South Wales were Scots, including the best of them, the rugged 'man from Mull', Lachlan Macquarie. In every sphere of Australian activity (except for the convicts), Scotsmen have led the way. The same is true of Canada and New Zealand. In a real sense, the British Empire became a Scottish domain.

The long-term effect of the Union on the domestic affairs of Scotland was quite another matter. Despite the benefits of freedom of trade, Scotland became a backwater. It had a far higher rate of unemployment than England and was even referred to as 'North Britain' for postal and other official purposes for a time. To this day, Scotland shows signs of

17

neglect. A Scot, McAdam, invented the modern road; another, Thomson the inflatable tyre; a third, Bell, the telephone; and a fourth, Baird, television, but Scottish communications are substantially worse than those of England. James Watt, born in Scotland, devised the modern condensing steam engine but Scottish railways are generally fewer, certainly slower and often grubbier than their English counterparts. Despite the largely successful (although fatal) efforts of the Scot, Percy Pilcher, in the 1890s to build the world's first practical aeroplane, the airports, with the exception of Prestwick, are inferior to those in England and incapable of accepting the largest aircraft. There are even more suicides and fewer teeth per head of population than in any other part of the United Kingdom. It is not surprising that so many Scots have emigrated, to the advantage of themselves and their adopted countries, but to the detriment of their homeland.

Members of the present royal family are descended from Mary Queen of Scots and her son, James VI, and, probably to their relief, not from Henry VIII. Yet, except for the brief visit of George IV in 1822, no reigning monarch came north in almost two centuries after Charles II in 1651. Then, in 1841, Prince Albert persuaded Queen Victoria to take a greater interest in Scotland and, in due course, buy and rebuild Balmoral as her Highland residence. Victoria grew to love Scotland and was happier there than anywhere else, even publishing several volumes of her Scottish diaries, *Leaves from the Highlands*. So began the rebirth of the involvement of the reigning house with Scotland, which continues to the present day.

Queen Mary's great-grandfather, Henry VII of England, made a prophecy while he was arranging the marriage of his elder daughter, Margaret, to James IV. Those who were hostile to the marriage pointed out that were his sons, Arthur and Henry, to die without heirs, the descendants of Margaret, the Stewarts, would rule England. The king shrewdly replied:

> Supposing, which God forbid, that all my male progeny should become extinct and the Kingdom devolve by law to Margaret's heirs, will England be damaged thereby? For since it happens that the lesser becomes subservient to the greater, *the accession will be that of Scotland to England*, just as formerly happened to Normandy which devolved upon our ancestors in the same manner and was happily added to our Kingdom by hereditary right – as a rivulet to a fountain.

Henry's prophecy was fulfilled, almost exactly one hundred years after he made it, fifty years after the death of Edward VI, his last male descendant, and four hundred years after the loss of Normandy to the French king.

Scotland was to be distinctly subservient to England from the accession of James VI as James I of England. His mother's determination to gain the English crown, if not for herself at least for her descendants, was totally inflexible and a central feature of her rule in Scotland. By a strange coincidence, two of the events which led inexorably to the dual monarchy and ultimately to the Union took place on the same day of the same month – 29 July 1565 and 29 July 1567. Furthermore, the most dramatic events of Queen Mary's life, when she was 'content to hazard all rather than forego her right', occurred in the two years between these dates. The period central to this book begins with her marriage to Darnley, James's father, and ends with her enforced abdication and the coronation of the baby James in her place. The story is of two terrible years, two marriages, two murders and the miscarriage of twins. It is the story of the birth and coronation of the infant king who displaced his mother and grew up believing she had murdered his father. Finally it is a story of two queens, cousins who never met.

Mary's pursuit of the glittering throne of her Tudor ancestors led her down a path on which she lost the respect of others, her freedom, her crown, her health, her beauty and finally her life – everything except her dignity, her faith and her belief in the right of others to follow theirs.

CHAPTER 1

Entrance

MARY QUEEN OF SCOTS WAS A STEWART AND THE STEWARTS WERE AN unlucky line. Time and again since they had first gained the Scottish crown, in 1371, they had been unable to fulfil the most important duty of kingship and ensure that one adult male monarch duly succeeded another. In the 161 years immediately before the infant James VI's coronation, the average age at which a Scottish king came to the throne was six and a half. His life expectancy at birth was thirty-six years and one month and his probability of dying peacefully in bed – or anywhere else – was exactly zero.[1] Whatever the Stewarts' other successes as rulers – and these were, at times, impressive – they could not be relied upon to produce anything other than immature heirs. This necessitated a series of regencies, the severest and most exacting test for a royal house. The results were often disastrous.

It was not that the Stewarts lacked advantages. When they did reach adulthood, their fifteenth- and sixteenth-century members – from James I to James VI – turned out to be intelligent and able people. The crown that they wore commanded respect and was reinforced by a series of religious and national sanctions. The monarch was the head of the state and, in Catholic times, the first son (or daughter) of the church. He or she was enthroned with proper ceremonial and anointed with holy oil. The Blood Royal had a mystical quality that set its possessor apart from ordinary mortals. The monarch chose the high officers of state, summoned and dismissed parliament, appointed the judges, called up and commanded the army, granted franchises and charters and protected the church. The Scottish monarch was a ruler indeed, in authority little different from, and in no way inferior to, other kings and queens in Europe.

James I, *artist unknown, oil
on panel (National Galleries
of Scotland)*

In no sense was a king in Scotland absolute in his power, nor was any other king in Europe. The constraints were historical and practical – if the king had privileges, so did his subjects. A whole network of customary rights and jurisdictions had long existed, the products of an ordered and graded society. The king, although at the apex of a very complex social pyramid, lacked the practical props to enforce his power. Money was generally scarce; only the king of Spain, with the wealth of the Indies in his pocket, could afford a large permanent army and navy – and even the Spanish state was plagued by frequent bankruptcies. A professional civil service, its members stationed throughout the realm, reinforced by detailed information, was not to appear until very much later. If European kings did not yet have such advantages, Scotland was worse off still. It was remote and small – the population did not reach one million until the eighteenth century; it was primitive – in the sixteenth century practically nothing was exported other than skins, wool and fish. Thus the pressure was greater on the Scottish ruler, as was the requirement for special personal qualities and a commanding physical presence. The monarch in Scotland was the leader of a team rather than the head of an institution. His job was to effect a balance between the competing sections of the nation, which were numerous, since Scotland was in no sense a unified country.

In the north and west, the Highlanders were a law unto themselves, at odds with one another as well as their neighbours. Later – much later – they were to gain renown and respect as wild, kilted warriors, fighting for the British Empire; in the sixteenth century, theirs was a primitive, xenophobic existence, their culture and political fabric still relatively undisturbed by external influences. A few clan chiefs had been ennobled by the crown, but there was little reciprocity by way of an increase in royal influence in the chief's domain. A prudent ruler left the Highlands alone.

In the far south, an artificial line separated the Borderers of Scotland and England. It had little influence on the vigorous practice of border raiding which both Scottish and English governments tried to ignore. There were fierce fighting men in these rugged uplands, ready to follow their leaders in any wider conflict.

The central belt of Scotland, and its extension up the east coast, was where the main national events took place. Here were the principal towns. By English standards, they were small; only Edinburgh, the

James II, *artist unknown, oil on panel (National Galleries of Scotland)*

capital, was of much consequence. They were, however, often fortified and had strategic significance; they possessed a degree of self-government and a certain amount of economic prosperity.

Scottish society was based on agriculture. The bulk of the population worked the land. The real economic power lay with the landlords whose control was all-pervasive. While there were numerous small lairds (the gentry), they were overshadowed by the nobility who were generally dignified by the titles of 'Earl' and 'Baron'. Possessed of military power and, by Scottish standards, wealth, the nobles formed a small group of inter-related families. Their weakness lay in their inability to unite, or even to refrain from constant feuding. Armed strife was a constant factor. The crown could do little to suppress it; nor, considering its own weakness, was it in its interest to do so.

The nobility stood for division and disturbance. Traditionally the pillar of peace and stability was the Catholic Church, of which Scotland was a province, its hierarchy headed by the Archbishop of St Andrews. The church was extremely wealthy; it was said to pay half of all the taxation levied in Scotland. It could, however, afford to do so; at the time of Queen Mary, its annual revenue was of the order of £400,000 per year, whereas the annual income of the crown was never more than £20,000. The poverty and turbulence of the Scottish kingdom naturally affected

JACOBVS·3·D·GRATIA
REX·SOTORVM

James III, *artist unknown,
oil on panel (National
Galleries of Scotland)*

the church but, on the other hand, enhanced the uniqueness of its position. The church not only held the keys to salvation but was the repository of culture and education and Scotland's principal link with the international world of Christendom.

In the High Middle Ages, church and state in the west had been at odds over the problem of authority and appointments. How great was the Pope's power over secular rulers to be? How much say was he to have in choosing religious officials? By early in the sixteenth century both questions had been answered. The Pope's spiritual primacy was asserted and, although James IV died excommunicated, the Pope was usually the political ally rather than the overlord of the kings. They, in turn, had strengthened their practical hold over the appointment of bishops, abbots and other senior clerics. For hard-pressed European monarchs, this was a distinct advantage. Churchmen were able, well educated and disposed to give loyal service. Often of humble origin and, of course, unable to found families, they usually drew substantial incomes from their benefices. It was, therefore, not at all uncommon to find ecclesiastics serving as ambassadors and ministers of the crown. Their dioceses and abbeys did not benefit from their long absences on royal business, but the kings gained much. The Scottish kings were somewhat less fortunate. They made good use of religious 'civil servants' but these were often men from high society. The nobles, as well as the crown, had gained entry to church appointments in the sense that the nobility received most of the best places. Ironically, James V encouraged this, by making almost all of his bastard sons commendators, abbots or priors. In 1547, during Queen Mary's infancy, John Hamilton, illegitimate half-brother of Regent Arran, became Archbishop of St Andrews; another half-brother, James, was provided to the see of Argyll six years later. In 1551, one of Arran's sons, John, became

Commendator of Arbroath, and in 1553 another, Claud, Abbot of Paisley. Such men could not be expected to give the monarch the unstinting loyalty that was rendered by churchmen of humbler origins. The Scottish crown could not rely without question on the church.

James IV, *artist unknown, oil on panel (National Galleries of Scotland)*

A kingdom which made the life of its king so difficult was unlikely to be strong. Weakness could prompt the attention of neighbours. In the case of Scotland, this meant England and France. Their interference was a constant factor in Scottish affairs although it was not the result of any intrinsic Anglo-French concern for Scotland. England had long abandoned any intention of a Scottish conquest and most Frenchmen knew little of Scotland. But the northern kingdom held the key to the defence of England; as such, it was crucial in the perennial rivalry between England and France. The English could brook no threat from across the border; the French were trying to create one. Scotland and its monarchy were presented with the choice of allies and enemies. On the whole they preferred France, thereby perpetuating the 'Auld Alliance' and important cultural links with the continent.

At the beginning of the sixteenth century James IV was King of Scots. It was a time when monarchy in western Europe was displaying itself with new power and splendour. Charles V, the Holy Roman Emperor and King of Spain (1516), François I of France (1515) and Henry VIII of England (1509), were making their appearance as rulers of a new kind, different from their medieval predecessors. Their grandeur was undoubted, the substance of their authority perhaps less so. But it was far more than a king in Scotland, where local and family loyalties were intense and purses shallow, could emulate. By Scottish standards, however, James was a prosperous and effective ruler, building up authority and resources at the nobles' expense, increasing the revenue from crown lands and making ample use of the church's wealth. A marriage alliance with

25

James V, *artist unknown*
(National Galleries of
Scotland)

Margaret, daughter of Henry VII, and his traditional friendship with France seemed to bolster his position. But his allies went to war with each other. James sided with the French against his brother-in-law, and met defeat and death at the hands of the English at Flodden in 1513. His son and heir, James V, was an infant. Minorities were not good for the nation; they were worse for the monarchy.

Scotland was ruled by Margaret, the Queen Dowager, then by the Francophile Duke of Albany, and finally by the pro-English faction of Margaret again with her second husband, the sixth Earl of Angus, in an uneasy coalition with the first Earl of Arran. Entanglements with European power politics and disputes among the governing group weakened the royal power built up by James IV. Finally, in 1528, James V took up the reins of government. The new king, moody and erratic but intelligent and vigorous, endeavoured to restore royal authority. With large grants extorted from the church, he set up the College of Justice (finally ratified in 1541) to aid efficient central administration. Shows of force and selective ruthlessness pacified, at least temporarily, the turbulent Highlands and Borders. The Auld Alliance was confirmed by James's marriages to Madeleine, daughter of François I and, on her early death, to Mary, daughter of the Duke of Guise. But James's French connections inevitably aroused English hostility. In 1542, the English defeated the half-hearted Scots at Solway Moss. James suffered a nervous collapse and died six days after the birth of his daughter, Mary. Referring to the Stewart dynasty, his last words were: '. . . it came with a lass, it will pass with a lass'. Although his prediction came true, he could never have imagined that it would not 'pass with a lass', until the death of Queen Anne, 172 years later.

Once more a minority, once more a contest between England and France for dominance in Scotland. At first, the English were uppermost through the efforts of the realm's governor and regent, James Hamilton, second Earl of Arran – he was the little queen's cousin and, despite some doubts about his legitimacy, heir presumptive. Soon, however, yet again, England became the enemy. The Scots were defeated at Pinkie in 1547, amid much destruction of towns and countryside. French help was sought to eject the English, in return for which, in 1548, the infant Mary was sent to France, to be betrothed to François the Dauphin. Arran was created Duke of Châtelherault and finally replaced as regent by Mary of Guise in 1554. The French triumph seemed complete.

Royal minorities, the shifting loyalties of noble factions, Anglo-French rivalry, English invasions and French troops – it was a monotonous litany. But now a totally new element was to intrude as a divisive force, historically the most powerful of all movements – religion.

The Reformation had come slowly to Scotland. Despite the admitted weakness, even the corruption, of the Catholic Church, the Lutheran movement made only a limited impact. James V criticised the churchmen but made full use of the church for his own purposes. After his death, Protestant feeling quickened. George Wishart was burned for heresy, Cardinal Beaton was assassinated and some Reformed leaders, including John Knox, suffered exile. This spell in England and on the continent, particularly in Geneva, gave Knox and a number of the other Reformed leaders a chance to absorb the clearly articulated doctrines of Calvinism. It was no less important that England began to assume a new role in Scottish affairs. Having long ago broken with Rome, England was Protestant under the boy king, Edward VI, who in infancy had been thought of as a husband for Mary. As far as Scotland was concerned, England was now the champion of the new religion, standing for something positive. Politics, foreign relations and religion were inseparable, for the French connection now meant the continuation of Catholic supremacy.

The role of Mary of Guise, Queen Dowager and Regent, meant a degree of French dominance which became more intense as the years passed. Yet her religious policy was mild. England had become officially Catholic once more under Mary Tudor (1553–58) and, though anti-French, posed no religious threat to Scotland. Leniency, however, encouraged the Protestants, who were growing more restive as French influence increased. Meanwhile, Archbishop Hamilton's attempts to reform and popularise the Catholic Church met with little success. Finally, in 1557,

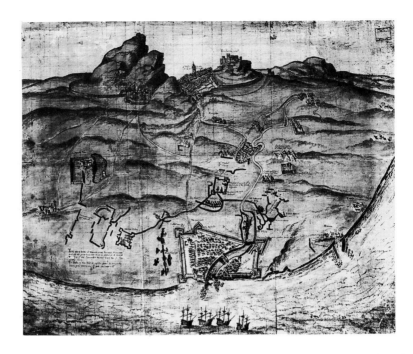

Siege of Leith,
(Lord Egremont)

some Protestant nobles, 'the Congregation of Christ', formed a band (a bond or covenant) to promote the pure Gospel and the Protestant faith. A distinct new church was being formed.

The work of the Congregation at home anticipated only briefly some momentous changes abroad. The Protestant Elizabeth succeeded her Catholic half-sister on the English throne. Mary Queen of Scots, nurtured in France, married the king's heir, François, and they promptly assumed the titles of King and Queen of England, holding that Elizabeth was illegitimate and that Mary, Margaret Tudor's grand-daughter, was the true heir. Aware of these movements and heartened by an aggressive Catholicism in France, Mary of Guise began to repress Scotland's Protestants. Anti-French feeling and Protestant fears saw a vigorous response among local Reformed churchmen. Enormously strengthened by the return of John Knox, they began to attack Catholic foundations. The nobles of the Congregation gathered an army to harry Mary of Guise's French occupation force. By 1559, there was civil war – Protestant against Catholic, pro-English against pro-French, the Congregation against the Regent. Back in France, Henri II died, leaving François and Mary to reign in Paris.

Wars of religion were by no means uncommon in the Europe of the time. They were soon to break out in the Netherlands and in France itself. In Scotland there seemed little chance of a Protestant victory, despite a growing popular feeling for the new cause. The Queen Dowager's army of French professional soldiers, reinforced by ships, was too strong to be driven out. The only hope of success for Protestant Scotland was in military and naval help from Protestant England. Elizabeth, ever cautious, was reluctant to intervene. But she had no real choice in the matter. The assumption by Mary and François of the English royal title was frightening; the Reformation in England needed a friendly neighbour. So an English army and navy (whose commanders were told to act on their own, not on the queen's, authority) entered Scotland and, aided by the convenient death of the Queen Dowager, prevailed. The Treaty of Edinburgh between England and France (the Scots were not officially a party to it) secured the withdrawal of the French and their recognition of Elizabeth as Queen of England. Religion was to be settled by local agreement. The result was a partial Protestant triumph. A parliament of somewhat dubious legality proceeded to abolish the Pope's jurisdiction and the celebration of the Mass; a Protestant Confession of Faith was sanctioned, a document which owed much to Calvin. But parliament did not endorse the first Book of Discipline, which dealt with the ecclesiastical structure and revenues of the Protestant religion. Thus, while the Reformed Church gained official recognition, the old institutions remained intact and retained most of their endowments. Meanwhile, across the sea in Paris, Queen Mary endorsed neither the treaty nor the proceedings of parliament.

In Edinburgh, there was a political vacuum. The Queen Dowager was dead and there was no local successor; the lawful queen was in France as consort to the king of that country. Scotland was run by a triumvirate of Congregation sympathisers: the Earl of Arran (now Duke of Châtelherault), Lord James Stewart (later Earl of Moray), half-brother to the queen, and the wily Maitland of Lethington, shrewdest of the three and the best administrator. Then, in December 1560, François II died. Unwilling to remain in France under the thumb of her powerful mother-in-law, Catherine de Medici, Mary, the eighteen-year-old widow, decided to return to her native land. For the first time since 1542, Scotland was to have an adult monarch in residence.

Henry VII, *M. Sittow, 1505*
(National Portrait Gallery)

Edward VI, *after Hans Holbein, c. 1542*
(National Portrait Gallery)

Queen Mary Tudor, *Gerlach Flicke,*
oil on panel, c. 1555 (Dean and Chapter
of Durham Cathedral)

Mary reached Edinburgh in August 1561, to rule Scotland and to press her claim either to the English throne or, at least, to be Elizabeth's successor. The Scots were doubtful about their new queen. While they had no objection to her ambitions for England many disliked her Catholicism and distrusted her French upbringing. Elizabeth, who always reacted violently to any talk about the succession, was deeply suspicious both of Mary's royal claims and of a possible weakening of England's hard-won influence in Edinburgh. In the short term, however, neither Scotland nor England had much to fear.

Mary's first years as Queen Regnant of Scotland were marked by moderation. She was eager to please and the charm of her manner was quite disarming. Even the dour John Knox, given to strident sermons against the court, could not resist her fascination and was greatly fearful of its effect on others. While not endorsing parliament's proceedings in the matter of religion, Mary issued her own proclamations against the Mass and even sanctioned financial aid to Protestant ministers. She maintained her faith and Catholic worship in her chapel but put Archbishop Hamilton into custody. The Reformation made rapid progress, unhindered by the widespread persecution that had marked its course in England under Mary Tudor. There was no return to an alliance with France, where civil war was weakening the country's international standing. Mary kept an open court and won over many of her suspicious nobles. These were good years.

There still remained two major questions: Mary's claim to the English throne and her marriage. The two were connected. Elizabeth did not wish her cousin to marry a powerful foreign prince[2] (although there were several ready to enter the lists) lest Mary's pretensions be bolstered. But long negotiations between the emissaries of the two sovereigns failed to reach a settlement; Mary's desire to be acknowledged as next in the English succession, at least until Elizabeth produced an heir, was not to be fulfilled. One possible husband was Don Carlos, son of Philip II of Spain. To Elizabeth's relief, and probably Scotland's as well, this came to nothing but it prompted a search nearer home. Elizabeth, to the general surprise and widespread disgust of the Scots, suggested her own favourite, Lord Robert Dudley (later Earl of Leicester). That Dudley was popularly believed to have murdered his wife, did nothing to enhance his cause – although it added to the stock of historical ironies, when later events are considered. Mary would have none of it, although it took a long time for the diplomatic comedy to play itself out. But she did proceed to make a kind of English match, one that avoided all international entanglements. Randolph, the English envoy, got wind of it when he told Cecil, Elizabeth's minister, that Mary would 'let fall her anchor between Dover and Berwick, though not in that port, haven or road that you wish she should'.

The royal anchor finally fell upon her cousin, Henry Stewart, Lord Darnley, the English-born son of the Earl of Lennox. Lennox, long exiled from Scotland, was invited to Edinburgh late in 1564. Darnley followed in February 1565. Events then moved quickly, ending in the arrangement of a marriage between Mary and Darnley. To the queen it was a sensible, as well as a deeply desired, step; the fitting climax to her time of prudent and popular rule. The widowed queen would have a husband, as everyone thought natural and fitting; hopefully there would be an heir for Scotland's throne and, since Darnley too had Tudor blood, the claim for that of England would be enhanced. What better move could Mary have made? As events were to show, what worse?

1. The following tables show contrasting comparative figures for Scottish monarchs and their English counterparts over the period between the accession of James I and that of James VI. It is noteworthy that the English monarchs had a two in three chance of dying peacefully.

Interestingly, despite being less likely to die violently, English monarchs could not anticipate living much longer than their Scottish counterparts. Nor, as the table indicates, could they expect to reign as long – ten English kings and queens ruled over the same period as did Mary Queen of Scots and the five Jameses who preceded her. Two of them ruled twice each, leading to twelve reigns in all. English monarchs were also just as likely as Scottish ones to have their reigns terminated by force, whether in battle, by imprisonment or murder. Over the period, there were five depositions with kings ending up in the Tower of London, or killed, or both. Four Scottish kings died by violence over the same period.

English monarchs, however, were as often as not succeeded by their brothers or cousins (or occasionally uncles) rather than their eldest surviving sons. This was in marked contrast to Scottish kings and queens. During the Stewart dynasty, there was a continuous line of succession from monarch to son (or daughter) from Robert II (succeeded 1371) to Charles II (1649). This was the root of Scotland's problems and is illustrated by the figures for age of succession. During the 161 years under examination Scotland was ruled by monarchs who were less than 21 years old for nearly 83 (51.3%) of them, whereas during the same period, England was ruled by a minor for only 29½ years (18.3%). If the age of majority is taken as being 12 rather than 21 the comparative figures are only marginally better (19.8% against 8.7%) and, if the period considered is extended to cover the 297 years between the accession of Robert the Bruce (1306) and the Union of the Crowns (1603), the picture for Scotland becomes even worse. No matter how the figures are cast, the conclusion always emerges that Scotland experienced royal minorities for about two and a half times as long as England.

SCOTTISH MONARCHS from JAMES I to JAMES VI

	DATE of BIRTH	DATE of SUCCESSION	DATE of DEATH	AGE at SUCCESSION	AGE at DEATH
JAMES I	1 Aug 1394	4 Apr 1406	20 Feb 1437	11 yrs 6 mths	42 yrs 6 mths
JAMES II	16 Oct 1430	21 Feb 1437	3 Aug 1460	6 yrs 4 mths	29 yrs 9 mths
JAMES III	10 Jul 1451	3 Aug 1460	11 Jun 1488	9 yrs 0 mths	36 yrs 11 mths
JAMES IV	17 Mar 1473	11 Jun 1488	9 Sep 1513	15 yrs 2 mths	40 yrs 5 mths
JAMES V	10 Apr 1512	9 Sep 1513	14 Dec 1542	1 yr 4 mths	30 yrs 8 mths
MARY	8 Dec 1542	14 Dec 1542	8 Feb 1587	6 days	44 yrs 2 mths
JAMES VI	19 Jun 1566	26 Jul 1567	27 Mar 1625	1 yr 1 mth	58 yrs 9 mths
AVERAGE between 1406 & 1567				6 years 6 months	36 years 1 month

ENGLISH MONARCHS from HENRY V to ELIZABETH

	DATE of BIRTH	DATE of SUCCESSION	DATE of DEATH	AGE at SUCCESSION	AGE at DEATH
HENRY V	9 Aug 1387	21 Mar 1413	31 Aug 1422	25 yrs 7 mths	35 yrs 0 mths
HENRY VI	6 Dec 1421	31 Aug 1422		0 yrs 8 mths	
EDWARD IV	28 Apr 1441	4 Mar 1461		19 yrs 10 mths	
HENRY VI		9 Oct 1470	4 May 1471	48 yrs 10 mths	49 yrs 4 mths
EDWARD IV		4 May 1471	9 Apr 1483	30 yrs 0 mths	41 yrs 11 mths
EDWARD V	2 Nov 1470	9 Apr 1483	23 Jun 1483?	12 yrs 5 mths	12 yrs 7 mths
RICHARD III	21 Oct 1450	23 Jun 1483	22 Aug 1485	32 yrs 8 mths	34 yrs 10 mths
HENRY VII	26 Jul 1455	22 Aug 1485	22 Apr 1509	30 yrs 0 mths	53 yrs 8 mths
HENRY VIII	28 Jun 1491	22 Apr 1509	28 Jan 1547	17 yrs 8 mths	55 yrs 7 mths
EDWARD VI	12 Oct 1537	28 Jan 1547	6 Jul 1553	9 yrs 3 mths	15 yrs 8 mths
MARY	18 Feb 1516	6 Jul 1553	17 Nov 1558	37 yrs 4 mths	42 yrs 8 mths
ELIZABETH	7 Sep 1533	17 Nov 1558	24 Mar 1603	25 yrs 2 mths	69 yrs 6 mths
AVERAGE between 1406 & 1567				24 years 1 month	37 years 11 months

2. In the table of most (but not all) of the prominent men who considered marrying Mary, during the period between her return from France and her marriage to Darnley, and those that she considered in that role, it can be seen at a glance that they do not represent the glittering array of handsome princes that many people imagine. With the benefit of hindsight, the most sensible choice would appear to have been Frederik of Denmark whose daughter, Anne, eventually

married Mary's son, James. The worst criticism that contemporary chroniclers levelled at him was that 'his drinking habits were those of his time', and he seems to have been one of the few on the list who was faithful to his wife, after he eventually chose one in 1572.

It is an interesting (if futile) intellectual exercise to speculate what might have happened if Mary had married Frederik. In 1563, Denmark-Norway embarked on the Nordic seven years war against Sweden, whose king was Frederik's cousin Erik XIV. This may have been one of the reasons why Mary does not appear to have considered either monarch for very long. Frederik won the war but was unsuccessful in realising his dream of uniting his kingdom with Sweden, which at that time included Finland and large areas around the Baltic, of what are now Lithuania, Latvia, Estonia, Poland and Germany. If Frederik had realised his aims with Scottish help, Mary and he would have ruled over a very substantial empire indeed.

QUEEN MARY'S SUITORS 1561–1565

JAMES HAMILTON, 3rd EARL of ARRAN	about 5 years older	Mad and getting madder
LORD JOHN HAMILTON, later 1st MARQUESS of HAMILTON	about 2 years older	Amiable, unambitious and indolent
LORD CLAUD HAMILTON, later 1st BARON PAISLEY	about 1 year younger	Devious and self-seeking, considered fratricide
SIR JOHN GORDON	about 5 years older	Homicidal criminal, already married
ROBERT DUDLEY, 1st EARL of LEICESTER	about 10 years older	Suspected uxoricide, the 'shop-soiled widower'
DON CARLOS, CROWN PRINCE of SPAIN	3 years younger	Hunchbacked, gluttonous, sadistic, megalomaniac, considered parricide
CHARLES IX, KING of FRANCE	8 years younger	Deranged, sickly, and indecisive
ANTOINE, KING of NAVARRE	24 years older	'*Faible et irrésolu*', already married
LOUIS de BOURBON, 1st PRINCE of CONDÉ	12 years older	Courageous, hunchbacked, licentious, already married
ERIK XIV, KING of SWEDEN	9 years older	Homicidally mad, personally murdered Nils Sture
JOHAN, DUKE of FINLAND, later JOHAN III, KING of SWEDEN	5 years older	Amiable but irresolute, sought unsuccessfully to mediate between Catholics and Protestants
FREDERIK II, KING OF DENMARK and NORWAY	8 years older	Sympathetic, winner of the Nordic seven-year war
CHARLES, ARCHDUKE of AUSTRIA	2 years older	Ruler of Styria, Carinthia, Carniola, Gorizia, Trieste and Eastern Istria
FERDINAND, ARCHDUKE of AUSTRIA	13 years older	Ruler of Tyrol and Swabia, already married

CHAPTER 2

'The lustiest and best-proportioned long man'

THE MARRIAGE OF MARY QUEEN OF SCOTS AND HENRY LORD DARNLEY WAS A triumph of dynastic diplomacy, bringing together the strands of family relationships. A web was woven covering the claim of Mary, and her Stewart descendants, to the throne of England. Both bride and groom were great-grandchildren of Henry VII through his daughter, Margaret Tudor. Darnley was also descended through his father, from James II. Both were therefore descended from Henry VII *and* James II. Scotland seemed set to provide the next King or Queen of England, so long as Elizabeth, the last of the Tudor line, did not produce an heir.

The principal architect of the marriage had been Darnley's mother, Margaret, Countess of Lennox, herself a granddaughter of Henry VII. She had been determined that her eldest son should marry Mary, the only surviving legitimate child of her half-brother James V. It seemed hopeless when the young queen married the Dauphin, but she still sent Henry to the French court just after their coronation. Eighteen months later, after François's death, more hopefully, she sent him again. There is no evidence, however, that Mary, whose attention was by then being directed towards Don Carlos of Spain, took any notice of the tall pale youth until long after her return to Scotland.

They next met at Wemyss Castle in Fife, two days after St Valentine's day 1565, shortly after Darnley's arrival from England. She was twenty-two and he was nineteen. Matters progressed with speed. On 15 May, Darnley was created Earl of Ross and something akin to betrothal (in those days, a binding agreement) may have taken place. Two months

THES BE THE SONES OF TH RIGHT HONERABLES TERLE OF LENOXE AD
TE LADY MARGARETZ GRACE COVNTYES OF LENOXE AD ARGWYSE.

1563

CHARLLES STEWARDE
HIS BROTHER. ÆTATIS. 6,

HENRY STEWARDE LORD DAR̄
LEY AND DOWGLAS. ÆTATIS. 17,

Henry Darnley, second husband of Queen Mary, with his younger brother Charles, later Earl of Lennox, in the great hall of their home, Temple Newsam in Yorkshire, *Hans Eworth (Reproduced by Gracious permission of Her Majesty the Queen)* later, Darnley became Duke of Albany and the banns of marriage were called. A week afterwards, Darnley was made King of Scots (subject to certain limitations and with dubious legality) and the following day the wedding took place. This easy process, whereby the prospective bridegroom stepped up in rank as he stepped towards his bride, masked a host of complications, local and international – of such stuff was Scottish politics made.

The announcement of Darnley as king at the instructions of Mary, who had not first consulted parliament, caused considerable resentment. The title was ostentatiously broadcast by heralds at the Mercat Cross, the centre of Edinburgh, where proclamations were made and punishments were meted out – everything from ear-nailing, branding and nose-pinching to tongue-boring and even death. Whatever the enthusiasm of Lady Lennox and the happy couple, there were many to whom the marriage was anathema. Foremost, and by far the most formidable, was Queen Elizabeth who was in no way reconciled to the prospect of being succeeded by anyone at all, let alone the Catholic Mary. For the Queen of Scots to wed Darnley was a threat indeed. As a son of the exiled Lennox, he had been born in England, a circumstance held by some authorities to strengthen his claim to the English throne. On the other hand, a statute of Henry VIII's time made it treasonable for any English subject of the Blood Royal to marry without the monarch's permission, strengthening Elizabeth's hold on him. Of immediate concern to Elizabeth was the threat that the marriage posed to England's hard-won position in Scotland. It was far from certain that the Protestant interest and the influence of Mary's existing advisers would remain. Elizabeth had every reason to deplore the union of Mary and Darnley, as she was to make abundantly clear.

Elizabeth had permitted Darnley and Lennox to leave England and travel to Scotland on English passports. Then, a month before the wedding, she changed her mind. She threw the Countess of Lennox into the Tower of London. She followed up this not unexpected action (many people, including some of her own relations, were in the Tower on numerous occasions) by sending an emissary to Edinburgh to demand the repatriation of Lennox and Darnley – their passports had expired. Of course, nothing happened. The travellers had much to gain by staying in Scotland and little, except a spell in prison alongside Lady Lennox, by a return to London. It was certainly worth gaining Mary's hand at the expense of Elizabeth's enmity.

37

Lennox had not come north to any safe haven. He was perhaps the most hated man in Scotland. In 1545, he had decided to reinforce his dynastic position by securing the hand in marriage of Henry VIII's niece, Lady Margaret Douglas. In order to obtain the king's permission, he had offered his services to England at the start of the 'Rough Wooing'. The Scottish parliament had declared him a traitor the same year. Two years later, on the eve of the battle of Pinkie, he joined the English invaders in the sacking of Annan in Dumfriesshire. He forced some Scottish horsemen into his ranks by holding their children hostage. When there were desertions, Lennox ordered some of the children to be hanged. The incident had not been forgotten. From then until his return in September 1564, Lennox had not set foot in Scotland.

In another sense the wedding was a Lennox triumph. His eldest son was to wed the child whom he himself had once planned to marry. For on the death of Mary's father, James V, in 1542, Lennox had been one of those who courted the widowed queen, Mary of Guise. She, to obtain his support, had offered him her baby daughter, the new queen, as a future wife. Lennox had accepted but then changed his mind and went to England in pursuit of Lady Margaret Douglas and dishonour. Now back in Edinburgh, he was more influential than ever – and even more unpopular.

Some of the unpopularity was dynastic. The Hamiltons hated him because the two families, both descended from James II, were rivals for the succession to the throne were the Royal Stewarts to die out. James Hamilton, Earl of Arran and Duke of Châtelherault in the peerage of France, was Lennox's mortal enemy. James Stewart, Earl of Moray, was of a somewhat different order. While he had the strongest ancestral reasons for hating Lennox, he was moved against him rather by political threat. As illegitimate half-brother to the queen and her principal adviser, he stood to lose his whole influence by the dominance at court of the Lennox faction. With Moray went the wise and devious Maitland of Lethington, ablest of Mary's counsellors. These three men were only the most prominent of a host of people who, for reasons both personal and political, had no reason to welcome Lennox's return and stayed away from the wedding.

Another absentee was the dashing bachelor, James Hepburn, fourth Earl of Bothwell, aged just over thirty. An adventurous man of action who belonged to a powerful old Border family with strong links with the

Stewarts, he was also sophisticated and much travelled. He had met Mary during her thirteen years in France, had been a loyal supporter of her mother and was in the fleet in which Mary sailed from France to Scotland four years earlier. Bothwell's father, Patrick, had courted Mary's mother at the same time as Lennox, and his grandfather, Adam, the second Earl, had stood proxy for James IV at the betrothal ceremony to Margaret Tudor. Adam's illegiti-

James Hepburn, 4th Earl of Bothwell, *miniature, artist unknown, c. 1566 (National Galleries of Scotland)*

mate and reprobate first cousin, another Patrick, had succeeded his uncle John Hepburn as Prior of St Andrews in 1525 and in 1538 became Bishop of Moray, dying in 1573 having had nine illegitimate children – as he claimed 'all by other men's wives'. It was at the bishop's hands that young James Hepburn received much of his training. James had lost favour with Mary after her return from France. Persuaded by Moray, who wanted all competition out of the way, she had him imprisoned in Edinburgh Castle after the discovery of a plot to abduct her. He had, however, made an enterprising escape and was now in Paris. Mary, realising that she needed Bothwell's abilities even more, now that she had lost the advice of Maitland and Moray, had a week earlier sent an emissary to France to recall him. As yet, he had not returned.

Moray, Maitland and Châtelherault were resolved to boycott the wedding ceremony, while others, only a little less hostile, attended with grave reservations. To make matters worse, it was of concern to many of them that the marriage would be celebrated according to the traditional rite. Many of the guests were recent converts to Protestantism and saw in the retention of the Catholic form an affirmation of Mary's religious preference and policy. Darnley himself was ambivalent enough – his life at the English court had taught him to dissemble, if nothing else. Religious doubts would, therefore, be much in evidence at the wedding. Curiously enough they were deepened by Rome itself. As Mary and Darnley were cousins, Catholic canon law required them to obtain a papal dispensation from 'the barrier of matrimony within the prohibited degrees'. The

Holyrood Palace, *c.* 1560
drawing by David Simon

dispensation was duly applied for, in the confident expectation that it would be granted. It would be a slow process, since the return trip to Rome took more than two months and the Vatican Chancery was notorious for its delays. Mary, however, fearful of the growing opposition, especially from Elizabeth, put the wedding date forward as far as possible. She thus further reduced the time for the journey and for the dispensation to be promulgated in Scotland. To Protestants, it was of little consequence as they denied that the Pope had any ecclesiastical authority in Scotland. To Catholics it was a matter better forgotten. But the irregularity was there, a constant reminder that the marriage of Mary and Darnley was fraught with religious problems. Few weddings were brought about in less propitious circumstances.

So began the fifth Scottish royal wedding of the century. With the exception of James IV's marriage to Margaret Tudor, no marriage had lasted more than three years and, apart from Mary, all the earlier participants were now dead. The one immediately previous had been that of Mary when only fifteen to the even younger Dauphin of France at Nôtre Dame. The one before that had been of Mary's father, James V, and her French mother, Mary of Guise, in 1540. Before that, in 1537, James married the daughter of the French king, Madeleine, who succumbed to the Scottish climate after only six weeks in the country in June of that year. In 1503, James IV had married Margaret Tudor, daughter of Henry VII and sister of Henry VIII.

None of these royal marriages had produced sufficient children to guarantee the future of the Stewart dynasty, nor indeed had any in the previous century. So thin had the Scottish royal line become that there had been an heir apparent to the throne for only six days out of the last fifty years and for only thirty-two years out of the previous hundred. James II succeeded at the age of six, James III at eight, James IV at fifteen, James V at one and Mary at just one week. The omens were not good.

* * *

The wedding took place early on the morning of Sunday, 29 July 1565. Despite the season, the weather was cold; winter had been dreadful and now the summer was little better. The sun was up as Mary made her way from her room on the second floor of Holyrood Palace, downstairs to her private chapel with its stained glass windows and the royal coat of arms.

She wore a black mourning gown, her hair completely covered by a black hood. In this sombre garb – a wedding dress reminiscent of widow's weeds – she was escorted by Lennox, her future father-in-law, and the Earl of Atholl, with footmen following in scarlet and yellow liveries.

At nearly six foot, the twenty-two-year-old widow who was about to become a bride was taller than the men beside her. She was finely built, with a clear white skin and a fresh, healthy complexion. Much given to outdoor exercise, she would often hold audiences in the garden, striding up and down with her visitors beside her. Her lips were too thin, her nose a little too long and pointed and there was a noticeable squint in her narrow hazel eyes. Yet everyone thought her ravishingly beautiful. She had great charm and an infectious zest for life, although she could be provoked to tears of rage and frustration, even when the occasion called for the most regal behaviour. The sumptuous splendour of her dresses and jewels was something not seen in Scotland for years and the dignity of her deportment made up for her lapses of temper. The inventories list, among her belongings, sixty gowns of silk, satin, velvet and cloth of gold or silver, and jewels from the French court including diamonds 'as big as the moon', rare rubies, black pearls and huge crystal rosaries. Small wonder that even her mighty adversary, John Knox, who denounced her 'joyousity' and her 'fiddling and flinging', could quote Robert Campbell's words that she had given Holyrood 'some enchantment by which men are bewitched'. Shaped by a childhood in the brilliant French court – Paris, Blois, Fontainebleau, Amboise – where gaiety and romantic intrigues were the order of the day, Mary glowed with feverish brilliance. In the midst of so much danger, she had got her own way. Lively, headstrong, and now in love, this was her morning of triumph.

It was after five in the morning when Mary was escorted to the chapel. Outside, the people of the city were already beginning to stir, to attend their devotions in the nave of the Abbey of Holyrood, which was the parish church of the Canongate. Here was Protestant plainness but in the chapel, built by Mary's father, with its wonderful ante-room and painted ceiling, the ancient splendour of the Catholic Church was everywhere. Leaving Mary in the chapel, Lennox and Atholl went to Darnley's chamber and brought the happy bridegroom to his bride. In his exquisite doublet and hose, Darnley, even taller than Mary, towered over his escorts. He was just over two years Mary's junior and immature, described as 'more like a woman than a man, for he was handsome, beardless and baby-faced'. Schooled like Mary in the intricate rituals of Renaissance court life (in his case the English court), in dancing, poetry and music, Darnley had a passion for sport – golf, croquet and hunting – and shared with his bride an enthusiasm for hawking. Mary, always ready to indulge him, had engaged two extra falconers on his behalf. She showed great affection for her future husband, behaving in such a familiar way that observers suspected that they were already secretly married or, at least, had become lovers. Mary was quick to defend Darnley against courtiers who sneered that he was vain, arrogant and perhaps stupid; her reply was that much had to be put down to his youth.

Then the trumpeters sounded, the music started and John Sinclair, soon to be Bishop of Brechin and Lord President, began the wedding service. Randolph, the English emissary, described how 'two priests there received them, the words were spoken, the rings which were three, the middle a rich diamond, were put upon her finger, they knelt together and many prayers were said over them'. So they were married. When the new 'King Henry' was referred to as joint sovereign with Mary, 'no man cried so much as Amen, saving his father, who alone cried out aloud ''God save His Grace'' '. Then the new king, quick to assert his now exalted position and show his apathy towards Mary's religion, refused to remain with her through the nuptial mass and left the chapel. Darnley was, at that time, said to be 'indifferent about religion'. His parents thought, and Mary hoped, that he was a Catholic but it was later remarked (with no great conviction) that 'he had always shown himself a Protestant'.

Randolph went on: 'He went to her chamber and within a space she followed and there, as was required according to the solemnity, she cast off her mourning and laid aside those sorrowful garments to give herself a pleasanter life. After some pretty refusal, more I believe, for manner's sake than grief of heart, she suffered them that stood by, every man that could approach, to take out a pin and so being committed to her ladies, changed her garments.' It was still quite early in the morning when Mary reappeared in a brightly coloured gown, symbolic of her newly married life. To share her rejoicing, the queen went outside the palace and, as tradition required, threw handfuls of money to the multitude. It is not recorded whether these were the freshly minted coins on which Darnley's head appeared. Some of the earliest of them had given rise to public indignation for placing King Henry's name before that of the queen. The ritual wedding breakfast provided by Mary for her guests then followed. Sixteen dishes were served. As so often, Mary ate sparingly, fearing poison. Later in the day, there was a banquet in the Great Hall, to the accompaniment of a masque, followed by music and dancing. The only blot on the occasion was a disturbance in the streets but Mary's fair words pacified the rioters.

As the king and queen went to bed on that memorable day of 29 July 1565, the Tudor roses around the English throne looked like wilting and being replaced by thorny Scottish thistles. Four hundred miles south in London, the angry Protestant queen was plotting. As the guests left the festivities, many had doubts. Others who had been invited had not attended at all. There was ample material for any plotter to work on. The most malleable material of all was the man whom Mary had just taken to be her lawful wedded husband.

CHAPTER 3

The Chaseabout Raid

WITH THE WEDDING OVER, MARY REACTED SHARPLY TO THE MENACES OF ITS chief opponents. Although she held two more masques on the nights immediately after the ceremony, she knew that the time was fast approaching when she would have to take up arms.

Moray had been supplanted. The real ruler of Scotland from the death of his step-mother, Mary of Guise, in June 1560 until the return of his half-sister, he had remained Mary's principal adviser and right-hand man. He was an experienced politician with a love of power. The Protestant cause had found a champion in him and consequently he strongly supported the connection with England. It had not been easy for him. Mary's Catholicism had meant that the government had lost control of the religious revolution without leading a Catholic revival. Moray's Protestantism put him at a disadvantage on both counts. He began to lean towards the religious activists led by the formidable John Knox. Such partiality gave scope to his numerous enemies among the nobles.

When Darnley appeared on the scene, Moray took an instant dislike to him. Darnley was openly offensive. Looking at a map of Moray's extensive lands, he remarked that they were 'too much'. Never careful of what he said or to whom he said it, he was so indiscreet as to direct the remark to Lord Robert Stewart, another of the queen's half-brothers. Lord Robert duly reported it to Moray who, in turn, protested to Mary. Darnley was told to apologise but the damage had been done. Moray was simply confirmed in his belief that Darnley was dangerous. By the time of the wedding he was saying that Darnley was plotting his murder. In return, rumours were being whispered that Moray was planning to kidnap Darnley and his father and send them both back to England and the tender mercies of Queen Elizabeth. Between Moray and Darnley there could be no peace. Moray was fighting for his political power, perhaps even his life.

The dislike of Châtelherault for the bridegroom was, if anything, more intense. It was also more dynastic in character. Darnley was a Lennox, Châtelherault was a Hamilton – the difference spelt generations of rivalry. Historically, when the Lennoxes had espoused the French cause, the Hamiltons had been pro-English and vice-versa. Now they were even rivals for the succession to the crown. Châtelherault was heir presumptive. Were Mary to die childless, causing the Stewart line of succession to fail, he would become King of Scots. Next in line to the Hamiltons was Darnley's father, the Earl of Lennox. For some time, the Lennoxes' response to the lineal superiority of the Hamiltons was to cast doubts on Châtelherault's legitimacy, and thus on his right to succeed. They suggested that his father, the first Earl of Arran, a man of a somewhat chaotic private life, had not quite got around to marrying his third wife before his son (Châtelherault) was born. Châtelherault, in turn, attacked Lennox's patriotism, accusing him of treachery and brutality when he fought for Henry VIII against his fellow-countrymen, twenty years earlier. Personal dislike was exceeded by dynastic enmity. The hatred between the two noble houses was implacable.

As early as March 1565, the plotting had begun. Moray had persuaded Châtelherault and another enemy of the Lennoxes, the fourth Earl of Argyll, to sign a bond of support should the Darnley marriage take place. It was not by chance therefore that, shortly after Mary's creation of Darnley as Earl of Ross, Moray made his last appearance at Council and retired to Lochleven Castle which had belonged to his step-father, Sir Robert Douglas. Sir Robert had married his mother, Margaret, second daughter of John, fifth Lord Erskine in 1527. Margaret became a favourite mistress of James V, by whom, in 1531, she had the child who was to become Moray. She still found the time, however, to give Sir Robert six legitimate children before his death at the battle of Pinkie in 1547. When the king had married the present queen's mother, she had hated her supplanter and now there was little love lost between Margaret Douglas and Mary Stewart.

From Lochleven, Moray sought help from England, his religious and political ally. The English ambassador, Randolph, was asked for a subsidy of £3,000, as a token of Elizabeth's approval. Moray, if not Châtelherault, was clearly bent on resistance to ensure his personal power and the continuation of his policies.

Three days after the wedding, Mary summoned Moray to Edinburgh, 'on pain of treason', to explain himself. He ignored her. Five days later, he was 'put to the horn' – declared an outlaw. Within a week, his properties, along with those of the Earl of Rothes and Sir William Kirkcaldy of Grange, were formally seized. Châtelherault and Argyll were given a stern warning that they might share the same fate. It was to no avail, since Moray was already in open revolt and had assembled troops at Ayr in the west. Mary responded with alacrity and ordered a muster of her supporters at Edinburgh on 22 August. Four days later, having despatched Atholl to hold off Argyll in the north, she rode out for the west at the head of her army. There was a pistol at her saddle and Darnley was at her side, affectedly posing in an elaborate suit of gilded armour. The classic course of a serious political dispute in Scotland had begun.

Armed rebellion was a matter of manoeuvre and posturing as much as bloody conflict. The purpose was to enlist allies, secure the necessary resources and deny them to the enemy. Since the soldiers were often less than keen and were obliged to live off the country, the campaigns tended to be short. On 31 August, the rebels entered Edinburgh. Their leaders, Moray, Châtelherault, Glencairn, Rothes and Kirkcaldy, hoped to enlist Protestant support for their cause and, by occupying the capital, to establish the credibility and legitimacy of their cause. But the people of Edinburgh, the largest body of citizenry in Scotland, showed no enthusiasm for the rebel nobles and their programme. They were tired of war – it was always bad for property and trade. Catholic and Protestant alike, they had little reason to be discontented with the four years of Mary's personal rule. Looming over the town was the castle commanded by Lord Erskine, recently created Earl of Mar by the queen and loyal to her. Its guns were a menace to any would-be invader. Moray soon realised that the occupation of Edinburgh was futile and started to withdraw to the south-west. Here he would be closer to any support that might be forthcoming from England. He had lost the first stage of the campaign without fighting a battle.

49

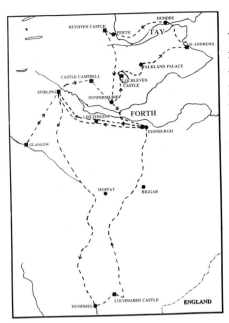

The Chaseabout Raid

Mary did not rush things. She waited in Glasgow for reinforcements from the north and spent the time reassuring public opinion. Moray's reason for revolt may have been his loss of influence with the rise of Darnley but he emphasised his championship of Protestantism. Now Mary re-issued her proclamation of August 1561, which promised a definitive settlement of the religious issue, when order had been restored. Meanwhile, on 6 September, Moray reached Dumfries on his southward march. He was moving away from his power base and could only hope for English help. Frantic messages to Elizabeth were of no avail; assistance did not come. With Mary's forces poised for the attack, Moray and Châtelherault recognised the hopelessness of their position. On 6 October they fled from Scotland, Moray to London and Châtelherault to France.

In London, Moray was carpeted by Queen Elizabeth in front of the politely cynical French ambassador. In a tremendous tongue-in-cheek display of righteous indignation she expressed her horror at his traitorous behaviour towards his anointed queen and told him he was lucky she did not send him to prison. It was made abundantly clear to him that he could expect no help from England; Elizabeth was not interested in backing a loser. Elizabeth knew that, however awkward the unwanted presence of Moray might be, in him she had a useful weapon. She did not throw him into prison but granted him asylum and allowed him to stay at Newcastle-upon-Tyne. She even promised to intercede with Mary for his return. Though nearly penniless – Elizabeth's frugality prevented her from giving him any money – he was now close to the border and could wait for a favourable turn of events at home. The 'Chaseabout (or Roundabout) Raid', as it came to be known, had been a disaster for Moray. Despite having the services of Kirkcaldy, the ablest soldier of the day, he had been outmanoeuvred at every turn – quite literally, since his army had never made contact with Mary's. He had only taken up arms after the wedding, being content to sulk and plot before the ceremony. Had he obtained the necessary English aid and gained a victory, it could scarcely have resulted in a dissolution of the royal marriage. For an adept politician, Moray's conduct had been singularly inept. This perhaps was the real reason for Elizabeth's anger.

The fiasco of the Chaseabout Raid gave Mary both the motive and the opportunity to harden her religious and diplomatic attitudes. This was not surprising. She had taken a remarkably relaxed line towards Protestant worship and done her best to conciliate the suspicious Elizabeth. Neither policy had achieved the desired result. Her reward had been a revolt of some of her nobles in the name of the Reformed religion, and the Queen of England was still covertly hostile. On the Continent there were old friends and potential allies in Rome, Madrid and Paris, all of them Catholic. Mary therefore released Archbishop Hamilton from prison where he had been since 1563. She then sent messengers to Pope Pius IV and Philip of Spain seeking aid. Then she announced her intention of seeking action by parliament to give some help to the old religion. Protestantism seemed to give no guarantee to her success as queen. The other side, at least in its European aspect, might be more helpful.

The raid had failed. But the mere fact that it had happened was a sign that the Darnley marriage was unpopular with many nobles and advisers. Moray and others had shown their disapproval openly and actively, to their cost. The prudent Maitland, cleverest of the queen's councillors, had been no less disgusted. He, however, simply immured himself at Lethington (Lennoxlove), remote from the affairs of state. Such absences, enforced or voluntary, were diminishing the group of responsible people who were regularly around the queen. Her father-in-law Lennox, Huntly, Bothwell and Atholl were now the only earls in regular attendance.

Darnley, the cause of so many abstentions, was of little use. Indolent and dissolute, he was rarely to be found when there was business to be done or advice to be offered. Hunting and carousing took up most of his time. Affairs of state were very low on his list of priorities. He remained sensitive to his privileges and neglectful of his responsibilities. As a result, the queen was obliged to rely on men of lower status. Sir James Balfour was an example – he was a well-born Scot but neither a noble nor an hereditary councillor. In other countries, monarchs were using such people as a matter of policy – better a loyal bourgeois than an arrogant aristocrat. Mary had somewhat less choice and she was descending further down the social scale, depending even on low-born foreigners. These were described by Ambassador Randolph as 'crafty vile strangers'. Thus it was that David Rizzio came to prominence.

CHAPTER 4

'Sauvez ma vie, Madame'

MARY WAS NEVER ALONE. SHE WAS ALWAYS SURROUNDED BY HER 'LADIES', who formed only a small part of her 200-odd domestic staff. An indication of how many were in attendance can be found in her household accounts; one bill is for 'saddles and bridles for twelve of the Queen's ladies', another is for 'fifteen black riding cloaks'. The 'four Maries', who were with her from infancy – Mary Fleming, Mary Beaton, Mary Livingston and Mary Seton – were still there. Mademoiselle de Pinguillon was her chief lady-in-waiting, and one of her new favourites was her illegitimate half-sister, the unhappily married Jean, Countess of Argyll. The queen was extremely fond of music and employed *valets de chambre*,[1] singers who performed for her regularly.

David Rizzio (or Riccio), born about 1533, a native of the Italian Duchy of Piedmont, had come to Scotland in 1561, in the service of Robertino Solara di Moreta, the ambassador of the Duke of Savoy. He was short, dark and hunchbacked. Contemporaries, not without malevolence, described him as 'hideously ugly' but his most authentic (but not contemporary) surviving likeness shows him with large soulful eyes and an engaging, if not appealing, expression – rather like that of some adoring dog. He was of uncertain age – indeed he appeared so twisted and bowed that many thought him to be fifty years old, although an examination of his body after his murder persuaded one chronicler that he could not be more than twenty-eight.

There was much in Rizzio to make up for his physical deficiencies; he was clever, he was witty and he had a talent to amuse. He was an accomplished musician with a fine bass voice. He was a skilful player of the rebec,[2] and accompanied himself in songs of which he composed both words and music. He spoke in the language of Ronsard[3] and reminded Mary of the charming Italians she had seen at the French court. It was his vocal ability, however, which brought him to the queen's attention. Her three *valets de chambre* needed a bass to complement their group. The result was that the ambassador's entourage was depleted by one and the queen's trio became a quartet. When Darnley came on the scene he initially liked Rizzio and, since he had no proper gentleman to attend him at their wedding, Mary appointed 'Seigneur Davie' to him for the occasion.

Had Rizzio been content to remain in that role, the history of Scotland might have been different. But he was ambitious for advancement, not in the field of music but in that of government. Over the next three years, he gradually but steadily insinuated himself into the queen's favour, and became as much a confidant as an entertainer. In 1564, Raullet, Mary's secretary for her French correspondence, died and Rizzio was appointed in his place. Mary's French connections meant that he became her secretary in her role as Queen Dowager of France, rather than as Queen of Scots. The post was important, and he was paid out of her French pension. What gave it real significance, however, was the place that Rizzio gained in the queen's confidence.

Personal favourites, whose main strength lay in their loyalty to the monarch, were not uncommon. They may or may not have been good at their jobs but they relied utterly on their patrons for their position and power. They may have been self-seeking and greedy – and Rizzio was both – but they could never be disloyal and undermine their only support. In courts so largely composed of ambitious nobles and grasping politicians, favourites were a relief to lonely and hard-pressed princes. The favourite's position was often powerful, but it was also frequently fraught with danger. Its holder was bound to be resented by the lords, who thought themselves to be the rightful advisers and counsellors to the throne. Resentment generally gave way to hatred if, as was usually the case, the favourite was socially inferior or alien in origin. These feelings were compounded by frustration when bribes had to be paid to gain access to the monarch, or to secure favours at court. It was not that cash transactions to get results were considered wrong or even unusual; fees and presents for services to be rendered were common enough. But there was a fine line between such payments and outright bribery; it was tempting for the favourite, who lacked any independent income, to over-step the mark. Rizzio ventured every hazard in the favourite's book. He did nothing to allay the consternation of the Scottish nobles.

Rizzio's power was in no way diminished by the marriage of the queen his protectress. Indeed her union with Darnley increased her reliance on him for company and advice. The Chaseabout Raid had deprived her of many of her nobles, who were now in exile. Maitland of Lethington, though still in Scotland, had withdrawn from court, disgusted by the marriage. As the months passed Darnley was becoming progressively more hopeless. The wretched man so often could not be found, when he was needed at court, that the queen had to have a wooden stamp of his signature made so that important documents could be processed in his absence.

Although Darnley had been friendly with Rizzio for some time after the wedding, he was becoming more and more resentful of the Italian's influence with the queen. He disliked Rizzio's arrogance, and was affronted by the favours showered on him. In particular, he was angry that Mary had made the prudent decision to deny him the Crown Matrimonial – at least for the time being. This honour would have meant that, in the event of the queen predeceasing him, his children by a later wife could still succeed to the throne. As it was, he was only King Consort for the queen's lifetime. As far as Darnley was concerned it was Rizzio's advancement which was the cause of the shabby treatment he was now receiving from the queen. Darnley's resentment was shared by many of the nobles who hated the Italian upstart. While they had little time for the king, they realised that they could use him in a campaign against court favourites in general and Rizzio in particular. His cousin, the cunning and unscrupulous James Douglas, fourth Earl of Morton,[4] led the way in sowing the seeds of suspicion and discontent in Darnley's immature and illogical but receptive mind.

There were family and political reasons (in Scotland, the two were often barely distinguishable) for a move against Rizzio. Parliament was to meet in March 1566. Its main item of business would be to consider a charge of high treason against Moray and the other rebel lords of the Chaseabout Raid. Their conviction seemed inevitable and, with it, the forfeiture of their lands and other possessions. To Morton, this result would have

55

been intolerable. He was the friend and ally of Moray and would undoubtedly have joined the rebels, had Darnley not been his cousin.
Moray's conviction would be a blow directed at the whole nobility and a
vindication of the royal marriage. On a personal level, there were
rumours that Morton would shortly be relieved of the office of Chancellor,
which he had held since the downfall of the fourth Earl of Huntly in 1562.

So an unlikely and unholy alliance was devised. Morton and others of
the Douglas family would ensure, by violence if necessary, that parliament
would take no action against Moray and the other rebel lords. In exchange,
the lords would support Darnley's claim to the Crown Matrimonial and
Darnley would enable the elimination of Rizzio. The favourite's doom
was sealed.

The lords did not trust Darnley. They insisted that he append his
signature (not just his stamp) to a bond agreeing, thus binding him to
the plot if anything went wrong. When they discovered that, further to
humiliate the queen, Darnley required Rizzio to be seized in her presence,
they extracted a second bond from him. By it, he accepted responsibility for
Rizzio's murder. The document was composed with unctuous hypocrisy:

> We Henry by the grace of God, King of Scotland and Husband to the
> Queen's Majesty, for so much we having consideration of the gentle
> and good nature, with many other qualities in her Majesty, we have
> thought pity and also think it great conscience to us that are her
> husband, to suffer her to be abused or seduced by certain privy
> persons, wicked and ungodly – especially a stranger called Davie – we
> have devised to take these privy persons, enemies of Her Majesty, us,
> the Nobility and Commonwealth, to punish them according to their
> demerits, and in case of any difficulty to cut them off immediately and
> to take and slay them wherever it happeneth.

A plan of such murderous intent, involving so many people, was bound to
be difficult to keep secret. Soon there were rumours at court that something involving the rebel lords was afoot. The courtier and diplomat, Sir
James Melville of Halhill, told the queen of them and pleaded with her to
pardon the rebels and thereby defuse the situation. Mary is reported to
have said that she had also heard the rumours but discounted them since:
'Although the Scots were great talkers, they rarely put their bragging into
effect.'

In the light of her experiences over the last four and a half years and her ancestors' tribulations over several centuries, with rebellious nobles in general and Douglases in particular, this alleged comment is extraordinary. It would indicate a blinkered naïvety most uncharacteristic of her and it is quite possible she never made it. It has to be said, however, that it is quite possible that she may have chosen not to believe what she did not wish to hear.

Mary opened parliament on 7 March but Darnley did not accompany her. He made it clear that he was still angry at not having received the Crown Matrimonial. His absence, however, was more likely to have been caused by his reluctance to be involved, as a Peer of the Realm, with the dispossession of Moray. This, and his foreknowledge of the fate that was to befall Rizzio, probably did more to keep him away than the withholding of an honour which, in the light of his recent behaviour, he could hardly have expected to receive anyway.

Rizzio's enemies struck quickly. On the afternoon of Saturday, 9 March, Darnley played tennis with Rizzio. That evening, the Queen gave a small supper party for some friends, relations and members of her entourage, in a little tapestry-lined room next to her bedchamber. Her half-brother, Lord Robert Stewart, Commendator of Holyrood, and her half-sister, Jean, Countess of Argyll, were there. In attendance were Mary Beaton's father, Robert Beaton, Laird of Creich, Keeper of Falkland Palace and Master of the Household, and Arthur Erskine of Blackgrange, Captain of the Guard, once described by John Knox as 'the most pestilent papist in the realm'. There were her French apothecary and one or two domestic servants. And there was Rizzio. Mary sat at one end of the table, with Rizzio at the other and her guests in between. It was cold and dark outside but the fire was burning, and the candles on the table gave enough light. The meal was substantial because, although it was Lent, Mary, now nearly six months pregnant, had been advised to eat meat. There had been music beforehand, and Rizzio had sung in what was to be his farewell performance. There was scarcely room for them all in the little chamber but the party was informal and relaxed so they settled down in the warmth to enjoy themselves with no inkling of what was to come.

Scarcely had they begun the meal when the tapestries at one end of the room parted and Darnley appeared, framed in the doorway behind, which was at the head of a narrow spiral stair to his apartment directly beneath. His appearance was totally unexpected since it was well known that he had been on bad terms with the queen for some time and, in any case, he was thought to be elsewhere in the palace with Lord Lindsay. He was, however, in good humour and, saying that he had already eaten and did not require supper, sat down next to the queen and affectionately put his arm round her. His presence cast a feeling of unease over the party, since there was no obvious reason for his good mood. Everyone must have thought that he had been drinking, since his alcoholic excesses had of late become famous.

Then the tapestries parted again. The feeling of unease gave way to one of stark horror as the appalling figure of Patrick, Lord Ruthven, appeared at the head of the stairs. Ruthven, described by one chronicler as a 'highly unsavoury character', due to his involvement in sorcery and the black arts, was widely thought to be on his deathbed, suffering from 'internal inflammation'. Now he stood in full armour over his nightrobe, his face pallid and ravaged; a macabre spectacle of debilitated malevolence. In a voice of doom, he addressed the queen: 'May it please your Majesty, to let yonder man Davie come forth of your presence, for he has been over-long here.' Mary's guests were later said to have thought that he was 'raving through the vehemency of a fever' but, more in anger than in fear, she said: 'What offence hath he made?' 'Great offence.' Mary then turned furiously on Darnley and demanded to know what part he had in all this. When he remained silent she retorted that, if Rizzio had been guilty of any offence, he would be tried and punished according to the law of the land. She then ordered Ruthven to leave or be tried as a traitor; ignoring her, he looked at Darnley and said: 'Sir take the Queen's Majesty, your Sovereign and wife to you.'

Mary rose to her feet only to be seized by Darnley who pinioned her arms. Rizzio could now see what was about to happen to him. He shrank back into the window embrasure, behind the queen, clutching at her skirts and drawing his dagger. The guests had by now risen to their feet and made for Ruthven but he drew his pistol and said: 'Lay not hands on me for I will not be handled.'

As if by a pre-arranged signal (which perhaps it was) the opposite door, leading from the main staircase, burst open. The conspirators rushed in, overturning the table and sending plates, food and candlesticks in all directions. Only the presence of mind of the Countess of Argyll, who snatched up a candle as it fell, prevented the *mêlée* from becoming a massacre in the flickering firelight. One of the conspirators, Andrew Ker of Fawdonside, seized the pregnant queen and held a loaded pistol to her stomach. Another, George Douglas, deftly removed the dagger from Darnley's belt and stabbed Rizzio over Mary's shoulder. She said later that the blows struck at the little Italian passed so close to her throat that she 'felt the coldness of the steel'. Rizzio was then dragged from the chamber crying: '*Justice, justice, sauvez ma vie, Madame, sauvez ma vie.*'

There were now about twenty men trying to strike at the wretched victim as he was hauled to the head of the stairs and on Darnley's order flung down them, dying or dead.

The body was carried to the porter's lodge, thrown across Rizzio's own trunk and divested of its fine clothing. It was found to have more than fifty wounds. Significantly and symbolically, Darnley's dagger was still embedded in it. The porter's servant, obviously enjoying the task of stripping the body, permitted himself the luxury of sententiously philosophising: 'This hath been his destiny, for upon this chest was his first bed when he entered this place and now here he lieth again, a very ingrate and misknowing knave.'

Inevitably an event which took place in such a short time and involved so many excited and murderous people came to be reported in many different versions. Ruthven later declared that no blow was struck in the queen's presence; this did not at all accord with Mary's account. It is clear that, whether Rizzio died screaming and clutching at the queen's skirts or silently at the foot of the stairs, there was neither courage nor dignity in the manner of his death. What did call for fortitude and presence of mind was the situation in which Mary now found herself.

While all this was going on Mary was remonstrating with Lord Ruthven and Lord Lindsay in the supper chamber. Soon Darnley joined them, having supervised Rizzio's last journey down the stairs. He at once voiced his usual complaints, demanding rather than pleading, that the exiled lords be pardoned, so that they might return home. The queen, still uncertain whether her secretary was alive or dead, acidly rejoined that it was largely for Darnley's sake that they had originally been forced to leave. This unrewarding conversation was brought to an end by the sounds of the city alarm bell and of a great multitude gathering outside the palace. The Provost had entered the courtyard with a crowd of townsfolk, many of them armed. They had heard the commotion in the palace and feared for the queen's safety. Mary made to go to the window but Lindsay brutally snarled that he would 'cut her into collops'[5] if she tried to speak to them. Darnley then leaned out and told the Provost and his people that the queen was safe and everything was under control. He urged them to disperse and go home.

It was not until much later that one of Mary's ladies-in-waiting brought her the news that Rizzio was indeed dead. 'How do you know?' she asked. 'I have seen his body,' was the reply. It was then that the queen showed her astonishing power of recovery and the fortitude which was to remain with her until the final hour at Fotheringhay. She dried her eyes, composed herself and said: 'And now we shall think on revenge.'

Mary's vengeance may not have been deliberately planned; nevertheless nearly all the conspirators died before her, most of them by violence.

Darnley perished in mysterious circumstances at Kirk o' Field less than a year later.

Morton became the most ruthlessly effective Regent of Scotland in Mary's lifetime and was executed in 1581, on 'the Maiden', the instrument of death, the design of which he himself had imported from Halifax.

Knox, who had no hand in the murder but probably knew of it in advance, and certainly loudly approved of it afterwards, died in bed in 1572. His young wife was immediately swept away and married by the murderous Ker of Fawdonside who had so nearly blown apart not only Mary but the unborn child who was to become James VI.

Maitland, who also had no hand in the murder but unquestionably knew of it in advance, died diseased and imprisoned in Leith, after the fall of Edinburgh Castle in 1573.

Moray, who was in England on the night of the murder but nevertheless very much a party to it, was shot to death by Hamilton of Bothwellhaugh in Linlithgow in 1570.

Lennox, who was to succeed Moray as regent, was undoubtedly told of the plot by Darnley and approved of the murder. He died of his wounds after a skirmish with the Hamiltons and Gordons near Stirling in 1571.

Lindsay, who threatened and brutalised Mary on the night of the murder and was to do so again at the time of her abdication, was one of the few who survived Mary. He died peacefully in 1589.

Mary Queen of Scots and Henry Darnley, *artist unknown, c. 1565*
(National Trust, Hardwick Hall)

Mary Queen of Scots and her first husband,
François II at the time of their coronation, a
miniature from the prayer book of Catherine de
Medici, artist unknown (Bibliothèque Nationale)

Diane de France *(daughter of Henri II and Diane de*
Poitiers, his mistress), half sister to François II and therefore
half sister-in-law to Mary. One of the earliest equestrian
portraits of a woman. Note the fleur-de-lys of France on her
saddle cloth (Lennoxlove)

Henry VIII, *Holbein (Lennoxlove)*

Queen Elizabeth, *English School (16th century) (Lennoxlove)*

James VI, *Adrian Vanson, 1595 (Scottish National Portrait Gallery)*

Mary Queen of Scots in White Mourning, *'Deuil Blanc', François Clouet, c. 1560 (Bibliothèque Nationale)*

Falkland Palace, *Alexander Kierincx, c. 1636 (National Galleries of Scotland)*

James Douglas, 4th Earl of Morton, Regent of
Scotland, *17th-century copy of original, Scottish
School (Lennoxlove)*

*French silver gilt casket ('The Casket'), a present on
marriage from the Dauphin (later François II) to
Queen Mary, later used for messages between her and
her third husband the Earl of Bothwell. Forgeries
and/or collages purporting to be these were used by
the prosecution in her first trial. The original letters
were taken by James VI in 1584 after the execution of
the Earl of Gowrie, and disappeared, although copies
exist (Lennoxlove)*

Henry Yair, a one-time priest, was an adherent of Ruthven, one of the small fry amongst the conspirators. Possibly because he could not get close enough to Rizzio to strike a blow he murdered a Dominican priest, Father Adam Black, the same night. He was executed in August 1566.

Tom Scott was another of Ruthven's adherents. But he was also Under-Sheriff of Perth and his official position caused his offence of 'warding the Queen within Holyrood' to be considered especially villainous. Since Ruthven was Hereditary Sheriff and elected Provost of the same town, as well as Sheriff-Clerk of Perthshire, Scott's fate was particularly unfair. He was also executed in August.

Patrick Bellenden was another who survived Mary. He died at a great age in 1607.

George Douglas, who is said to have struck the first blow, continued his ecclesiastical career, but was not a credit to the Reformed Church. He survived Mary by at least two years. There were several other Douglases involved but they were also small fry and, although some of them were brought to justice, it seems that none of them paid the supreme penalty. There does not appear to be any record of their dates of death.

The Ruthvens were another matter.

James VI was to exact terrible vengeance on the Ruthven family. In 1584, William, fourth Lord Ruthven and first Earl of Gowrie, who accompanied his father at Rizzio's murder, was executed. In 1600, James took further reprisals. In an incident at Gowrie Castle, Alexander, Master of Ruthven, and his brother John, third Earl of Gowrie, were killed. Their corpses were hanged and quartered and fragments were sent to be displayed on spikes in Edinburgh, Perth, Dundee and Stirling. Later that year an act was passed abolishing the name of Ruthven for all time. Even then, the king was not satisfied. He issued orders for the apprehension of the younger sons of the first Earl of Gowrie, who were only school-children at the time. One escaped to the continent where he died without returning to Scotland. The other was arrested and sent to the Tower of London. He eventually died in the King's Bench prison as late as 1652.

The last word must be reserved for the Ruthven who started it all. Patrick, third Lord Ruthven, was clearly close to death as he stood at the head of the stairs – a ghastly figure of doom, in full armour, terrorising the queen and her companions. This stalwart and indomitable noble who, in defiance of the frailty of his own body, strove so hard to do what he saw to be his duty, died at Newcastle a few weeks later. His last words were: 'I see the heavens open and a choir of angels come to take me.' He may have been mistaken about his destination.

1. A 'valet de chambre' is described as a domestic servant 'attaché plus spécialement au service de son maître'. In the sixteenth century, the term was often applied to the personal musicians of a monarch or nobleman.

2. A rebec was a three-stringed, bowed instrument, made in several sizes, depending on which it was held against the chin, chest or thigh. Rebecs had a slightly unpleasant but fortunately muted sound and, about the time of Queen Mary, were being superseded by instruments of the viol family.

3. Pierre de Ronsard (1524–85). Attached to the French and then the Scottish court, he was one of the best, and probably the most prolific of the poets of the French Renaissance.

4. Morton and Darnley's mother were both grandchildren of Sir George Douglas, Master of Angus, who was killed at Flodden. Sir George's father was the famed Archibald 'Bell the Cat', fifth Earl of Angus. Darnley's grandfather, the equally famed Archibald, sixth Earl of Angus, husband of Margaret Tudor, was Morton's uncle. Morton was therefore Darnley's first cousin once removed.

5. Collop: A slice of meat.

CHAPTER 5

'A fair son and I am but a barren stock'

THE CONSPIRACY HAD, AT LEAST PARTIALLY, SUCCEEDED; RIZZIO WAS DEAD. But this was the beginning, not the end, of the affair. The true object of the plotters was to secure power for themselves and maintain it against all comers. The removal of Rizzio was but a preliminary move in a complicated game. Darnley had been neutralised by being enlisted as a conspirator. But it was the marriage of the two cousins which was the real target of the conspiracy. Rizzio's death was only an incident.

It was not even a decisive incident. His murderers had intended to round up those of Mary's supporters who were in Holyrood and kill them on the spot. Sir James Balfour, one of the queen's lower-born advisers, was to be hanged. Before the *mêlée* in Mary's chamber, they had arranged for the palace doors to be guarded. So Huntly, Bothwell, Atholl, Livingston and Fleming climbed out of a back window and made their escape. Thoroughness was not a characteristic of the conspirators. They had to content themselves with Henry Yair's killing of the Dominican, Father Adam Black. The unfortunate priest, who was being harboured by the queen, was murdered for no better reason than that he was a Catholic who happened to be around.

Mary had a miserable night. The Douglases, who now held the palace, would not allow her medical attention, not even a midwife, nor the presence of any of her accustomed servants. Only Lady Huntly, the redoubtable widow of the fourth Earl, remained with the pregnant queen. Next morning, a Sunday, found a chastened Darnley back in Mary's apartments. His bravado of recent days had gone. Having been a witness and accessory to the murder of the previous night, he had begun to realise that he was simply not in the same league as men like Lindsay and Ruthven; he now knew that, if it suited them, they would kill him as cheerfully as they had Rizzio. A matter of considerable concern to him was what the conspirators had determined to do next. He knew that the queen was to be taken to Stirling and kept there until the birth of her child. Thereafter, they would rule in the infant's name and Mary would continue to be detained, probably until she died. What he did not know was what his role was to be in this grim scenario.

The queen extracted this information from her pusillanimous husband during their morning's meeting. She had been thoroughly fed up with him before the events of the previous night, and now her main feelings towards him were of disgust and revulsion. There remained, however, a lingering sense of compassion for the pitiable creature, who had found himself so far out of his depth with the determined and unscrupulous plotters. She resolved to make use of him and his knowledge of the schemes directed against her.

Mary's main aim was to escape. Clearly her chances were much better from Holyrood; at all costs she had to avoid being taken to Stirling. So although her baby was not due for another three months, she pretended to go into labour. So convincing was she that Lord Ruthven and the others were obliged to send for a midwife and all hope of moving her was abandoned, at least for the time being. While this was going on, Darnley, at Mary's instance, issued a proclamation in the joint names of the queen and himself, cancelling the meeting of parliament on 12 March. It was an important move. The purpose of the intended parliament had been to proceed against those involved in the Chaseabout Raid; among them were Moray, Châtelherault, Argyll, Glencairn, Rothes, Ochiltree, Boyd and Kirkcaldy. These men were now free to return. They might link up with the Rizzio conspirators, but Mary believed that they were more likely to prove loyal to her.

Moray lost no time in returning from England. As soon as he arrived in Edinburgh he was summoned to Holyrood, where he had a meeting with Mary, who was still pretending to be in labour. Having no idea how deeply, if at all, he had been involved with the conspirators, she desperately wanted to distance him from them. Moray was so overcome by his half-sister's distraught state that, in her words, he was 'so moved that tears fell from his eyes'.

The next day, Monday, 11 March, Moray came again, this time with Morton and the other leaders of the conspirators, who knelt before her asking to be forgiven. It was an arranged scene. Darnley, naïve as ever, had suggested that pardoning the murderers was the only way out of this dangerous situation. Mary had no intention of making such a turnabout but she desperately needed to buy time. In response to their entreaties, she said that she could not grant them an immediate pardon but declared that if, by their future actions, they tried to atone for the past, 'I give you my word – that on my part, I will endeavour to forget what you have done'.

Moray then delivered a sententious homily on the virtues of clemency and Mary, feeling her temper rising, prudently feigned labour pains again, in order to avoid saying something she might later regret. The interview was at an end. It was time for the queen to plan her escape.

Mary had already convinced Darnley that the danger to him was no less than that to her and that, if they stayed in Holyrood much longer, they might both end up imprisoned indefinitely in Stirling Castle. Escape to a secure place, where they might rally supporters, was now crucial. Accordingly, at eight o'clock that evening, she sent for John Stewart of Traquair, who was Captain of the Royal Guard, her equerry Arthur Erskine, and Anthony Standen, one of her pages. She persuaded them to help her and Darnley escape; they agreed to stand by with horses near the abbey at the back of the palace at midnight. Getting out of Holyrood would be the least of their problems, since Darnley had told the conspirators that he would prevent his wife from descending the private staircase from her apartments to his own. Now that she had convinced him of his own danger, the escape should be comparatively simple.

Just before midnight, Mary and Darnley made their way down the spiral staircase, the same staircase that the murderers had come up two nights before. They moved silently through store rooms, wine cellars and servants' quarters to an unguarded door at the back of the palace. From there it was only a short walk past the abbey to the meeting place. Traquair, Erskine and Standen were there with horses and a few soldiers. Mary's intention was to go to Seton House to pick up some loyal nobles who had already been alerted and then go with them to Dunbar Castle, a stronghold on the coast, thirty miles east of Edinburgh.

All went according to plan. Mary, being six months pregnant, rode pillion, not with her husband but with Erskine. Darnley had a horse of his own and behaved abominably during the journey. Panicking at imaginary pursuers, he whipped up his horse and Erskine's, crying, 'Come on! come on! By God's blood, they will murder both you and me if they can catch us!'

Mary pleaded with him to remember her condition but he replied callously that if she lost this child, they could always get others. Given the political turmoil of the time it was not an expectation to be relied upon. The journey took an exhausting five hours. Nonetheless, Mary was able to call on hidden reserves of energy. On arrival, she sent for eggs and cooked breakfast for everyone.

Over the next five days at Dunbar Mary consolidated her position. She wrote letters to her friends abroad, including a particularly long one to Queen Elizabeth, describing Rizzio's murder and appealing for help. On 15 March, she awarded Bothwell the lands and lordship of Dunbar. Meanwhile, Atholl, Fleming and Seton came to her with supporters and, by 17 March, she had 4,000 men at her command. On the same day she issued a Royal Proclamation calling on the inhabitants of the surrounding districts to meet her at Haddington with provisions for eight days. In the eight months since her marriage, Mary was raising her second army; once again not to defend the nation against a foreign invader but to subdue her unruly nobles.

For the conspirators, this was the final straw. It was bad enough that Bothwell, Huntly, Balfour and others should have escaped on the night of the murder. It was worse that Darnley should have betrayed them and allowed the queen to escape. Now that she had raised so much popular support, their position had become untenable.

Mary made a triumphant entry to Edinburgh on 18 March. Her second army was now 8,000 strong but it did no more fighting than the first – the conspirators had left the day before. Ruthven, Ker, Lindsay and Morton went to England, where Ruthven died shortly afterwards. Maitland, who knew of the plot but took no part in it, went to Dunkeld. Knox, who probably did not know in advance but issued a trumpeting approval after-wards, acted as so often on his almost uncanny sense of danger and went to Ayrshire. Only Moray, who had been in England on the night of the murder and had made his peace with Mary the following day, remained in Edinburgh. The queen could not face returning to Holyrood so soon after the events of the previous week so she lodged in the High Street with Lord Herries; she felt safer there, among the ordinary people, than in the palace, among her rapacious nobles.

Mary made a further attempt to divide the opposition. On the day after her return, she sent a message to Moray, the new apostle of reconciliation. She was willing to come to terms with the leaders of the Chaseabout Raid but there would be no forgiveness for the Rizzio murderers. Darnley was still claiming ignorance of the conspiracy and news of this soon got to Morton and his friends. Vindictively, but not surprisingly, they sent to the queen a copy of the incriminating bond, signed by Darnley. Mary, of course, already knew the full extent of her husband's involvement but, much as she despised and detested him, was not going to give the murderers the satisfaction of seeing her take any punitive action against him. She was also unwilling to antagonise Darnley unnecessarily since she believed him quite capable of casting doubts on her unborn child's legitimacy.

So Mary ignored the bond while she took steps to rehabilitate what was left of Rizzio. His body was exhumed from the common grave in the Holyrood cemetery and re-interred according to Catholic rites in the abbey church at Holyrood.[1] His eighteen-year-old brother Joseph, who had recently arrived with the French ambassador, was appointed French Secretary in his place. Mary's attention however was now focused not on the past but the future – the birth of her child. At the beginning of April she moved to Edinburgh Castle, which was thought by her council to be the safest place, and there she started to make detailed preparations.

On 3 June, Mary took to a small panelled chamber to await the birth and, while waiting, made her will. If she died and the child survived, everything was to go to the child. If they both died, her property was to be divided up, with her best jewels going to the crown of Scotland. There were many other bequests to her French and Scottish relatives and several to her friends. There were more than twenty-five to Darnley.[2]

On 18 June, the queen went into a long and difficult labour. The Countess of Atholl tried to help by using her skill in sorcery to transfer the pains to Lady Reres who was in a bed nearby. This ingenious exercise caused much suffering to Lady Reres but did nothing to alleviate that of Mary. At last, between ten and eleven o'clock the following morning, after more than twenty hours in labour, the queen gave birth to an impressively healthy boy.[3]

The birth of Prince James was the occasion for immense rejoicing

James VI, *Arnold
Bronkhorst, c. 1580
(National Galleries of
Scotland)*

throughout Scotland and particularly in Edinburgh. Five hundred bonfires were lit, all the artillery of the castle was discharged and lords and commons gathered in St Giles to give thanks to God for an heir to the throne of Scotland. For Mary, it was important to make a statement. Summoning Darnley to her chamber, she displayed the baby to him in the presence of her assembled household and said, 'My Lord, God has given you and me a son, begotten by none but you – here I protest to God, as I shall answer to him at the great day of judgement, that this is your son and no other man's son. I am desirous that all here, with ladies and others, bear witness.'

Then she added gloomily, 'For he is so much your own son that I fear it will be the worse for him hereafter.'

The good news soon crossed the border but it was not improved by travel. Sir James Melville was despatched to inform Queen Elizabeth. He took four days to get to London and arrived on a Sunday evening to find the English queen dancing after supper. When he gave out his tidings, there was a long silence. Then Elizabeth said: 'The Queen of Scots is lighter of a fair son and I am but a barren stock.'

1. George Buchanan suggests that Rizzio was interred in the Chapel Royal. The suggestion is untrue.

2. Buchanan asserts that Mary totally ignored Darnley in favour of Bothwell in her will. In fact, there are only two bequests for Bothwell and over twenty-five for Darnley.

3. The 'bones in the wall' story is sensationally resuscitated, usually by the less responsible newspapers, at frequent but irregular intervals. It tells of the discovery in the 1840s of a baby's bones, wrapped in cloth of gold or in a tiny coffin or both, during repairs and alterations to the part of Edinburgh Castle where Queen Mary was confined in 1566. The implication is that Mary's child was still-born, James VI was a changeling and the whole of the subsequent royal family illegitimate. The crown of Scotland should therefore have passed to the Hamilton family in 1587 and more than 300 years later, through the daughter of the twelfth Duke of Hamilton, to the Dukes of Montrose. The story is dubious in the extreme. Bones were certainly discovered but there is absolutely no evidence that they were wrapped in cloth of gold (or anything else), in a coffin, or even that they were human.

CHAPTER 6

Baptism of the Prince

THE BIRTH OF PRINCE JAMES ON 19 JUNE 1566 WAS THE OCCASION FOR GREAT rejoicing throughout the country. The Scots had every reason to celebrate. Their queen had performed her fundamental duty: she had provided a male heir to the throne. Mary was young and there was good reason to believe that her realm would be spared the dangers of yet another royal minority. If the nation was more secure, so also was the House of Stewart. Mary's position, as next in line to the crown of England, had become stronger now that there was a prince to follow her. The popularity of the queen had never been higher and she consolidated it by the care that she lavished on the infant James. He was taken to Stirling Castle with the utmost pomp and circumstance and given into the custodianship of John, sixth Lord Erskine, recently created Earl of Mar, and the hereditary guardian of royal princes. Her subjects, encouraged by the concessions that the Catholic queen was making to the Protestant Church, and sharing her enthusiasm for the welfare of her son, did not even object to paying additional taxes to reduce the cost to the crown of the baptism.

There was, however, one man in the kingdom who did not view the new era of goodwill with much satisfaction. To Darnley, the birth of his son brought no joy. It displaced him in the order of succession and reduced his importance in the realm. Mary viewed him with scorn and he responded with tantrums, drunkenness, and petty exhibitions of jealousy directed towards those nobles who were in her favour, especially Moray and Bothwell. Darnley and Mary were not often in each other's company and rarely, if ever, intimate. On one occasion at Traquair, they had a

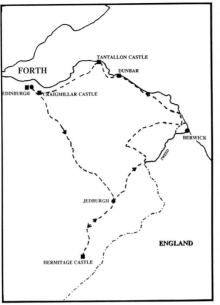

Jedburgh and Hermitage

mortifyingly public quarrel, with Darnley speaking to her in such coarse terms that he had to be rebuked by their host, John Stewart, the Captain of the Queen's Guard. He was becoming, in the eyes of the queen and the leading men in the country, a nuisance and an embarrassment. At the end of September, in response to Darnley's repeated threats to leave Scotland altogether, a conference[1] was held between the queen and her husband, in the presence of the French ambassador du Croc, at the Privy Council. It failed to reconcile any differences, although Darnley did not leave the kingdom which, he asserted, was not showing him proper respect. With the exception of his father, it is doubtful if any of those present thought him entitled him to any.

Mary's growing estrangement from her foolish, wilful husband was one cloud in the summer of 1566, the season of the prince's birth. As autumn drew on, the sky darkened further for the queen. At the beginning of October she went to Jedburgh, about forty miles south-east of Edinburgh, on judicial business. The visit was expected to last about a fortnight and she stayed in the town.[2] About the time of her arrival, news came through that Bothwell had been wounded in a skirmish in Liddesdale with some Border thieves, and was lying seriously ill in his castle of Hermitage. On 16 October,[3] with her retinue, including Moray but not Darnley, Mary rode more than twenty miles across the moors to the stronghold of her lieutenant on the Borders. Hermitage was not equipped for a royal visit – certainly not an overnight one – so the party had to ride back to Jedburgh on the same day.

Mary had not been well before going to Jedburgh; she had never properly recovered from the rigours of giving birth, three months earlier, and her health had not been improved by the mental stress imposed on her by her ever-worsening relationship with Darnley. The exertion of the

*Hermitage c. 1560,
drawing by David Simon*

fifty-mile ride brought on a severe illness, from which many around her thought she would not recover. There was however a temporary improvement but, on 25 October, this was followed by a relapse; funeral arrangements were discussed and prayers were said for her in churches as far away as Edinburgh. At one point her servants thought she was dead, and opened the windows of her room to let her spirit escape. Moray was alleged to have been seen avariciously – and prematurely – fingering her jewellery. At this stage, Arnault, her physician, went into action, administering wine and medical potions alternately orally and anally. Whether or not this saved her life is questionable; at any rate she started to recover.

Within a fortnight the queen was well enough to make a circuit of the eastern border and east coast, ending up at Craigmillar Castle on 20 November. On this journey, in addition to her normal retinue, she was accompanied by a large body of nobles. Moray was still with her, as was Bothwell, who had also just recovered. During the whole episode Darnley only visited his wife once, when he stayed in Jedburgh on the night of 28 October. It has been suggested that he was out hawking and hunting near Glasgow and did not hear of his wife's illness until 27 October, whereupon he immediately rode to Jedburgh, arriving the

71

following day. This would explain his apparently callous behaviour in reaching her so late, but it would not mitigate his lack of concern for his sick wife's welfare when he left so abruptly the next day. His departure was probably precipitated, as so often, by some imaginary but deeply perceived slight.

Mary's illness had at least cleared the air regarding the state of her marriage. Darnley's visits to her had been becoming rarer and briefer and now any real communication between them had effectively ceased. In fact, the queen had begun to suspect her husband of plotting against her. At the height of her illness, alarmed by her collapse, she had told Moray and the other attendant nobles that it was her wish that, in the event of her death, Prince James was to succeed her, to the exclusion of Darnley: furthermore she attributed her sickness to her husband's 'ingratitude'. The rupture was complete. So much so that, at a meeting at Craigmillar in late November, the still ailing queen could discuss formally with a broad array of the notables of the kingdom the removal of Darnley from the political scene. There were two matters of great concern to her; first the legitimacy of the young prince, which could be called into question in the event of divorce or annulment; and second her own honour, which could be compromised if a more drastic method of neutralising Darnley was arrived at. Mary, deeply depressed, was not thinking with her customary clarity, but she did have enough of her wits about her to restore to Archbishop Hamilton a temporary jurisdiction in matrimonial causes. The way was open for the final solution to the Darnley problem.

It was not all grim foreboding. The serenity of the summer returned briefly on a wintry day in December. At the chapel in Stirling Castle, the baptism of Prince James took place. It was a grand occasion, suitably royal and international in character. Queen Elizabeth was a godparent and donated a massive golden font. Mary's brother-in-law, King Charles IX of France, was also a godparent, representing the other side of Mary's ancestry, and the other nation concerned with Scottish affairs. The Duke of Savoy, who was married to Charles's aunt, Marguérite, was the third godparent. While none of the royal sponsors could be present, nor were they expected to be, their acceptance was a sign of the importance attributed to the prince's birth in the European context.

The ceremony followed the rites of the Catholic Church, with all the splendour of the ancient ritual. John Hamilton, Archbishop of St Andrews, that doughty ecclesiastical survivor and a member of the family next in line to the throne, was the officiating clergyman. Mary struck a jarring note by refusing to allow him to mix his spittle with the baby's. A 'pocky priest' was not to endanger the health of a child so important to the future of Scotland. The christening was Catholic, but the congregation was ecumenical. Nobles of the old faith carried the implements used in the ceremony. The principal Reformed nobles attended, clad in fine costumes provided at the queen's expense. It was a national occasion, and differences in religion were minimised. During her illness, Mary had asked for the same tolerance for her fellow Catholics that she had given the Protestants, although this was scarcely the spirit of the Counter-Reformation. Survival, not supremacy, was Mary's expectation for her faith. It was therefore easy enough for George Buchanan, ally of John Knox and later one of the queen's most trenchant critics, to compose verses for the masques that were the highlight of the christening party.

Mary presided with maternal pride over what was to be the last great ceremonial occasion of her reign. To her, it was the beginning of a new era, in which Darnley would no longer be a feature. It must have been significant to the queen that the father of the royal child was not among those present. Darnley was in Stirling, but not in the chapel. He had objected to Queen Elizabeth as a godparent, since she had opposed his marriage and never paid any heed to him as king. Now Elizabeth's subjects were to be seen everywhere, contemptuous witnesses to the low esteem in which his countrymen held him. The king of France had ignored him, and his ambassador, du Croc, had refused him an interview that very day. Darnley was not at the christening because he did not want to be there, and felt that no one else wanted him to be there either. The admission to the Christian religion of the son coincided with the humiliation of the father, who skulked away to Glasgow shortly after the ceremony.

1. Had there been any suspicion at this stage of any impropriety between Bothwell and Mary, it would almost certainly have been aired. Clearly there was not.

2. As in the case of 'John Knox's House' in Edinburgh, there is little evidence that the house now known as 'Queen Mary's House', which is set back from the main street a few hundred yards from the town centre in Jedburgh, is the actual house referred to by contemporary chroniclers. There is no doubt, however, that the existing building is of the correct period, and a fine example of the sort of fortified house in which she would have stayed.

3. The Jedburgh visit has become famous in Marian history, not least for George Buchanan's racy account of the trip to Hermitage and the events surrounding Mary's illness. According to him, as soon as the queen heard of Bothwell's condition she dropped everything and hurried to his side. She lingered with him at Hermitage before bringing him back to Jedburgh and installing him in a room directly under her own in the house where she was staying. Buchanan implied that her illness was brought on by excessive 'indulgence in their passion'. Apart from being contemptible, the story is highly suspect, in that 'indulgence in passion' would have been a highly improbable, not to say dangerous pastime, whether lying severely injured at Hermitage or nearly dead at Jedburgh. In any case the dates simply do not fit. Bothwell was wounded on 7 October. Mary arrived at Jedburgh before the 9th, was probably told about it immediately, but did not ride out for Hermitage until the 16th. She fell ill on her return to Jedburgh the same day, was despaired of on the 25th and started to recover shortly afterwards. Bothwell was brought to Jedburgh on a litter, also about the 25th, and Darnley arrived, for his one-night stay, about three days later.

CHAPTER 7

'Pity me Kinsmen'

DARNLEY MAY HAVE STARTED HIS JOURNEY TO GLASGOW IN A FIT OF PIQUE, but before he arrived he was a very sick man indeed. He took to his bed on Christmas Eve suffering, according to contemporary reports, from smallpox. There is now some evidence that his ailment was syphilis and this would certainly accord with his promiscuous behaviour over the previous year or so.[1] However, from Christmas till 20 January, Mary did not seem to take his illness too seriously and, naturally, she was still furious with him over his outrageous behaviour at the christening.

During that period, Mary restored the powers of Archbishop Hamilton – probably in order to enable him to facilitate her separation from Darnley without making the young Prince James illegitimate. However, there was such an outcry from Protestant circles that she revoked the archbishop's powers again a week later. At the same time, although this went very much against her personal feelings, she finally gave in to pressure from Moray to pardon the murderers of Rizzio.

Then on 20 January, after sending her own doctor to see and report on Darnley, Mary suddenly and unexpectedly decided to make the two-day journey to Glasgow. Her decision may have been taken in the light of the doctor's report that Darnley was sicker than had originally been thought, but a more likely explanation is that she had taken notice of certain sinister rumours that had been gaining strength since his departure from Stirling; rumours of a plot to imprison or kill her and place her infant son on the throne with Darnley as regent. It is difficult to imagine anything more likely to cause chaos than an attempted coup of this nature, and

Mary may have thought it prudent to bring her wayward husband back into her orbit.

The journey was not without danger; Glasgow was the heartland of the Lennox family, whose head was Darnley's father. Mary was, however, well protected by her troop of well armed soldiers picked by Bothwell, and the trip was uneventful. Glasgow was then a charming village on the banks of the Clyde with an imposing castle and an even more imposing cathedral with an archbishop's palace nearby. This last was empty since the archbishop, James Beaton, had been in voluntary exile in Paris since 1560, and Mary immediately made it her headquarters.

When Mary saw Darnley in the castle, he presented a pathetic sight. While he was clearly recovering, the illness, whatever it was, apart from having had a general wasting effect, had caused appalling facial disfigurement, and the wretched patient had elected to wear a taffeta mask to prevent his visitors from seeing the ravages inflicted by the disease on his once pretty face. He greeted Mary with a mixture of gratitude and reproach. He was clearly glad to see her, but fearful that she might have brought with her some of the lords he most hated and feared – those whom he had betrayed at the time of Rizzio's murder.

The queen stayed in Glasgow until the end of January but immediately began a campaign to persuade her husband to return to Edinburgh with her. Darnley was initially hesitant but eventually the attraction of the promised resumption of married life as King of Scots outweighed the fear of leaving his father's protection and returning to Edinburgh where so many of his enemies were. Mary explained gently that it was quite impossible for him to come back to Holyrood for fear of infecting the infant prince who had recently been moved there. She had arranged for him to stay at Craigmillar Castle, just to the south of Edinburgh, where she could come and visit him regularly.

When he was well enough, Darnley was loaded on to a horse litter and the journey back to Edinburgh began. Almost immediately he started to complain and said he would not go to Craigmillar. He was clearly worried about the isolated position of the castle and fearful of what might befall him when Mary was not with him. Eventually a compromise was reached and it was agreed that he should go to the old Provost's lodging at Kirk o' Field, a smaller house much closer to Holyrood, just inside the city wall on the south side of Edinburgh. Word was sent ahead to make the place ready.

On Saturday, 1 February the party arrived at Kirk o' Field and Mary set about making her husband comfortable. Furniture and supplies had been brought up from Holyrood and the doctors had decided that he should be there till the tenth of the month, which was the Monday after the end of the following week. Then he was to be given a bath, which would mark the end of his convalescence, after which, so they believed, he could return to Holyrood without any fear of spreading infection. Over the next few days Mary visited Darnley frequently and even slept in the house in the room below his on the nights of 5 and 7 February. But she was not the only one taking a vigilant interest in the progress of the king. Argyll, Huntly, Maitland, Morton, Bothwell and certain other lords and lairds were keeping a close watch on events, and none of them had any wish to see Darnley recover and resume his place at Mary's side. At the end of January, they met at Craigmillar Castle, and a bond was signed agreeing to Darnley's liquidation. Sir James Balfour was there and, as a qualified lawyer, probably drew up the bond to which he too was a signatory.

Bothwell was particularly active during the week after Darnley's arrival in Edinburgh, supervising his men who were moving huge quantities of gunpowder into the vaulted cellars of the building. This was probably carried out from the next door building, which belonged to Sir James Balfour's brother, Robert, and had interconnecting cellars with the king's lodging. About a hundred yards away was Hamilton House, the town residence of the Duke of Châtelherault, who was still in France and had lent it to his half-brother, Archbishop John Hamilton. The archbishop was as concerned as Bothwell and the other signatories of the Craigmillar Bond to see that Darnley did not resume his former position.

Bothwell's men toiled away for several days in their task of converting the lower part of Darnley's quarters into a mine and were almost ludicrously inept in concealing what they were doing. They left an empty powder barrel in the yard where inevitably it would be found and its origin traced; they bought candles at the last minute from a shop a few yards from the house; they obtained lint (fuse) from soldiers of the guard. Their activities have been described as 'dropping clues like drunken sailors scattering their money'.[2] They were later to pay dearly for their carelessness.

Morton, too, was active on the night of 9/10 February and had an assassination team stationed in the neighbourhood of the house. It is not certain whether Bothwell's men and Morton's had any knowledge of the activities nor even the existence of each other. What is clear is that their instructions were only subtly different. Bothwell's men were charged with killing the king inside the house, whereas Morton's were instructed that he should not leave the vicinity alive.

For the queen, the evening of Sunday 9 February was a busy time. She attended a farewell supper party given by the Bishop of Argyll for the Savoyard ambassador, Robertino Solara di Moreta. It was in Moreta's retinue that Rizzio had first come to Scotland and the party must have brought back memories of the man who was dragged, bleeding and screaming, from her presence exactly eleven months before. Many of her leading nobles were with her, including Argyll, Huntly, Bothwell and Cassilis. Morton and Maitland were absent, as was Moray, who made the last minute (and quite plausible) excuse that his wife, who was in a late stage of pregnancy, was ill, and needed him by her side.

After the party, the queen and her court, accompanied by Moreta, rode to Kirk o' Field and stayed for two or three hours with Darnley. The presence of so many people must have made it easier for her to excuse herself at about midnight. She had promised to attend a midnight masque at Holyrood in honour of the wedding of her favourite servant, Bastien Pages, who had been married that morning. Darnley grumbled, but was mollified when she reminded him that the next day he would be out of quarantine and they would sleep together at the palace. After the queen had left, Darnley called for some wine and sang a few songs with his servants, as was his custom. Then his valet, a young Englishman called Taylor, who was sleeping in the same room, put out the candles and they all retired.

At about two o'clock on the morning of Monday, 10 February, a mighty explosion occurred. So loud was it that at Holyrood, nearly a mile away, it was thought to be cannon fire. People from all over the town rose from their beds and hurried to the scene. The sight that met their eyes was one of utter destruction. All that remained of Darnley's quarters was a pile of rubble and it seemed that no one could have survived the blast. But someone had. Darnley's servant, Nelson, was found wandering about in the wreckage and many of those present began to dig in the rubble for other survivors. Two bodies were found, soon identified as servants. There was no sign of Darnley or Taylor. Then, considerably later, a search of the grounds was mounted and the two missing men were found in a

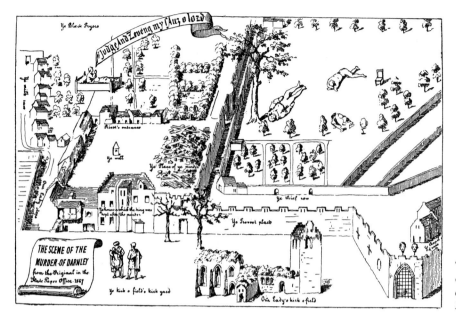

The Scene of the Murder of Darnley, *from the original in The Public Record Office*

garden beyond the town wall. They were clad only in night shirts and were both dead, but there was no sign of the cause of death on their bodies.

Much has been made of the fact that the bodies of Darnley and Taylor were discovered so far from the centre of the explosion. It was also thought to be strange, if not sinister, that not only did the bodies show no sign of blackening or charring from the explosion, but there were no external signs of the cause of death on either of them.

From the many explanations, of varying degrees of plausibility, that have been offered for these phenomena, the two that seem the least outlandish are:

1. The two unfortunate men were blown there by the explosion. If they were in their beds at the moment of the blast, they would probably have been reasonably well protected from any scorching effects. After the volcanic eruption in Martinique in 1902 and the subsequent *'nué ardente'* which claimed more than 40,000 lives, it was established that inhalation of gas at temperatures of 400°C (750°F) is necessary for less than one second to effect total destruction of the lungs. Under these circumstances, no visible cause of death need be evident. Darnley and his servant were immediately above the gunpowder when it ignited, and it is at least

79

possible that they inhaled the combustion products at such temperatures. It has to be said, however, that the likelihood of them being propelled so far without sustaining any visible injuries on impact with the ground, or any of the objects that must have been flying through the air, at the same time as they were, is extremely small. There is also more than an element of coincidence in the fact that both men were found so close together and in the same condition.

2. Perhaps a more likely explanation is that the men heard or smelt something which frightened them into beating a hasty retreat from the house. Morton's men, Douglases, all related to Darnley through his mother, Lady Margaret Douglas, were hiding in the grounds or just outside the city wall, determined to see that the king did not get far. It would not have been difficult for them to seize the two frightened and breathless men and suffocate them. If this is what happened, it would account for Darnley's pathetic last words, allegedly heard by some women who lived nearby: 'Pity me kinsmen for the sake of him who had pity on all the world.'

If the latter explanation is correct, it says much for the presence of mind of Morton's men. They had been quietly lurking in the shadows of the old Provost's lodging, patiently waiting to carry out one or possibly more murders – a business not unfamiliar to them – when the whole house blew up. Whether they thought it a form of divine retribution or a warning must have depended on whether they had just murdered Darnley, or were just about to. In any event, unlike Bothwell's blundering cronies, they completed their task with consummate efficiency, and melted into the dark. Apart from Morton himself, who was almost certainly not at the scene of the crime, only one of them, John Binning, the servant of Archibald Douglas, Parson of Glasgow, paid the price for the Douglases' role in the evening's work, and that some fourteen years later.[3]

Whether Bothwell's, Morton's or even someone else's men were the immediate cause of Darnley's demise is largely irrelevant since so many interests had been conspiring towards the removal of the embarrassing and dangerous twenty-one-year-old. Had there been no gunpowder plot that night, and had Morton's men not been in the garden, there seems little doubt that others would have ensured that Darnley did not see his twenty-second birthday.

Bothwell was at Holyrood at the moment of the explosion and, by the time that he had made his way to Kirk o' Field, a large crowd had gathered, some to help with digging in the rubble for the bodies and survivors and some merely to gaze at the unfortunate victims. Eventually the corpse of the man who was king for a year and seven months was carried into the house next door to be examined by doctors in the presence of some of the lords of the Privy Council. Then it was put on a board and carried to Holyrood.

Bothwell returned to Holyrood and broke the news to Mary. It caused her to go into a sort of collapse, not unlike her father's shortly before his death after the battle of Solway Moss. It was a state most uncharacteristic of one who might have conspired in the death of her husband. A theory which has been advanced is that from early January she believed she was pregnant, almost certainly by Bothwell. Fearful of the scandal that would ensue, since everyone knew that she had not cohabited with her husband for many months, she decided to entice him home. She went to all the trouble to go to Glasgow and persuade him to come back to Edinburgh, not in order to have him killed, but to sleep with him and legitimise the baby she believed she was carrying. This theory, allied to the likelihood that she had inherited her father's tendency to go into a catatonic state,[4] when under extreme stress, has the merit of explaining the fact that her behaviour, over the next two months, was almost suicidally irrational.

In any case, pregnant or not, Mary was most convincing in her demonstrations of shock, grief, anger and fear. She made it quite clear that she believed the plot was aimed at her as well as her husband, and that it was only by chance that she was not staying at Kirk o' Field on the fatal night. This was not unreasonable since she had spent the nights of 5 and 7 February there and the explosion occurred in the early hours of 10 February. Her depression continued for at least a month and it is a matter of conjecture whether it had completely lifted by 15 May, the day on which she made what was, up to that time, the worst and most damaging decision of her life.

1. It is debatable whether Mary knew, or even suspected, the nature of Darnley's illness. There is plenty of evidence that she was familiar with the subject of venereal disease – many of her contemporaries were afflicted by it and, at her son's christening, she would not let the 'pocky priest', Archbishop John Hamilton, spit in the child's mouth, presumably for risk of infection. The evidence indicating that Darnley had syphilis is considerably less conclusive; much of it depends on the examination of pitting on a skull said to be his. Since the skull was taken from Holyrood after 1688, when the royal vault was vandalised, its authenticity is in some doubt. In the second casket letter, Mary (allegedly) referred to Darnley's breath,

which 'nearly killed her', and compared it with that of Bothwell's uncle the reprobate Bishop of Moray who, in the light of his age and admitted sexual proclivities, was extremely likely to have had the disease in its tertiary stage. The treatment at the time (which was often more dangerous than the disease) was the oral administration of a salivation of mercury, which had an unpleasant odour. There were however other causes of bad breath – not least rotten teeth, which were very common. Darnley's facial rash or pustules, which required him to wear a mask, are more indicative of smallpox than syphilis, which only rarely breaks out in such a way.

More important than what the nature of Darnley's ailment was, however, is what Mary thought it to be. The most that can be said is that those of her contemporaries who believed in the authenticity of the casket letters, also believed that she thought, or at least suspected, that her husband had syphilis. If she did, it is almost impossible to understand her evident enthusiasm to resume normal marital relations with him on the evening of 10 February (he was killed that morning). If she had any idea of the contagious nature of the disease, this plan would seem to amount to foolhardy lack of concern for her health, and that of any child she was carrying. It is just possible, however, that her frantic desire to legitimise the child overcame her fear and revulsion.

2. George Malcolm Thomson in: *The Crime of Mary Stuart*.

3. Archibald Douglas was careless enough to leave one of his slippers at the scene of the crime. Despite this incriminating piece of evidence, he was cleared of the charge of regicide at his trial in 1581. His acquittal may have been something to do with the number of Douglases who packed the court, some of whom were even on the jury. He lived to a fair age and was still active in the 1590s.

4. Catatonia is a syndrome of motor abnormalities associated with an atypical mental state. It manifests itself in two different manners – the excited and the inhibited. The syndrome often leads to behaviour being modified by suggestion. See next chapter.

CHAPTER 8

'Wantons marry in the month of May'

IN THE CAREERS OF FAMOUS PEOPLE, THERE IS OFTEN ONE ACTION WHICH appears, in the light of hindsight, to have been a turning point, a parting of the ways. From that one incident there may be traced a steady movement towards fame and fortune or dishonour and disaster. Shakespeare was to put such a sentiment into the mouth of Hamlet; a generation earlier, Mary had confirmed its truth. The action was her marriage to Bothwell.

The abrupt removal of Darnley from the terrestrial scene was no great tragedy except for the unfortunate king. It was far from being the first assassination of one of Scotland's rulers; the kingdom had survived many worse incidents. Indeed, there was good reason to expect that the explosion at Kirk o' Field might clear the political atmosphere. Mary was no less at the head of affairs because of the death of her unreliable and erratic husband. On the contrary, the strong opposition which had been aroused by her second marriage might now be expected to melt away. So long as she could keep her indignation over Rizzio's death under control, she stood to regain much of the support that her alliance to Darnley had forfeited.

The problem lay with Mary herself. From the time that she heard of her husband's death, she was in deep shock. Her reaction, far from being that of a woman who had conspired to murder her spouse, bore every sign of a paralysis of fear and anxiety, similar to that of her father at the end of his life. Her doctors began to be troubled by the depth of her depression. It was the practice of European courts for a widow to go into formal mourning for forty days, confined to her chamber and cut off from the world. The medical advice given to Mary was to break with custom and leave Edinburgh for some 'good wholesome air'. On 16 February the queen left the capital to stay with Lord Seton at his house on the Firth of Forth. Here, she may have played a little golf; if she did, it was to no avail. Her black mood persisted. As late as 8 March, she received an envoy from England in audience in a darkened room; there was a suspicion that she had arranged to be impersonated by one of her ladies. There was no sign, in these weeks of mourning when Mary might have consolidated her position, that she was capable of decisive action.

Her lassitude was no reflection of the state of public opinion. In Edinburgh, there was a ferment of suspicion. At first, it was directed solely at Bothwell. Placards began to appear, on the door of the Tolbooth and in other places, accusing him of Darnley's murder. This was straightforward enough and wholly to be expected, but from the beginning of March they became more sinister. They implied that the queen had known of the intended crime in advance and was therefore an accessory to the murder. Such an accusation had to disturb Mary's lethargy, and it did. Righteous indignation replaced apathy. She did not keep her distance from Bothwell; on the contrary she showered him with gifts and contrived to be seen with him in public.

Mary was adopting an attitude. But it was one thing to give Bothwell support in the face of popular indignation. It was wholly another to allow him and his followers to be brought to trial for regicide. If she believed him innocent, the queen would not go that far, and if she suspected he was guilty, she would do nothing at all. But there were others who were not disposed to remain inactive. The Earl of Lennox had ended sixteen years of bitter exile in England when he had come to Scotland to pave the way for his son. It was a time of honour after disgrace. Now his son was dead and he wanted revenge. Since the queen would do nothing, he applied to the Privy Council for a trial. To prevent any confusion, he cited Bothwell as the perpetrator. The council, in turn, required Lennox to act in the matter as if he, rather than the commonweal of Scotland, were the aggrieved party.

The date fixed for the hearing was 12 April. So badly had law and order broken down, and so weak had the queen's government become, that it was clear that the case was to be a trial of strength, rather than of fact. Bothwell packed Edinburgh with his supporters. Lennox marched towards the capital from Glasgow with 3,000 men but, on arriving at Linlithgow, he was informed that he could proceed no further with more than six companions. Unwilling to risk a confrontation against such massive odds, he turned his army around and went home. The hearing was held in the absence of the principal accuser, with Bothwell himself a Privy Councillor, active behind the scenes. Evidence was heard over eight hours; the result was a declaration of Bothwell's innocence. The Lennox counter-attack had failed.

The initiative in a confused situation had passed to Bothwell. Now was the time for him to push ahead in his quest for power by marrying Scotland's queen. A week later, he gave a supper party at Ainslie's Tavern in Edinburgh. An extraordinarily large and influential group of men was assembled – among them eight bishops, ten earls and eleven lords. Influential in a different way were the 200 soldiers, loyal to Bothwell, who surrounded the tavern. Here Bothwell encouraged his guests to sign yet another bond, this time committing them to favour his marriage to the queen. There was much talk, then and later, about coercion and Lord Eglinton was said to have slipped out, when no one was looking, to avoid adding his signature. But Argyll, Huntly and Morton, who did sign, were not men likely to be coerced by a passing show of force. The real coercion lay in their belief that Bothwell, wholly unsuitable though he was to be the queen's consort, was the only man strong enough to give the country a measure of desperately needed stability. Their belief was to be short-lived, but their consent was enough to encourage Bothwell to act.

On 24 April, Mary was returning to Edinburgh from Stirling, where she had spent a few days with James, her infant son. In her company were about thirty people, among them Huntly and Maitland of Lethington and Sir James Melville. As they approached the capital, they were met by Bothwell and several hundred troopers. Seizing Mary's horse by the bridle, he declared that a dangerous situation had arisen in Edinburgh and that he was going to take her to Dunbar for her safety. Some of her party prepared to resist this high-handed action, but Mary stayed them, saying that she would have no more bloodshed. Accordingly, she allowed Bothwell to take her to Dunbar, with Huntly, Maitland and Melville attending her. The rest of her party continued their journey to Edinburgh.

Mary stayed at Dunbar for nearly a fortnight and returned to Edinburgh on 6 May. There was much talk at the time, and there has been endless argument ever since about Bothwell's 'abduction'. But the word seems inappropriate. Whatever she may have felt, Mary gave no credence to the accusations by anything that she did. In fact, she did nothing at all; she neither resisted going to Dunbar nor attempted to escape while she was there.

Meanwhile, the way was opening for the next step to be taken. Her husband's removal had made Mary free to marry again. Bothwell had a living wife, Lady Jean Gordon, sister of the Earl of Huntly, but this impediment was swiftly removed. While her husband was at Dunbar, Lady Jean obtained a divorce from him on the grounds of his adultery with one of her servants. The decree, of 3 May, was given in the Commissary Court and was a Protestant ruling. To the Catholics, on the other hand, divorce was an impossibility, but an annulment, a declaration that a marriage had never properly taken place, was a long established procedure. To make possible his nuptials with Lady Jean, who was a member of a traditionally Catholic family, Bothwell had earlier secured a dispensation from all impediments from John Hamilton, Archbishop of St Andrews. Now the same Catholic prelate, on 7 May, silently ignored his own dispensation and annulled the marriage. In the eyes of both the new and the old religions, Bothwell was available for matrimony.

There can be no doubt that Bothwell was determined to marry the queen. What is not so clear is what Mary wanted. She was several months pregnant, almost certainly by Bothwell. It was vital that the child (or, as it turned out, the twins) be legitimised by the marriage of the parents. A more persuasive factor was Mary's belief that here was a man who was strong and loyal, the only man in Scotland in whom she could place implicit trust, and the man who less than a month earlier had received the signed endorsement of his declared intention from at least twenty of the most influential men in Scotland. It is highly probable that the object of her confidence and affection had not yet confided to her the part he had played in her husband's murder. The question arises as to whether Mary suspected the truth. It is quite possible that she did, but so desperate was her need for a strong man she could trust, and so suitable did Bothwell appear to be in that role, that she willed herself to bury her doubts.

On 11 May, John Craig, Knox's colleague at St Giles, reluctantly read the banns of marriage. John Brand, the minister of the Canongate, had earlier courageously refused to do so. The following day, Mary elevated

Bothwell to the dukedom of Orkney, making him the first duke in Scotland since the simultaneous extinction of the dukedom of Albany and the life of Darnley three months earlier. Then at ten o'clock in the morning on 15 May, the pair were married, according to Protestant forms, by Adam Bothwell,[1] Bishop of Orkney and a friend of the bridegroom.

It was not only the religious rite which was novel at Mary's third wedding. There were few important guests, even fewer of the signatories to the Ainslie Tavern bond. There was no masque, no dancing, no popular rejoicing. Very soon the mood touched the bride. She wrote to the Pope, professing herself his 'most devoted daughter'. Later that day she broke down in front of John Leslie, the Catholic Bishop of Ross, and told him that she already deeply regretted marrying by Protestant form. Her regrets were to haunt her for the rest of her life.

Mary had private regrets but in the Catholic world, that she believed she had betrayed, there was public denunciation. The saintly Pope Pius V declared that he would have nothing to do with her until she mended her ways. Philip of Spain refused to have dealings with a woman who had married a divorced Protestant. In France, her Guise relations expressed horror and washed their hands of her. But long before the news had reached foreign parts, the streets of Edinburgh buzzed with disapproval. The placard campaign started once more, and soon there was a sign outside Holyrood scornfully inscribed, 'Wantons marry in the month of May'.

The only break in the blank wall of opposition came from England. Queen Elizabeth had some words of comfort for Mary and discouraged the flow of rumour around her court. She recognised Bothwell as an implacable foe of England and disliked him accordingly. Yet perhaps she preferred to see Mary married to an awkward Scottish nobleman than to a Catholic prince from the continent. It is even just possible that she had some sympathy; she could well remember the time when everyone had expected her to marry a man whom the world suspected of murder.[2] But Elizabeth's apparently compassionate attitude was deceptive. Exactly one year later, Mary was to allow it to influence her into making another mistake and casting herself on the English queen's mercy.

For the present, it was the mistake of her 'abduction', followed by her marriage to Bothwell that alienated many of Mary's nobles. Most of those who had been at Ainslie's Tavern were having second thoughts about Bothwell and the bond disintegrated under the stress. On 1 May, while

Mary was still in Dunbar, Argyll, Atholl, Morton, Murray of Tullibardine (the queen's comptroller) and others had signed a bond to rescue the queen. Their concern was needless. Some days after the wedding there was another bond, this time to secure the support of Sir James Balfour, a vital commodity, since at that time he was keeper of Edinburgh Castle. Finally, on 6 June, a very powerful group, including twelve earls and fourteen lords, the 'Confederate Lords', signed yet another bond agreeing to rescue Mary from Bothwell's 'captivity' and to punish the murderers of Darnley.

So within three weeks of her third wedding, the queen had alienated almost all of her allies in Europe and most of her supporters in Scotland. It was the marriage to Bothwell that caused the trouble. Suspicion of complicity in the murder of the appalling Darnley was something that she could have lived down. Had she acted with resolution and independence after the event, all might have been well. But she married Bothwell. From that moment, everyone firmly believed that she and her lover had murdered her husband. With that, her cause was lost.

1. Despite their friendship and the similarity in their methods of address (although not their surnames), James Hepburn, Earl of Bothwell and Duke of Orkney, and Adam Bothwell, Bishop of Orkney were not related.

2. Robert Dudley, Earl of Leicester (*c.* 1533–88), suspected of murdering his wife Amy Robsart.

CHAPTER 9

Confrontation, Abdication, Coronation

ON 15 JUNE 1567, A MONTH TO THE DAY AFTER MARY AND BOTHWELL MARRIED, their troops encountered those of the Confederate Lords at Carberry, six miles east of Edinburgh and just to the south of Pinkie, where the Scottish army had been so shamefully routed by the English twenty years earlier. Here, from two low hills, the rival forces faced each other for what might have become the decisive battle of the time.

Mary's soldiers formed up under the saltire of St Andrew; the queen herself had the flag of the Scottish lion. Her army was proclaiming that it was the upholder of the royal cause against those who would affront the dignity of the crown. The Confederate Lords had their family emblems but they also carried a white banner depicting the murdered Darnley with the infant James crying out for vengeance. They too were fighting for a cause – to extract their queen from the evil clutches of Bothwell.

It had been a month of hectic manoeuvring and of some achievement. Bothwell had proved less arrogant in public and more positive in policy than his enemies affected to believe. Mary had recently given express protection and security to the Reformed Church, something she had never done before. But to no avail; the Lords had made their bonds and gathered their soldiers. Mary and Bothwell had been surrounded in Borthwick Castle early in June and forced to make separate exits. Mary had parleyed with the besiegers long enough for her husband to make his escape and then, disguised in male attire, had slipped out, rejoined him and gone on to Dunbar.

Secure in Dunbar Castle, the royal couple had the opportunity to gather

Seton House from the
south-west

their forces and rally those nobles who were still uncommitted. But they were lured from their coastal stronghold by the promise of Sir James Balfour to protect them at Edinburgh Castle. Not for the first time, Balfour was playing them false. The little army, mostly recruited from East Lothian and the Borders, was without the support of their Hamilton allies or Huntly's Highlanders, who had no time to get there. The previous day, the soldiers had camped at Prestonpans while Mary and Bothwell had spent their last night together at Seton House nearby. On a hot Sunday morning, the royal troops took up their position on Carberry Hill, facing the soldiers of the Confederates who had marched out from the capital to block their progress.

There was no battle. Throughout the day, the armies eyed each other from their vantage points. The only action was a war of words. First of all, du Croc, the long serving and respected French ambassador, presented the rebel lords' case: they would reaffirm their allegiance if Mary were to dispose of Bothwell and deliver herself up to them. Mary's anger became as hot as the day. Bothwell was her rightful husband; had not these rebel lords urged her to marry him? Why should she entrust herself to these men, now in arms against her, rather than to her own loyal and lawful spouse? Not surprisingly, she did not add, although by now she knew, that she was pregnant by Bothwell. Du Croc's mission had failed.

Then began a series of challenges. It was suggested that the issue might be decided by single combat between champions of each side. Bothwell eagerly accepted, to find Sir William Kirkcaldy of Grange, not only willing but enthusiastic to meet him in single combat in front of both armies. Bothwell however, not unaware of Kirkcaldy's awesome reputation, declined to fight him on the grounds that it was beneath him, as a duke and consort to the queen, to fight someone as lowly as a mere knight. He then issued a counter-challenge to James Douglas, Earl of Morton. Morton, who was now over fifty, was under no illusions about his chances of success against the thirty-one-year-old Bothwell, so he deputed Patrick, Lord Lindsay of the Byres, who, although only a few years younger than Morton, had a reputation almost as impressive as that of Kirkcaldy. Lindsay accepted with alacrity and Morton presented him with the mighty two-handed sword which had once belonged to his famous ancestor Archibald Douglas, 'Bell the Cat'. At this stage, Mary, alarmed at what might happen, intervened. She forbade Bothwell to accept or issue any more challenges.

So nothing happened at the front. What was of significance was happening at the rear. Here there were no heroic posturings, no time-wasting histrionics. Mary's army was beginning to melt away. The heat of the day, the lack of food and drink, the stalling of the opposing army, the absence of reinforcements from the west and north were all taking their toll.

The fear of desertion forced Mary to think of negotiation. Although Bothwell was prepared to meet Lindsay, he agreed with her that they should live to fight another day. It was better to retreat to Dunbar and wait for their army to be reinforced and the opposition to be weakened by disaffection. Mary went further. She submitted to the rebels' latest offer, brought by Kirkcaldy: Bothwell would be allowed to leave the field, Mary would surrender to the Confederate Lords and they would acknowledge her sovereignty. Trusting in Kirkcaldy's integrity, the queen said that she believed that, given peaceful conditions, a parliamentary enquiry might acquit Bothwell of Darnley's murder. If the findings of the enquiry went the other way, 'it would be [for Mary] an endless source of regret that, by her marriage, she had ruined her good reputation'; then she added: 'from this she would endeavour to free herself by every possible means'.

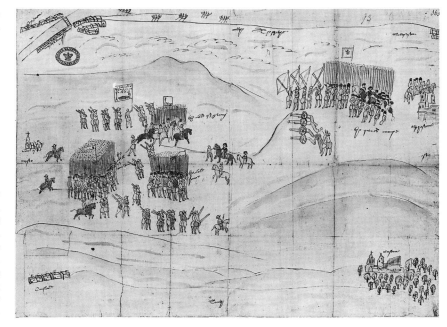

Carberry Hill, *primitive
drawing showing Queen
Mary being led towards the
Lords of the Congregation
under the delusion that she
was returning to Edinburgh
in triumph. Instead, she
was imprisoned in Lochleven
the following day
(Public Record Office)*

Bothwell then made his last contribution to the Darnley saga. He gave
Mary the bond signed at Craigmillar, which made clear the intention
of Maitland, Morton and the other conspirators to kill the king. It also
clarified, or so he hoped, his own reliance on their counsel in the whole
gruesome affair. Then he embraced his wife and rode off towards
Dunbar. They never met again.

The queen was now in the hands of the Confederate Lords. She had
relied on Kirkcaldy's word that they would respect her person and accept
her authority. But some of them wished to detain her person and usurp her
authority. Mary soon saw that she had made a terrible mistake. As
evening fell, she was taken to the rebels' camp amidst the jeers of the
soldiers. As a prisoner, she was taken to Edinburgh to meet insults and
abuse from the populace. Shrieks of 'whore' and 'murderess' accompanied her up the High Street. Only now did the appalling consequences
of her marriage to Bothwell begin to dawn on her.

The Sunday night at Edinburgh and the following day were, for Mary,
a time of humiliation and total disillusion. Her regality was at an end, she
was subjected to insults and her future seemed black indeed. Taken, not
to Holyrood in state but to the Provost's house as a captive, she spent a

troubled time, surrounded by soldiers, unable to sleep, shunned by Maitland and other possible sympathisers and taunted by the crowd. The spectacle of the Queen of Scots, Dowager of France, descendant of a hundred kings, heir to the thrones of England and Ireland, now dishevelled and in disarray, screaming for help to the crowd below her window, and being brutally dragged back by the guards – this scene has appealed to the dramatic instinct of every historian of Scotland. How much further could the mighty fall? What was there left of the dignity of the crown of Scotland?

To the resolute among the Confederate Lords, there was more work to be done. Their seizure of practical power had to be made legitimate, and this could only happen if Mary were out of the public gaze. Their own part in Darnley's murder had to be concealed, above all, from any official enquiry. On that fateful Monday, Morton, Maitland and their associates decided to pack the queen off to the island fortress of Lochleven. To justify this decision in the face of moderate men such as Kirkcaldy of Grange, who believed in honouring the arrangement made at Carberry, Morton and his friends broadcast the story that Mary, far from abandoning Bothwell, as she had promised, had written him a letter promising to stand by him. Kirkcaldy, rightly, could not believe this but was overruled. Late in the evening, Mary was taken to Holyrood. Thinking herself safe, she broke the fast that she had maintained since leaving the field of Carberry but it was not long before her hopefulness was shattered by the news that she was now to be taken to Stirling. She was then escorted to Leith by two of the coarser and more ferocious of her enemies, the Lords Lindsay and Ruthven. She tried delaying tactics on the road in the hope of rescue by the Hamiltons but her efforts came to nothing. The destination was not to be Stirling, where she could be reunited with her infant son, but the castle of Sir William Douglas, remote on its island in Loch Leven. This was to be Mary's prison as ordained by Morton and other lords who, only two months earlier, had signed the Ainslie bond, favouring her marriage to Bothwell. She must have wondered if it was to be her tomb.

For more than ten months, until 2 May 1568, Mary was a prisoner in the grim castle, secure in the middle of the loch. Her gaoler and the castle's owner was the younger half-brother of her own half-brother, the Earl of Moray. Their mother, the redoubtable Margaret Erskine, the widowed chatelaine, had hated Mary's mother, who had replaced her in James V's

Lochleven Castle, *from an
old print in the British
Museum*

affections and now felt under no obligation to make the queen's stay a
pleasant one. When she arrived, Mary was in a state of shock as a result
of the events of the previous week, so she took to her bed and fell into a
stupor, as she had done at earlier crises in her life.

Beyond the confines of the castle and the loch, there was a welter of
activity. Much of it centred round Bothwell. After leaving Carberry in the
direction of Dunbar Castle, he had tried to gather support, although there
was a price on his head. For a time it seemed that he might meet with
some success. But his official outlawry turned the tide against him. He
moved northwards and came to Spynie, the palace of his uncle, the disreputable Bishop of Moray. Betrayed by the bishop's illegitimate sons,
and pursued to Orkney by the resolute Kirkcaldy of Grange, he escaped
to Norway in September.

Bothwell left a legacy. On 24 July, Mary had a miscarriage and gave
birth to stillborn twins. Ever since, there has been controversy about the
date of conception. It was (and still is) argued that if conception occurred
before the death of Darnley, her complicity in her second husband's
murder was highly probable. This postulation seems far from being
proven and, in any case, an examination of the relevant dates indicates
that it is quite possible that conception took place about the time that
Bothwell 'abducted' Mary to Dunbar. The main result of the miscarriage,
however, was immediate and clear. In her weakened state after giving
birth, the queen became less and less concerned for the absent Bothwell.
This made it easier for the Confederate Lords to remove her from the
throne.

It appeared to Queen Elizabeth that Mary's imprisonment might lead to her enforced abdication. Dismayed at this threat to a fellow-monarch, she tried to have the young Prince James sent to England, and dispatched Sir Nicholas Throckmorton to Scotland with instructions to try to effect this. The new ambassador could make little headway. Before the birth (and death) of the babies, Mary would not agree to divorce Bothwell nor to preserve her own life by abdicating. But Throckmorton smuggled her a message, concealed in a scabbard. He entreated her to agree, under duress, to renounce her crown. Such an enforced abdication, he assured her, would be invalid in law, yet might save her life. By no other means could her safety be ensured.

It was with these words in mind that Mary, enfeebled after childbirth, met the crude threats of Lindsay: she must abdicate or die. On 24 July the queen put her signature to three documents of abdication, whereby Prince James would assume the crown, Moray would become regent, with Morton ruling as his deputy until Moray's return from abroad, and a council would act in conjunction with both. Mary signed these instruments without reading them, thereby stressing her contempt for their legality. But they served the lords' purpose. On 29 July, at the parish church at Stirling, after a formal reading of the abdication documents, Prince James became King of Scots. Morton and Home acted for the thirteen-month-old king, and John Knox preached the coronation sermon. It was two years to the day since Mary had married Darnley.

CHAPTER 10

Exit

MARY WAS A PRISONER AT LOCHLEVEN; JAMES WAS KING; THE CONFEDERATE Lords were in control. Mary had lost her throne; there was the prospect that she would lose even more. Already, Throckmorton had reported that if the lords ventured 'to touch their sovereign in honour or credit, they will never think to find any safety so long as she lives, and so not only deprive her of her estates, but also of her life'. Now that the estates had gone, what was the prospect for that life?

In August, just under a month after her imprisonment, Mary was visited by her half-brother Moray who had recently returned from England. Over the next two days, he lectured her in terms that were far from fraternal. Referring to the murder of Darnley, he told her that while she might be innocent in the eyes of God, she certainly was not in the eyes of her people. With mountainous hypocrisy, he said that it was not enough to refrain from committing a crime; it was also necessary to avoid the suspicion of it. As far as is known, he gave no reason why this, by now useless advice, had not been offered two months earlier. Nor did he explain why so many of those, who at that time had enthusiastically encouraged her to marry Bothwell, were now denouncing her. At the end of the first day, he made it clear to Mary that she was in grave danger of execution; he later informed Throckmorton that he had left her 'with the hope of nothing but God's mercy'. Then, adopting a posture, in Throckmorton's words, 'of leading his people like the ancient prophets of Israel', he told her that, although his private tastes led him to shun grandeur and personal ambition, he had reluctantly decided to accept the regency.

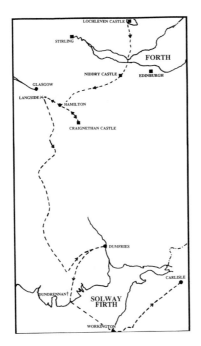

Lochleven–Langside–Carlisle

After the interview, Moray returned to Edinburgh, made a full report to Throckmorton for the benefit of Queen Elizabeth and, on 22 August, was proclaimed Regent of Scotland. One of the pettier things he did over the next few weeks was to pilfer his half-sister's jewellery. His eyes had been on the collection, since (and possibly before) Mary and he had been in Jedburgh the previous October, and now his opportunity had arrived. Some of the pieces he gave to his wife, and others he sold to Queen Elizabeth in order to alleviate his parlous finances. The one thing he did not do was carry out Mary's wishes and ensure that, on her death, most of them 'be permanently united with the Crown of Scotland'.

Back in Lochleven, Mary's situation did not look promising. Parliament would not help her and refused her an opportunity to appear before it; Mary was confronted only with the legislature's confirmation of her abdication and Moray's regency. External aid was no more hopeful; neither England nor France would give practical assistance. Meanwhile the prospect of rescue from the grim fortress seemed remote. The queen's supporters were dispirited and disorganised. Nor was that all. In confirming James's accession and Mary's imprisonment, the Privy Council and parliament declared Bothwell to have been the 'chief executioner of the horrible murder' of Darnley, and Mary to have been 'privy, art and part of the actual devise and deed of the forenamed murder of the King her lawful husband'. It was not being Bothwell's wife, but his accomplice that was Mary's alleged transgression; indiscretion was one thing, murder quite another.

On 2 May 1568, the situation changed abruptly. After a few false starts, Mary escaped from Lochleven, chiefly by the contrivance of its owner's brother, the dashing George Douglas, one of the queen's would-be suitors, and his orphaned cousin, Willy. Only a few nobles, including Lord Seton

and probably Lord Claud Hamilton, had prior knowledge of the intended
escape, but both the news and the support for Mary spread with amazing
speed; the French ambassador declared that he had never seen anything
like it. Suddenly, there was not only sympathy for Mary in Scotland,
there was a Marian army in the field. Over the next eleven days, Mary
became once more, and for the last time, in a position of power.

The end came on 13 May. Mary was keen to skirt Glasgow and go to
Dumbarton with her army to await reinforcements from the Highlands
generally and Huntly's Gordons in particular. But the Hamiltons were
keen to settle the matter on their own territory, especially as Mary's forces
outnumbered those of the regent by about three to two. So they insisted
on doing battle at Langside, a small village between Hamilton and
Glasgow. In a brief contest which, though decisive, did not produce
many casualties on either side, the generalship of Kirkcaldy and Morton,
the suicidal impatience of the Hamiltons, the physical collapse of Argyll
and the consequent desertion of the Campbells ensured Mary's defeat.
These were the fortunes of war. It might have been otherwise. For all
their passivity during her imprisonment at Lochleven, Mary's supporters
and sympathisers were numerous and widely distributed. There were
those, such as the Hamiltons, who had for some time stood by her. There
were others – Argyll was one – who thought that Bothwell's expulsion
was sufficient reason to give her full support. Moray's rule had not
endeared him to everyone in Scotland. The Langside fight might have
been averted until the Marian party was stronger in the field. Even after
Langside, there was the strong chance that the struggle might have been
continued with vigour if Mary had remained in Scotland. It died away
because it lacked royal leadership. Instead of going to Dumbarton or
another of her strongholds, Mary fled to England.

The journey south was arduous. In all probability, Mary was in fear for
her life, remembering the fate that befell her great-grandfather, James III,
who was murdered trying to escape from the battle of Sauchieburn eighty
years earlier. Mary reached Workington via Dumfries and Dundrennan
on 16 May. There were many arguments along the way. Her advisers
were in favour of her remaining in her native land or taking temporary
refuge in France. They especially remonstrated against her precipitous
decision to cross the Solway into England. Elizabeth may have shown
sympathy during the Lochleven episode, but which Scottish monarch

had ever been safe among the English? But Mary insisted that the English queen would receive her with kindness and provide her with the resources to regain her throne. It was a fatal mistake. Only death was to release her from the clutches of Elizabeth's hospitality.

Thereafter, the story of Mary Queen of Scots falls into two parts. There was the captive queen, under house arrest (or worse) in England, waiting on the pleasure of Elizabeth. There were her supporters in Scotland, holding out against the authority of King James and his regents. Since both the king's and the queen's parties had a close interest in Mary's English fate and fortunes, the two parts are inextricably linked.

One element in the story had now disappeared inside a Danish prison. Bothwell, on the run from Scotland, had landed in Norway, where he had the misfortune to meet some of his former creditors and the relatives of his discarded mistress, Anna Throndsen. Love and money – or rather, the shortage of both – were a powerful combination. Soon he found himself the prisoner of Frederik II, King of Denmark and Norway, who saw in his captive a potential pawn in the game of international politics. In time, Bothwell's diplomatic value faded but, despite Scottish attempts at extradition, he remained a prisoner in increasingly squalid conditions. He died, broken and insane in Dragsholm Castle in 1578, still the lawful husband of Mary. There were attempts by Mary's supporters to get the marriage annulled. But nothing happened since Pope Pius V and then Pope Gregory XIII, who succeeded him in 1572, were fearful that Mary would be further endangered rather than assisted by an annulment.

The flight of Mary to England did not mean that support for her cause in Scotland had come to an end. It is true that the king's party was in a strong position. At its head was Moray, now regent. His government had the backing of many nobles and lairds and most, but by no means all, of the Reformed clergy. The re-enactment of the Reformation legislation of 1560, never ratified until now, albeit seven years late, ensured the sympathy of some ministers. The queen's party, however, still commanded respect. There were Reformers, both clerical and lay, in its ranks. Some of the greatest nobles – Argyll, Châtelherault and Huntly – were on her side. Nor was Queen Elizabeth, Mary's reluctant hostess, wholly in favour of Moray and the infant James VI. In all probability, she would have preferred Mary to be in Scotland rather than England where she could be a source of trouble. So she ordered a conference to be held at York, where Regent Moray's charges against Queen Mary, and hers against him, could be assessed.

At York, and later at Westminster and Hampton Court, Mary's commissioners, including Bishop Leslie and Lord Herries, and those of Moray, including Maitland of Lethington and the regent himself, met commissioners appointed by Elizabeth, who included the Earl of Sussex, Sir Ralph Sadler and the Duke of Norfolk. Moray presented his case with vigour; Mary was not permitted to attend. During the tortuous proceedings, the emphasis gradually shifted from Moray's acts of rebellion against his anointed queen to Mary's complicity in the murder of her husband. Her commissioners protested against the change in direction, but to no avail. Before the 'trial' had begun, Elizabeth had been talking of Mary's return to Scotland on strict conditions; towards its end, she was allowing her commissioners to consider the possibility of the Scottish queen's guilt.

The conclusions turned out to be negative. As a consequence of the commissioners' report, it was declared that nothing had been proved against Moray which impaired his honour. Mary too was exonerated; as Cecil said, there was no evidence produced by Mary's accusers 'whereby the Queen of England should conceive, or take any evil opinion of the Queen her good sister'. But there the similarity ended. Moray was granted an audience with Elizabeth and went home to Scotland with English money in his pocket and the regency still in his possession. Mary was not permitted to meet her royal cousin – then or ever – and remained under detention in England. She was merely moved from Bolton Castle, which she disliked, to Tutbury Castle, which she hated.

Elizabeth's commissioners had been unimpressed by the evidence which came to be known as the 'Casket Letters'. The originals of the eight letters, two marriage contracts and 158 lines of verse were appropriated by James VI in 1584, and have never been seen since. All that remains are copies and copies of copies in Scots, English or the original French. These purport to show collusion between Mary and Bothwell in planning the death of Darnley. According to Morton, no friend of Mary, they had been taken from Geordie Dalgleish, a tailor in Bothwell's service, and exhibited to some of Mary's opponents in June 1567. Their existence was not mentioned during Mary's arrest and imprisonment or at the time of her flight to England. Only in December 1568 were they officially produced at Westminster, by which time Dalgleish had long been executed for his part in the outrage at Kirk o' Field. They did nothing to sway the commissioners' judgement. But these documents, some forged, some doctored, most more or less irrelevant, and all now disappeared, came to stir the imagination of later historians. Mary's contemporaries were less impressed by what may have been a hasty piece of unscrupulous 'editing'. The final verdict, however, delivered in January 1569, was dictated chiefly by English policy. It suited Elizabeth to maintain Regent Moray in Scotland, without so alienating Mary's supporters as to drive them into the arms of the French.

The king's party remained in control of the government of Scotland. It won over some of Mary's supporters and showed no sign of losing its place in the country. But the queen's party was still formidable. Some influential notables were to be found in its ranks, now augmented by Maitland of Lethington and Kirkcaldy of Grange, hitherto Mary's opponents. The Marians were in possession of Dumbarton Castle, which controlled the traffic on the Clyde, and Edinburgh Castle, whose guns dominated the capital. Moray, meanwhile, was ineffectual in rounding up Elizabeth's rebel subjects, who fled across the border after the collapse of the rebellion of the northern Catholics in England. Before he was able to re-establish his credibility with London, he was assassinated in January 1570.

Elizabeth, in any case, had lost her enthusiasm for a strong anti-Mary policy. She withdrew her raiding troops from Scotland, secured the appointment of the anglophile Lennox as regent and arranged an armistice between the factions. These pacific moves were followed by an offer to restore Mary to the Scottish throne, albeit on stringent conditions. Given the international situation of the time, England needed peace in Scotland. But England's and Scotland's requirements have rarely been in harmony and they were not in 1570. The king's party would have none of the suggestion that Mary should return to Edinburgh. Morton and Mar gained parliamentary support for their stand. The truce was soon broken; civil war once again plagued the country. The king's party knew that it could afford to ignore Elizabeth's proposals. England needed its help in keeping Scotland neutral and the English rear secure in the event of trouble on the Continent. There was little that Elizabeth could do to enforce a truce. The struggle in Scotland was a contest for power between rival groups; England's concern was for security amid the tangle of European power and religious politics. The scenario was not new.

The new, and possibly crucial, factor was the presence in England of the captive Mary. There was a sense in which Mary was more important as a helpless prisoner in Tutbury or Chatsworth than she had ever been as the ruling Queen of Scots. On the face of things, Mary was bereft of power. She was kept under ever tighter control, her retinue whittled down, her freedom of movement constricted. She had few means of gaining accurate information about affairs; she could not communicate readily with the outside world. The cloak and dagger diplomacy to which she had to resort did little to promote her interests. But Mary's personal qualities gave strength to her cause. Despite bouts of that depression and inertia which afflicted her throughout her life, she generally maintained her spirits and her courage. Despite some flirtation, probably for political reasons, with the Anglican Church, she consolidated, and even intensified, her Catholic faith. There was also that personal fascination which ensnared the unlikeliest of men, even Cecil himself. It was in no way diminished by the woes of captivity; if anything, they gave it a further dimension, that of the tragic heroine.

If Mary the imprisoned princess had some strengths, then Mary the Catholic queen had others. She was an anointed sovereign, whose sacrosanctity was treated with respect by her fellow monarchs. She was next in succession to the throne of England. Were Elizabeth to die unmarried or childless or, as it turned out, both, who else could succeed her? In fact, Mary had never wholly abandoned her claim to have a better right to the English throne than Elizabeth herself. She was thus at the centre of the activities of the queen's opponents. She was a Catholic, whereas the Protestant Elizabeth had been excommunicated in 1570, and her Catholic subjects therefore released from their allegiance to her by Pope Pius V. Catholic plotters and Catholic princes could only take advantage of Mary's role. She was half-French and formerly the consort of a Valois king. France could not ignore the incarceration of one of its two Queens Dowager. She was a threat to the English establishment and therefore useful to England's emerging enemy, Spain. Her husband, Bothwell, had disappeared into a Danish dungeon. A divorce was a strong possibility and would make Mary an intriguing marriage prospect. She was a Stewart, forced to abdicate. There was some prospect that Scottish events would require her presence in Edinburgh. Mary's prison, seemingly remote from the rest of the world, was the focal point for every kind of local, national and international political and religious interest from 1568 to 1587. The more powerless Mary became, the more her influence increased. And so did her vulnerability.

As a prisoner in England, Mary was more important as Elizabeth's rival for the English throne than as the predecessor of James VI in Scotland. Around the captive queen were local rebels, political malcontents, Catholic recusants, international adventurers, foreign diplomats and churchmen – all ready to use Mary's desire for freedom for their own purposes. Mary was significant because she was Catholic rather than because she was Scottish.

Even as Mary's name was being cleared by Elizabeth's commissioners, England's relations with Spain reached their first crisis point. This prompted Don Guerau de Spes, who had taken over from de Silva as Spanish ambassador, to concoct an elaborate scheme which included marrying Mary to the Duke of Norfolk and making her Queen of England. The plan inevitably failed but the involvement in it of dis-affected English nobles was ominous. In 1569 the great 'Rising of the North' broke out, a large-scale movement both feudal and religious. Norfolk lacked the resolution to lead it, but the rebels thought of Mary as England's new queen. With the rebellion crushed, and some of its leaders fugitives in Scotland, Elizabeth once more sought peace on the border by suggesting that Mary be returned to Scotland as queen. Morton and the king's party would have none of it.

Before Elizabeth could take further action, the discovery of another plot, a complex and ambitious conspiracy by the hare-brained Florentine, Ridolfi (who had been involved with de Spes), once more implicated Mary and Norfolk and some of the Marian party. Norfolk was executed and Mary was more closely confined. To isolate her further, in April 1572, Elizabeth made the treaty of Blois with the French. Meanwhile the tide began to turn against the Marians in Scotland. Dumbarton Castle fell in 1571 and Archbishop Hamilton who had taken refuge there was escorted to Stirling where he was hanged in his vestments. The Hamiltons' response was the killing of Regent Lennox. The massacre of St Bartholomew's Eve in France, in August 1572, renewed England's fears of French aggression in Scotland on behalf of Mary and her party.

At Edinburgh, Maitland and Kirkcaldy still held the castle for the queen. After toying with the notion of returning Mary to the new regent, Mar, for trial, Elizabeth determined to promote a general peace in Scotland. Mar's successor, Morton, was persuaded to resolve his differences with the

Edinburgh Castle 1573,
drawing by David Simon

Hamiltons and Huntly at the Pacification of Perth in February 1573. But Edinburgh Castle still held out. In May 1573 the English siege guns under Sir William Drury finally overcame it and, at the same time, the hopes of the Marian party. Kirkcaldy was executed and Maitland died of disease or poison, possibly self-administered. Thereafter, the ruthless Morton ruled in England's interest and Queen Mary remained under the control of Shrewsbury at Sheffield Castle. She maintained a certain degree of grandeur and, despite her keeper's vigilance, kept up a ceaseless correspondence with Catholic potentates. But disappointment and confinement took their toll. Despite the consolations of her religion, her health and spirits declined and she began to age prematurely.

From 1580, the pace of events quickened. In December that year, Morton was overthrown for the second time and put on trial for complicity in Darnley's murder. He was executed the following June and replaced, as the most powerful man in Scotland, although not as regent, by the king's favourite and cousin, Esmé Stewart, Duke of Lennox. Stewart's ascendancy meant a revival of French and Catholic influence, and led to an elaborate plan for a many-pronged assault on England and, inevitably, Elizabeth's replacement by Mary. The 'Ruthven Raid' overthrew the regime and the youthful king was captured. It did not last as

The Execution of Mary
Queen of Scots, 1587,
artist unknown
(British Library)

James proved uncooperative with England. But another version of the international plot, associated with Francis Throckmorton (nephew of Sir Nicholas), surfaced and was exposed. Elizabeth, now jettisoning her most recent offer to restore Mary to the Scottish throne, came to regard Mary as incorrigible – as, from her point of view, she was. James, whose concern for his mother did not extend to any wish for her return to Edinburgh as queen, became an English pensioner. After all, was he not (after his mother) next in line to Elizabeth's throne? With the gathering of storm-clouds of war with Spain, Mary came to be regarded as a menace to national security.

A 'Bond of Association' (the Scottish habit had spread across the border) was formed against any attempt on the queen's life, threatening death to those who might profit by it. Mary, now guarded by the strict and puritanical Sir Amyas Paulet, was moved to Tutbury, and then to Chartley. Here, in 1586, hints of intrigue congealed into the Babington conspiracy. The plot was doomed to failure, but Walsingham's counter-espionage service gathered sufficient information to implicate Mary. Her final fate was sealed.

Mary was tried at Fotheringhay for her part in the plot to kill Elizabeth. She denied the competence of the court and the truth of the charge. This was to no avail, as a second trial confirmed. Parliament called for Mary's death; so did the ministers of the crown. Elizabeth hesitated. In an agony of indecision she tried to get others to take responsibility, or to plead international pressure for a reprieve. Neither Scotland nor France would oblige and Spain, now the enemy and preparing for war, was in no position to do so. Finally the queen's council sent off the warrant. At eight o'clock in the morning of 8 February 1587, Mary Queen of Scots, serene, dignified and devout, met her death. She had undeniably been the victim of the grossest injustice since she fled to England. Arriving in search of political asylum, she was put on trial for a crime that was committed outside England. She was allowed neither to attend nor confront her accusers. She was not found guilty and no sentence was passed against her. Nonetheless, she was detained against her will for nineteen years without a shred of legality. Finally she was executed, ostensibly for plotting against a queen to whom she owed no allegiance and whose kingdom she wished to leave. In fact, she died because of something beyond her control – her dynastic proximity to the English crown.

There were storms of belated protest in Scotland and France. They did nothing to weaken the determination of England in the face of the apparent act of retribution, the long-delayed Spanish Armada, the following year. Essentially a creature of Spanish imperialism, it was a failure. Mary lay buried at Peterborough, unavenged. Yet the House of Stewart was the ultimate victor. In 1603, sixteen years after her death, Mary's son, James, fulfilled her dynastic ambition by becoming King of England. Nine years later, he brought what was left of his mother's mutilated body to Westminster Abbey where it lies near to that of the last of the Tudors, Elizabeth, the cousin she never met. In death, she achieved the ambition that eluded her in life.

EPILOGUE

Scotland

MARY QUEEN OF SCOTS' PERSONAL REIGN WAS SHORT, TROUBLED AND tragic, but it had a long-lasting effect, not only on Scotland and the Scots, but on England and the British Empire. As well as becoming the ancestress of all the seventeen monarchs to rule Great Britain since her deposition, her reign led directly to the Union of the Crowns in 1603, and inexorably, if less directly, to the Union of the Parliaments in 1707. It has to be said, however, that one of the factors that made the Union of the Crowns possible in 1603 was the fact that Mary was by then no longer Queen of Scots. Had she been alive when Elizabeth died, it is unlikely that most Englishmen would have accepted her.

It is worth giving brief consideration to what has happened to Scotland since her death. Sixteen years later, the country lost its resident monarch for all time. Scotland and England were united under one crown but tensions between the two kingdoms remained high. In 1639 and 1640, there were two brief campaigns between Mary's grandson Charles I and the Covenanting Scots. Their cause was the attempt by the Scottish bishops, as much as the English authorities, to enforce Anglican observances and in particular a new prayer book on the Scottish Church. The Covenanters' response to this was a demand for the abolition of episcopacy. The 'Bishops' Wars', as they came to be known, were the run-up to the civil wars, which were to last on and off until 1651, and for a time it appeared that Presbyterianism would become the official religion of the whole of Britain. On New Year's Day[1] 1651, almost two years after the execution of his father, and nine months before the end of the civil war, Charles II was crowned King of Scots at Scone. Just over ten years later, after the death of Oliver Cromwell and the resignation of his son Richard, he was crowned king at Westminster.

On Charles's death in 1685, he was succeeded by his younger brother James VII whose intransigent Catholicism led to his deposition in the 'Glorious Revolution' three years later, 101 years after his great-grandmother's death. For the next thirty-nine years, Britain was ruled by four of Mary's great-great-grandchildren: William III, Mary II, Anne and George I. It was during these reigns, and that of George II who succeeded his father in 1727, that at least four unsuccessful Jacobite risings took place, all designed to restore James VII or his son to the British throne. The last, and most serious, ended at Culloden on 15 April 1746, with the defeat of James's grandson, Bonnie Prince Charlie. On that day all hopes of seeing a Stewart (as distinct from a Catholic)[2] monarch, once more on the British throne, evaporated forever. In January 1788, the prince died, drunk and dissolute in Rome, a week before the 201st anniversary of Queen Mary's execution.

Despite the oppressive English response to Jacobitism, Scotland developed a high level of intellectual and educational life in the second half of the eighteenth century. Edinburgh became the 'Athens of the North' and Scottish universities and schools clearly outstripped those of England. By 1800, Scotland was exporting large numbers of professional men to England and the Empire.

The Industrial Revolution made its mark of the Lowlands, where Glasgow became a major industrial centre, drawing migrants from the Highlands and Ireland. While it depressed the agricultural economy and caused acute urban social problems, industrialisation conferred many benefits. Mining, manufacturing, shipbuilding, commerce and banking flourished. Yet the Industrial Revolution brought southern Scotland into the northern English orbit – there was no distinctive Scottish economy. All the time, the dream of younger people of opportunities across the border and overseas went on. Because many Scots were skilled workers or men of learning or astute in business, they felt the call of bigger opportunities beyond their national boundaries. The result was good for the Scots but not always beneficial to Scotland. An analysis of the population statistics of Scotland compared with those of other English-speaking countries makes this very clear.

with more than 1,000,000 inhabitants

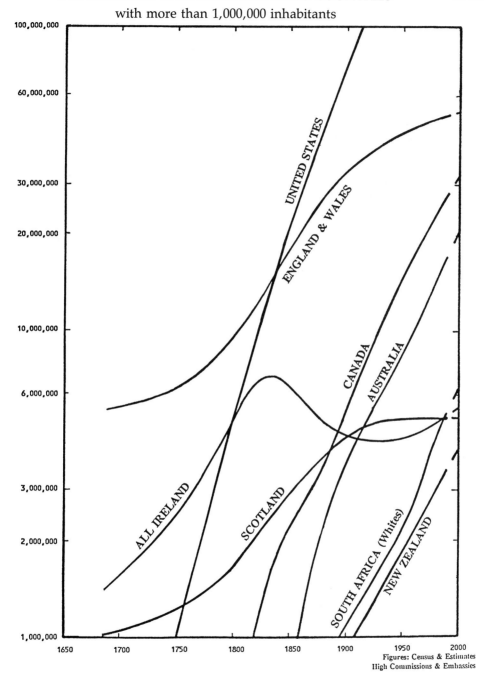

Figures: Census & Estimates
High Commissions & Embassies

The population figures are plotted logarithmically, since a linear display would give a distorted impression. For instance, an increase of, say 1,000,000 people in 1900, would have had an imperceptible impact on the United States but would have been cataclysmic for New Zealand. Due to the scarcity of reliable figures, no attempt has been made to show information much before 1700. The famines of the late seventeenth century would, in any case, make Scotland's curve look like a switch-back. The best estimates give its population at the time of Queen Mary, as in the order of 600,000. England at that time had six or seven times as many people, as indeed it had until nearly 1900, although the ratio since then has risen to nearly ten to one. Interestingly, the curve for All Ireland gives a clear picture of the effect of the potato famines, which started in 1845, on the number of people living in Ireland, many of whom migrated to Scotland. The curve for Scotland, on the other hand, shows the steepest gradient, indicating the greatest *rate* of population increase, during the period usually associated with the highland clearances. The devout belief, held by so many people, that the clearances precipitated massive depopulation, is not supported by the facts. Clearly they were aggravated by, and to a degree caused by, a population explosion. In any case, a large proportion of those cleared from the Highlands settled elsewhere in Scotland; especially in or near the industrial centres.

It can be seen from the table that the population growth of Scotland more or less kept in line with that of England and Wales throughout the eighteenth and nineteenth centuries. It was in about 1900 that the trouble really started. Scotland is the only country under examination where there has been practically no growth in the last eighty years. Population stagnation and economic stagnation are not necessarily synonymous but often go hand in hand. The latest forecasts for births, deaths and migration indicate no foreseeable change. Scotland's population was overtaken by that of the United States in about 1760, by Canada in 1880 and by Australia in 1905. The next census results are likely to show that there are more whites living in South Africa and more Irish living in the whole of Ireland than there are Scots living in Scotland. The population of New Zealand will probably exceed that of Scotland by the year 2015.

The sterile argument that Scotland's decline in general, and its low standard of communications in particular, compared to other developed countries, are a result of too few people inhabiting too large an area, can be demolished by inspecting the following table:

	AREA (Sq miles)	POPULATION	PEOPLE per sq mile
AUSTRALIA	2,967,909	16,676,800	5.62
CANADA	3,849,646	25,309,330	6.57
EIRE	27,136	3,503,000	129.09
ENGLAND	50,363	50,562,500	1,003.97
NEW ZEALAND	103,934	3,328,490	32.03
NORTHERN IRELAND	5,452	1,575,200	288.92
SCOTLAND	30,414	5,112,000	168.08
SOUTH AFRICA	471,445	32,392,000	68.71
UNITED STATES	3,623,461	231,106,727	63.78
WALES	8,018	2,836,000	353.70

Figures: Census & Estimates 1986–90

Scotland has five times the population density of New Zealand and thirty times that of Australia. Despite this, it takes about the same time, using public transport, to travel from Edinburgh to Ullapool (150 miles as the crow flies) as it does to travel from Auckland to Queenstown (555 miles) or Sydney to Geraldton (2170 miles). Innumerable other examples can be cited. The telephone system in Scotland, although much improved over the last few years, is not exactly an example to the rest of the world. It is usually quicker to telephone Oodnadatta Airfield ground services from Brisbane (a distance of 1070 miles), than to call British Rail Enquiries at Waverley Station from the Balmoral Hotel (150 yards). Again, many other instances can be given. It need scarcely be said that this is not a criticism of British Telecom, but of Scottish communications in general.

It is not necessary to be bearded, kilted, Gaelic speaking, play the bagpipes, eat haggis and vote for the Scottish National Party to recognise that all is not well. There are about 25 million Scots in the world and it is ridiculous that only a fifth of them find it worth their while to live in Scotland. In 1603, Scotland exported its king to England. Since (and even before) then, it has been exporting its people and their expertise all over the world, but mainly to England and the countries that were once part of the British Empire.

James VI wearing the
order of St George,
Scottish School, c. 1630
(Lennoxlove)

Queen Mary made four major conscious decisions in her life and several decisions were made about her, which were beyond her control. Had she decided to remain in comfort and retirement as Queen Dowager of France after the death of her first husband and relinquish her rights to the English and Scottish thrones, James Hamilton, or possibly Matthew Stewart and their descendants would have become Kings of Scots. It is highly doubtful that any of these men (and certainly not Darnley) would have been acceptable to the English on the death of Elizabeth in 1603. The Union of the Crowns would have occurred much later, if at all. Many young women, in Mary's position in August 1561, would have adopted a low profile. Courageously she did not.

If she had decided not to marry at all, continued a policy of tolerance and moderation, and survived Elizabeth, she would probably have succeeded to the English throne in 1603, and in turn have been succeeded by a member of the Lennox family (the Hamiltons had no Tudor blood and no right to the throne of England). If she had married a Scotsman (a Hamilton, Gordon, Campbell or even a Hepburn), she could have had a long, happy and successful reign as Queen of Scots and still succeeded Elizabeth in 1603. If she had married one of the Scandinavian kings, there might now be a Common Market of the North incorporating Scotland, Norway, Sweden, Denmark, Finland, the Baltic states, parts of Poland and northern Germany, Iceland and Greenland. If she had married a Frenchman, whether Bourbon or Valois, ironically it is possible that France would have become and stayed Protestant. It is even possible to argue that if she had married a Hapsburg, whether Austrian or Spanish, World War One might have been averted. But she courted disaster and the Anglo-Scot Darnley.

If she had remained unmarried for a period after Darnley's death in 1566, her position would have been much the same as it was in 1561, except for the fact that she had gained experience from, and respect for, five years of wise government. But she was desperate and married one of her late husband's murderers. If she had admitted her mistake and publicly renounced Bothwell, it is possible that she would not have spent so long incarcerated in Lochleven and could have recovered her position and respect. But she did not.

Even after the battle of Langside, if she had remained in Scotland or gone to France, disaster might have been averted. But like so many Scots before her, she trusted the English and cast herself on the mercy of Elizabeth.

The foregoing series of 'ifs' may be accurately described as 'futile speculation', but they are nowhere near as futile as the widely held beliefs that Mary had little effect on the Britain of today – it is truly astonishing how many people, especially English people, think that the present Royal Family is descended from Henry VIII and not Mary Queen of Scots. Queen Mary can scarcely be blamed for what is happening to the Scotland of today, more than four hundred years after her murder but during her imprisonment in England, she used to say: 'En ma fin est ma commencement'. She never spoke a truer word.

1. In 1600, James VI decreed that New Year's Day in Scotland should thenceforth fall on 1 January. Previously, it had fallen on 25 March, as indeed it continued to do in England until 1752. In that year, in order to come into line with the rest of Europe, both countries (as Great Britain), amidst much public consternation, made the change from the Julian calendar (introduced 46 BC) to the Gregorian (1582 AD). At the same time, England took the opportunity of coming into line with Scotland and 1 January became New Year's Day throughout Britain. When Charles II was crowned, therefore, it was New Year's Day 1651 in Scotland, but in England, 1650 still had nearly another three months to run.

2. By no means were all Jacobites Catholic – in fact it is quite possible that most were Protestant. They were not interested in restoring James VII because he was Catholic but because he was the rightful Stewart king.

Biographical Sketches

118

ADAMSON, PATRICK, ARCHBISHOP of ST ANDREWS 1537–1592

Patrick Adamson, Archbishop of St Andrews

Adamson graduated from the University of St Andrews in 1558 as Patrick Constyne and qualified as a Reformed minister under the name of Cousteane. In 1563 he held the Fife parish of Ceres and came to public notice as an anti-papal writer. His horizon widened in 1566 when he went as a tutor to France. The birth of Prince James, in June of that year, prompted him to compose a thanksgiving poem, describing the child as Prince of Scotland, England, France and Ireland. It earned him the displeasure of Queen Elizabeth and a spell in a French prison, from which Mary's influence secured his release. He then went to Geneva, met the Reformer Beza, and studied the best of Calvinist theology. By the time of his return to Scotland in 1572, Adamson (who had dropped his earlier names) was an accomplished theologian.

The final two decades of Adamson's career were filled with conflict and controversy. Minister at Paisley, he became titular Archbishop of St Andrews four years later. He was James VI's principal apologist against the strict Presbyterians and suffered much at their hands. Andrew and James Melville were his strongest opponents. More than once he faced excommunication, only to be rescued by the king. Adamson was a learned and eloquent defender of the episcopal, conservative position. In an age of knockabout controversy, in which the soft answer rarely turned away wrath, he pulled no punches. His enemies said he was crude and gross. They may have been right, but Adamson was effective. In the end, with death at hand, he was forsaken by the king, who gave his episcopal revenues to a courtier. Pressured by Andrew Melville, he is said to have recanted. For so tough a divine, this is very hard to believe. He died in February 1592.

Adamson married Elizabeth, daughter of William Arthur of Kernis, who bore him two sons and a daughter. There was a strange episode with the 'wisewoman', Alison Pearson, who helped him recover from sickness in 1579. In return, he shielded her from a witchcraft charge but, in the end, he could not save her, and she was burnt at the stake in 1583.

Antoine King of Navarre,
François Clouet
(Bibliotheque Nationale)

ANTOINE de BOURBON,
KING of NAVARRE
1518–1562

Navarre was a small independent country, known until the twelfth century as the kingdom of Pamplona, occupying what is now the Spanish province of Navarra and the western part of the French *département* of the Basses-Pyrénées. It had an importance out of all proportion to its size since it controlled the main pass from France to Spain in the western Pyrenees and was a buffer state between Gascony, Castile and Aragon. In 1512, the southern portion was occupied by Spain although the northern part remained a separate kingdom.

Antoine was born on 22 April 1518, the son of Charles de Bourbon, Duc de Vendôme, and Françoise d'Alençon. In 1548, he was married at Moulins to Jeanne d'Albret, daughter of Henri II, King of Navarre, and Marguérite, the sister of François I of France. Jeanne was, therefore, first cousin of Henri II (q.v.) of France as well as heiress of Béarn and Navarre. When her father died in 1555, Jeanne inherited the throne and Antoine became King Consort. Henri II of France's son François II (q.v.), who, as Dauphin, married Mary Queen of Scots, died in 1560. The forty-two-year-old Antoine then had the notion of divorcing the wife who had made him king, and marrying the eighteen-year-old widow, despite the fact that she had been married to his wife's cousin. This grotesque scheme did not find favour with Mary, whose first husband, had he survived, would have become Antoine's son, Henri's brother-in-law, in 1572.

Described as *'faible et irrésolu'*, Antoine vacillated between the Catholic and Huguenot parties, finally embracing the Catholic cause in time to command the army at the siege of the Protestant stronghold of Rouen. Here he received wounds from which he died at Andelys on 17 November 1562.

Antoine is best remembered as the father of Henri III of Navarre, who was born in 1553 and became Henri IV (the Great) of France in 1589.

120

BALFOUR, SIR JAMES, of PITTENDREICH
c. 1525–1583

John Knox (q.v.) referred to him as 'Blasphemous Balfour' and a later writer described him as 'the most corrupt man of the age'. Nonetheless Balfour was a capable lawyer who contributed much to the regularisation of the Scottish legal system. A son of Michael Balfour of Montquhannie in Fife, in 1546 James, along with several other local lairds, was an associate of the murderers of Cardinal Beaton (q.v.) at St Andrews Castle. He later helped defend the castle against the French and, on its fall the following year, was sent to the galleys with John Knox but was released, or escaped, about two years later.

Balfour is next referred to as 'Parson of Flisk' and an ecclesiastical lawyer. This does not mean that he was in holy orders, although he was qualified to be one of the clerical judges in the Court of Session. In 1564, when Queen Mary set up the new Commissary Court of Edinburgh to take over the church's old jurisdiction in matrimonial cases, he was Chief Commissary. Appointed Privy Councillor in July 1565, he was one of the middle-class men on whom Mary was forced to rely after she had alienated so many of the nobility. Although not a party to the plot against Rizzio, he was at Holyrood on the night of the murder and escaped from the palace with Bothwell (q.v.) and others. MacGill, the Lord Clerk Register, was deprived of his office for alleged involvement and Balfour succeeded to the vacancy.

Balfour was widely believed to have been involved in the plot against Darnley in February 1567 and probably drew up the bond signed by the conspirators. Apart from motive (of which many people had plenty), he had the opportunity, since his brother's house was next door to the old Provost's lodging, Kirk o' Field, where the king was lodging. Soon after the murder, he was appointed Captain of Edinburgh Castle at the instance of Bothwell. A few months later, however, he changed sides and refused to let Mary and Bothwell take refuge there. He also made arrangements with Moray (q.v.) to surrender the castle and joined the lords who rose in rebellion against the queen in June 1567.

After Mary's enforced abdication, Regent Moray made Balfour Commendator of Pittenweem and President of the Court of Session with a pension of £500. He fought at the battle of Langside in the regent's army. In June 1569 he changed sides again and was one of only nine out of forty-nine at the Perth convention to vote for Mary's return to Scotland. In the 1570s, he came temporarily to terms with Regent Morton but late in the decade had to withdraw to France, not to return until Morton's fall in 1580. However, it was during this period that he took part in attempts to revise and codify Scots law. His *Practicks*, a digest of decisions of the Court of Session, was not published until 1754 but is still of great value.

He married Margaret, heiress of Michael Balfour of Burleigh, and by her had three daughters and six sons, the eldest of whom was created Lord Balfour of Burleigh in 1606. This unscrupulous but able man died peacefully in 1583.

Cardinal Archbishop
David Beaton, *artist
unknown, Scottish School
(University of St Andrews)*

The first James, who was born about 1470, held several abbeys at an early age and in 1505 became Treasurer to James IV and Archbishop of Glasgow in 1509. Chancellor of Scotland from 1513 to 1526, he played a predominant role in the minority of James V, strongly supporting the traditional alliance with France. In 1522, he was translated to the Primatial See of St Andrews. Here he had to encounter the first stirrings of the Reformation; he met the threat with vigour, sending Patrick Hamilton to be burnt at the stake. On his death in 1539, he was succeeded at St Andrews by his nephew, David, who was already his coadjutor.

BEATON, JAMES,
ARCHBISHOP of GLASGOW
and ST ANDREWS
c. 1470–1539
BEATON, DAVID,
ARCHBISHOP of
ST ANDREWS and CARDINAL
c. 1494–1546
BEATON, JAMES,
ARCHBISHOP of GLASGOW
1517–1603

The Beatons (or Bethunes or Betouns) had a dominating influence on the affairs of the Catholic Church in sixteenth-century Scotland. Apart from one short break (1546–52), there was always an archbishop of that name from 1509 to 1603. They came from a lowland family but were not of noble lineage. They were thus in the line of ecclesiastical statesmen who owed their importance to their relationship with the crown rather than to inherited positions.

David Beaton, like his uncle, had been a minister to James V and a proponent of the French alliance. He played a major part in arranging James's successive marriages to Princess Madeleine and Mary of Guise (q.v.), and maintained a pro-French stance after the king's death in 1542. During the first four years of Queen Mary's minority, David Beaton was at the zenith of his power. At first, there had been a contest with the second Earl of Arran (q.v.) for the leading position. Indeed there was the strong belief that Beaton had forged a royal instrument (sometimes inaccurately called James V's will) giving himself control. The instrument was not upheld and Arran became Governor, although Beaton was Chancellor and Papal Legate and exercised his authority with fervour. When the English invaded in 1544, they saw him as their chief enemy. The incipient Scottish Protestant movement felt his full force, since it was opposed to the

Catholic Church and had links with the hated English. George Wishart (q.v.), who was burnt for heresy in 1546, was Beaton's most famous victim and it was Wishart's friend, John Leslie, who ended the cardinal's life at St Andrews Castle five months later. David Beaton was able and patriotic but proud, cruel and immoral. While he kept his church in power, he helped to bring it into disrepute.

The second James Beaton, nephew of the Cardinal, was different in almost all respects. Appointed Archbishop of Glasgow in 1552, he was a trusted adviser to Mary of Guise and, on her death in 1560, went to France and remained there for the rest of his long life. He died in 1603, the year that James VI's accession to the English throne finally ended French influence on Scotland. He continued a firm friend of his native land, managing the income that Mary enjoyed as Queen Dowager of France and giving her advice when he could. To Beaton, the murder of Darnley had been a disaster for the queen's cause, and her subsequent behaviour filled him with dismay. Yet he remained in Paris as spokesman, and indeed ambassador, for Scotland. At home, his church fell into decay, his ecclesiastical title had long been forfeited and regimes came and went, but Beaton held on. His fellow countrymen began to admire his work and, in 1598, five years before his death, restored to him his Scottish dignities. This in no way implied that Beaton's strong Catholicism had weakened; he had long been a benefactor of the Scots College in Paris. The Scots admired this honest

James Beaton,
Archbishop of Glasgow,
artist unknown

and devout man. Had the earlier Beatons possessed a modicum of his decency and devotion, the Catholic Church in his homeland might not have collapsed so readily before the Protestant assault. The last Beaton was the only one to be an ornament of his church.

BEATON, MARGARET, LADY RERES

The daughter of John Beaton of Creich, Margaret was the aunt of Mary Beaton (q.v.). She married Arthur Forbes of Reres. She was wet-nurse to the future James VI. Mary Fleming's sister, the Countess of Atholl, who was said to be a sorceress, cast labour pains on her before the birth. This caused intense discomfort to Lady Reres without in any way alleviating that of Mary.

Lady Reres was accused of facilitating a nefarious relationship between Mary and Bothwell at the Exchequer House in

123

Edinburgh, while Darnley was still alive. Since the exercise would have involved climbing down a rope from a first-floor window, and she was extremely stout, the story is highly unlikely.

She is often confused with her elder sister Janet, the five-times married Lady of Buccleuch, an ex-mistress of Bothwell who was also said to practise witchcraft and who married, among others, Crichton of Cranston Riddell, Simon Preston of Craigmillar and Walter Scott of Buccleuch.

BOTHWELL, ADAM,
BISHOP of ORKNEY
c. 1529–1593

One of the three bishops who joined the reformers and organised the Reformed Chuch in their dioceses. (The others were Alexander Gordon of Galloway (q.v.) and Robert Stewart (q.v.) of Caithness.) Son of Francis Bothwell provost of Edinburgh who was also a judge of the Court of Session, he numbered clerics and lawyers among his near kinsmen on his father's side. His mother, Katharine Bellenden, was sister of one justice-clerk and mother of another, and by her second marriage she became sister-in-law to John and Henry Sinclair, bishops of Brechin and Ross (q.v.). By the marriage of his sister he was related to the Napiers of Merchiston, the Melvilles of Raith, and Kirkcaldy of Grange (q.v.). He married Margaret Erskine. He was therefore linked to many members of the queen's intimate circle.

Born probably in 1529, Bothwell was trained in law and theology. Appointed by the pope to the bishopric of Orkney on 2 August 1559, he was consecrated shortly thereafter and in the spring of 1560 he set out for the islands, where he remained for a year, while Scotland was making its choice for the Reformation. Bothwell decided for the Reformed cause and forbade the Mass. In April 1561 he went to France to see Mary and he returned to Scotland in August, as she did.

Bothwell continued to administer his diocese, now in the interests of the Reformed Church. He visited Orkney most years from 1562 to 1566 and staffed the Church with ministers and readers. The General Assembly gave him a commission in 1563, but after he became a Lord of Session in 1564 its attitude to him cooled, and he displeased it more when he officiated at the marriage of Mary to the Earl of Bothwell (although it was a Protestant ceremony). He made amends by taking part with Kirkcaldy of Grange in the pursuit of Bothwell after Carberry (when he suffered shipwreck in Shetland) and by anointing James VI at his coronation.

However, in 1568 Lord Robert Stewart (q.v.), who held the crown lands in Orkney, compelled Bothwell by violence to resign to him the bishopric revenues, in exchange for those of the Abbey of Holyrood, and although Bothwell retained the title of Bishop of Orkney he was never again in the islands. He was a member of the Commission which represented Moray's party in the investigations at York and Westminster in 1568-9. He spent his later years in Edinburgh as Commendator of Holyrood and Lord of Session.

BOYD, ROBERT, 5th BARON BOYD
c. 1517–1590

The only son of Robert, the fourth Baron, and Helen, daughter of Sir John Somerville of Cambusnethan, he succeeded to the title on the death of his father about the end of 1557. His father had helped defeat William the third Earl of Glencairn at the battle of Glasgow in 1543, giving much help to Regent Arran (q.v.) in putting down the insurrection of the Earl of Lennox (q.v.). Thereafter, the Glencairns (q.v.) had withdrawn their support for Lennox.

Boyd supported the Lords of the Congregation against Mary of Guise (q.v.) in the civil war. He was with them at Perth in May 1559, and wrote to Sir William Cecil (q.v.) and Queen Elizabeth, asking for their support. He then took part in the unsuccessful negotiations for a compromise with Mary of Guise. In February 1560, he was one of the signatories of the Treaty of Berwick, whereby Elizabeth undertook to send troops to Scotland, in order to drive out the French. In April of that year, he joined the English army at Prestonpans, and in May, he took part in the unsuccessful attack on Leith. In 1563, Boyd and Hugh Montgomerie, the third Earl of Eglinton (q.v.) entered into a mutual bond of defence, ending the Boyd-Montgomerie feud which had lasted nearly eighty years.

Shortly after the marriage of Queen Mary to Darnley, Boyd joined other Lords in the 'Chaseabout Raid', for which he was declared guilty of lese majesty in December 1565. However, he received a pardon from 'Henry King of Scots' in March 1566, and was commanded to repair to court. At this stage, his political attitude underwent a complete change. He was probably privy to, if not involved in, the murder of Darnley, in February 1567, and, although a member of the jury which acquitted Bothwell of the crime, he joined the nobles who bound themselves to protect the young Prince James against Bothwell's sinister designs after his marriage to Mary. In May 1567, however, he was made a permanent member of the Privy Council, and became an energetic partisan of the queen. In June, with Huntly (q.v.), the Archbishop of St Andrews (q.v.) and the Commendator of Kilwinning, he tried unsuccessfully to hold Edinburgh for her. In August, Boyd, Argyll (q.v.), Livingston (q.v.) and the Commendator negotiated with Moray (q.v.) for the release of the queen from Lochleven. On 13 May 1568, after Mary's escape, Boyd fought for her at Langside and, after the battle, was forced to retire to his castle at Kilmarnock, which he was shortly compelled to surrender to the council. On 6 January 1569, Mary, by then in England, made him a member of her Council, and he was involved in her intrigues with the Duke of Norfolk.

In 1569, Mary expressed a desire to have Boyd and John Leslie, Bishop of Ross (q.v.), permanently about her, but Boyd was in Scotland, actively endeavouring to foment a general uprising in her favour. He was widely suspected of involvement in the murder of Regent Moray in January 1570. The following year, he defected again, possibly with Mary's approval, since she wished to have a loyal friend declaring support for the new *de facto* government of Scotland. On 5 September, Boyd became a consenting party to the election of Mar (q.v.) as regent and, on the 7th, was made a member of the Privy Council.

Shortly after the death of Mar, and before the death of Knox (q.v.) and the election of Morton (q.v.) to the regency (which happened on the same day), Boyd visited Knox on his deathbed and endeavoured to make peace with him. Knox's response is not recorded. At this stage, Boyd appears to have realised the hopelessness of the Marian cause and, from then on, became a firm adherent of Morton. On Morton's eclipse, he was appointed or e of the commission to capture Lords John and Claud Hamilton (q.v.). This exercise was unsuccessful. He then became involved in the Ruthven Raid for which he was banished in June 1583. He was allowed to return in 1586 and the following year was appointed commissioner to raise money for the expenses connected with the king's marriage to Anne of Denmark. In 1589, he became a member of the commission to enforce the statute against Jesuits.

Boyd died on 3 January 1590, survived by his wife Margaret, daughter and heiress of George Colquhoun, fourth of Glens, by his wife Margaret Boyd. By her he had two sons, Thomas, who succeeded him, and Robert and six daughters. He also had a natural son.

BUCHANAN, GEORGE
1506–1582

Buchanan, one of the leading scholars of his time, was a great educator and an historian of wide reputation. He was no less a man of affairs, active as a religious reformer and powerful in controversy. Born in 1506 at Killearn, Stirlingshire, son of a poor landowner, Buchanan studied briefly in Paris, returned to Scotland as a soldier, became a pupil of the famous humanist John Major at St Andrews and then at Paris and came home to tutor a natural son of James V. Buchanan's satires on monasticism, in Renaissance vein, were approved by the king but met with vehement opposition from Cardinal Beaton (q.v.). Imprisoned at St Andrews, Buchanan escaped to England and thence to France. For twenty years after 1540 he remained on the Continent, writing Latin poems and satires, conversing with scholars, teaching and tutoring. Most of his time he spent in Catholic countries, not always to the satisfaction of the Church authorities.

After Mary's assumption of personal rule in Scotland, Buchanan, now an established scholar well advanced in years, returned home. A new career of action and argument opened up. Appointed to the University of St Andrews, Buchanan drew up a scheme for the reform of its colleges, while playing a prominent part in the affairs of the church's General Assembly. Though now openly Protestant, he was in favour at court, writing poems for the Darnley marriage and other occasions. He played no part in the events of Mary's fall or flight, but emerged as secretary to the Scots Commissioners at the York enquiry in 1568.

The display of the casket letters at York touched Buchanan deeply. It is very unlikely that he was directly involved in their compilation but, from that time, he became closely associated with them. Certainly he gave strong support to Moray's (q.v.) case and affirmed that the letters were in Mary's hand; having been a tutor to her, his word carried weight. Henceforward, Buchanan devoted much effort to ramming home the case against her. Soon after the murder of Moray, Buchanan became tutor to the young King James and was also installed as Principal of the University of St Andrews. He signalised his appointment by publishing, in Latin and Scots (later in French), his *Detection*, based on the *Books of Articles* exhibited by the Commissioners at Westminster. It was an elaborate polemic, replete with serious and largely unsubstantiated charges against Mary. While he was later to resent the literary treatment of his mother, James admired the classical scholarship of his tutor. Buchanan ceased to hold the post of tutor in any more than nominal fashion in 1578. In the same year, he resigned the office of Keeper of the Privy Seal, which had allowed him to play a part in legal and educational reform.

Buchanan was now an old man, complaining of his infirmities. Yet he now published his two most important works. *De Jure Regni* (1579) was immediately popular though it was attacked by conservative critics because of its exposition and criticism of limited monarchy, even an elected one. It was, however, of enduring importance in the

George Buchanan, *artist unknown (University of St Andrews)*

history of political thought. In 1582, Buchanan's *History of Scotland* appeared in Latin. For its time, it was a remarkable production, the result of many years of labour. Its classical and medieval sections stood the test of time for several centuries. Its account of sixteenth-century events, especially those of his own manhood, was vivid and partisan; Buchanan spared nothing in his criticism of Mary. The *History* gained a permanent place in the intellectual life of Scotland and did much to establish national attitudes to the developments of his time.

The publication of his *History* was the last event of Buchanan's life. He died, universally acclaimed as a scholar, but surrounded by controversy as a political writer and man of affairs, on 29 September 1582.

CAMPBELL, ARCHIBALD, 4th EARL of ARGYLL
c. 1505–1558
CAMPBELL, ARCHIBALD, 5th EARL of ARGYLL
1530–1573

Archibald, fourth Earl, was the eldest son of Colin, third Earl, and Lady Jane Gordon, eldest daughter of Alexander, third Earl of Huntly. Archibald succeeded his father in 1530, and was immediately sent in command of an expedition to subdue an insurrection in the southern Hebrides. The show of force caused the principal chiefs to submit without a substantial struggle, but Alexander MacDonald of Islay, the prime mover of the revolt, was able to convince the king that the disturbances had principally been caused by the Earls of Argyll making use of the office of lieutenant over the Isles for their own personal aggrandisement.

The Earl was summoned before James V and imprisoned. He was soon liberated but his offices were not restored to him until after the king's death in December 1542. With his cousin, the fourth Earl of Huntly (q.v.), and others, he was named as one of the Council of the Kingdom, in the forged document purporting to be the will of James V. The document, which was produced by Cardinal Beaton (q.v.), proclaimed the cardinal himself Governor. The plan failed, Beaton was arrested in January 1543 and the Earl of Arran (q.v.), who was in any case heir presumptive, was chosen Governor.

When it became known that Henry VIII had arranged a treaty of marriage between his son (later Edward VI) and the young Mary, Argyll, Huntly, the fourth Earl of Lennox (q.v.) and the third Earl of Bothwell marched to Perth and forced the governor to surrender the infant queen, whom they triumphantly took to Stirling. In 1544, Lennox, who had gone over to the English side, unsuccessfully sought to capture Dumbarton Castle. He plundered the Isle of Arran and captured the Castle of Rothesay and most of the rest of Bute but as he sailed down the Clyde, he was fired on by Argyll who was holding Dunoon Castle with 4,000 men. Lennox then effected a landing and despite Argyll's opposition burnt Dunoon village and church. He went on to lay waste large parts of Kintyre but, as he had failed to take Dumbarton Castle, the expedition was a failure and he was forced to retire. His estates were forfeited and the largest share awarded to Argyll.

At the disastrous battle of Pinkie on 10 September 1547, Argyll with a force of 4,000 West Highlanders, commanded the right wing of the Scottish army. He was later unjustly suspected of defection to, or at least sympathy with, the English, which he soon afterwards disproved by fighting alongside the French at the siege of Haddington. Along with the sixth Earl of Angus (q.v.) and the fourth Earl of Huntly, he was made a Knight of St Michael by the French king.

In the early stages of the Reformation, Argyll came under the influence of Knox (q.v.) and was one of the first supporters of the Reformers. In 1556, Knox stayed with him at Castle Campbell and taught there on his way to Geneva. Archbishop Hamilton made great efforts to persuade him to renounce the Reformed faith, but to no avail, and Argyll encouraged much Reformed teaching in his house.

Argyll died in August 1558. By his marriage to Lady Helen Hamilton, eldest daughter of the first Earl of Arran, he had one son, Archibald, who became the fifth Earl (q.v.), and two daughters. By his marriage to Lady Margaret Graham, only daughter of the third Earl of Menteith, he had one son, Colin, who became the sixth Earl.

Archibald, fifth Earl, was educated at the University of St Andrews under John Douglas, the first Protestant archbishop, and this early training ensured his support for the Reformed faith. In 1556, with Lord James Stewart (q.v.), he attended the preaching of John Knox at Calder and was so highly impressed, that, the following year, he signed the invitation for Knox to return from Geneva and, along with his father, subscribed to the first band of Scottish Reformers. Despite this, he had an early career in the party of the Queen Regent, who appointed him one of her commissioners to treat with the Lords of the Congregation, which led to the Treaty of Perth. Soon afterwards, he and Moray withdrew their support from her and joined the Lords openly, although Argyll's zeal was by no means as fanatical as some of the others, for which Knox publicly rebuked him.

He and the other lords shared Knox's apprehensions of the intentions of the Queen Regent, fears which proved well founded when, in May 1559, she restored the Mass, at the same time installing a garrison of French troops in Edinburgh Castle. Argyll, with Lord James Stewart (q.v.) supported by 300 troops, withdrew from Edinburgh to St Andrews, where the sacking of the cathedral and monastery by a 'rascal multitude' roused the queen to attack them at Cupar, where they had withdrawn. The superior forces of Argyll and his supporters led to her withdrawal first to Perth, then by way of Linlithgow, to Dunbar. Argyll and Lord James then successfully entered Edinburgh without resorting to force, an act which led to their being denounced as rebels on 2 July. They agreed to deliver the city to the Queen Regent, pending the meeting of parliament in the following January, but while Argyll was in the west dealing with his ancient enemy, Macdonald of Islay, the Queen Regent used this time to fortify Leith, and only the timely arrival of Argyll with a force of 700 of his Highlanders stopped a French incursion upon the forces of the Lords of the Congregation. Notwithstanding this, they were eventually forced to withdraw to Stirling in November.

Subsequently, they sought English help, and Elizabeth sent a force to their aid in the siege of Leith. During the siege, the Queen Regent died, but not before she had sent for Argyll and the other lords to express her regret that matters had come to such a pass. Peace was declared shortly afterwards. In the following August, parliament sanctioned the Confession of Faith, and Argyll was the third member of the nobility to sign the Book of Discipline. He, Arran and Glencairn were made responsible for the destruction in the west of 'all monuments of idolatry'. On the arrival of Queen Mary at Leith, Argyll was one of those who received her, and shortly afterwards was sworn a member of the Privy Council, acting as before in concert with Lord James. He stood high in Mary's favour, and for his tolerant attitude towards her Catholic faith was denounced by Knox, and estranged from him until reconciled by Mary herself, who used Knox in an attempt to heal the rift between Argyll and his wife, Mary's half-sister.

He was strongly opposed to the Darnley marriage and used every effort to try to prevent it. He and Moray vainly sought the aid of Elizabeth, and it was strongly rumoured that he contemplated kidnapping both Mary and Darnley. After the marriage, he joined Moray in the 'Chaseabout Raid' and they were both declared traitors and forced to flee to England. Elizabeth declined to help them, and this refusal was largely the cause of Argyll's rejection of Elizabeth's cause and his subsequent reconciliation with Queen Mary. On his return to Scotland, shortly after the murder of Rizzio, he found the queen in an agreeable mood and as proof of their reconciliation, she ordered lodgings, next to her own, to be prepared for him when she went to Edinburgh for the birth of her child.

Argyll now became a collaborator in the scheme to remove Darnley; he signed the Craigmillar Bond, and was one of those in attendance on the queen on the night of Darnley's murder. Despite his complicity in the assassination, he not only signed the proclamation offering a reward for the apprehension of the murderers, but also presided at Bothwell's (q.v.) trial. On Bothwell's

release, Argyll attended the Ainslie Tavern supper, and signed the bond agreeing to Bothwell's marriage to the queen, although he afterwards exhibited remorse by signing the bond for the defence of Prince James.

He was estranged from Mary until after the flight of Bothwell, when he joined the other nobles of her party at Dumbarton to plan her release from Lochleven. On her reluctant agreement to the establishment of Moray's regency, he was appointed one of the members of council, although he manifestly disagreed with the arrangement and initially declined to meet Moray on his return, submitting only when he found that further resistance was ineffective. His dispute with the kirk over his divorce led to further disagreement with Moray, his brother-in-law, and again estranged him from Knox and the more extreme faction of the Reformed Church. Perversely, this may have bound him closer to the queen's cause, despite his own misgivings.

He signed the bond for her deliverance in May 1568 and, on her escape, joined her at Hamilton, and was appointed Lieutenant of her forces. He suffered a seizure, whether real or feigned, at a critical moment during the battle of Langside, which significantly contributed to the defeat. After the queen's flight, Argyll retired to his stronghold at Dunoon, where he continued to work for her restoration, but on the refusal of Elizabeth to lend support, he eventually submitted to Regent Moray at St Andrews in 1569. He was suspected of complicity in Moray's murder, although he denied this in a letter sent to Morton, but his continued involvement with the Hamiltons caused grave suspicion in the minds of many.

Eventually deciding that Mary's cause was hopeless, he was reconciled to the king's party, and was an unsuccessful candidate for the regency after the death of Lennox, being chosen as a Privy Councillor instead and eventually becoming Lord High Chancellor on the appointment of Morton to the regency. Through his agency the two parties were reconciled, but with the secret proviso that no further inquisition should be made into his part in the murder of Darnley.

Argyll died in 1573 of the stone. He married twice: first to Jean Stewart, daughter of James V and Elizabeth Beaton of Creich, and half-sister to the queen. There were no children of this marriage, which was not a happy one, ending in divorce in June 1573. He married secondly, in August 1573, Johaneta Cunningham, second daughter of Alexander, fourth Earl of Glencairn, but had no issue by her. He had several illegitimate children, and this was one of the causes of his divorce from his first wife. He was succeeded by his half-brother Colin as sixth Earl of Argyll.

CARLOS, DON, CROWN PRINCE of SPAIN 1545–1568

Born at Valladolid on 8 July 1545, Carlos was the son of Philip of Spain, later King Philip II, (q.v.) and his first wife, Mary of Portugal. In 1560, he was recognised as heir to the throne of Castile and three years later to that of Aragon. He

Don Carlos of Spain, *A. Sanchez Coello (Prado)*

was sickly from birth and suffered from a progressive form of mental derangement which was to manifest itself as gluttony, sadism and megalomania, leading him to contemplate even the murder of his own father.

Until his madness became widely recognised, Don Carlos was considered as a possible husband for the daughters of Henri II of France (q.v.), Elisabeth and Marie of Valois, and Mary Queen of Scots. Despite the attraction of a match leading to the union of the Spanish and Scottish crowns, Philip had reservations as he had no desire to offend Queen Elizabeth by marrying his son to her rival for the English throne. Nevertheless, negotiations continued until April 1564, although they ceased to be realistic after the end of 1563, when it became clear that Don Carlos was mad and getting madder.

Eventually Philip had to admit that his heir was a danger to the state and on 18 January 1568 had him arrested and sent to prison in Madrid where he died on 24 July. It has been suggested that his death was hastened by his father's marriage to his erstwhile betrothed, Elisabeth of Valois, but his habit of sleeping on ice in his stifling prison and his gluttony are more likely causes. Despite many contemporary rumours, even in court, there is no evidence that Don Carlos was murdered.

CARSWELL, JOHN
c. 1525–1572

A scion of the Carswells of Carnassary, Argyllshire, he was educated at St Andrews in 1541 and, as an early adherent to the Reformed faith, benefited from the patronage of the fourth Earl of Argyll (q.v.) and his son, later the fifth Earl (q.v.), when they became prominent in the movement. By 1551, he was Treasurer of the Diocese of Argyll, and parson of Kilmartin, his home parish, and after the success of the Lords of the Congregation in 1560, became Superintendent of Argyll.

In March 1565, Mary made Carswell Bishop of the Isles. In return, he took her side in the dispute between her supporters and those of her son. For this, he was censured by the General Assembly, which reproved him for not seeking its permission before accepting the bishopric. He popularised the Reformed faith in his diocese by translating into Gaelic the *Book of Common Order*, which had been prepared for the English congregation in Geneva, and which had been prescribed by the General Assembly for use in public worship in 1562, and approved and received by the Church of Scotland in 1564. This, when it appeared in 1567,

was the first book ever printed in Gaelic.

He died in 1572, and was buried at Ardchattan Priory on Loch Etive.

CATHERINE de MEDICI, QUEEN of FRANCE
1519–1589

'Hate – and wait' was one of the mottoes of this indefatigable and devious woman. Catherine was born in Florence on 13 April 1519, the daughter of Lorenzo de Medici, Duke of Urbino, and Madeleine de la Tour d'Auvergne. She was closely related to Pope Clement VII and related by marriage to John, Duke of Albany, Regent to James V. In 1533, the Pope arranged her marriage to the Duke of Orleans (later Henri II of France (q.v.)) with his father François I, then king of France, who was happy to strengthen his position on the Italian peninsula. After ten years of childlessness, there was talk of using sorcery to produce an heir, and even of divorce, but over the next seventeen years she gave birth to five sons and five daughters. Of her ten children, three died in infancy and five became kings or queens. She herself became queen on the death of François and the accession of Henri II in 1547.

During Henri's reign, she played little part in politics since he was completely under the influence of his mistress Diane de Poitiers, Duchess of Valentinois. She was, however, nominated regent in 1552 when Henri left the country, but was given very limited powers. This state of affairs continued after Henri's death in 1559 since her eldest son, now François II (q.v.), was under the spell of his wife Mary Queen of Scots who, little disposed to meddle in French politics, tended to refer matters to her uncles, the Cardinal of Lorraine and the Duke of Guise. During this period, although relatively politically inactive, Catherine had not been idle. Despite the rigours of having so many children, she had been keeping a close watch on events, filing away information for future use.

On the death of François on 5 December 1560, Catherine became regent again during the minority of her second son, Charles IX (q.v.). She was forty-one years old and, despite having had so many children, still vigorous and active. Although her regency ended in 1563, she dominated Charles for the rest of his life. Initially she listened to moderate counsels and adopted a policy of conciliation between the Catholics and Protestants. She was by habit a Catholic but her religion was always secondary to her appetite for power. She was determined to prevent the Protestants from gaining the upper hand, yet resolved not to allow them to be annihilated since she needed them as a counter-balance to the powerful Guises.

The renewal of civil war in 1567 frightened Catherine into supporting the Catholic party but in 1570, when she realised that the Huguenots could not be crushed by force of arms, she again resorted to a policy of conciliation. She started negotiations with a view to marrying her daughter Marguérite to the Protestant Henri of Navarre. By 1572, the pendulum had swung the other way. Fearful that the Protestants

Catherine de Medici,
François Clouet
(Bibliotheque Nationale)

were becoming too powerful, she fell back on the Guises and at the same time persuaded Charles to sanction the St Bartholomew's Eve massacre on 24 August 1572. This appalling atrocity was to haunt Charles until he died less than two years later. Catherine, however, was made of sterner stuff and revelled in the congratulations of the Catholic powers, especially the Pope, who ordered a special medal to be struck.

Henri III, who succeeded Charles in 1574, showed himself more independent of his mother but was unable to control the Guises who soon eclipsed both of them. Henri attempted to re-assert himself by arranging the assassination of Henri de Guise on 23 December 1588 but Catherine died at Blois a few days later on 5 January 1589. Henri did not survive the assassination or the death of his mother for long, since he was stabbed to death by a fanatical monk on 1 August. With his death, the male line of the House of Valois became extinct to be succeeded by the Bourbon dynasty with Henri III of Navarre, who became Henri IV (the Great) of France.

Like many Italians of the time, Catherine looked upon statesmanship as a career in which finesse, lying and assassination were the most effective weapons. It is ironic that, within a year of her death, the family for which she had struggled so hard should have been extinguished.

William Cecil, 1st Lord Burghley, *attributed to M. Gheeraerts the Younger, after 1585 (National Portrait Gallery)*

CECIL, WILLIAM, LORD BURGHLEY 1520–1598

William Cecil was born at Burleigh, Northants, the son of a minor courtier who amassed a large estate. He attended St John's College, Cambridge at an early age, coming under the influence of the Protestant scholars Ascham and Cheke. He fell even more under the influence of Cheke's sister, Mary, and had to leave the university to marry her. It was Cecil's only impetuous action in a long life distinguished by its circumspection. Fortunately for his relationship with his angry father, Mary, having given birth to a son, died before Cecil could be disinherited. Cecil's second marriage, to Mildred, daughter of Sir Anthony Cooke, was both judicious and happy. In 1547 Cooke became governor to the young Edward VI and Cecil's career blossomed.

He accompanied Protector Somerset to Scotland and came close to death at the battle of Pinkie. He became Somerset's secretary but survived his patron's fall and served Northumberland. On the death of Edward VI he resigned rather than condone the plan to place Lady Jane Grey on the throne. In the reign of Mary Tudor, Cecil had to exercise prudence, a quality that he possessed in abundance, and he was entrusted with several diplomatic missions.

With the accession of Elizabeth in 1558, Cecil came into his own. As Secretary of State, he exercised wide control, always subject to the queen's decisions, over foreign and domestic affairs. Scotland inevitably claimed his early attention. While, as a convinced Protestant, he sympathised with the Reformers, he saw Scottish affairs in the light of the security of England and the succession to its throne. Though restrained by the non-intervention provisions of the Treaty of Cateau-Cambrésis, he encouraged the Lords of the Congregation against the Queen Regent and the French. He travelled north to negotiate the Treaty of Edinburgh, but could not persuade Elizabeth, who was always reluctant to part with money, to buy the loyalty of the Protestant nobles.

The return of the widowed Mary to Scotland involved Cecil and Elizabeth in the double problem of arranging an acceptable marriage for the young queen while resisting any public recognition of her claim to the English crown. Cecil opposed a continental match, frustrated the efforts of Maitland of Lethington (q.v.) to reach a concordat on Mary's succession and, with Elizabeth's consent, offered the prospect of a marriage with the Earl of Leicester (q.v.). Elizabeth was less than enthusiastic about losing her own court favourite, but Cecil managed to drag out the negotiations for as long as possible. When Mary riposted by inviting Darnley to Scotland, it was probably Cecil who arranged for the new suitor to leave England. In so doing, he miscalculated. The subsequent marriage of the two cousins strengthened their joint claim to the throne of England. Moray's (q.v.) rebellion enlisted Cecil's Protestant sympathies but neither he nor Elizabeth could give much support, and after the Chaseabout Raid they were obliged to disown Moray in public. The plans for the Rizzio murder were known to Cecil well in advance of the deed.

While Elizabeth and her minister were generally at one on Scottish affairs, Cecil had a greater concern for the Protestant (and pro-English) cause while the queen remained sensitive to Mary's royal status and prerogatives. It was Elizabeth who implored Mary to remember her queenly duty during the Bothwell affair; it was Elizabeth who ignored Cecil's remonstrances and raged at the Scottish lords for imprisoning Mary at Lochleven, declining to recognise Moray's government and intriguing with the Hamiltons against him. Cecil's realistic policies did not always prevail.

Mary's flight to England began a new chapter in Cecil's Scottish activities. At the enquiries in York and Westminster, he was generally critical of Mary and disposed to give qualified support to Moray and her accusers. He was involved in the transcription and presentation of the casket letters. Elizabeth's 'not proven' verdict would not have been wholly to Cecil's satisfaction, and certainly, from then on, Mary regarded him as one of her chief enemies.

Cecil's hope for Scotland was the Protestant regency. The murder of Moray meant three years of civil war, a time of perplexity for English diplomats. Cecil sought only peace north of the border but it was never easy to obtain and it was not until 1573 that the Marian party was finally subdued. By this time Cecil, created Baron Burghley in 1571, had become Lord Treasurer. Scottish affairs – especially the policy of James VI – passed to Walsingham (q.v.) and other ministers. However, Burghley remained at the centre of policy-making, although there were occasions when he did not always agree with Walsingham on the best methods of dealing with the devious James.

There remained the captive Mary; her

claim to the throne, her position as a focus for opposition to Elizabeth and her government, her international connections, and her Scottish background, all made her of vital importance. Cecil distrusted and wished to neutralise her. To provide information about the many intrigues which centred on her, he gathered an army of spies and informers, and did not scruple to torture those Catholics who came into his hands in an effort to gain evidence which would incriminate her. He stage-managed the Commissions of Enquiry and, although unable to prevent Elizabeth returning a 'not proven' verdict, was successful in keeping Mary a prisoner. Several times, Cecil appeared to contemplate Mary's restoration to her throne, believing it might serve England's interests, while at others, he was her resolute opponent.

In 1570 Cecil, having been warned by Elizabeth not to succumb to Mary's charms as so many others had done, reluctantly visited the imprisoned queen at Chatsworth. He took with him excessively severe conditions for her restoration. Naturally nothing came of them. A further attempt after the St Bartholomew's Eve massacre in 1572, when anti-Catholic fears flared in England, produced no result. By the 1580s, it was becoming more important to conciliate James VI, the probable heir to the English throne, than to restore Mary. Cecil managed to persuade the king of his goodwill and, by 1584, was even considering giving Mary more freedom within England. But the growth of international tension, the shrill demands of the Puritans, who saw themselves as the guardians of Protestant nationalism, and the urgency of the House of Commons, convinced Cecil that Mary must not only be neutralised but eliminated. The Babington Plot gave credence to his determination. To sway the wavering Elizabeth was no mean feat, but Cecil's involvement of her entire council was a political masterstroke. In this sense, the decision to execute Queen Mary must be laid squarely on Cecil's shoulders.

William Cecil, Lord Burghley, remained the queen's principal minister until his death on 4 August 1598. His younger son Robert, later Earl of Salisbury, succeeded him as Elizabeth's chief adviser. He had outlived all his significant contemporaries, save the queen herself. No English, or for that matter Scottish, statesman held office for so long with the full confidence of his sovereign.

CHARLES IX,
KING of FRANCE
1550–1574

It was inevitable that on the death of his elder brother, François (q.v.), Charles should be considered for the hand of his sister-in-law, the widowed Mary Queen of Scots, although he was nearly eight years younger. However, within nine months of François's death, she was back in Scotland and Charles was only one of several candidates.

Born at St Germain-en-Laye on 7 June 1550, the second son of Henri II (q.v.) and Catherine de Medici (q.v.), Charles became king on the death of his brother in 1560 under the regency of his mother. He was proclaimed of age on 17 August

1563, when he was thirteen, but still remained under his mother's domination, being incapable of choosing and following a policy of his own. Despite a taste for violent exercise inherited from his father, his health was poor and he was mentally unstable.

In 1570, Charles married Elizabeth of Austria, daughter of Emperor Maximilian II, but she bore him no children. There followed a period of intrigue when he was persuaded to favour the Huguenot plan for intervention against Spain in the Netherlands. Catherine, however, induced him to drop this plan, and instead sanction a move against the Protestants. This was to become known as the St Bartholemew's Eve massacre.

Shortly before dawn on 24 August 1572, the killing started. It continued over the next five weeks, spreading over most of France. Up to 70,000 Protestant men, women and children were killed. Catherine received congratulations from all the Catholic powers and a jubilant Pope Gregory XIII ordered a medal to be struck. Elizabeth of England was horrified by the atrocities, which did much to confirm her fears of the Catholics and harden her attitude towards Queen Mary.

Charles was haunted by the massacre for the rest of his life. His health deteriorated and he became increasingly melancholy. He died of tuberculosis at Vincennes on 30 May 1574, leaving no legitimate children but a son, Charles, Count of Auvergne, later Duke of Angoulême, by his mistress Marie Touchet. Despite his mental instability, he was no imbecile. In 1572, he said of Mary: 'The poor fool will never cease

Charles IX of France,
François Clouet (Louvre)

[from plotting] until she loses her head. In faith they will put her to death. I see it is her own fault and folly.'

CONDÉ, LOUIS de BOURBON, 1st PRINCE of
1530–1569

Louis was born a hunchback at Vendôme on 7 May 1530, the fifth son of Charles de Bourbon, Duc de Vendôme, and Françoise d'Alençon. The youngest brother of Antoine King of Navarre (q.v.) and the first of the famous House of Condé, he was brought up among Huguenots and, in 1551, married

137

Louis de Bourbon Prince de Condé

Louis de Bourbon, 1st
Prince of Condé,
*18th-century engraving
(British Museum)*

Éléonore de Roye, herself a Huguenot.
Brave though deformed, light-hearted
though extremely poor for his rank, he
was destined from an early age for a
military career.

He served with distinction in the
armies of Henri II (q.v.) in the campaigns of 1551–57 but received no recognition since the Bourbons were looked
on with suspicion at the French court.
On Henri's death, he became the military leader of the Huguenots – they
needed a resolute princely patron
although they thoroughly disapproved
of his licentious way of life. He was
involved in the *'Tumulte d'Amboise'* in
March 1560, which was designed to
force the king, then François II (q.v.), to
give recognition to the reformed
religion. For that he was condemned to
death and only the timely death of the
king saved him before the sentence
could be carried out. On the accession

of Charles IX (q.v.), he was back in
favour since Catherine de Medici (q.v.)
needed him as a counter-balance to the
Guises with whom he was formally
reconciled in August 1561.

After the massacre of the Huguenots
at Vassy in March 1562, he occupied
Orléans and marched on Paris but was
defeated and captured by François de
Guise at Dreux on 19 December. For the
three years following the Peace of
Amboise in March 1563, he tried to
restrain the Huguenots and collaborated with the government although he
was much preoccupied with his love
affairs. His first wife died in 1564, but he
cannot have been a candidate for Mary
Queen of Scots' hand for long, since he
married Mlle de Longueville (Françoise
d'Orléans) in 1565. He became alarmed
at the government's dealings with
Spain and left the court again in July
1567 to lead the Huguenots in another
unsuccessful attack on Paris. From then
on, he was constantly at war with the
Catholics until his death. At the battle of
Jarnac on 13 March, 1569, in an act of
lunatic gallantry, he charged the whole
Catholic army with only 400 horsemen.
He was captured and shot through the
head on the spot.

He left three children by his first wife:
Henri, 2nd Prince of Condé; François,
Prince of Conti; and Charles, Cardinal
of Vendôme and one by his second,
Charles, Count of Soissons.

CROC, PHILIBERT du, FRENCH ENVOY

Du Croc, described by the English
historian Holinshed as 'a wise aged
gentleman', was frequently in evidence

at the queen's court during her personal rule in Scotland. A French diplomat of long standing, he was closely associated with the Guise interest, especially that of the powerful Cardinal of Lorraine.

Du Croc represented France in Edinburgh in 1563, and again in 1566, when he reported on the queen's illness and attended Prince James's baptism. He probably took the news of Darnley's murder to France. The French government then sent him back to Scotland to compile a full report. In accordance with his country's policy, du Croc did not attend Mary's marriage to Bothwell. Instead, he tried to mediate between the Royal army and the forces of the Confederate Lords as they faced each other at Carberry Hill. He followed the lords out of Edinburgh and pleaded with both sides to keep the peace. Neither side paid him much heed but his intervention probably reduced the likelihood of military action that day. Thereafter, he made no contribution to Scottish history.

CUNNINGHAM, ALEXANDER, 4th EARL of GLENCAIRN
c. 1510–1574

Alexander was the eldest son of William, the third Earl, by his first wife, Catherine, daughter of William, third Lord Borthwick. As Lord Kilmaurs, he was, like his father, a supporter of the Reformed faith as early as 1540. In May 1544, with his father and the Earl of Lennox (q.v.), he made an agreement with Henry VIII which resulted in all three of them receiving substantial pensions from the

Alexander Cunningham, 4th Earl of Glencairn, *18th-century engraving*

English king. Shortly afterwards, however, they were defeated by Regent Arran (q.v.) at the battle of Glasgow, and Alexander's younger brother Andrew was killed. In September of that year, Alexander and his father declined to assist Lennox on his expedition to the west of Scotland.

Alexander succeeded to the earldom on his father's death in 1547, and became one of the most fervent supporters of Knox (q.v.). He was one of the few nobles motivated purely by religious zeal. After Knox's return to Scotland in 1555, Glencairn invited him to his house at Finlayston near Glasgow, where he preached and celebrated the Lord's Supper. Glencairn's name appears as first of the four signatories on the letter sent to Knox in March 1557, inviting him to return from Geneva. His signature also appears second, after the fourth Earl of Argyll (q.v.), of the five on the first bond of the Scottish Reformers subscribed on

139

3 December 1557. When Mary of Guise (q.v.), outraged by the destruction of the monasteries by the 'rascal multitude', attempted to march on Perth in May 1559, Glencairn barred her way with 2,500 men.

After the parliament of August 1560, Glencairn, Morton (q.v.) and Maitland of Lethington (q.v.), were sent as ambassadors to Queen Elizabeth to request her assistance against the French invaders and propose a marriage between her and the third Earl of Arran (q.v.). They obtained a favourable reply as far as the former was concerned, but the latter was flatteringly declined. In June 1561, Glencairn, Arran and the fifth Earl of Argyll (q.v.) were commissioned to carry out the edicts of the lords for the destruction of 'all places and monuments of idolatry' in the west. This resulted in the ruthless demolition of, among others, the abbeys of Paisley, Fulford, Kilwinning and Crossraguel.

On the return of Mary Queen of Scots at the end of 1561, Glencairn was appointed Privy Councillor but he was always intolerant of the queen's papal practices. With other Reformers, he vigorously opposed the Darnley marriage in June 1565, joined Moray (q.v.) on the 'Chaseabout Raid' and in December was declared guilty of the crime of lese majesty. He then went to Berwick but was back in Scotland early the following year. He was in Edinburgh at the time of the Rizzio conspiracy but was not involved, and was one of the first of the lords to join Mary at Dunbar after the murder. Thereafter Glencairn became one of the queen's chief opponents. He had nothing to do with Darnley's murder, was not in Edinburgh on the night of the signing of the 'Ainslie Bond', and strongly disapproved of the Bothwell marriage. He was one of the leaders of the army under Morton against the queen and Bothwell, at Carberry on 15 June 1567. A few days later, in an act of futile vandalism, he and his servants demolished the altar, ornaments and images of the Chapel Royal at Holyrood. On 29 July, after Mary's abdication, he carried the sword at the coronation of the infant king.

Glencairn commanded one of the divisions against Mary at Langside in May 1568. He was taken prisoner at Stirling in September 1571, on the night that Regent Lennox was killed, but was rescued soon afterwards. He frequently visited John Knox on his deathbed and on 24 November, the day of Knox's death, was nominated along with Morton as a candidate for regent but was substantially outvoted.

Glencairn died on 23 November 1574. In 1526, he married Lady Johanna Hamilton, natural daughter of James, first Earl of Arran. By her he had three sons, including William who became the fifth Earl, and a daughter, Margaret, who married John Wallace of Craigie after whose death about 1570 she became the second wife of Andrew, second Lord Ochiltree. Glencairn divorced Johanna before 1546 and married Janet, daughter of Sir John Cunningham of Caprington. They had a son, Alexander, and a daughter Johaneta who, in 1573, married the widowed Archibald fifth Earl of Argyll, after whose death she married Humphry Colquhoun of Luss.

DOUGLAS, ARCHIBALD, 6th EARL of ANGUS
c. 1489–1557
DOUGLAS, DAVID, 7th EARL of ANGUS
c. 1515–1557
DOUGLAS, ARCHIBALD, 8th EARL of ANGUS
c. 1555–1588

Archibald Douglas, 6th Earl of Angus, *second husband of Margaret Tudor, French School (Reproduced by Gracious permission of Her Majesty the Queen)*

Archibald, sixth Earl was the eldest son of George, Master of Angus, killed at Flodden in 1513, and Elizabeth, daughter of John, first Lord Drummond. He succeeded to the earldom on the death of his grandfather, the formidable Archibald 'Bell the Cat', at the end of the same year. His younger brother George was the father of Regent Morton (q.v.). In 1509, he had married Margaret, daughter of Patrick Hepburn, first Earl of Bothwell, but she also died in 1513.

On 6 August 1514, Angus married Margaret Tudor, the Queen Dowager, and they became the centre of a series of intrigues for the control of the young King James V as they tried to rule the country. James IV, however, had stated in his will that Margaret's rights as tutrix to her son should expire on her re-marriage and friction arose between her and the pro-French Regent Albany, who arrived from France in 1515. She returned to England the same year and, while there, gave birth to a daughter, Margaret (q.v.), later to become the Countess of Lennox. While she was away, Angus and the regent had a good working relationship.

When Albany went to France in 1517, Angus, who was by now estranged from Margaret, was appointed to the commission of regency but showed little statesmanship and was unable to get on with the other regents, especially the first Earl of Arran. Conflict, amounting almost to civil war, arose between the Douglases and the Hamiltons, culminating in 1520 in the affray in Edinburgh known as 'Cleanse the Causeway', in which the Douglases drove the Hamiltons from the town.

Following the return of the regent in 1522, Angus withdrew to France, where he remained until Albany's final departure in 1524. On his return he found Margaret in power, and the young King James on the throne. He effected an outward reconciliation with the Queen Dowager, and was restored to all his former rights and privileges. Appointed one of the lords to have guardianship of the king, Angus proceeded to 'obtain control of his person' at the end of 1525, and kept him in confinement over the next two and a half years. During this period, he was the *de facto* ruler of

141

Scotland, despite two attempts to recover the king from his custody.

The king escaped early in 1528, and the same year, Margaret obtained a divorce. Angus, together with his brother George, his uncle Archibald and his kinsman Alexander Drummond, were banished, their estates forfeited and divided up among the chief nobles. The king thus accomplished a *coup d'état* which established him as the master of his kingdom. Angus retreated to his stronghold of Tantallon and twice resisted sieges led by the king in person, who lost his guns on the second occasion although most of them were chivalrously returned along with his master of the artillery who had been taken prisoner.

This inconclusive conflict continued for several months, although several attempts at reconciliation were made. A condition of the renewal of the truce with England was that Tantallon should be surrendered, but although Angus confirmed the surrender of the castle, James refused to carry out his part of the treaty and Angus retired to Berwick, whereupon Henry VIII attempted to procure his pardon, but without avail. James demanded that Angus should leave the Borders and that Berwick should be restored. This was treated by Henry as a declaration of war, and Angus was summoned to the English court, where he remained until the death of James in 1542. During this time, Angus took part in several border raids, and made frequent attempts to obtain remission, but such was the hatred of the king for the name of Douglas that no pardon was ever granted. Instead the Master of Forbes

was tried, condemned and executed for 'attempting the king's life with a culverin' in 1537, and three days later, his mother-in-law, Lady Jane Glamis, who happened to be Angus's sister, was burnt at the stake for her part in the conspiracy. Sir James Hamilton of Finnart (the Bastard of Arran) was beheaded in 1540 on a similar charge.

With the deaths of Queen Margaret in 1540, and the king in 1542, Angus's two principal enemies were removed, and he returned to Scotland, where his lands and possessions were restored. He was made a Privy Councillor, although he continued to contend with the Hamiltons, now led by Regent Arran (q.v.). His support for the policies of Henry VIII caused grave suspicion and continued until 1544, when the savage attack on Leith, Fife and the Lothians by the English under Hertford caused him to embrace the patriotic cause. In 1544, he was appointed Lieutenant of Scotland south of the Forth, in which capacity he proved himself a valiant commander, being largely responsible for the Scottish victory at Ancrum Moor. He commanded the van at the Battle of Pinkie in 1547 but complained that he had not been properly supported by Regent Arran, whom he blamed for the defeat. Although now aged over sixty, he continued to take the field against the English until the peace in 1550, but played no active part in the military operations.

Angus was not on good terms with Mary of Guise, who was appointed regent in 1554. He insisted on being accompanied by a bodyguard of 1,000 men when attending council to the discomfiture of the constable (George, seventh Earl of Erroll) and the annoyance of the regent. His later years were comparatively peaceful, and he died at Tantallon Castle in January 1557.

The sixth Earl married three times. By his first wife, Margaret, daughter of Patrick, first Earl of Bothwell, he had no surviving issue. By his second, Margaret Tudor, he had one daughter, Margaret, who married the fourth Earl of Lennox (q.v.). By his third, Margaret Maxwell, daughter of Robert, fifth Lord Maxwell, he had a son, James, Master of Angus, who died in February 1548. The earl, having no surviving male issue, was succeeded by his nephew, David Douglas.

David, seventh Earl, was the elder son of Sir George Douglas, who died in 1552, and Elizabeth, only daughter and heiress of David Douglas of Pittendreich. His younger brother James became by marriage the fourth Earl of Morton, and was later Regent of Scotland. Although he negotiated with the Earl of Hertford for the surrender of Tantallon in 1544, little else is known about him, apart from the facts that he was of a studious disposition, suffered from ill health, and took little part in public life.

He died in June 1557, only six months after his uncle. It is doubtful whether he was ever recognised as Earl of Angus, since he is not so designated in any surviving legal document. He married in about 1552, Margaret Hamilton, daughter of John Hamilton of Samuelston, a natural brother of James, Duke of Châtelherault. They had one son, Archibald, who succeeded as eighth Earl, and two daughters: Margaret, who married first Sir Walter Scott of Branxholm and Buccleuch, and second Francis Stewart, Earl of Bothwell; and Elizabeth, who married first John, eighth Lord Maxwell, second, Alexander Stewart of Garlies; and third John Wallace, elder, of Craigie.

Archibald, eighth Earl, succeeded his father at the age of two in 1557, only a few months after the death of his great-uncle the sixth earl. Two years later, his uncle, James, Earl of Morton, became his guardian. The young earl's early life was beset by the efforts of his cousin, Margaret Douglas, Countess of Lennox, daughter of the sixth earl to appropriate her father's estates which had passed to him along with the earldom through his father. Margaret, however, was also extremely keen to see her son Darnley married to Queen Mary. In May 1565, a contract between all the parties concerned, including Mary herself, was signed. Margaret renounced all her claims in return for the support of Morton and Angus for the marriage. Morton's guardianship was interrupted in 1566, when he had to take refuge in England after Rizzio's murder and he was briefly supplanted by the fourth Earl of Atholl although he returned the following year and resumed his responsibilities.

Angus took part in public life at an early age, carrying the crown at the coronation of King James VI at the age of twelve in 1567. In 1575, he was appointed Lieutenant-General on the Borders, and in May 1577, Warden of the West Marches and despite his youth, justified the confidence placed in him by his administration of the border.

His old guardian's early influence ensured Angus's support when Morton became regent, and on Morton's final fall from power, in 1580, Angus found himself the subject of political attack from the king's favourites, Esmé Stewart, now the Earl of (later Duke of) Lennox, and James Stewart, the new Earl of Arran. Angus plotted with Randolph (q.v.), the English ambassador, to make a counter-attack, but his plans were betrayed to Lennox, and he became a fugitive. On Morton's execution in 1581, Angus took refuge at the court of Queen Elizabeth, where he formed a friendship with Sir Philip Sidney.

The Ruthven Raid of 1582, in which the king was seized by the Earls of Mar and Gowrie (q.v.), enabled Angus to return to Scotland, although his forfeiture was not rescinded, and on the king's escape, he was again banished from court and retired to the north where he conspired with Mar and Gowrie to stage a *coup d'état* in 1584. But the plot was discovered, Gowrie was seized and executed on 2 May the same year, and the remaining conspirators were obliged to seek refuge in England. There, they received the support of Elizabeth, who recognised their value to her. Arran sought their return, but a further plot had been hatched involving not only Angus and Mar, but also Lords Claud and John Hamilton (q.v.), whose ancestral estates had been seized by Arran. This had the support of Sir Francis Walsingham (q.v.) and Sir Edward Wotton, the English ambassador, and led ultimately to the downfall of Arran.

On the return of the banished lords, the standard of rebellion was raised in the Borders by Lord Maxwell and quickly spread to the towns. Stirling fell in November 1584, and Arran fled. The office of chancellor was offered to Angus but he declined so it was conferred on Sir John Maitland of Thirlestane, the late William of Lethington's (q.v.) younger brother.

Angus's early education at St Andrews inclined him towards the doctrines of the Reformed Church, of which he became a staunch partisan. He devoted his remaining years to the support of the Presbyterian clergy. In July 1587, parliament ratified to the earl the lands, honours and title of his uncle, the late regent. In 1587 and 1588, he acted vigorously in controlling the Borders and administering justice to thieves, even taking part with the king in person in an expedition against Lord Maxwell, which ended in Maxwell's capture but contributed towards a breakdown in Angus's health. His death in 1588 was probably from consumption but at the time it was attributed to witchcraft. Two women were arrested on suspicion, one was released and the other burnt some years later.

Despite dying at the age of thirty-three, the earl married three times. By his first wife, Mary Erskine, daughter of John, Earl of Mar, Regent of Scotland (q.v.), whom he married in June 1573 and who died in May 1575, he had no children. Nor did he by his second, Margaret Leslie, daughter of the fifth Earl of Rothes (q.v.), whom he married on Christmas Day 1575 and divorced early in 1587. He married, thirdly, on 29 July 1587, Jean Lyon, daughter of John, seventh Earl of Glamis, by whom he had a daughter, who was born after his death, and died unmarried at the age of fifteen. On his death, the title and estates of Douglas passed to his cousin, Sir William Douglas of Glenbervie, while those of Morton eventually passed to Douglas of Lochleven.

DOUGLAS, GEORGE, BISHOP of MORAY
c. 1530–1589

Natural son of the sixth Earl of Angus and therefore half-brother of Margaret, Countess of Lennox, Douglas was for many years in contention with James Beaton (q.v.) for the abbacy of Arbroath. Beaton became Archbishop of Glasgow in 1552, but Douglas then had to deal with another rival, Lord John Hamilton (q.v.), second son of Regent Arran (q.v.), who was said to have been given the abbey as early as 1541. By 1570, Hamilton was styled Abbot and Commendator, while Douglas was only styled Postulate but Douglas had been in possession of the abbey for many years. That year, Hamilton enlisted aid to eject him and an unsuccessful siege of the abbey took place. In 1572, Douglas sat in the Privy Council as Commendator of Arbroath.

It was while he was in possession of the abbey that Douglas became involved in the Rizzio conspiracy. He was among the murderers and was said to have struck the first blow at the queen's favourite.

In 1573, he was chosen Bishop of Moray, but found it hard to come up to the standards of the Reformed Church, partly because he was accused of fornication and partly because he was a poor preacher. He died in 1589.

James Douglas, 4th Earl of Morton, *later Regent of Scotland, attributed to Arnold Bronckhorst, c. 1580 (National Galleries of Scotland)*

DOUGLAS, JAMES, 4th EARL of MORTON CHANCELLOR and REGENT of SCOTLAND
c. 1516–1581

James was the second son of Sir George Douglas (1490–1552). He was the great-grandson of Archibald 'Bell the Cat', the fifth Earl of Angus (*c.* 1449–1514); nephew of Archibald, sixth Earl of Angus (q.v.); younger brother of David the seventh Earl (q.v.), and the uncle and guardian of Archibald, the eighth Earl. His mother was Elizabeth, daughter and heiress of David Douglas of Pittendreich. In 1543, he contracted marriage with Elizabeth Douglas, daughter of James, third Earl of Morton, on whose death in 1552 (the same year as that of his father), he succeeded to the earldom, having previously been styled 'Master of Morton'.

145

His father was one of the Douglases forced to flee to England in 1528 after the sixth Earl of Angus surrendered Tantallon Castle to James V. Young Morton went into hiding, took the name of Innes and worked as a grieve and overseer on an estate in the far north of Scotland. This enabled him to acquire a knowledge of business which stood him in good stead for the rest of his life.

In 1545, he took part in the invasion of England, which was unsuccessful, largely due to his father's mishandling of the campaign. Taken prisoner on the capture of Dalkeith Castle in 1548, he did not regain his liberty until the pacification two years later.

During the 1550s, Morton's attitude towards the Reformation was equivocal. Although he subscribed the first bond of Scottish Reformers on 3 December 1557, he would not assist them against Mary of Guise (q.v.) and withdrew his backing altogether in November 1559. He did not, however, give the Queen Regent anything more than moral support and on 10 May 1560, with the other Lords of the Congregation, including Moray (q.v.) and Argyll (q.v.), he ratified the Treaty of Berwick with England against France. Mary of Guise died on 11 June 1560 and in October of that year, Morton accompanied Maitland (q.v.) and Glencairn (q.v.) to London to propose the marriage between Elizabeth and the third Earl of Arran (q.v.).

After Queen Mary's return to Scotland, he became a member of the Privy Council. With Lord Lindsay (q.v.), he raised 100 horse and 800 foot-soldiers in support of Mary's campaign against the fourth Earl of Huntly (q.v.) in the autumn of 1562. The campaign culminated in the battle of Corrichie and the death of Huntly on 28 October. On 1 January 1563, Morton was appointed Lord Chancellor in Huntly's place.

Morton supported the queen's marriage to Darnley, partly because the latter's mother, Lady Lennox, was his first cousin and had, in May 1565, renounced her claim on the earldom of Angus, which Morton was holding in trust for his nephew, the young eighth earl. His support, however, was never more than lukewarm and Randolph (q.v.), on 19 February, reported that Morton 'much misliked [Darnley] and wished him away'. Nonetheless, he was present at the wedding on 29 July 1565 and, in the autumn of that year, assisted Mary in the 'Chaseabout Raid', acting as military commander. Despite his support, the queen was gravely suspicious of him on account of his earlier friendship with the rebels Moray and Argyll.

With Lord Ruthven (q.v.), Morton led the conspiracy to murder Rizzio and was in the chamber when the queen's favourite was killed on 9 March 1566. The plan to detain Mary and take her to Stirling was frustrated when she escaped with Darnley to Dunbar. Morton and his fellow murderers immediately went to England.

Most of the conspirators, including Morton, were pardoned by the queen at the end of December 1566. Almost as soon as he returned to Scotland, Morton became involved in the plot against Darnley. The murder took place in the early hours of 10 February 1567 and, although Morton was out of Edinburgh on the night, there is much evidence of his complicity. In his confession, just before his execution in 1581, he admitted that he had known in advance of the plot although he had 'neither art nor part in it'.

Never on good terms with Bothwell, Morton's attitude hardened when Mary was forcibly abducted on 24 April 1567. He formed a 'secret council [of lords to] seek the liberty of the Queen, to preserve the life of the Prince and pursue them that murdered the King.' After Mary's marriage to Bothwell on 15 May, exasperated at her folly, he did everything he could to detach her from her husband. At Carberry on 15 June, he was finally successful. The queen surrendered and was taken to Lochleven.

After Mary's abdication on 24 July, Morton played a major role in the regencies of Moray, Lennox (q.v.) and Mar (q.v.). Mar died on 29 October 1572 and on the 24th of the following month, Morton was elected regent. On the same day, John Knox (q.v.) died. Morton later uttered the graveside eulogy saying that 'he neither feared nor flattered any flesh'.

The last of the Marians, including Maitland (q.v.), Kirkcaldy (q.v.) and Home (q.v.), were holding out in Edinburgh Castle. With the help of money and troops from Elizabeth, Morton stepped up the siege and on 28 May 1573 the castle fell. Home was sentenced to be confined to the castle, Maitland died almost immediately and saved the executioner a job, but Kirkcaldy was 'hanged against the sun' on 3 August; a tragic end for such an able soldier.

The fall of the castle was a deathblow to Mary's cause, and for several years Morton was able to rule in peace. He kept firm control of the nobles, maintained order in the Borders and above all resolutely adhered to the English alliance despite highly fickle support from Elizabeth.

Briefly overthrown in March 1578, he soon regained his position and ruled from June 1578 to December 1580 when he was suddenly arrested. His position had latterly been undermined by his numerous enemies, including the Hamiltons and the new royal favourites Esmé Stewart, Duke of Lennox and James Stewart, Earl of Arran. He was charged with complicity in the murder of Darnley fourteen years earlier and found guilty.

Morton had been responsible for the introduction of a machine called 'the Maiden' for the humane beheading of wrongdoers. It was a development of the 'Halifax gibbet' and a forerunner of the guillotine. It was on this instrument of death that, with great courage, he met his end in June 1581.

His wife had been insane for many years before her death in September 1574 and he was not survived by any legitimate male children. The title passed to John, first Lord Maxwell, grandson of the third earl, and later to the Douglases of Lochleven on Maxwell's death in 1593.

DOUGLAS, LADY MARGARET, COUNTESS of LENNOX 1515–1578

Born at Harbottle in Northumberland in October 1515, the importance of the young daughter of Margaret Tudor,

*Lady Margaret Douglas,
Countess of Lennox,
mother of Darnley and
grandmother of James VI,
artist unknown, late 16th
century (Reproduced by
Gracious permission of Her
Majesty The Queen)*

widow of James IV, and her second husband, Archibald, sixth Earl of Angus (q.v.) was recognised from the moment of her birth. Taken to London in the following May, she was lodged at Greenwich with her young cousin Princess Mary Tudor, with whom she formed a staunch friendship. On the separation of her parents in 1520, three years after her return to Scotland, her father seized her, and from then on she became a pawn in the deadly game of the succession to the throne of England.

After the birth of the Princess Elizabeth in 1533, she was made the first lady of honour, and when both princesses were declared illegitimate, became the lady of highest rank. Despite the claims of her half-brother James V to be next in line to the English throne, the fact that she was born in England, and was under the protection

of Henry, made her consider that her claim was the stronger. The birth of Prince Edward in 1537, however, made Henry determined to place her in the same category as the two princesses, and he obtained sufficient evidence to declare her mother's second marriage unlawful. This done, she was restored to Henry's somewhat mercurial favour and, in arranging her marriage to Matthew Stewart, Earl of Lennox (q.v.), himself a claimant to the Scottish throne, Henry secured a match which gave satisfaction to all parties. Lennox promised to surrender his claim to the Scottish throne to Henry, and in return was granted the governorship of Scotland in Henry's name, while Lady Margaret gained not only a husband for whom she felt genuine affection, but also strengthened her own claim to both thrones.

When Henry sent Lennox on an expedition to Scotland immediately after the marriage, Margaret seized the opportunity to escape from the king's influence and returned to Yorkshire, where her husband later joined her. Their home at Temple Newsam became the focus of Catholic intrigue, causing great offence to Henry, who, in his last will, disinherited the countess from the succession. With the accession of Mary Tudor, however, her star was once more in the ascendant. Not only was she granted annual revenues from the wool trade, but she was restored to the succession, being given precedence over Princess Elizabeth. On the death of Mary, she was received with seeming kindness by Elizabeth, but neither was deceived as to the true feelings of the other and, although permitted to leave court, she and her husband were kept under constant surveillance in Yorkshire.

Again she was precluded from the succession and, in addition, Elizabeth also resurrected the question of her legitimacy. Lady Lennox was not unduly concerned by these actions; she had determined to advance her dynastic ambitions and secure both thrones through the marriage of her son, Lord Darnley, to Mary, Queen of Scots, who had a strong claim to succeed if not supplant Elizabeth. Although the plans proceeded in secret, Elizabeth learned of them through her network of spies, and for some time it seemed that they would miscarry. The Lennoxes were summoned to London, where the earl was placed in the Tower, and the countess and Darnley were confined to the house of Sir Richard Sackville in Sheen. An enquiry was mounted as to whether the intentions of the countess were treasonable. Lady Lennox wrote moving and flattering letters to Elizabeth which, while the queen was not deceived as to their sincerity, were sufficient to promote a reconciliation between the two, and secure the liberty of the countess and her family.

In 1564 Lennox was permitted to return to Scotland, and at the very time that Elizabeth was urging Mary to marry Leicester (q.v.), she made the fatal mistake of allowing Darnley to join him. Lady Lennox, meanwhile, had skilfully impressed Melville (q.v.) whom she used as a conduit for her wooing of the Scottish queen. By her renunciation of her claim to the earldom of Angus, she also gained the support of the Earl of Morton (q.v.) for the marriage. Nothing now stood in her way. Elizabeth, on discovering the duplicity of the countess, immediately committed her to the Tower, where she was confined until after Darnley's murder. Shortly afterwards she regained her liberty and, while her husband made vain efforts to secure the conviction of Bothwell for the murder, she denounced Mary to the Spanish ambassador in London. This had the effect of suspending the quarrel with Elizabeth, but when she learned that Mary had sought the protection of the English queen, the countess and her husband hastened to accuse her of the crime, with a vigorous demand for vengeance for the death of their son.

It suited Elizabeth's policy that Lennox should be appointed regent on the death of Moray (q.v.) in 1570, while the countess still remained hostile to Mary. The feelings of the earl towards Mary had always been stronger than those of his wife. Following his death, when his last words were a desire to be remembered to his wife, a reconciliation took place between the countess and Mary, the queen promising in a letter to 'love her as her aunt, and respect her as her mother-in-law'. The countess, always a devout Catholic, had by now a strong desire to be reconciled with the mother of her grandson.

In 1574, having been given permission to set out for Scotland, Lady Lennox sought permission to visit Chatsworth on the way, where Mary was imprisoned. This was denied, since Elizabeth suspected ulterior motives, despite the countess's protestations that she had no wish to meet Mary. The true cause of the proposed visit was revealed when the marriage hastily took place between her younger son, Charles, by then the sixth Earl of Lennox, and Elizabeth Cavendish, daughter of the equally ambitious Bess of Hardwicke, wife of Mary's gaoler, the Earl of Shrewsbury. Elizabeth immediately ordered her return and, in December, both she and the Countess of Shrewsbury were sent to the Tower. Here she stayed until early in 1577, receiving her pardon shortly before the death of her son from consumption. She did not long survive him, dying in March 1578.

The Countess of Lennox had four children, all of whom predeceased her, although her two grandchildren, James VI, and Arabella Stewart, daughter of her younger son Charles and Elizabeth Cavendish, survived her. Arabella died in the Tower in 1615, but the main objective of the countess's life was fulfilled by James, who succeeded to the crowns of both England and Scotland. She also achieved royal burial, being interred in Westminster Abbey alongside her son Charles.

DOUGLAS, SIR WILLIAM, of LOCHLEVEN, later 5th EARL of MORTON 1540–1606

The eldest son of Sir Robert Douglas of Lochleven, who was killed at the battle of Pinkie in 1547, his mother Margaret, second daughter of John, fifth Lord Erskine, had been one of the mistresses of James V and was mother of James Stewart, later Regent Moray (q.v.). Sir William was thus closely related to three nobles each of whom became regent of Scotland: Moray was his half-brother; Mar (q.v.) was his uncle; and Morton (q.v.) was so closely related that he made Sir William his heir.

Following her marriage to Darnley, Mary demanded that Douglas give up his fortress of Lochleven, but Douglas pleaded ill-health and was permitted to keep it on the understanding that it would be delivered with all its armaments on request at twenty-four hours' notice. He had sufficiently recovered, however, to be present on the night of Rizzio's murder, and was denounced as one of the murderers. A year later, he joined the Confederate Lords to protect the young king and avenge Darnley's murder. Following Mary's surrender at Carberry Hill on 15 June 1567, because of his close relationship with Moray and Mar and the impregnable position of his fortress, he was appointed her gaoler, receiving a warrant for her commitment on 16 June. It was through no lack of vigilance on his part, or that of his mother (who as Moray's mother had a double interest in keeping Mary incarcerated) that the queen made her escape, aided by at least two of Sir William's kinsmen, nor was he ever charged with collusion or complicity.

He was present at the battle of Langside in May 1568 bringing reinforcements to the right wing. Later that year, he accompanied Moray and Morton to the queen's trial in York and when, following the Rising of the North in 1569, Thomas, seventh Earl of Northumberland was taken prisoner in Liddesdale, at Elizabeth's request it was to Lochleven that he was taken. In a shameful act, Douglas accepted the sum of £2,000 to deliver the earl to Elizabeth, rejecting the offer of the same sum from the Countess of Northumberland for her husband's freedom.

On the murder of Moray, Douglas and his half-brother Lord Robert Stewart (q.v.), as next of kin of the murdered man, unsuccessfully sought vengeance against the assassin, Hamilton of Bothwellhaugh (q.v.). During Morton's regency, Douglas became closely involved with the regent. It was to Lochleven that Morton retired when he demitted office in 1578. When Morton was apprehended and charged with the murder of Darnley, Sir William, together with others of his kinsmen, were also summoned to appear. In March 1581 he was banished beyond the Firth of Cromarty. He took no part in the Ruthven Raid, although his son was involved, and in December 1583 he was again banished, and went to France with the principal conspirators, where they organised a plot which resulted in the capture of Stirling Castle and the overthrow of James Stewart, Earl of Arran in 1585.

In 1588, on the death of Archibald Douglas, eighth Earl of Angus (q.v.), Sir William succeeded to the title of Earl of Morton since Lord Maxwell's title had been revoked in 1585. In 1592, however, Lord Maxwell's title was revived, so that for a time there were two Earls of Morton. Despite assurances that this revival should not prejudice the rights of Sir William, the situation was not satisfactory to either claimant, and the two came to blows over the right of precedent in a church in Edinburgh in February 1593. As one of the leaders of the Presbyterian party, Douglas

exercised considerable influence at court after the marriage of the king to Anne of Denmark.

He died in September 1606 having married Lady Agnes Leslie, eldest daughter of George, fourth Earl of Rothes. They had four sons and seven daughters. The sons were: Robert, who predeceased his father, and whose son, William, inherited the title of Earl of Morton; James, Commendator of Melrose; Sir Archibald Douglas of Kellour; Francis, who died young; and Sir George Douglas of Kirkness. The daughters, who were known as the seven pearls of Lochleven were: Margaret, who married John Wemyss, son and heir of Sir David Wemyss of that Ilk; Christian, who married first Laurence, Master of Oliphant, and second Alexander, first Earl of Home; Mary, who married as his second wife Walter, Lord Ogilvy; Euphemia, who married as his second wife Thomas Lyon of Baldukie, Master of Glamis; Agnes, who married Archibald, seventh Earl of Argyll; Elizabeth, who married as his third wife Francis, ninth Earl of Erroll; and Jean, who died unmarried.

DRURY, SIR WILLIAM
1527–1579

The third son of Sir Robert Drury of Hedgerley, Buckinghamshire, and his wife Elizabeth Brudenell, Drury was educated at Gonville Hall, Cambridge and gained early military experience in the retinue of the Earl of Bedford during the campaign in France in 1544, when he was taken prisoner. A supporter of the Reformed faith, he thought it

151

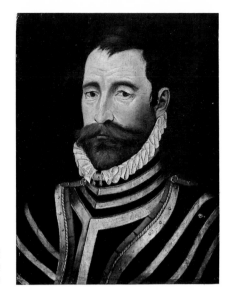

Sir William Drury, *artist
unknown, mid-16th century
(National Portrait Gallery)*

prudent to retire from court during the reign of Mary Tudor, but returned with the accession of Elizabeth who, recognising his talents, despatched him secretly to Scotland to report on the state of the parties there, and to view the fortifications of Leith, which were then nearing completion. His report strengthened Elizabeth's determination to support the Lords of the Congregation, and he returned to Scotland to take part in the siege of Leith, where he had the misfortune to be captured yet again, but the duration of his incarceration was brief. He was then appointed Governor of Berwick in 1564, an office which he held until 1576. During the Rising of the North in 1569, he suppressed with great firmness the rebellion of the northern earls under Percy and Westmorland in support of Queen Mary.

In January 1570, he was appointed one of the commissioners to treat with Regent Moray for the surrender of the Earl of Northumberland, but on his way to the meeting, Moray was assassinated, and it was rumoured that the same fate was intended for Drury. He accompanied the Earl of Sussex in the retaliatory raid on the Borders and reduced Liddesdale and Teviotdale, before marching on Edinburgh with a strong force, but failed to persuade Lethington and Kirkcaldy to agree to terms. Similar negotiations with Lord Fleming at Dumbarton were halted by a further attempt to assassinate Drury with, it was hinted, the connivance of Fleming himself. His disapproval of his unfriendly reception was shown by his razing the principal castles belonging to the Hamiltons and ravaging Clydesdale on his return journey to England.

The effect of this punitive act was short and, in 1571, Elizabeth again found it expedient to despatch him to Scotland to examine the state of the country, and he was instructed to negotiate with the king and Regent Lennox, but without success, his efforts again attracting the attentions of unsuccessful assassins. These repeated attempts on his life, in all there were to be eight, not unnaturally caused him some anxiety, and he besought the protection of Cecil, for his wife and family, in the event of his untimely death. Further attempts at negotiation were thwarted by the arrival of du Croc, and Drury requested that he should be recalled, saying that he would 'rather serve in Constantinople than among such an ingrate people'.

In April 1573, Elizabeth decided that it was necessary to use force against the recalcitrant lords, and again Drury was despatched to Edinburgh, this time at the head of a strong force, supported by a heavy train of artillery. Kirkcaldy who was holding the castle refused to submit, so Drury trained his guns on it, choosing the siting with highly professional skill. The assault started on 21 May, and continued for eight days and nights until, on 29 May, the castle surrendered. With its capture, and the deaths of Maitland and Kirkcaldy of Grange, the civil war came to an end. Before his execution, Kirkcaldy praised Drury, saying that he had ever found him upright in his sovereign's cause. Drury, in turn, considered Kirkcaldy to be a plain man of war, for whom he had the highest regard. An allegation was made that, in the confusion, Drury had misappropriated the Scottish crown jewels, but the charge was malicious and quite without foundation.

Having established peace in Scotland, Drury then turned his attentions to Ireland. In 1576 he accepted the position of President of Munster, where he quickly subdued the province to obedience and fortified the garrisons, which had been allowed to fall into disrepair. His tenure in Munster was short, Sidney obtaining the appointment of Lord Justice for the Council in Ireland for him in 1578, but shortly after Drury's return to England, rebellion broke out in Ireland, and he determined to return to the field, despite failing health. He died in Waterford on 13 October 1579, and was buried, without ceremony, in St Patrick's Cathedral in Dublin. Nothing now remains of the monument erected to this man of honour, whose calling was to serve his queen and country to the best of his ability.

Drury married, in October 1560, Margaret, daughter of Thomas, Lord Wentworth, and widow of John, last Lord Williams of Thame.

Robert Dudley, Earl of Leicester, *by Nicholas Hilliard, 1576 (National Portrait Gallery)*

DUDLEY, ROBERT, EARL of LEICESTER
1533–1588

Robert was the fifth and youngest son of John, Earl of Warwick and Duke of Northumberland, the real ruler of England in the latter years of the boy-king, Edward VI. Northumberland and several others were executed for treason at the beginning of Mary Tudor's reign, for trying to place his daughter-in-law, Lady Jane Grey, on the English throne. The Dudley family, or what remained of it, continued to be in a dangerous position even after the accession of Elizabeth. No Tudor monarch could be expected to take kindly to a family likely to attempt to alter the very doubtful succession to the crown. Yet Robert surmounted these difficulties and his place at court, though variable, was never in serious doubt. Indeed, given other circumstances, he might have become King Consort of England.

He was educated by the great teacher-scholar, Roger Ascham, who also tutored Princess Elizabeth, and was taken to the court of Edward VI, where he met Elizabeth, and was knighted. On 4 June 1550, when only seventeen, he married Amy, daughter of Sir John Robsart. Although his father's attempt to enthrone Jane Grey led to Robert's condemnation for treason, he was reprieved, visited Europe and even did military service for the suspicious Queen Mary. On Elizabeth's accession, he immediately came into favour and was showered with offices and lands. That he formed a close relationship with Elizabeth is beyond doubt and her affection for him was genuine. His influence at court grew to the detriment and dismay of Cecil (q.v.) and many others.

On 8 September 1560, Amy Dudley was found dead at the foot of a staircase; her neck had been broken. She had lived away from court despite being on good terms with her husband. A jury gave a verdict of accidental death. Dudley did not attend the funeral and inevitably, intense gossip and speculation followed. Allegations that Dudley had caused his wife's murder continued to be made for years to come. Elizabeth, however, was unmoved and her relationship with him remained unchanged. Dudley tried to get Spanish help to promote his marriage to the queen but such a marriage, in the light of his wife's death, was impossible. Mary Queen of Scots was later to find her marriage to Bothwell – in not dissimilar circumstances – congenial to herself but to no one else.

By 1563, Elizabeth had come to realise that she could not marry Dudley herself, but Mary Queen of Scots could. That year she suggested that Mary marry Dudley and in September 1564, created him Earl of Leicester. The only merit Mary could see in the scheme was that it might win English friendship and smooth her path to the succession. Leicester, still wishing to marry Elizabeth, was aghast and the Scots were no more enthusiastic about the project, Leicester being referred to as 'the shop-soiled widower'. For Elizabeth, however, the plan would neutralise a potentially hostile Scotland and it was revived in 1565, after there had been a suggestion that Ambrose Dudley, Earl of Warwick, Robert's older brother, be a substitute bridegroom. Leicester was no more enthusiastic and the proposition, made desperately to forestall Mary's marriage to Darnley, came to nothing.

Leicester, meanwhile, remained high in Elizabeth's favour but at odds with Cecil and the old nobility. His own behaviour was erratic and inconsistent. He sometimes supported proposals for her marriage; at other times he opposed them. He was entirely reliant on her support, and she found him handsome, grave, devoted and a comfort. Yet he was not above becoming involved in movements against her, however indirectly, such as the proposed marriage of Norfolk and Mary, and the northern earls' rebellion. In 1571, he imperilled his own standing by a mysterious liaison with the widowed Lady Sheffield, which she alleged was a marriage. It produced a son, Robert, whom he acknowledged as his own.

Although often disappointed in his tremendous ambitions and rarely able to influence the principal policies of Elizabeth, Leicester generally remained in favour at court. Even his marriage in 1578 to Letticia Knollys, the widowed Lady Essex (and mother of Elizabeth's last favourite, the second Earl), did not incur more than her temporary wrath. By this time, Leicester was adopting a stance as a Puritan nationalist and trying to influence government policy through Sir Francis Walsingham. This led him to advocate a strong anti-Spanish attitude in the Netherlands. Disappointed in his wish to command there in 1577–78, he eventually became commander in the great expedition of 1585–86. He fell out with the Dutch, displeased Elizabeth and proved a negligent general. He arrived home to find the final agitation against Mary Queen of Scots at its height. Though earlier in favour of lenient treatment for her, he now strongly supported calls for her execution.

In 1588 the Armada arrived. Leicester was made Captain-General and set up camp at Tilbury. Never easily able to exert authority and always touchy about his dignity, he proved a difficult commander. But he did stage-manage Elizabeth's visit to her army and her rousing address of defiance. Flushed by the Armada's defeat, Elizabeth considered giving Leicester the unprecedented office of Lieutenant-General of the kingdom. However, characteristically, she delayed and Leicester died, on 4 September 1588, without this final accolade that in no sense would he have deserved. In addition to his son by Lady Sheffield, he had another son, also named Robert, by Letticia Knollys.

Erik XIV, *King of Sweden, by S. van der Meulen, 1561 (National Swedish Portraits Collection, Gripsholm)*

ERIK XIV, KING of SWEDEN 1533–1577

Born in Stockholm on 13 December 1533, Erik was the only son of Gustavus Vasa by his first wife, Catherine of Saxe-Lauenburg. He was therefore first cousin of his great rival for control of the Baltic, Frederik of Denmark and Norway (q.v.).

He was crowned at Uppsala on 29 June 1561 and almost immediately started to show signs of insanity, quarrelling with his younger half-brothers and other members of the nobility. To free Swedish trade from Danish domination, he sought contacts with Western Europe and made unsuccessful approaches to both Queen Elizabeth of England and Mary Queen of Scots, with a view to marriage.

In 1562, he imprisoned his half-brother Johan, Duke of Finland (q.v.) for signing a marriage treaty with Poland and in September 1563, Frederik of Denmark, now allied with Poland, declared war on Sweden. Thus began the Scandinavian Seven Years War. Erik's conduct of the war was ineffective and marked by his suspicions of treason amongst his nobles, many of whom he had killed or imprisoned at Uppsala in 1566 and 1567. He even went so far as to personally assist in the murder of one of them.

In July 1568 he had his mistress, Karin Månsdotter, crowned queen, but his insanity had become so pronounced that a committee of senators was appointed to govern the kingdom. On 30 September 1568, Erik was replaced by Johan (whom he had released from prison a year earlier).

In spite of several rebellions, Johan III, as he now was, managed to retain his throne. Erik died in prison at Orbyhus, at the end of February 1577, allegedly poisoned by the governor on Johan's orders.

ERSKINE, ARTHUR, of BLACKGRANGE
c. 1514–c. 1570

The fifth son of John, the fifth Baron Erskine, and Lady Margaret Campbell, daughter of Archibald, second Earl of Argyll, he was the younger brother of John, sixth Lord Erskine (q.v.), who later became the Earl of Mar and Regent of Scotland. One of his four sisters was Margaret, who married Robert Douglas of Lochleven, but was a mistress of James V, and bore him a son, James Stewart, who later became Regent Moray (q.v.).

Robert Douglas was cousin of James, fourth Earl of Morton (q.v.), and his son William (q.v.) became the fifth Earl in 1588, so Erskine was related to three men who were to become regents of Scotland; Moray, his nephew; Mar, his brother; and Morton, his cousin by marriage. His sister, Margaret, had detested Mary of Guise (q.v.) for replacing her in the king's affections, and there was consequently little love lost between her and Queen Mary.

It was therefore ironic that Erskine should have become Mary's favourite equerry, and that in the light of his brother Mar's religious persuasion, he should have been described by Knox (q.v.) as 'the most pestilent papist in the realm'. He was in attendance on the queen in Holyrood on the evening that Rizzio was murdered in March 1566, and the following night helped organise her escape from the palace and escorted her to Dunbar.

In January 1562, Erskine married Magdalen Livingston, whose sister was one of the 'four Maries' and whose brother, William, sixth Lord Livingston (q.v.), was another of the queen's most constant and faithful supporters. The marriage was childless, and Erskine died at the end of 1570.

ERSKINE, JOHN, of DUN, 1508–1591

The son of Sir John Erskine, fifth Laird of Dun, and Margaret Ruthven, Dowager Countess of Buchan, John belonged to the family which also included the earls of Mar. His father, grandfather, great-uncle and uncle were all killed at the battle of Flodden, so John had as guardian Sir Thomas Erskine, secretary to James V. He received an excellent education in Scotland and France and became an accomplished Greek scholar. In 1535, he married Elizabeth Lindsay, daughter of the eighth Earl of Crawford, but she died in 1538. Sometime during the next five years, probably during his extensive European travels, he married Barbara de Beirle.

On his return to administer his estates in Scotland, Erskine became friendly with the Reformer and martyr, George Wishart (q.v.). In 1555 he met Knox who strengthened his Protestant understanding. Although he had given considerable support to the Queen Regent, apparently fearful that the nation would be weakened by religious dissension, he was, in 1557, along with Argyll (q.v.), his son Lorne (q.v.), Glencairn (q.v.) and Morton (q.v.), one of the signatories of the 'First Bond'. Erskine's own faith was clear enough and he was one of the Protestant Commissioners at the marriage of Queen Mary and François II of France (q.v.). Henceforward, as the Reformed cause gathered momentum, Erskine emerged as one of its leaders. In 1560 he became superintendent of Angus and Mearns, despite his layman's status.

During the personal rule of Mary, Erskine achieved distinction. He was popular with the queen, partly because he tried to tone down Knox's attacks on her and partly because he could serve as a bridge between the court and the Protestant aristocracy. He served as Moderator of the General Assembly on several occasions. He was, however, no Marian supporter. He attended the coronation of the infant James VI and upheld the regency. As the issue of episcopacy became acute, Erskine took a moderate line. A promoter of the *Second Book of Discipline*, he was nonetheless unwilling to make the elimination of an active episcopate the test of true Presbyterianism. A member of the royal council in 1579, he could not approve of James VI's later attempts to strengthen the position of the bishops, but he would not support those who were violently opposed to the royal policy. John Erskine was a leader of the Reformation whose long career served to show that an influential layman could promote the Protestant cause without having ulterior political motives.

He died early in 1591, leaving a son, John.

ERSKINE, JOHN, 6th BARON ERSKINE, 1st EARL of MAR, REGENT of SCOTLAND c. 1510–1572

The third and eldest surviving son of John, the fifth Baron, and Lady Margaret Campbell, daughter of Archibald, second Earl of Argyll, his family traced its descent from Christiana, sister of

John Erskine, Earl of Mar,
Regent of Scotland, *artist
unknown, mid-16th century
(National Galleries of
Scotland)*

Robert the Bruce. The fifth Baron had been guardian of James V during his minority, and later of Queen Mary during hers. He had also been keeper of Edinburgh Castle before his death in 1552.

The sixth Earl had been educated for the church, and became heir unexpectedly, after the death of his two brothers. After the death of his father, Edinburgh Castle came into the hands of the Duke of Châtelherault (q.v.), who however relinquished it when Mary of Guise (q.v.) became regent in 1554. The custody of the castle was then delivered to Erskine by parliament, with the proviso that he should prevent it from falling into the hands of the French.

Erskine had not at this stage become a supporter of the Reformed doctrines, although he did so later. In 1557, with Lord Lorne, later fifth Earl of Argyll (q.v.), Lord James Stewart, later Earl of Moray (q.v.), and the Earl of Glencairn (q.v.), he invited John Knox (q.v.), to return from Geneva. In 1559, however,

he supported Mary of Guise in her vain effort to prevent the surrender of Perth. It is clear that his chief motive was to prevent the miseries of civil war. Although his sympathies were by now entirely with the Reformers, he remained courteous to Mary of Guise, and even received her into Edinburgh Castle in the interest of peace.

On the return of Queen Mary in 1561, Erskine was appointed a member of the Privy Council, and received a grant of several church lands. He favoured the proposal for the marriage of Queen Mary to Leicester (q.v.), but on discovering her feelings, cordially supported the Darnley match. On 23 June 1565, Erskine was created Earl of Mar. He was present at the marriage of Mary and Darnley, and thereafter assisted Mary in the Chaseabout Raid. Shortly after the birth of Prince James, the queen stayed with him and the Earl of Moray (q.v.) at his castle near Alloa.

Mar had nothing to do with the murders of either Rizzio or Darnley, but while lying ill at Stirling, shortly before the trial of Bothwell, consented that Edinburgh Castle should be delivered up to Bothwell at the instance of Mary. On 19 April 1567, he was confirmed in his captainship of Stirling Castle, so that he should be entrusted with the guardianship of the young prince there. He was not even asked to be a signatory to the Ainslie Bond and later refused to deliver up the young prince to Bothwell.

Mar was present at the surrender of the queen at Carberry on 14 June 1567, and two days later signed the order for her commitment at Lochleven Castle. On the 24th, he was one of the council to whom she demitted the government, and on the 29th, he carried the young prince in his arms to his coronation.

On Mary's escape from Lochleven, he sent a supply of men to Regent Moray from Stirling, and was present at the battle of Langside on 13 May 1568. After Moray's murder, he was one of those who bore the regent's body at the funeral. On 3 September 1571, the king's party was surprised by the Hamiltons and others near Stirling. Mar gallantly opened fire on the intruders and drove them off, but not before Regent Lennox (q.v.) was killed. Mar was then by general consent chosen regent.

On 10 September, he came to Leith where he proclaimed Morton (q.v.) lieutenant-general of the forces, and from then on until his death, he was effectively Morton's pawn, albeit occasionally unwillingly. The remainder of his short regency was undistinguished and notable only for his efforts to secure the surrender of Edinburgh Castle, which was still being held for the queen. On 9 October 1572, a conference took place between Morton, Mar and Killigrew (q.v.) when the proposal was mooted on behalf of Queen Elizabeth that Mary should be delivered up to her enemies in Scotland with a view to her execution. Mar did not express much enthusiasm for this plan.

Shortly after this conference, Mar was seized with a violent sickness from which he died on 29 October 1572. Remarkably he had succeeded in winning the respect of both the king's and the queen's parties. By his wife, Annabella Murray, he had one son,

John, who succeeded to the earldom, and a daughter, Mary, who became Countess of Angus.

FLEMING, JAMES, 4th BARON FLEMING
c. 1534–1558
FLEMING, JOHN, 5th BARON FLEMING
c. 1536–1572

James, fourth Baron, the eldest son of Malcolm, third Lord Fleming and Johanna Stewart, natural daughter of James IV, succeeded to the title when his father was killed at the battle of Pinkie.

His mother, who later had a scandalous affair with Henri II of France (q.v.), was governess to the young Queen Mary, and his sister was one of her 'four Maries'. In 1548, he and Lord Erskine (q.v.) accompanied the queen to France. He also accompanied Mary of Guise (q.v.) there in 1549. On 21 December 1553, he was made Great Chamberlain of Scotland for life in succession to his father. About the same time he was appointed guardian of the East and Middle Marches.

In February 1558, he was one of eight commissioners sent to France to represent Scotland at the marriage of Queen Mary to the Dauphin François (q.v.). The fact that they did not send for the crown of Scotland caused much ill feeling and four of them, including Fleming, mysteriously died on the way home, supposedly poisoned by the Guises. Fleming died in Paris on 18 December.

By his wife, Lady Barbara Hamilton, eldest daughter of James, Duke of

Châtelherault (q.v.), he had one daughter, Jane, who married first, John, Lord Thirlestane (died 3 October 1595) and second, John, fifth Earl of Cassilis, but had no children. Fleming was succeeded by his younger brother John.

John, fifth Baron, the second son of Malcolm, third Lord Fleming, succeeded to the title on the death of his elder brother on 18 December 1558. He is mentioned by Randolph (q.v.), in a letter to Cecil (q.v.) of 3 June 1565, as having 'shamefully left Moray when he endeavoured to prevent the marriage between Mary and Darnley'. On 30 June, he was appointed Great Chamberlain of Scotland like his brother and father before him. He joined the queen's army in the 'Chase-about Raid' in the autumn of that year.

Fleming was one of the nobles who were in waiting on the queen, on the night of 9 March 1566 when Rizzio was murdered, and were forced to escape from Holyrood through a window at the back of the palace. In 1567 he received the important office of Governor of Dumbarton Castle. Although in Edinburgh at the time, he was not involved in the murder of Darnley on 10 February 1567. He did, however, sign the 'Ainslie Tavern Bond' on 19 April, in favour of the marriage of Mary and Bothwell. He was in the queen's army on 15 June, at Carberry; with Lord Seton (q.v.), he accompanied Bothwell from the field to the north of Scotland, where they eventually abandoned him.

Fleming then joined the party of the Queen's Lords who resolved to free her from Lochleven, refused to attend parliament on 15 December, and withdrew to Dumbarton Castle. On Mary's escape, on 2 May 1568, he went with other lords to Hamilton. The queen would have preferred to shut herself up in Dumbarton under the protection of Fleming, until all her supporters had time to assemble, but the Hamiltons insisted on doing battle with Moray's (q.v.) army immediately. The result was the catastrophe at Langside on 13 May. Fleming, Herries (q.v.) and Livingston (q.v.) watched the battle with the queen and, when it was obvious that the day was lost, escorted her from the field. They crossed the Solway into England on 15 May and lodged her at Carlisle Castle.

Mary sent Fleming to London, to make representations to Queen Elizabeth on her behalf, and at the end of 1568 he went to York as one of her commissioners to represent her at her first trial. In January 1569, he returned to Dumbarton Castle, which he held in the queen's name in defiance of his denunciation as a traitor by parliament on 17 November.

In January 1570, Moray (q.v.) came to Dumbarton to negotiate the castle's surrender but went away empty handed. It was in the castle that Moray's assassination by James Hamilton of Bothwellhaugh (q.v.) on 23 January was planned. Archbishop John Hamilton (q.v.), kinsman of the assassin and accomplice in the murder, sought refuge there afterwards. Suddenly, on the morning of 2 May 1571, the castle fell after a daring attack by Captain Thomas Crawford and his men, who scaled the cliffs and overpowered the garrison. Fleming escaped by a postern gate, and proceeded to

Argyll and then to France where he tried to raise support for Mary. An expedition under his direction was mounted but its ships were wrecked on the English coast. Fleming escaped although his papers fell into the hands of the English.

Finally, he made his way to Edinburgh Castle, which was still being defended by supporters of the queen. There, on 5 July 1572, he was fatally wounded in the knee by an accidental ricochet shot fired by a French soldier. He lay for some time in the castle before being taken on a litter to Biggar, where he died on 6 September. By his wife, Elizabeth, daughter of Robert, Master of Ross, he had three daughters and one son, John, who became the first Earl of Wigtown.

Dauphin François, *later King François II of France, first husband of Queen Mary, François Clouet (Bibliotheque Nationale)*

FRANÇOIS II, KING of FRANCE 1544–1560

A sickly youth of limited understanding and weak will, François's main claim to distinction was that of being Mary Queen of Scots' first husband. He was born at Fontainebleau on 19 January 1544, the eldest son of Henri II of France (q.v.) and Catherine de Medici (q.v.).

Mary and he had been playmates since he was four and they were married at Nôtre Dame when he was fourteen on 25 August 1558. He became king on the death of his father on 10 July 1559. During his short reign, he was completely under the domination of Mary and therefore her uncles,

François, Duke of Guise, and Charles, Cardinal of Lorraine, into whose hands he virtually delivered the reins of government.

To break the power of the Guises, the Prince de Condé (q.v.) planned the *'Tumulte d'Amboise'* in March 1560. Some Huguenot gentlemen surrounded the château of Amboise and tried to kidnap the king. The coup was abortive and served only to further strengthen the Guise family's position.

François died of an ear infection on 5 March 1560, aged sixteen, leaving Mary Queen Dowager of France. His death ended the domination of the Guises and saved Condé, who had been condemned to death for high treason. François had no children and was succeeded by his younger brother who became Charles IX (q.v.).

161

*Frederik II, King of
Denmark and Norway (a
king much beloved by his
people) Hans Knieper, 1581
(Museum of National
History, Frederiksborg,
photo Lennart Larsen)*

FREDERIK II, KING of
DENMARK and NORWAY
1534–1588

Born at Halderslev on 1 July 1534,
Frederik was the son of Christian III
of Denmark and Dorothea of Saxe-
Lauenburg. His mother's sister
Catherine was the first wife of Gustavus
Vasa and mother of Erik XIV of Sweden
(q.v.) who, although they were cousins
born within a year of each other, was to
become his lifelong rival for control of
the Baltic.

At the age of two, he was proclaimed
successor to the throne at the Danish
Rigsdag and homage was paid to him at
Oslo for Norway when he was fourteen.
He became king on his father's death on
New Year's Day 1559, aged twenty-
five.

The first eleven years of his reign were
years of war, first with the annexation
and partitioning of Ditmarsh in Western
Holstein and then with the Scandinavian Seven Years War against
Sweden. Denmark emerged victorious
from the latter but the Peace of Stettin,
which reconciled all parties, ended his
dream of re-uniting Sweden with
Denmark-Norway. It was during this
period that both he and Erik of Sweden
transferred their suits from Elizabeth of
England to Mary Queen of Scots. It is
highly probable that Mary did not take
their approaches very seriously since
she did not wish to become embroiled in
a Scandinavian war.

During the ensuing peace, which was
to last the remaining eighteen years of
his reign, Frederik sought to dominate
the seas around Scandinavia and
cleared the Baltic of the pirates which
haunted it. Married eventually in 1572,
to his cousin Sophia of Mecklenburg,
he was one of the few Oldenburg kings
not to keep a mistress. Much beloved
by his people, he died at Antvorskov on
4 April 1588. His daughter, Anne of
Denmark, married Queen Mary's son,
James VI, in 1589.

GORDON, ALEXANDER, BISHOP of GALLOWAY, ARCHBISHOP of ATHENS
c. 1516–1575

The younger son of John, Lord Gordon, and Margaret, natural daughter of James IV and Margaret Drummond, he was the younger brother of George, the fourth Earl (q.v.). Like his elder brother, he was educated at court, alongside James V, under the guardianship of the king's step-father, Archibald Douglas, sixth Earl of Angus (q.v.).

He administered the see of Caithness from 1544 and, although he failed to secure the archbishopric of Glasgow in 1547, Pope Julius III gave him the titular archbishopric of Athens, with the promise of the next vacant bishopric in Scotland. He was appointed Bishop of the Isles in 1553, and in 1558, he was elected to the see of Galloway. After the final Provincial Council at Blackfriars in 1559, Gordon emerged as a Protestant supporter. On 27 February 1559, he joined in ratifying the Convention of Berwick; on 27 April, he formally joined the Reformers; and in the August parliament, he voted for the new acts which, among other things, renounced the jurisdiction of the Pope and prohibited the Mass.

Gordon continued to work effectively in his diocese after the triumph of the Reformation. In 1562 he asked to be made superintendent over an area more extensive than his see. The assembly refused, but allowed him to perform superintendent's duties. Clearly, there was some tension involved in being a Reformed bishop, and the queen was led to believe that Gordon was not to be trusted. Yet he soon became a Lord of Session and a Privy Councillor, while holding to his episcopal title. Thenceforth, Gordon's life was dominated by his concern for Mary and his uneasy relations with the General Assembly.

Although the fourth Earl of Bothwell had married his niece, Lady Jean Gordon, the bishop signed the Ainslie Bond in April 1567, supporting the earl's marriage to Queen Mary. The imprisonment of the queen at Lochleven in June obliged Gordon to go along with Regent Moray (q.v.). This he did to the extent of attending the parliament which confirmed Mary's enforced abdication but, on the queen's escape, he resumed his work on her behalf. He was a Queen's Commissioner in England in 1570 and 1571, and a member of Kirkcaldy of Grange's (q.v.) Marian parliament at Edinburgh in 1571. He continued to pray for the queen in public, and even preached from Knox's pulpit to Kirkcaldy's adherents. For this, in August 1573, he was ordered by the assembly to do public penance for three successive Sundays in sackcloth, although, in March 1574, the judgement was commuted to one day's penance without sackcloth. He attended the assembly of August 1575 when, for the first time, objections were raised, but not sustained, to the lawfulness of any form of episcopacy.

Gordon's relations with the General Assembly, never good, worsened after Mary's flight to England. He died on 11 November 1575. By his wife, Barbara Logie, daughter of the Laird of Logie, he had at least four sons. The known ones were: John, Dean of Salisbury;

Alexander (died young); Lawrence, Commendator of Glenluce; George, who succeeded to the revenues of the see of Galloway, and was its bishop-designate until his death in 1605; and Robert, killed in a duel while in the service of Queen Margaret of France. He also had a daughter, Barbara, who married Anthony Stewart, Rector of Penninghame.

GORDON, GEORGE, 4th EARL of HUNTLY 1514–1562
GORDON, GEORGE, 5th EARL of HUNTLY c. 1535–1576

George, fourth Earl, was the eldest son of John, Lord Gordon, and Margaret, natural daughter of James IV and Margaret Drummond. His father, who was the second son of Alexander the third Earl, died in 1517 and his uncle, the third Earl's eldest son, had died in childhood. George therefore succeeded to the title on the death of his grandfather in 1524.

He was brought up with his exact contemporary James V, under the guardianship of the king's step-father, Archibald, sixth Earl of Angus (q.v.), who had married Margaret Tudor after James IV's death at the battle of Flodden in 1513. Angus fell from grace in 1528, whereupon, at the king's direction, Huntly was placed under the direction of the ablest masters for the remainder of his education.

In 1535, Huntly became a Privy Councillor, and the following year, when the king went to France to marry Princess Madeleine, he was appointed to the Council of Regency, which governed the country, until James returned with his bride in May 1537. Shortly afterwards, he received the important appointment of Lieutenant of the North and in 1540, accompanied the king on his journey to the Hebrides. On 24 August 1542, at Hadden Rig, with the assistance of George, fourth Lord Home, he totally defeated an English force of 3,000 men, which included his former guardian, the now disaffected Earl of Angus, and other Scottish rebels. When the Duke of Norfolk, with an army of 30,000 advanced to avenge the defeat, he kept the English at bay, not allowing them to advance more than two miles beyond the Tweed. Since Huntly was preoccupied with this when the battle of Solway Moss took place on 24 November, he was unable to be present at what turned out to be the shameful rout, the news of which precipitated the king's death.

With Cardinal Beaton (q.v.), he was one of the four named as regents for the infant Queen Mary in King James's 'forged will', but the plan misfired, the cardinal was arrested, and James Hamilton, second Earl of Arran (q.v.) became regent in March 1543. Later that year, the cardinal escaped and Huntly collaborated with him in a conspiracy to kidnap Mary and her mother. A reconciliation between Arran and Beaton took place, however, and Huntly attended the coronation at Stirling on 9 September. At about the same time he was appointed Lieutenant-General of the North and of Orkney and Shetland. He used these positions to effect a vast increase in the power and wealth of his family.

After Beaton's murder, Huntly was, on 5 June 1546, chosen to succeed him as Lord High Chancellor and was again appointed a Privy Councillor. In the battle of Pinkie on 10 September 1547, he was in charge of the rear, which broke and fled at the first charge, largely contributing to the Scottish defeat. Huntly was taken prisoner by the English but allowed to return to Scotland the following year in time to be granted the earldom of Moray on 13 February and given a charter of hereditary bailiary of all the lands in the bishopric of Aberdeen. He attended the parliament held in the Abbey of Haddington on 1 July, and was among those who voted for the marriage of Mary to the Dauphin of France (q.v.). Shortly after this, he was given the Order of St Michael by the French king.

Soon after Mary of Guise (q.v.) assumed the regency in 1554, Huntly fell into disgrace, allegedly for laxness in quelling a rebellion of the Clanranalds, and suffered imprisonment in Edinburgh Castle for five months. He was also forced to pay a heavy fine and was deprived of the governorship of Orkney. As a special friend of both James V and Cardinal Beaton, Huntly had always leaned towards Catholicism but he was also highly suspicious of the Queen Regent's policies towards the nobles. On 25 April 1560, he withdrew his support from her altogether, joined the Lords of the Congregation at Leith and signed a bond for the defence of the Reformed doctrines and the expulsion of the French. He took great care, however, to stipulate that his own powers in the north be protected and even enhanced. His defection inflicted a blow on the Catholic cause from which it never recovered and Mary of Guise died six weeks later.

Huntly's support for the reformers was, however, a façade. After his downfall, it was proved that he had preserved, at his Castle of Strathbogie, the utensils of Aberdeen Cathedral, so that they might be brought back into use on the restoration of Catholicism. When the Dauphin, now François II, died in December 1560, he sent John Leslie, later Bishop of Ross (q.v.) to persuade the widowed Mary Queen of Scots to return to Scotland via Aberdeen, and promised to have 20,000 men at her disposal to convey her to Edinburgh. He also formed a plot for the seizure of Edinburgh Castle, although the attempt was never made. On 19 August 1561, Mary returned to land at Leith, and Huntly became a Lord of the Privy Council but, aware of the fact that he was largely motivated by self-interest, she bestowed no special favours on him. She had decided to place herself entirely under the guidance of her half-brother, Lord James Stewart (q.v.) and make it clear that she would not countenance Huntly's schemes.

As it became increasingly evident that Huntly was going to continue challenging her authority in the north, and was even planning a state of near-independence for his territories, Mary secretly bestowed on Lord James the earldom of Moray and decided to mount an expedition to re-establish royal control. In August 1562, she rode into the Highlands at the head of an army, arriving at Inverness on 11 September. Alexander Gordon,

Inverness Castle's captain, refused to allow the queen entry to her own castle until he received Huntly's authority the next day. For this, he was hanged over the battlements, on Moray's orders.

Then for six weeks a game of cat and mouse was enacted as Huntly disappeared and reappeared, sleeping every night under a different roof while the royal army searched for him. His third son, Sir John Gordon, had been exhibiting an infatuation for Mary and had even been rash enough to threaten to abduct and marry her. He was, in any case, a wanted man as he had, in June 1562, been imprisoned for severely wounding Lord Ogilvy in the streets of Edinburgh, but had escaped. He had then made his way north, gathered a force of 1,000 men and was now harrying Mary's soldiers as they looked for his father.

The game could not go on indefinitely however and, on 28 October, Huntly, with 1,000 Highlanders, met the royal army which greatly outnumbered them, at Corrichie, about fifteen miles from Aberdeen. He is reputed to have prayed: 'O Lord, I have been a bloodthirsty man and by my means has much innocent blood been spilt; but thou give me victory this day and I shall serve thee all the days of my life.' The Lord was not convinced, the rout was complete and Huntly and two of his sons were taken prisoner. One of the most bizarre and macabre episodes of Mary's reign followed. The great northern earl, corpulent, weary and unfit, was brought before her on horseback. Before he could speak, he suffered a seizure, and rolled from his horse, stone dead.

Sir John was beheaded the next day. Very much against her will, Mary was forced to witness the event, which was so badly mismanaged by the executioner that he took several strokes, and the queen fainted and had to be carried away. Nor was the dead earl to be left in peace. Ancient Scots law stipulated that the death of an offender did not excuse him from trial for treason. The body was taken to Aberdeen, where it was embalmed, sent by ship to Edinburgh, and kept in Holyrood for over six months. On 28 May 1563, it was propped up in front of the full session of parliament with the queen sitting on the throne at the other end of the chamber.

The trial was a foregone conclusion; the corpse was solemnly pronounced guilty and an act of forfeiture and attainder was passed declaring Huntly's 'dignity, name and memory to be extinct' and his posterity 'unable to enjoy any office, honour or rank within the realm'. The body then lay unburied at Blackfriars monastery in Edinburgh until April 1566 when it was permitted to be taken north to the tomb of the Gordons in Elgin Cathedral and finally laid to rest.

By his wife Elizabeth, eldest daughter of Robert Lord Keith, he had nine sons and three daughters. The sons were: Alexander, who married Lady Margaret Hamilton, second daughter of the Duke of Châtelherault, but died without issue about 1553; George, fifth Earl (q.v.); Sir John, executed 1562; William, died about 1566; James, a Jesuit who died in 1620; Sir Adam, died 1580; Sir Patrick, killed at the battle of Glenlivet, 1594; Robert and Thomas. The daughters were: Elizabeth, married to John Stewart, Earl of Atholl (q.v.); Jean, married to (1) James Hepburn, fourth Earl of Bothwell (2) Alexander Gordon, eleventh Earl of Sutherland (q.v.) (3) Alexander Ogilvy of Boyne; and Margaret, married to John, eighth Lord Forbes.

George, fifth Earl, the second son of George, fourth Earl of Huntly, succeeded after his father was defeated and died at the battle of Corrichie, his elder brother having died earlier. Following the battle, at which it is unlikely that he was present, he fled to the Duke of Châtelherault, his father-in-law, but was placed in custody in Dunbar and convicted of treason in February 1563. Only his long friendship with the queen saved him from execution. He remained in prison until, following the marriage of Mary and Darnley, it was necessary for her to strengthen her faction to counter Moray's rebellion.

He then entered into an alliance with Bothwell and both were at Holyrood on the night of Rizzio's murder, although neither took part in the deed. They were in attendance on the queen at Dunbar, following her escape with Darnley from Holyrood. On the exile of Morton after the murder, despite Huntly's forfeiture, which was not repealed until 1567, Mary appointed him Lord High Chancellor, a post once held by his father, which he held only until November 1567 when Regent Moray reappointed Morton to the post. In the reconciliation between the opposing parties which took place in April 1566, both Huntly and Moray privately regarded the arrangement as merely a temporary

truce. Huntly was determined to avenge himself upon Moray for the death of his father and the ruination of his house. To this end, both he and Bothwell endeavoured to make the queen imprison Moray during her pregnancy on the grounds that during that time, Moray might try to usurp her authority. They also plotted to murder Moray while he was with the queen at Jedburgh, Huntly being promised by Bothwell to use his influence to ensure that his estates would be restored.

Huntly accompanied Bothwell when he went to inform the queen of Darnley's death on the morning after the murder, and his complicity in the furtherance of Bothwell's schemes extended to persuading his sister, Lady Jean Gordon, who was Bothwell's wife, to agree to a divorce. Despite being Bothwell's constant companion, Huntly was appointed one of the commissioners at his trial, and it was following Bothwell's acquittal that parliament restored Huntly to his estates on 19 April 1567. As a matter of course he signed the Ainslie Bond and his signature appeared on the second marriage contract between Bothwell and the queen, one of the documents discovered with the 'Casket Letters'. Although he appears to have had doubts about the prudence of the marriage, he accompanied Bothwell and Mary into Edinburgh on 6 May 1567, and was one of the few noblemen present at the ceremony, where he signed his name as a witness.

When the Confederate Lords entered Edinburgh following the marriage, Huntly was permitted to leave and hastened north to collect his followers.

His failure to arrive in time led directly to the disaster of Carberry Hill and Mary's imprisonment in Lochleven. He then joined the party of nobles who met at Dumbarton in June to plot her escape, and unsuccessfully attempted to raise the north in her support, but came to terms with Moray in September, and was chosen one of the Lords of the Articles at the meeting of parliament in December.

On Mary's escape from Lochleven, he became a prominent supporter of her cause in the north, but on reaching Perth with 2,000 men he found all the passes along the Tay strongly defended and was forced to return home. With Argyll (q.v.), Huntly held the north and west for Mary, and it was not improbable that, with the help of the Hamiltons and the Borderers, they would have defeated Moray had not an order from Mary commanded them to disband on the grounds that a similar order had been delivered to Moray from Elizabeth. Either the order had not been received by Moray, or he deliberately disregarded it, and the time he gained by this was fatal to Mary's cause. Huntly then realised that he had no alternative but to submit to the regent, which he did in May 1569. In spite of this, Mary appointed him her Lieutenant of the North, and he again took up her cause, not only in the north but also in Edinburgh, where he took part in various raids against the regent's forces. He was one of the leaders of the expedition to Stirling when Regent Lennox was fatally wounded. Argyll effected a reconciliation between Morton, who had been chosen Regent, and Huntly and the Hamiltons, on the basis that no

further inquiry would be made into the murder of Darnley, and those concerned in the murder of Regent Lennox would be pardoned.

The withdrawal of Huntly and the Hamiltons led to the collapse of the queen's cause, and virtually ended the civil war. Later there were suspicions of Huntly being involved in a plot with the French, and for this he was confined to Galloway in 1574. Thereafter he retired to the north, where he lived quietly, taking no further part in public affairs. On 25 October 1576, while apparently in the best of health, he enjoyed a strenuous morning's hunting and in the afternoon played a game of football. In the middle of the game, he appeared to suffer a seizure and started to vomit blood 'black like soot'. He died early that evening.

Huntly married in 1558 Anne Hamilton, third daughter of the Duke of Châtelherault, by whom he had three sons and a daughter: George, sixth Earl and first Marquess of Huntly; Alexander of Strathaven; William, a Franciscan; and Jean, who married the fifth Earl of Caithness.

GORDON, JOHN, 10th EARL of SUTHERLAND 1525–1567 GORDON, ALEXANDER, 11th EARL of SUTHERLAND 1552–1594

John, tenth Earl, was the son of Alexander Gordon, Master of Sutherland and his wife, Janet, eldest daughter of John Stewart, second Earl of Atholl, and his wife Janet Campbell. He succeeded his grandfather, Adam Gordon of Aboyne (second son of George, second Earl of Huntly), who had assumed the title of Earl of Sutherland in right of his wife, Elizabeth, Countess of Sutherland, daughter and heiress of John, ninth Earl of Sutherland.

Even before his majority, the earl took an active part in politics and, as an ardent Catholic, with the fourth Earl of Huntly (q.v.), his kinsman, signed the Cardinal's Bond in 1543, undertaking to support Cardinal Beaton's policies. In the same year, he also sat in parliament, although still a minor. In 1547, he was appointed Lieutenant north of the Spey, and in the following year was present at the battle of Pinkie, where he escaped from the rout, although Huntly was taken prisoner.

He stood high in the esteem of the Queen Regent and, in 1550, both he and Huntly accompanied her to France, returning to Scotland in 1553. During his absence his brother, Alexander, to whom he had entrusted the care of his estates, engaged in hostilities with the neighbouring Mackays, which continued after the earl's return, matters not being resolved until 1556 with the submission of Iye-du Mackay. On 15 July the Queen Regent granted him the earldom of Ross, in addition to that of Sutherland, while in 1557 many church lands in Caithness were conveyed to him. Thus, with Huntly, the Gordons had control of the whole of the north.

Strongly under the influence of Huntly, he was sent by him in 1559 to offer assistance to the lords in their dispute with the Queen Regent but shortly after his arrival was shot by a hagbut in a skirmish with French auxiliaries and retired. He supported Huntly's proposal that Mary's return to Scotland should be at Aberdeen, and throughout her progress in Huntly's domain, remained in attendance on her. Despite his apparent loyalty, there were continuing suspicions about his relations with Huntly, which were proved to be well-founded when, on the death of Huntly at the battle of Corrichie, letters were found implicating Sutherland in a plot to carry off the queen. Before the battle Sutherland had fled to Flanders, but in his absence, in June 1563, was condemned and he was forfeited by parliament. At the same meeting, Huntly's embalmed corpse was also attainted. The earl remained in Flanders until, after the marriage of Mary with Darnley, he was recalled, but on his way home his vessel was captured and he was taken as a prisoner to Berwick, where he languished until Moray induced Elizabeth to release him in 1566.

He had been pardoned in December 1565, although his forfeiture was not finally rescinded until 1567, and he returned to Scotland on 7 March 1566, two days before the murder of Rizzio. He had supported Bothwell in all of his projects and, after Bothwell had been cleared of the murder of Darnley, was one of the signatories of the Ainslie Tavern Bond. He was one of the few nobles who actually attended the marriage ceremony on 15 May 1567, probably his final public act.

From Edinburgh, he proceeded north to Helmsdale, home of his uncle, Gilbert Gordon of Garty. While there, he and his countess were poisoned by Isabel Sinclair, Gilbert's wife, who hoped by this act to ensure the succession of her own son. However, Alexander, the earl's heir, escaped the plot. Out hunting, he came late to the meal, and was warned by his father, who already felt ill, not to eat nor drink. The earl and his countess were carried from Helmsdale to his castle of Dunrobin, where they died on 23 June 1567.

The earl was described as being of a 'fair and good countenance, kind, courteous, mild and affable', rare epithets in a violent time. He married three times. Through his first wife, Elizabeth Campbell, only daughter of Colin, third Earl of Argyll, and widow of James, Earl of Moray, a natural son of James IV, he acquired an interest in the earldom of Moray, and later obtained a lease in other of her lands. They had no children, and she died in May 1548. Shortly afterwards, he married Helenor Stewart, daughter of John, third Earl of Lennox, and widow of William Hay, sixth Earl of Erroll. Countess Helenor died in November 1564. The earl married, thirdly, Marion Seton, daughter of George, fourth Lord Seton, and widow of John, fourth Earl of Menteith. It was she who was poisoned with the earl when they both died in 1567. By his second marriage the earl had two sons: John, who died young, and Alexander, who succeeded him. There were also three daughters of the marriage: Margaret, who died unmarried; Jean, who married, first, Alexander Innes of that Ilk, and second, Thomas Gordon, son of George, fourth Earl of Huntly; and Eleanor, who was betrothed to Robert Monro, younger of Foulis, but died the night before her wedding day.

Alexander, eleventh Earl, the second, but only surviving, son of John, tenth Earl, by Helenor Stewart, his second wife, was only fifteen when his father died and he succeeded to the title. He narrowly escaped the fate of his father and stepmother, and was sent for safety to the castle of Skibo. On the death of his father, his wardship had been purchased by George, fourth Earl of Caithness (q.v.), kinsman of Isabel Sinclair who had murdered his parents, and it is not beyond the bounds of possibility that thereby the earl hoped to accomplish what his kinswoman had failed to achieve, to obtain possession of the Sutherland lands by any means at his disposal. Caithness established himself at Dunrobin and sought to destroy the family writs, but was foiled in this. Following further attempts on his life, friends helped the young Earl of Sutherland to escape from Dunrobin and he took refuge with the fifth Earl of Huntly. In 1573 he attempted to recover his estates which he accomplished after much difficulty on 8 July, but only with the intervention of the Privy Council. At this time the counties of Caithness and Sutherland were in turmoil, but he succeeded in pacifying his own tenants, and eventually reduced the influence of the Earl of Caithness over his territories.

Sutherland took little part in public life, appearing at court rarely, and most of his life was spent in trying to alleviate the frequent disputes which disturbed his lands, and those of his neighbours, the Earl of Caithness and Mackay of Farr. He died at the age of forty-two in December 1594, and was buried in Dornoch Cathedral.

The earl married twice: first, in 1567,

to Barbara Sinclair, daughter of his guardian, George, fourth Earl of Caithness, who forced his ward into the marriage. It was, understandably, not a happy one, Sutherland being only fifteen at the time, and his bride thirty-two, and it ended in divorce in 1572, on the grounds of her adultery. In December of that year, he married Jean Gordon, daughter of George, fourth Earl of Huntly, who had previously been married (very briefly) to James Hepburn, fourth Earl of Bothwell. She, too, was older than the earl, by some six years, and outlived him, not dying until 1629, when she was eighty-three. By his second marriage the earl had five sons: John, twelfth Earl; Alexander, and Adam, who both died in infancy; Sir Robert, who entered the service of James VI in 1605 and contributed largely to the Nova Scotia colonisation scheme, becoming the Premier Baronet of Nova Scotia; and Alexander, who was knighted by King James in 1617. They also had two daughters: Jane, who married Hugh Mackay of Farr, and Mary, who married David Ross, son of George Ross of Balnagown.

GRAHAM, WILLIAM,
2nd EARL of MONTROSE
c. 1500–1571
GRAHAM, JOHN,
3rd EARL of MONTROSE
1548–1608

William, second Earl, the son of William, first Earl of Montrose, by his first wife, Annabel Drummond, one of the five daughters of John, Lord Drummond, succeeded his father in 1513,

while he was still a minor. His qualities of diplomacy and prudence were early recognised, and led to his being appointed in 1525 by parliament as one of the lords to attend the king. An ambassador to France in connection with the king's marriage to Princess Madeleine in 1535, he was a member of the Commission of Regency to conduct the government of the country during the king's absence. As a reward for his support of the king against the Earl of Angus (q.v.) and the English party, he obtained a grant of royal lands.

Notwithstanding his support for Cardinal Beaton (q.v.) in his dispute with Regent Arran (q.v.), he was a leading member of the Regent's Council, and was with him at the siege of Broughty Ferry in 1547. When Arran was deposed by the Queen Dowager (q.v.), he was one of the nobles who signed a bond in Arran's favour. He was not present in parliament when the supremacy of the papacy in Scotland was ended in August 1560, and was the only nobleman to attend the queen at her first Mass after her arrival in Scotland in 1561.

He was made a member of the Privy Council in September 1561, but it is not recorded that he attended any of the parliaments after Queen Mary's return from France. He remained aloof from the intrigues of the time and appears to have been trusted by both parties, although Cecil (q.v.) named him as a possible threat to the newly-restored Earl of Lennox (q.v.) in 1565. Notwithstanding this, he favoured the marriage of the queen to Darnley. In June 1565, he was identified with the Marian cause, and was one of the party of

171

noblemen who came to Edinburgh to avenge the murder of Darnley, and to seek the separation of the queen from Bothwell, but he did not assent to her deposition and imprisonment in Lochleven. After her escape, he joined her at Hamilton and signed the bond for her support on 8 May 1568. His absence from the battle of Langside was notable, although he was by then an old man, but may have been caused by the fact that his grandson, and heir, John, was on the opposing side. The earl disappeared from public life after Mary's defeat, and died in Kincardine in 1571, still ostensibly a Catholic.

In 1515, the earl married Janet Keith, daughter of William, third Earl Marischal (q.v.). By her he had four sons and six daughters. The sons were: Robert, Master of Graham, who was killed at Pinkie, leaving a posthumous son; John, who succeeded his grandfather as the third Earl of Montrose; Alexander, who died without issue; William, an ecclesiastic; Mungo, Master of the Household to King James. The daughters were: Margaret, who married Robert, Master of Erskine; Elizabeth, who married George, fourth Earl of Caithness (q.v.); Nicolas, who married John Moray of Abercairny; Agnes, who married Sir William Murray of Tullibardine; Janet, who married Sir William Murray of Balvaird; and Christian, who married Robert Graham of Knockdolian.

John, third Earl was the posthumous son of Robert, Master of Graham, and Margaret, daughter of Malcolm, third Lord Fleming. John succeeded to the title on the death of his grandfather on 24 May 1571 during the short and troubled regency of the Earl of Lennox.

On 24 July 1567, he was one of the procurators authorised by Queen Mary at Lochleven to receive her renunciation of the crown in favour of her son. On the same day, he refused to allow the English ambassador, Sir Nicholas Throckmorton (q.v.), access to her. He fought against her at Langside after her escape. In 1569, Regent Moray (q.v.) directed him to capture Dumbarton Castle but this he was unable to do. Montrose was at the skirmish near Stirling on 3 September 1571, when Regent Lennox was killed, and when Mar (q.v.) was elected regent a few days later, he was chosen as a Privy Councillor.

He was one of the commissioners sent by Morton (q.v.) in July 1572 to conclude the Pacification of Perth with the Hamilton party, and was appointed one of the judges north of the Forth, and was thus identified with the leaders of the Reformed party for many years. He was, however, at the convention called by Atholl (q.v.) and Argyll (q.v.) at Stirling on 8 March 1578 when the young king took the government into his own hands, with a council of twelve to assist him, of which Montrose was one. He was one of the nobles upon whom the king relied most and did much to effect Morton's execution in 1581.

In 1584, with James Stewart, Earl of Arran, he attempted to arrange the deaths not only of Morton's nephew, the eighth Earl of Angus (q.v.), who had taken refuge in England on his uncle's death, but also of the second Earl of Mar and the Abbot of Cambuskenneth. In November 1585, however, they were both overthrown by the return of Angus and his supporters. Arran fled for his life and the king, Montrose and other lords shut themselves up in Stirling Castle. A reconciliation took place between Angus and Montrose in May 1587 and in November 1591, Montrose was again admitted an Extraordinary Lord of Session.

In 1598, he became president of the thirty-one members of the Privy Council. In January 1599, he was named Chief Officer under the Crown, Lord Chancellor, after the post had been vacant for over three years following the death of Lord Thirlestane. The same year, he was also made Chancellor of St Andrews University.

When James ascended the English throne, in 1603, the administration of Scottish affairs was entrusted to Montrose and Lord Fyvie. Montrose had to go south to London but on his return in December 1604, he was appointed Viceroy or High Commissioner in Scotland for life, although in practice the real administration of affairs was conducted by Lord Fyvie. In 1607, ill health compelled him to delegate his duties as commissioner of the Scottish parliament to his former protégé, the second Duke of Lennox, who presided until parliament rose towards the end of the year.

Montrose died on 9 November 1608 and was buried with great solemnity. By his wife, Jean, daughter of David, Lord Drummond, he had three sons: John, who became the fourth Earl; Sir William Graham of Braco; and Sir Robert Graham of Scottistown. He also had a daughter, Lilias.

John, fourth Earl was the father of James, first Marquess of Montrose, who was to fight so valiantly and die for Mary's grandson, Charles I, forty-two years later in 1650.

James Hamilton, *2nd Earl of Arran, Governor of Scotland and later Duke of Châtelherault, second cousin once removed to Queen Mary and Heir Presumptive before the birth of James VI, Arnold Bronckhorst, c. 1573 (Lennoxlove)*

HAMILTON, JAMES, 2nd EARL of ARRAN, 1st DUKE of CHÂTELHERAULT GOVERNOR and REGENT of SCOTLAND
c. 1516–1575
HAMILTON, JAMES, 3rd EARL of ARRAN
c. 1537–1609
HAMILTON, JOHN, 1st MARQUESS of HAMILTON
c. 1540–1604
HAMILTON, CLAUD, 1st BARON PAISLEY
c. 1544–1622

James, second Earl of Arran, later first Duke of Châtelherault, eldest son of James Hamilton, second Lord Hamilton and first Earl of Arran, by his third wife, Janet Beaton of Easter Wemyss, succeeded to the earldom on the death of his father in 1529. His legitimacy was

173

Pictorial genealogy showing James III (centre), Princess Mary (top left), her husband Lord Hamilton (top right), 1st Earl of Arran (bottom left), and Regent Arran (bottom right), in the manner of David Paton, 18th century (Lennoxlove)

always in some doubt due to the uncertainty as to whether his father, who was the grandson of James II, had actually married his mother by the time of his birth. During his minority, he was under the guardianship of his half-brother, Sir James Hamilton of Finnart, who was tried and executed on extremely dubious charges in 1540 on the orders of James V.

Arran was one of the nobles who accompanied James V on his matrimonial expedition to France, and shortly after the king's death, he was appointed governor of the realm, despite the violent and unscrupulous opposition of Cardinal Beaton (q.v.) and other nobles. Beaton even went so far as to arrange a forged legal instrument declaring himself co-regent but the plot failed and Beaton was briefly imprisoned. Arran's appointment was

confirmed but everyone was aware that it was due to his position as heir-presumptive to the throne, rather than innate ability, although John Knox (q.v.) preferred to believe that his leanings towards the Reformed Church had some influence. Initially in favour of the alliance with England, he prepared a treaty in July 1543 to arrange the marriage of the infant queen with the young Prince Edward, but Mary's capture and removal to Stirling alienated him from the English king and, although he ratified the treaty in August, he shortly afterwards joined Cardinal Beaton's party and renounced the Reformed faith.

Since Arran's vacillation gave satisfaction to neither party, an attempt was made to oust him and replace him with Mary of Guise (q.v.), but in March 1545, he prevailed and his supremacy was

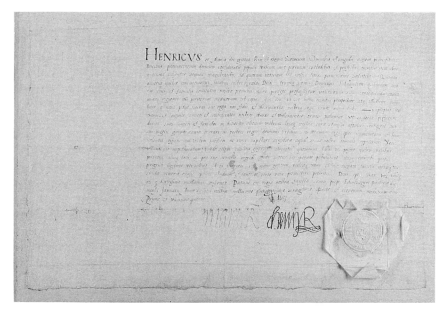

Passport, allegedly permitting James Hamilton, Duke of Châtelherault, to go abroad for the sake of his health, but in effect banishing him (Lennoxlove)

175

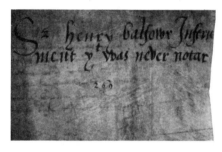

*Putative will of James V,
forged at the behest of
Cardinal Beaton. The
signature is that of Henry
Balfour who was not, in
fact, a notary but one of
Beaton's monks
(Lennoxlove)*

was granted the dukedom of Châtel-herault. Nonetheless, despite this and other pressures on him to do so, he did not finally resign the regency until 1554.

He lent his support to the Queen Dowager until her conduct led him to support the Protestant nobles and sign the second Reformation Covenant on 27 April 1560. This infuriated her and led her to try to discredit him at the English court; a forged letter purporting to be from the duke to the French king assuring him of his allegiance came to the notice of the English Privy Council and there was some inclination to believe it, given Châtelherault's reputation for insincerity. But in another letter, intercepted on its way to the Cardinal of Lorraine, Mary of Guise acknowledged the plot, and Châtelherault was exonerated.

After the death of François in 1560, the duke, in the hope of the marriage of the queen to his eldest son, opposed her marriage to Darnley, especially as he saw this as a threat to his claim to the succession. Initially friendly, his relationship with the queen soon deteriorated, until in 1565 he was declared a traitor, and fled for his life. Mary eventually forgave him on condition that he went into exile for five years. In February 1566, he went to France where he remained until 1569. With the death of Darnley, his attitude to Mary changed materially. He no longer regarded her as his enemy and even went so far as to offer her his support, although his attempts to raise a French force were frustrated by Throckmorton (q.v.). Early in 1569 he landed in England, and after initial hindrance, made his way to Scotland,

confirmed. Meanwhile, the repudiation of the treaties had inevitably led to the renewal of hostilities, and after the defeat at Pinkie in 1547, the situation of the Scots was grave. Arran lost the support of many of the nobles through his continuing weakness, and the Queen Dowager gradually assumed power. Although Arran continued to be titular regent, the arrangement of the marriage between Mary and the Dauphin François (q.v.) strengthened the French party (and Mary of Guise). In July 1548, the arrangement was confirmed and, to ensure his support, he where his return posed a threat to Regent Moray (q.v.). Shortly after his return, he was committed to Edinburgh Castle, and was not released until after Moray's assassination in January 1570.

During the civil war which followed the assassination, he acted as chief of the Marian party, with substantial losses to his own property, his castles of Kinneil and Cadzow being razed to the ground. He continued faithful to the queen until February 1573 when, at the Pacification of Perth, he was reconciled to the king's party. Châtelherault did not long survive this treaty, and died at Hamilton on 22 January 1575.

He married, in 1532, Margaret, eldest daughter of James Douglas, third Earl of Morton, by whom he had five sons and three daughters: James, Lord Hamilton, Earl of Arran; Gavin, who died young; John, first Marquis of Hamilton; David, who died without issue in 1611; Claud, Lord Paisley; Barbara, who married James, fourth Lord Fleming; Janet who married Hugh Montgomery, Earl of Eglinton (q.v.); and Anne, who married George, Lord Gordon, afterwards fifth Earl of Huntly (q.v.).

James, third Earl of Arran, was the eldest son of James, second Earl, and was born in about 1537, since he was under twenty-three in April 1560, when Randolph (q.v.) wrote to Cecil (q.v.) praising his good qualities. He succeeded his father in 1575.

Simultaneously with the proposal to marry the infant Queen Mary to Prince Edward, Henry VIII suggested that the young James should marry the Princess Elizabeth, but although his father initially agreed enthusiastically to the

Said to be James Hamilton, 3rd Earl of Arran, *Spanish School, mid-16th century (Lennoxlove)*

proposal, Cardinal Beaton (q.v.) later persuaded him to reject the idea in the hope that a marriage would take place between his own illegitimate son and Mary. Indeed, such was his importance in the line of succession that, while he was in captivity following the assassination of Cardinal Beaton, an act was passed debarring him from all rights of succession, lest he should fall into the wrong hands.

Shortly after the betrothal of the queen to the Dauphin François (which his father did not dare to oppose), Arran left for France where, in 1550, he was appointed to the command of the Scots Guards and, in 1557, distinguished himself, and his regiment, at the defence of St Quentin. While in France, he kept on good terms with Mary. However, his conversion to Protestantism while he was there caused great scandal, and to escape arrest, he fled to Geneva, and from thence to England with the connivance of Cecil and Knox. His return to

Scotland, under an assumed name, encouraged the Lords of Congregation, who marched on Edinburgh on 15 October 1559, forcing the Queen Dowager to retire to Leith. A series of disasters forced their retirement to Stirling, on 7 November, where they awaited help from Elizabeth. When the Queen Dowager regained Edinburgh on 9 November, Arran was escheated. Warning of the impending French invasion, Arran, together with Lord James Stewart, assembled their forces at Cupar, and marched to Dysart, where, with a force of about 600 men, they kept the French at bay for twenty-one days. Disheartened, the French prepared to march on St Andrews, but were prevented from doing so by the arrival of the English fleet in the Forth. Thus the persistence of Arran and Stewart saved Fife, for the French then retreated to Leith. Arran was present at the siege of the town.

After the death of the Queen Regent on 10 June, parliament proposed that Arran should marry Elizabeth, and that Mary should renounce her throne and, to this end, Morton (q.v.), Glencairn (q.v.) and Maitland of Lethington (q.v.) went, albeit reluctantly, to England to support the proposal. Mary and her party had nothing to fear from this, since Elizabeth 'was indisposed to marry at present'.

The king of France's death on 6 December 1560 focused the attention of the nation on their queen, and renewed Arran's determination to marry her. Knox supported his suit, deeming it of the highest importance that her next husband should be a Protestant. Mary, however, refused him, but named him

one of her Privy Councillors on her arrival in Scotland. He strongly opposed the celebration of the Mass in her private chapel, and publicly protested the protection of her servants from prosecution for their religious beliefs. He even went so far as to declare his intention to absent himself from court, 'so long as the Mass remained'. Later events were to prove that his strong condemnation was an early sign of the mental aberration which was to lead to his being pronounced insane in April 1562.

Arran's feud with Bothwell, which had been deepened by Bothwell's theft of English money sent for the support of the Protestant lords in October 1559, led to Bothwell asking Knox to mediate in March 1562 but, although outwardly they were reconciled, Arran accused Bothwell of trying to persuade him, Arran, to kidnap the queen and forcibly marry her. At the time, this was treated as a symptom of his madness, but Bothwell's subsequent career showed that he adopted the plan himself. From this time, Arran lapsed in and out of madness, and was confined to prison, where Mary paid him a friendly visit. He was released in 1566, although he was by then in a weak state, and remained at liberty until 1568, when he was arraigned with other members of his family. He was permitted to live in retirement with his mother at Craignethan Castle, and on the death of his father, in 1575, came into possession of the family estates, which were, however, administered by his second brother, Lord John. In 1579, the government, on the pretext of freeing him from wrongful imprisonment, besieged

Craignethan, and he was transferred to Linlithgow. After the apprehension of Morton in 1580, he was placed under the protection of James Stewart of Bothwellmuir, shortly himself to be created Earl of Arran, but the estates were restored to the family on the downfall of Stewart in 1585. Arran died, still insane, in March 1609. He never married.

John, first Marquis of Hamilton was the second surviving son of James, first Duke of Châtelherault. In 1551, he was provided with the well-endowed, and extensive, abbacy of Arbroath and styled Commendator shortly afterwards, although this was disputed by George Douglas, a quarrel which continued until 1571, when the abbey was seized by Douglas.

In 1561, Lord John was one of those who ratified the Treaty of Berwick, and also lent his support to the scheme to marry his brother, Arran, to Queen Elizabeth. Following his brother's imprisonment, Lord John, together with other members of the family, fell into disgrace, but he was reconciled to the queen in 1563. In the following year, he went to Italy, where he remained for two years, but had returned to Edinburgh when Darnley was murdered, and served as a member of the Assize which formally acquitted Bothwell of the murder.

Like all the members of his family, he was an adherent of the queen, and, with Huntly, raised a force of 800 men to support her at Carberry. After her imprisonment at Lochleven, it was rumoured that he and Huntly were secretly plotting to rescue her, although some suspected that the Hamiltons were plotting her

Said to be John, Lord Hamilton, *later Marquis of Hamilton (Lennoxlove)*

death to further their own dynastic claims. He refused to attend the General Assembly in 1567, pleading that he could not come into Edinburgh while it was in possession of those who favoured the queen's detention, and was also absent from the coronation of James in Stirling. He continued to work for the release of the queen, and left for France, without the leave of the regent, in furtherance of her cause. He was still in France at the time of her escape from Lochleven, and was not present at Langside.

At the end of 1568, Lord John, with other members of the Hamilton family, were forfeited, an act which did nothing to heal their breach with Regent Moray, and which, doubtless, further fuelled their feud with him. He was present in Stirling when Regent Lennox was assassinated, an event in which his brother, Lord Claud, was said to have taken an active part, and later represented the family interests at the Pacification of Perth.

179

His father's death in 1575 meant that Lord James became head of the family because of his eldest brother's insanity, to the disadvantage of his brother Lord Claud, who entertained ambitions towards the throne, and who, it was said, even considered his brother's assassination. During this year, a reconciliation took place between the Douglases and the Hamiltons, but, given the involvement of the Hamiltons in the assassination of Regent Moray, it did not find favour with all members of the Douglas family and was short-lived. Lord John was attacked by William Douglas of Lochleven (q.v.) on several occasions, and eventually both families were summoned by Regent Lennox (q.v.) and bound over to keep the peace. Douglas, refused to comply with the order, and was incarcerated in Edinburgh Castle.

In 1579, the Hamiltons were again prosecuted for the slaughter of regents Moray and Lennox, the charge having been kept on the books and not discharged by the Pacification of Perth. Lord John escaped to France with the connivance of the French ambassador, Castelnau. There, he was harboured by the king, who bestowed a pension upon him, but the Marian party were still suspicious of his motives, especially since, unlike his brother, Lord Claud, he had remained a Protestant. While he was in France, his abbey of Arbroath had been bestowed on King James's new favourite, Esmé Stewart, Duke of Lennox, and even worse, the baronies of Hamilton and Kinneil, together with other estates belonging to the Hamiltons, had been given to Captain James Stewart, another favourite, who, as an ultimate

insult, had also been created Earl of Arran. This was the nadir in the fortunes of the House of Hamilton. Lord John felt that he could no longer trust King Henry III of France, but resolved instead to place his trust in Elizabeth, who had long proved to be his friend. He therefore joined his brother, Lord Claud, at the English court.

In 1584, he joined Lord Claud in his unsuccessful attempt on the (Stewart) Earl of Arran, and made a further, again unsuccessful, attempt the following year. From then on, Lord John followed a different path from his brother. As a Protestant, he distanced himself from the intrigues of France and Spain, and being by nature somewhat indolent and unambitious, devoted his time to the restoration of the Hamilton fortunes. He joined with the banished lords to meet the king at Stirling on 4 November and was re-admitted to the king's favour, the king confessing that Lord John had 'been most wronged'. By a special act of parliament, he was again placed in possession of the family estates, and made guardian of his insane elder brother.

The death of Mary strengthened the hopes of the Hamiltons with regard to the throne. She had left Lord John, as a souvenir of her regard, a sapphire ring, but whatever his private feelings, Lord John seems never to have swerved in his loyalty to James, with whom he enjoyed a good relationship. He denounced the plans of his brother, Lord Claud, for the Spanish invasion of Scotland, and it was at this time that Lord Claud considered his brother's assassination to further his own ambitions.

In 1588, he was appointed to the embassy which negotiated the marriage of James to Anne of Denmark, and in the following year, when the king went to Denmark to bring home his bride, Lord John was appointed governor of the Borders. At the coronation of the queen, the Hamiltons played a significant part. He continued high in the king's favour and, in 1597, the king, in consideration of the great loss to Lord John and his family of the French dukedom of Châtelherault, granted him the temporalities of the abbacy of Arbroath, although at the same time the castle of Dumbarton was taken from him and granted to the Duke of Lennox. In 1599, he was, with great ceremony 'in His Majesty's Great Chamber at Holyrood' installed as Marquess of Hamilton. He survived to enjoy his honours until 1604, his last act being to commend his son to the king's favour. His unfortunate brother, the Earl of Arran, was still alive, and his care was bestowed on James, Lord Abercorn, son of Lord Claud, Baron Paisley.

Lord John married in 1577, Margaret, daughter of John Lyon, seventh Lord Glamis, widow of Gilbert, fourth Earl of Cassilis (q.v.), and by her had two sons, Edward, who died young, and James, afterwards second Marquess of Hamilton, and one daughter, Margaret, who married in 1597, John, ninth Lord Maxwell, from whom she was divorced. He also had two natural children.

Claud, first Baron Paisley was the fifth and youngest son of James, second Earl of Arran and first Duke of Châtelherault. In 1553, he was appointed Commendator of Paisley on the

Lord Claud Hamilton, *later Baron Paisley, ancestor of the Dukes of Abercorn, attributed to Bronckhorst (The Duke of Abercorn)*

resignation of his uncle, John Hamilton (q.v.), a natural son of the first Earl of Arran, who had succeeded Cardinal Beaton as Archbishop of St Andrews six years earlier. A member of the queen's party, in 1568, he took a leading part in the plot to help her escape from Lochleven, and after she crossed the Firth of Forth on 2 May met her with a force of fifty horse and escorted her first to Niddry Castle and then to Hamilton. At the battle of Langside, he led the vanguard following which he was declared traitor on 9 August and forfeited, his abbey lands being bestowed on Lord Sempill.

After his uncle, the Archbishop of St Andrews, was hanged at Stirling in 1571, Lord Claud was one of the leaders of the conspiracy to capture Regent Lennox in that city, and after the raid, during which the regent was fatally wounded in the back by Captain Calder, was said to have been the instigator of his murder. At the Pacification of Perth in February 1573, a pardon was issued for those involved in the killing of Lennox, and Hamilton and other members of his family were restored to their possessions, although force had to be used against Lord Sempill to ensure their return. However, the charges of complicity in the murders of the two regents remained against Claud and his brother John, and these were later used by Regent Morton in April 1579 to obtain an act of council ordering that they be apprehended, using whatever armed action might be necessary, and their possessions confiscated again. In so doing, Morton sought to break the power of the Hamilton party, of which John and Claud were the leaders, since their elder brother was by now hopelessly insane.

Harried by Morton, Lord Claud fled to the north of England, and placed himself under the protection of Elizabeth, who intervened on his behalf, but without success. He was forfeited on October 1579, and joined the 'banished lords' in their attempt to overthrow James Stewart, the new Earl of Arran. In October 1584, he reached an accommodation with the king which permitted him to return to Scotland, but he was too much of a threat to Arran to be allowed to remain and, in April 1585, he was ordered to leave for France. He was in Paris when the second attempt on Arran was successful, and an act was passed for the restitution of the banished lords and their adherents. He returned to Scotland, took his seat and oaths and became a member of the Privy Council.

Hamilton had become a Catholic, and his ability and ambition caused him, rather than his brother John, to become the agent of the Marian party. He also hoped that he might supplant his brother as the heir to the throne, and it was even suggested that an assassination might be arranged to ensure this. With the sixth Earl of Huntly, he shared the leadership of the Catholic faction, and tried to effect a reconciliation between Mary and her son. More importantly, he was involved in the Babington Conspiracy and sought the assistance of the king in this enterprise. He had also been in touch with the king of Spain, seeking his aid to dethrone James and restore Catholicism to Scotland. The Catholic lords also supported the Spanish Armada and, even after its destruction, they continued to support Spain. In February 1589, their plot was discovered, and despite Lord Claud's denial, he was imprisoned in Edinburgh Castle on 7 March, although he was at liberty again by January 1590.

Throughout this period he had been on good terms with James, who restored him to his abbacy of Paisley, and on 29 July 1587 raised him to a temporal barony as Lord Paisley. Lord Claud's later years are obscure; his son obtained a commission to act for him, and it was suggested by the English ambassador, Sir Robert Bowes, that he suffered from the insanity which had earlier beset his elder brother. He died in 1622, and was buried in the St Mirren Chapel of his abbey of Paisley.

In 1574, he married Margaret, daughter of George, fifth Lord Seton (q.v.). They had, besides three children who died in infancy: James, created Earl of Abercorn, ancestor of the Dukes of Abercorn; Sir John, who married

Johanna, daughter of Levimus Everard, Councillor of State to the king of Spain; and Sir Claud of Shawfield, Gentleman of the King's Privy Chamber, and member of the Privy Council, who married Janet, daughter and heir of Sir Robert Hamilton of Leckprevick and Easter Greenlees. They also had a daughter, Margaret, who, in 1601, married William the first Marquess of Douglas, when he was only twelve years old. Margaret died in 1623, and, in 1632, the marquess married Mary, daughter of George Gordon, sixth Earl and first Marquess of Huntly, by whom he had a son, William, who was created Earl of Selkirk in 1646, married Anne, Duchess of Hamilton in 1656, and in 1660, was created Duke of Hamilton for life.

HAMILTON, JAMES, of BOTHWELLHAUGH c. 1540–c. 1580

A great-great-nephew of Sir James, first Lord Hamilton, his father was David Hamilton, a 'gudeman of Bothwellhaugh' and, according to Buchanan (q.v.), his mother was the sister of Archbishop John Hamilton (q.v.), despite the fact that her name was Catherine Schaw. He was the eldest son and married to Alison Sinclair, co-heiress of Woodhouselee.

Bothwellhaugh fought for the queen at Langside, was taken prisoner and sentenced to death, but was pardoned because of the intercession of Knox (q.v.). His lands were, however, forfeited and his wife was violently expelled from her house, and is alleged to have gone mad and died from the cold, although there is evidence that she was alive thirty years later. Although there is no reason to believe that Regent Moray (q.v.) had any knowledge of, let alone responsibility for, the eviction, Bothwellhaugh resolved to kill him, with the full connivance of the chiefs of the House of Hamilton and others of the queen's friends.

Moray was lured to Dumbarton Castle on the false pretext that the keeper, Lord Fleming (q.v.), who was holding it for the queen, might be prepared to surrender. On reaching Glasgow, though, he discovered he had been misled, and decided to return to Edinburgh. As he passed through Linlithgow on 23 June, Bothwellhaugh, who was hiding in a house which belonged to Archbishop Hamilton, shot him and he died from the wound later that day. The assassin, who had a horse in readiness at the back of the house, made a dramatic escape and eventually found refuge in France. Queen Mary, by now in detention in England, expressed fervent approval of the act, although she stated that the deed had been committed without her knowledge. She also declared her desire to bestow a pension on Bothwellhaugh, whenever her circumstances permitted.

In France, Bothwellhaugh, who was nearly penniless and writing to his Hamilton kinsmen for assistance, received several approaches to commit other assassinations of Mary's enemies, most notably that of Admiral Coligny. All of these he contemptuously rejected, saying that his dispute with Moray was a personal one which he had avenged, and that he was no hired killer. He was, however, involved in other intrigues on the queen's behalf.

183

He is thought to have died in France in about 1580. His possessions were not finally restored to his family until 1609.

HAMILTON, JOHN, ARCHBISHOP of ST ANDREWS
c. 1511–1571

A natural son of James, first Earl of Arran, as a boy he became a monk in the monastery at Kilwinning and in 1525, at the instance of James V, was appointed Abbot of Paisley. In 1540, he went to Paris for three years to study at university. On his return, he became Secretary of State and two years later, Bishop of Dunkeld.

With the murder of Cardinal Beaton (q.v.) in 1546, Hamilton was nominated as Archbishop of St Andrews and *ex officio* primate. The appointment was confirmed in 1549 after considerable opposition and negotiation; he was also papal legate *a latere*, which was by no means *ex officio*. Since he also held the position of Treasurer, Hamilton was able to exert great influence.

Hamilton had come back from the Continent a strong opponent of Protestantism. He soon had his half-brother, Regent Arran (q.v.), adopting a like policy. Hamilton's unbending attitude during the upheavals at St Andrews in 1546–47 stiffened the Catholic cause. Three years later, he had Adam Wallace burned for heresy in Edinburgh. But Hamilton was neither a religious reactionary or an enthusiast for the Counter-Reformation. He held three provincial councils, between 1549 and 1559, in an effort to reform the Church and strengthen popular Catholicism. In theology, he was liberal; his catechism made some concessions to the Lutheran position and omitted reference to papal authority. Plans for better clerical and lay education anticipated some of those proposed and eventually effected by the Reformers. But the primate could not halt the spoliation of Church property by the crown and the nobles. Hamilton's liberalism did not extend to the Protestants themselves. In 1558 the aged priest Walter Mylne was condemned for heresy and became a local martyr, being burnt at the stake in St Andrews.

Already the regime of Mary of Guise (q.v.) had weakened Hamilton's authority. She disliked the archbishop and took the treasurership from him. Interested in church lands rather than church reforms, she was relatively lenient to the Protestants when England became Catholic again under Mary Tudor. With the return of Knox (q.v.) at the accession of Elizabeth, the Queen Dowager's attitude hardened, but not to Hamilton's benefit. The presence of members of his family among the Lords of the Congregation did not help his cause. Yet in the 1560 parliament he did not condemn the Confession of Faith in its entirety: parliament only prohibited Roman authority over the bishops and Hamilton was never strongly pro-papal.

The return of Mary saw the official continuation (subject to financial constraints) of the Catholic Church alongside a rapidly developing Reformed Church. Hamilton's position became very awkward. He was not a part of the Catholic circle at court – indeed, he criticised the court's levity – but he could not follow some of his episcopal colleagues in co-operating with the Reformers. He was imprisoned at one stage for saying Mass in public and lost most of his consistorial powers. The open immorality of his personal life (though not unusual for the time) made Hamilton an easy mark for preachers' ridicule and invective. He lived with Grizzel Sempill, wife and then widow of James Hamilton, Provost of Edinburgh; she bore him three children, two of whom were legitimated.

Hamilton presided at the baptism of Prince James in December 1566, somewhat to Queen Mary's dismay. His legal powers were restored temporarily so that he might issue the necessary dispensation to clear the way to the queen's marriage with Bothwell. In the events of Mary's fall from power, imprisonment and escape, Hamilton naturally supported her. Two of his sons were captured at Langside; he urged Mary to remain in her kingdom, being confident that she would eventually prevail over the opposition. Denounced by Regent Moray (q.v.) as a traitor, he took refuge in Dumbarton Castle after the regent's assassination. On 2 April 1571 the castle was captured and the archbishop with it. After a summary trial for complicity in the deaths of Darnley and Moray, Hamilton was hanged, in his episcopal vestments, at Stirling on 7 April 1571. Two years later, one article in the Pacification of Perth, which ended the struggle between the king's and the queen's parties, required the rehabilitation of Archbishop Hamilton from the charges laid against him.

Hamilton was a man of many parts and many contradictions. In quieter times, he would have been a successful administrator in church and state, the looseness of his morals readily condoned or at least overlooked. But in the troubled and rapidly changing times in which he lived, this the ablest of the Hamiltons, found his imperfections and shortcomings brought to the test although it was his support for the queen rather than his private life that was his undoing.

Sir Christopher Hatton, *favourite of Queen Elizabeth, witness to the baptism of James VI, artist unknown, mid-16th century (National Portrait Gallery)*

HATTON, SIR CHRISTOPHER
1540–1591

Like so many of those who rose to eminence under the Tudors, Hatton was a member of the squirearchy rather than the aristocracy. Second son of William Hatton of Holdenby Northampton and his wife Alice, Sa(u)nders, he was educated at St Mary Hall,

185

Oxford, left without taking a degree, but then became a member of the Inner Temple. He is not recorded as having been admitted to the Bar, but his time there was useful since, at the Inner Temple Revels in 1561, he met Robert Dudley, later Earl of Leicester (q.v.), who became a lifelong friend.

Tall and handsome, with a natural talent for dancing, he attracted the attention of Queen Elizabeth, who in 1564 made him one of her Gentlemen Pensioners. He was one of the English guests at Stirling for the baptism of Prince James – here a masque had been produced, with satyrs pretending to be Englishmen, wagging their tails. This so enraged him that he declared that, had it not been for the presence of the queen, he would have put his dagger into the heart of the knave who devised the performance.

Thereafter, Hatton was showered with offices and estates, being made a Gentleman of Elizabeth's Bedchamber and captain of her bodyguard in 1572. In 1577 he became Vice-Chamberlain of her Household, and in December that year was knighted. Having been elected to parliament in 1571, he acted as the queen's mouthpiece there, a role which he filled until he lost his seat in 1586. At the time of the passing of the bill against Jesuits and Seminary priests in 1584, he prayed loud and long in the House for the safety of the queen. As with so many other of her courtiers, his name was linked romantically with that of Elizabeth, and his behaviour indicated that he had hopes in that direction. Appointed one of the commissioners to treat with the French envoys at the time of her suggested marriage with the

Duke of Alençon and Anjou in 1581, he at first appeared to favour the match, but later displayed signs of jealousy and beseeched her to terminate the affair. He showed further signs of jealousy when Sir Walter Raleigh's star began to rise, and when, in 1584, it became obvious that Hatton had lost the queen's favour, he withdrew from the court to Holdenby and did not return until enticed back by her cajoling letters.

Hatton was a member of both commissions to try Anthony Babington and others for plotting for Mary Queen of Scots in September 1586. When she was tried at Fotheringhay, he was again one of the commissioners, and persuaded her that it was in her best interests to submit to the jurisdiction of the court. On the pronouncement of the sentence, he immediately went to London, where he spoke in parliament at great length on the 'horrible and wicked practices of the Queen of Scots so-called'. The following day his eloquence was rewarded when the House voted to petition for Mary's execution, despite Elizabeth's express wish that she might be spared. When William Davison, who had been given the responsibility of despatching the warrant for the execution, spoke to Hatton about his doubts about the propriety of the matter, Hatton, who had no misgivings whatsoever, took Davison before the council to be persuaded, and the warrant was duly despatched. The matter did not end there; Hatton suspected Davison of sympathy towards Mary and later interrogated him in the Tower.

In April 1587, Elizabeth appointed him Lord High Chancellor, delivering the seal to him personally. Given his scanty knowledge of the law, the news of the appointment was met with some surprise, although he took office on 3 May, attended in great state, not only by his own retainers and officers of the court but by Burghley (Cecil (q.v.)) and Leicester. He took care, however, never to sit on the bench alone, and although none of his cases have been preserved, certain of his speeches show that, while his knowledge of law might have been slight, there was not much wrong with his wit. In January 1588 he conducted the examination of Moody, a supposed assassin, accused of having been sent by the French to murder Elizabeth, and in a long speech to the House of Commons on 22 February 1588, inveighed at length about the imminence of a Spanish invasion. On 24 April 1588 Hatton was created a Knight of the Garter, and on the death of Leicester, with whom he had always been on close terms, in September that year, Hatton succeeded him as Chancellor of Oxford University. As Lord Chancellor, he opened proceedings in parliament in February 1589 with a long speech celebrating the destruction of the Armada, and asking for the navy to receive an increase of funds.

Hatton died on 20 November 1591 at Ely House of diabetes, allegedly aggravated by owing Elizabeth large sums for tithes. He was buried in St Paul's Cathedral on 20 December. His funeral was as lavish as his life: 100 poor people preceded the corpse, in gowns paid for by his executors, and it was followed by 400 gentlemen and yeomen, the Lords of the Council and eighty Gentlemen Pensioners. Hatton never married, and

his estates passed through two of his relations, eventually ending up with his cousin who became Christopher, first Lord Hatton.

Henri II of France, *who died after a tournament held to celebrate the Treaty of Cateau-Cambrésis, François Clouet (Bibliotheque Nationale)*

HENRI II,
KING of FRANCE
1519–1559

Born at St Germain-en-Laye on 19 March 1519, Henri was the second son of François I and Claude de France. Although physically robust, he was cold, haughty, melancholy and dull and lacked the brilliance of his father, whose policies, nonetheless, he successfully continued. On 27 October 1533 he married the Florentine princess, Catherine de Medici (q.v.). He became dauphin on the death of his elder brother, François, three years later and from then on was dominated by his scheming mistress, Diane de Poitiers.

His father died on 31 March 1547 and he became king, immediately dismissing most of his father's ministers and raising, among others, the Guise family to favour. The Guises, the family of Mary Queen of Scots' mother, were to retain this favour until the death of Henri's son (and Mary's husband), François II (q.v.). Henri maintained a strongly Catholic stance but in external affairs, the traditional French hostility to the Hapsburgs, rulers of the Austrian and Spanish domains, led him to make periodic alliances with the Protestant princes of Germany. The Valois-Hapsburg rivalry extended to Britain. Whereas the Holy Roman Emperor Charles V was generally the ally of England, François I and Henri II of France maintained the traditional connection with Scotland. So Henry VIII married Charles's aunt, Catherine of Aragon, and his daughter, Mary I, married Charles's son and heir, Philip of Naples and Spain. James V on the other hand married Princess Madeleine of France, and on her death, Mary of Guise. It was the natural consequence of French policy that Henri's eldest son François should marry Mary Queen of Scots. The wedding of the Dauphin and Mary took place on 24 April 1558. The marriage was to be pitifully short, and Mary's time as queen of France even shorter.

At home Henri showed himself to be a bigoted Catholic, and persecuted the Protestants with vigour. In October 1547 the *'Chambre ardente'* for trying heretics was created in the Paris *parlement*, although in June 1551 the Edict of Châteaubriand transferred the trial of notorious cases to the secular courts. In foreign affairs he continued the policy of warfare against the Holy Roman Empire. In January 1552 he even went so far as to sign the Treaty of Chambord with the German Protestant princes, promising them troops and subsidies for use against Charles. But by 1559 the war had caused financial difficulties in both France and Spain, and this, as well as Henri's determination to fight heresy at home, led to the Treaty of Cateau-Cambrésis in April of that year. The Franco-Spanish peace that followed meant that Henri no longer needed to consider the sensibilities of his German allies. In June 1559 the Edict of Écouen laid the ground for the systematic persecution of the Protestants on a scale precedented only by the Spanish Inquisition.

The treaty was cemented by the marriages of Henri's daughter Elizabeth to Philip of Spain, and his sister, Marguérite, to Emmanuel Philibert of Savoy. In a tournament during the festivities on 30 June Henri was riding against Gabriel, Count of Montgomery, Captain of the Scottish Guard, whose lance shattered. Splinters entered the king's eye and throat and he died of blood poisoning in Paris on 10 July.

By Catherine de Medici, he left four sons: the future kings François II (q.v.), Charles IX (q.v.) and Henri III of France, and François Duke of Alençon and

Anjou (the young suitor of Elizabeth of England, to whom she referred as 'my frog'). He also left three daughters: Elizabeth Queen of Spain; Claude Duchess of Lorraine; and Marguérite who, in 1572, became queen of Navarre. One of his natural children by Diane de Poitiers was Diane de France.

PATRICK HEPBURN,
BISHOP of MORAY
?–1573

Patrick Hepburn was probably an illegitimate son of the first Earl of Bothwell. Certainly he profited by his family connections, becoming Prior of St Andrews in 1522. Hepburn was a court official, secretary to James V and, as a churchman, was involved in the death of the Protestant Patrick Hamilton. He rose further in both church and state, becoming Bishop of Moray, Commendator of Scone and, in 1546, a Privy Councillor.

Life took on a hectic quality for Hepburn in the late 1550s. He offered assistance to the Lords of the Congregation but was also involved in the martyring of Walter Mylne. When the enraged Dundee townsmen sacked his abbey at Scone, his Protestant sympathies waned. Instead, he went to France where, with Bishop Leslie, he tried to persuade the newly widowed Queen Mary to join an army at Aberdeen and rule her kingdom by force. In the first religious settlement, he retained two-thirds of his revenues.

Disreputable in the extreme – he had nine illegitimate children all, as he boasted, by other men's wives – Hepburn's religion sat lightly upon him. The Pope thought him too unreliable to summon to the Council of Trent; on the other hand, he was able to attend the parliament in 1567 which gave legal establishment to the Reformed faith. The latter event may have been helped on by his involvement with his nephew, the fourth Earl of Bothwell. He had nurtured the young man and was believed to have assisted his flight after Carberry, despite the treachery of his own sons who tried to betray the fleeing earl (now the Duke of Orkney). He was acquitted of involvement in the Darnley murder only a month before parliament met.

Hepburn took little part in the complex events in the years after Mary's flight to England. He died at Spynie Castle in 1573, having secured the legitimation of most of his offspring.

HOME, ALEXANDER,
5th BARON HOME
c. 1528–1575

The eldest son of George, fourth Baron Home, Alexander was captured by the English at the battle of Pinkie on 9 September 1547. While still a prisoner, he succeeded to the title and estates on the death of his father from wounds received in a skirmish on the day before the battle. He regained his freedom later that year, and in 1548 took part in campaigns against the English and assisted the French at the siege of Haddington.

Although not a strict Catholic, Home never became a Protestant, refusing to join the Lords of the Congregation and

189

expressing a wish to remain neutral. On the return of Queen Mary in 1561, he became a Privy Councillor and for the early years of her reign was her staunch supporter, although he declined to attend Mass in her chapel.

He supported the queen's marriage to Darnley on 28 July 1565 and joined her army on the Chaseabout Raid in the autumn. In the following year, Mary visited his castles of Home, Wedderburn and Langton with her retinue. Home was not involved in either the Rizzio or the Darnley conspiracies. Mary's marriage to Bothwell on 15 May 1567, on the other hand, was anathema to him mainly because Bothwell was his principal rival for authority in the south of Scotland. He withdrew his support from the queen and was not among the signatories of the 'Ainslie Tavern Bond'.

After the marriage, Home joined the Confederate Lords, and with Morton (q.v.) commanded the van of the army at Carberry under Moray (q.v.) on 15 June. He received the queen on her surrender and signed the order for her committal to Lochleven. On 21 June, with Morton and several other lords, he witnessed the opening of the casket allegedly containing Mary's letters to Bothwell. He was present at her abdication on 26 July. He was also at the coronation of James three days later, where he and Morton took the oath on behalf of the infant king to maintain the Protestant religion.

On Mary's escape from Lochleven on 2 May 1568, Home foiled an attempt of the Hepburns to hold Dunbar Castle on her behalf. At Langside, eleven days later, he was at the head of 600 spearmen in the van against her, fighting much of the battle on foot wielding a pike.

Over the next two years, Home's enthusiasm for the king's party waned. With the removal of Bothwell, his hostility towards the Marian cause had lost its focus, and he was disillusioned by the English, who had captured and pillaged two of his castles. He still felt loyalty to Regent Moray, but after Moray's assassination on 23 January 1570 he rejoined the party of the queen. He took refuge in Edinburgh Castle, which was under siege and being held for Mary by Kirkcaldy of Grange (q.v.).

From then on, he was a resolute supporter of Mary, virtually acting as lieutenant to Kirkcaldy until the end of the three-year siege on 28 May 1573, when he was taken prisoner. Though convicted of treason, he was not executed with Kirkcaldy, but confined to the castle where he died on 11 August 1575.

By his first wife, Margaret, daughter of Sir Walter Ker of Cessford, he had one daughter. By his second wife, Agnes, daughter of Patrick, fourth Lord Gray, he had a son, Alexander, sixth Baron and first Earl of Home. His second wife later married Thomas Lyon of Baldukic, Master of Glamis.

JOHAN, DUKE of FINLAND, later KING JOHAN III of SWEDEN
c. 1537–1592

The oldest of the ten children of Gustavus Vasa by his second wife Margareta Leijonhufvud, Johan spent much of his life in dispute with his mad, brutal older half-brother Erik King of Sweden (q.v.).

In his will, Gustavus had bequeathed to his younger sons large duchies semi-independent of the crown, and on his death Johan became Duke of Finland. It was in this capacity that he was considered for the hand of Mary Queen of Scots but not for long, since in 1561 he married Katerina, the sister of Sigismund Augustus, the Polish king. As security for a loan to his brother-in-law, Johan was given some Polish castles in Livonia (a state composed of what is now north Latvia and south Estonia) but Erik looked on Poland as his enemy and, after a brief civil war, Johan and Katerina were imprisoned.

In 1567, Erik's insanity became acute. He had many of the foremost nobles imprisoned or murdered but suddenly became penitent and ordered Johan's release. It was not a wise move. Within a year Johan, in alliance with his youngest brother Charles (later Charles IX of Sweden), had risen in rebellion and Erik was in prison where he was to remain until his death nine years later.

Johan ascended the throne as Johan III in 1568 and ruled for twenty-four years. He was an amiable man, learned in theology but a weak and irresolute king. His reign was marked by the end of the Scandinavian Seven Years War and a sporadic war with Russia.

His religious policy was designed to pave the way for a general reconciliation between the Protestant world and Rome. The policy was unacceptable to both Rome and the Lutheran Church in Sweden.

Johan, Duke of Finland, later Johan III, King of Sweden (National Swedish Portraits Collection, Gripsholm)

He died in 1592 leaving Sweden with a Catholic heir (his son Sigismund) and many other problems.

KEITH, WILLIAM, 4th EARL MARISCHAL
c. 1507–1581

The eldest son of Robert Lord Keith, by Lady Elizabeth Douglas, eldest daughter of John, second Earl of Morton, he was also the grandson of William, third Earl Marischal. His father was killed at the battle of Flodden in 1513, and he succeeded to the title on the death of his grandfather in about 1530. In January 1531, he received a grant of lands in Kincardine.

In 1535, he accompanied James V on his trip to France for the royal marriage to Madeleine, daughter of King François I. On 2 July, he was made an extraordinary Lord of Session. In March 1543, he became a Privy Councillor, and one of the keepers of the infant Queen Mary, although he was unwilling to have her 'delivered out of the realm' to England or France. In June 1543, he gave his support to Mary of Guise (q.v.) who he hoped would become regent rather than the Earl of Arran (q.v.). Nevertheless, he not only continued to support an English alliance but maintained a favourable attitude towards the Reformers.

He attended a sermon in 1544, preached by George Wishart (q.v.), in Dundee, despite being forbidden to do so by Mary of Guise. In the following year, he was consulted by Henry VIII about the plot to murder Cardinal Beaton (q.v.), but refused to become involved. He was present at the battle of Pinkie in 1547, and after the pacification in 1550 accompanied Mary of Guise to France.

He was so impressed with Knox (q.v.) that he tried to effect a reconciliation between the Reformer and the Queen Dowager, although he exercised a policy of neutrality between them. He entered Perth with her in 1559, but nonetheless gave her no substantial help against the Lords of the Congregation. In 1560, he remained with her when she withdrew to Edinburgh Castle on the arrival of the English forces, and was with her at her deathbed, where she appointed him her executor, which duty he declined on the grounds of ill-health.

On the return of Queen Mary from France, he was elected a member of the Privy Council and opposed the moves to deprive the queen of the Mass. Nevertheless, he continued to support the kirk, and was a constant supporter of the principles of the Reformation. Although the father-in-law of Lord James Stewart (q.v.), he never became involved in the plots of the day. At the time of the murder of Darnley, he practically withdrew from public life, to his stronghold of Dunottar. His place on the Privy Council was taken by his son, William, Master of Marischal. He had the reputation of being the wealthiest man in Scotland, being able to travel from Berwick to the northern limits of Scotland eating and sleeping on his own estates.

He died on 7 October 1581. By his wife, Margaret, daughter of Sir William Keith of Inverugie, he had two sons: William Lord Keith, who predeceased him in 1580, and Robert Lord Altree, and seven daughters, of whom the eldest was married to Regent Moray. He was succeeded by his grandson, George, who became the fifth Earl Marischal.

KENNEDY, GILBERT, 3rd EARL of CASSILIS
c. 1517–1558
KENNEDY, GILBERT, 4th EARL of CASSILIS
c. 1541–1576

Gilbert, third Earl, the eldest of seven sons of Gilbert, second Earl of Cassilis, succeeded to the earldom on the murder of his father on 22 December 1527. While briefly attending St Andrews University, in February 1528, he subscribed the death warrant of Patrick Hamilton. In April 1530, he went to Paris and studied under George Buchanan (q.v.), who returned with him in 1535 and stayed at his seat in Ayrshire.

At the battle of Solway Moss on 25 November 1542, Cassilis was taken prisoner and, after a short time in the Tower of London, was placed on parole with Archbishop Cranmer, who converted him to Protestantism. With fifteen others, he was released on 26 December, on condition that he effect the marriage of Prince Edward and the infant Queen Mary. He had to leave two of his brothers and his uncle as hostages with the Archbishop of York and give an undertaking to return to England if he was unsuccessful. Not only was he unsuccessful, but he failed to return and abandoned the hostages.

A supporter of Wishart (q.v.), whom he invited to come from Dundee to Midlothian, Cassilis failed to meet him at the appointed time. Wishart fell into the hands of Cardinal Beaton (q.v.) and was burnt at the stake on 3 January 1546. Cassilis collaborated extensively with the English during the 'Rough Wooing', and made secret terms with the Duke of Somerset after the battle of Pinkie on 9 September 1547.

In October 1552, he agreed with Angus, Glencairn (q.v.) and the Sheriff of Ayr, 'to stand with the Dowager [Mary of Guise (q.v.)] against the Governor [Châtelherault (q.v.)]'. In 1554, he was appointed Lord High Treasurer. In 1557, he, Châtelherault, Huntly (q.v.) and Argyll (q.v.) refused to aid the Queen Regent in an invasion of England.

In February 1558, he was one of eight commissioners sent to France to represent Scotland at the marriage of Queen Mary to the Dauphin François (q.v.). The fact that they did not send for the crown of Scotland caused much ill feeling and four of them, including Cassilis, mysteriously died on the way home, supposedly poisoned by the Guises. Cassilis died in Dieppe on 18 November.

By his wife, Margaret, daughter of Alexander Kennedy of Bargany, Cassilis had three sons, of whom the eldest, Gilbert (q.v.), became the fourth Earl. He also had two daughters.

Gilbert, fourth Earl was the eldest son of Gilbert, third Earl whom he succeeded in November 1558. After Queen Mary's return, he was in 1562 appointed to the Privy Council. At the end of 1566, he went openly to hear Mass in the queen's private chapel. In 1567, however, he married Margaret Lyon, only daughter of John, seventh Lord Glamis, who converted him to Protestantism.

On 9 February 1567, he was with the queen when she visited Darnley at Kirk o'Field just before his murder. He sat on the mock assize that acquitted Bothwell on 12 April, and signed the Ainslie Tavern Bond a week later. Nevertheless, he was one of the nobles who signed the bond against Bothwell at Stirling on 1 May. He was not at Carberry on 15 June but fought bravely for the queen at Langside on 13 May the following year.

Cassilis, always keen to increase his family's land holdings, was sometimes less than scrupulous how he achieved this. He had his eye on the abbey lands of Glenluce and when the abbot died, persuaded one of the monks to counterfeit the late abbot's handwriting in a document making over the lands to him. Then to prevent the monk from talking, he arranged for a carl to 'stick' him. Finally, to keep the carl quiet, he persuaded his uncle to falsely accuse him of theft and hang him.

On another occasion, he wished to obtain the sole rights on the lands of Crossraguel which he had received from Mary and Darnley on 10 February 1566. Unfortunately, there were three other people interested in the concession, including the commendator, Allan Stewart. To force him to renounce his rights, on 29 August 1570, he enticed the unfortunate Stewart to his Castle of Dunure. In the 'black vault', Cassilis on 1 September and again on the 7 September 'set his bare legs to a great fire and extremely burnt him, that he was ever thereafter unable of his legs'.

Stewart was rescued by one of Cassilis's kinsmen and complained to the Privy Council, which directed the earl to lodge £2,000 as security to leave the commendator in peace. This was not forthcoming, and in 1571 Regent Lennox (q.v.) came to Ayr, declaring that he would destroy Cassilis if he did not fulfil the council's order. But Lennox's days were numbered and Cassilis, who on 12 August had come to an agreement with Morton (q.v.) to serve the young king, was present when the regent was killed in a skirmish near Stirling on 3 September.

Cassilis did not long survive his aquisition of Crossraguel and died at Edinburgh, on 14 December 1576, after falling from his horse. His eldest son John became the fifth Earl. His widow later married John Marquess, of Hamilton (q.v.).

KENNEDY, QUENTIN
1520–1564

Quentin Kennedy was one of the most serious and effective Catholic apologists during the successful rise of the Scottish Reformation. The fourth son of the second Earl of Cassilis by his wife, Isabella, second daughter of Archibald, second Earl of Argyll, Kennedy was educated at St Andrews and Paris as a theologian and lawyer. In 1547 he became Abbot of Crossraguel, a family foundation. He held this office until his death in 1564, despite the partial destruction of the house three years earlier.

Kennedy achieved prominence in 1558 with his *Compendious Treatise*, an elaborate justification of the Catholic Church from scripture, natural reason and history. It made little mention of the papacy, being content to regard the church as the proper component of Scottish society. Henceforward, with the serious onset of the Reformation, Kennedy was involved in public disputation, chiefly about the validity of the Mass.

In 1559 a planned debate with John Willock did not eventuate, but much correspondence ensued. Three years later, there was a famous confrontation with John Knox (q.v.), over three days, at Maybole, near Crossraguel. Kennedy came out of it so well that Knox felt obliged to publish his own version. By continuing to celebrate the Mass, Kennedy was going against the law, but was excused on account of his 'age and quality'. Since he was only in his early forties, his social and theological eminence, and the purity of his life, must have been the true reasons for such toleration. Had he lived much longer, he might have mounted quite a formidable challenge to the intellectual supremacy of the Reformers.

KILLIGREW, SIR HENRY
c. 1530–1603

The fourth son of John Killigrew of Arwenack and Elizabeth, second daughter of James Trewenard of Trewenard, he was probably educated at Cambridge. On 18 February 1553, he became member of parliament for Launceston. He was in exile during most of Mary Tudor's reign.

Killigrew was recalled to England on the accession of Queen Elizabeth and she employed him on various diplomatic missions. In June 1566, he was sent to Queen Mary for the 'declaration of sundry things necessary to be reformed between them for the preservation of their amity'. After the murder of Darnley, he was sent again with a special message which he delivered to her 'in a dark chamber', which gave rise to the belief that she was being impersonated by one of her ladies.

In September 1572, he returned in connection with the negotiations for the surrender of Queen Mary to the Protestant Lords, the implication being that they would execute her. Mar (q.v.) who was regent at the time was unenthusiastic about the plan and it came to nothing. Killigrew did, however, succeed in persuading Elizabeth to send an English force to assist in the siege of Edinburgh Castle which was being held for Mary. He remained in Scotland until the castle fell.

He was employed on other diplomatic missions in Scotland, the Low Countries, Germany and France. He was knighted on 22 November 1591 and died in the spring of 1603.

By his first wife, Catherine, fourth daughter of Sir Anthony Cooke, he had four daughters, and by his second, Jaél de Peigne, he had a daughter and two sons, the elder of whom, Joseph, succeeded to his estates at only ten years of age.

Sir William Kirkcaldy of Grange, *attributed to Clouet (Private Scottish Collection)*

KIRKCALDY, SIR WILLIAM, of GRANGE
c. 1520–1573

The eldest son of Sir James Kirkcaldy, Lord High Treasurer to James V, and Janet Melville, elder half-sister of Sir James Melville of Halhill (q.v.), William was therefore Melville's nephew despite being fifteen years older than

195

him. Apart from the fact that he was a student in Paris with Thomas Randolph (q.v.), nothing is known about his education. After the disaster of Solway Moss, James V stopped at his father's house at Hallyards on his last journey to Falkland Palace. Sir James was away, so young William waited on the king, who was to die a few days later.

On his father's instructions, he set up the assassination of Cardinal Beaton (q.v.) at St Andrews Castle on 29 May 1546. Going to the castle early in the morning, before the other conspirators, he gained access while the drawbridge was down to admit building materials and engaged the porter in conversation. When Norman, Master of Rothes (q.v.), and his accomplices, including his uncle John and brother William, arrived, the porter was thrown in the moat and, while the others went in search of Beaton, Kirkcaldy guarded the privy postern to prevent his escape.

After the assassination, the murderers held the castle but Kirkcaldy went to England to seek assistance from Henry VIII. He was only partly successful and returned to the castle, which fell to the French on 31 July 1547. He was taken to France and confined at Mont St Michel, but escaped with other Scottish prisoners on 5 January 1549 and made his way back to Scotland.

Kirkcaldy then went to England where Edward VI gave him a pension and employed him on secret diplomatic service. On the accession of Mary Tudor in July 1553, he was deprived of his English pension and entered the service of France, distinguishing himself in the campaigns against the Holy Roman Emperor, Charles V. He was described as 'one of the most valiant men of our time', by Henri II (q.v.), who conferred a pension on him although, according to Sir James Melville, he never drew it. Despite being a favourite of the French king, he was always hostile to the influence exercised by the French in Scotland and had 'a good mind to England'.

In June 1557, the act of forfeiture against him and the other murderers of Beaton was rescinded, and he returned to Scotland. His 'good mind to England' was soon severely taxed when his cousin, John Kirkcaldy, who had been taken prisoner in a border skirmish, was severely maltreated by the English. To avenge his kinsman, he challenged Lord Rivers, the English commander at Berwick, to a duel. The challenge was taken up by the commander's brother, Sir Ralph Rivers, and the combat was fought within sight of both the English garrison of Berwick and the Scottish garrison of Eyemouth. Kirckaldy ran his adversary through the shoulder and unhorsed him.

He took part in the discussions which led to peace with the English in May 1559 and then, at the instigation of John Knox (q.v.), entered negotiations with Cecil (q.v.) to secure English support for the Reformation in Scotland. In July of that year he made clear his support for the Protestants, and in November he led some horsemen and checked the French advance at the skirmish of Restalrig.

The following spring, the French burnt Kirkcaldy's house of Grange in Fife to the ground. Kirkcaldy and the Master of Lindsay, later the sixth Lord Lindsay of the Byres (q.v.), lost no time and surrounded the French force under Capitain le Battu at a village near Kinghorn. In a ferocious fight, le Battu and fifty Frenchmen were killed and the remainder taken prisoner. Shortly after this, according to Knox, he was shot under the left breast at Lundy but quickly recovered from the wound. On the arrival of the English fleet, he attempted to hinder the French retreat to Stirling by breaking down the bridge across the river Devon at Tullibody, but the French ingeniously repaired it using material from the roof of the local parish church.

In the autumn of 1562, at Queen Mary's request, Kirkcaldy joined her army on the operation against the fourth Earl of Huntly (q.v.). He played a substantial part in the campaign, which ended with the earl's defeat and death at the battle of Corrichie. At the parliament of May 1563, his estates were formally restored to him. He opposed the queen's marriage to Darnley, and joined the Earl of Moray (q.v.) on the 'Chaseabout Raid' in the autumn of 1565, after which he had to take refuge in England.

Kirkcaldy knew about, but did not take part in, the plot against Rizzio in March 1566, and arrived in Edinburgh with Moray on the day after the murder. He then took part in the deliberations about the future government of Scotland, which were rendered meaningless by the queen's escape from Holyrood. He was not involved in the murder of Darnley on 10 February 1567, nor was he a signatory to the Ainslie Bond, which approved Mary's marriage to Bothwell. He is the authority for her famous remark that she would 'follow [Bothwell] to the world's end in a white petticoat' and he attributed her 'ravishment' by Bothwell to her own instigation.

At Carberry, Kirkcaldy joined the Confederate Lords and commanded the horse, which he placed in such a position as to prevent Mary and Bothwell from escaping to Dunbar. Mary requested a conference with him, and while they were talking, a soldier sent by Bothwell took aim at him but the queen, horrified by such treachery, prevented any shot from being fired. When Bothwell issued his challenge to fight any man in single combat, Kirkcaldy accepted with alacrity but Bothwell, who cannot have been unaware of Kirkcaldy's awesome reputation, declined to fight someone so far beneath him in rank and challenged the Earl of Morton. Morton, who was then over fifty years old, nominated Lord Lindsay of the Byres, and presented him with the famous sword which had belonged to his great-grandfather, Archibald, 'Bell the Cat'. The queen put a stop to these proceedings and, having seen Bothwell safely off the field, finally surrendered to Kirkcaldy.

Kirkcaldy had pledged his word for Mary's safety, and consequently was strongly opposed to her harsh treatment after her surrender, especially her imprisonment in Lochleven Castle. He believed that all problems might be solved by the capture or elimination of Bothwell, and on 11 August was given a commission to fit out ships for the latter's pursuit. He caught up with him in the Orkneys but, by his own admission, was 'no good seaman' and Bothwell outsailed him and escaped to Norway.

197

On his return, Kirkcaldy succeeded Sir James Balfour (q.v.) as Governor of Edinburgh Castle and on Mary's escape from Lochleven joined Moray, who was now regent, for whom he commanded the army against the queen at Langside on 13 May 1568. His skilful generalship of an outnumbered army was the most important factor in the regent's victory.

There were three main reasons which brought about his decision to transfer to the queen's party. The first was Mary's agreement to a divorce from Bothwell, after which he became convinced that an accommodation with her was not only possible but highly desirable. The second was the fact that he had secured the deliverance, as a prisoner to himself, of William Maitland of Lethington (q.v.), who convinced him that it was possible to effect a reconciliation between Mary and the regent. The third was the murder of the regent himself on 23 January 1570. Although Kirkcaldy bore the standard before the body at Moray's funeral, he was not disposed to subject himself to any surviving member of the king's party, let alone Lennox (q.v.), who became the next regent – in fact, when Lennox was chosen, he refused either to come to the election, or to allow a salute to be fired in his honour.

In April 1571, Lennox issued a proclamation forbidding anyone to serve Kirkcaldy, who immediately announced that for his own security and that of the castle, he was forced 'to join with such of the nobility as would concur with him'. He set about fortifying the approaches to the castle, even mounting cannon on the steeple of St Giles, and appointed his son-in-law Andrew Ker of Ferniehurst, Provost of the City, which was now also held for the queen.

In September 1571, Kirkcaldy sent a force from the castle to Stirling with orders to intercept and capture leading members of the king's party, including the Earl of Morton (q.v.) and Regent Lennox. In a skirmish near the town, Lennox received wounds from which he died, but the deed was carried out against the express instructions of Kirkcaldy, who declared that if he knew who had committed the act, he would personally avenge it.

The Earl of Mar (q.v.) succeeded Lennox as regent and a truce which lasted five months was declared on 1 August 1572. Knox, on his deathbed, sent word to Kirkcaldy that unless he 'was brought to repentance', he would be 'disgracefully dragged from his nest to punishment and hung on a gallows in the face of the sun'. Morton, who succeeded Mar on the day of Knox's death, 24 November 1572, employed Sir James Melville to discuss an agreement for the surrender of the castle, but Kirkcaldy learned that Morton did not intend to include the other members of the queen's faction, especially the Hamiltons, in the negotiations, and they were suspended.

Meanwhile, Morton had negotiated assistance from England, and a force of 1,500 men with cannon under Sir William Drury (q.v.) arrived. They were complemented by 500 Scottish soldiers and a continuous cannonade started on 17 May 1573. The position of the defenders, who lacked water and provisions, was hopeless. On 28 May, Kirkcaldy sent word to the commanders of the Scottish contingent of the besiegers and delivered the castle into their hands, thus avoiding surrendering it to the English. The next day, he gave up his sword to Drury, who treated him with every courtesy.

On 18 June, Kirkcaldy and Maitland were delivered up to Morton. Maitland died in prison in Leith three weeks later. Kirkcaldy's friends, especially Lindsay, made every effort to persuade Morton to spare his life but to no avail. On the afternoon of 3 August 1573, Kirkcaldy was 'hanged against the sun' on the gibbet at the cross as Knox had predicted. He was described by Melville as 'humble, gentle and meek, like a lamb in the house and like a lion in the field, a lusty, stark and well-proportioned personage, hardy and of magnanimous courage'.

KNOX, JOHN
c. 1514–1572

Little is known for certain of the early years of John Knox. He was probably born in 1514, probably near Haddington, and probably of humble parentage. St Andrews was his university, though it does not appear that he ever took a degree. He was ordained, presumably in his twenty-fifth year, and appears in the *Haddington Protocol Books* on 13 December as 'sir John Knox' ('sir', from *dominus*, was the usual designation of a priest who had not obtained the university distinction of 'master', *Magister*).

In 1546 he first appears in his own *History of the Reformation in Scotland* as waiting upon George Wishart 'from the time he came to Lothian', and bearing before Wishart a 'two-handed sword'.

Said to be John Knox, *attributed to Thomas Key (Lennoxlove)*

Said to be Marjory, *John Knox's first wife, attributed to Thomas Key (Lennoxlove)*

Wishart persuaded him to relinquish the sword and encouraged him to return to his employment as a tutor of the 'bairns' of two of the local lairds, adding significantly, 'One is sufficient

199

for the sacrifice'. On the very night of that encouragement, Wishart was arrested and taken to Cardinal Beaton and martyrdom, which he suffered in St Andrews on 1 March 1546. Three months later, Beaton was himself killed there after his murderers occupied the castle while waiting for help from England. Many men joined their garrison, including Knox and his 'bairns' in the Easter of 1547. From these men, Knox received his call to be a preacher, and it was to them he delivered his first sermon.

Almost immediately afterwards, however, instead of the expected help from England, a French fleet anchored off the west sands of the bay, and four weeks later the defenders of the castle, including Knox, were prisoners in the French galleys. Of the nineteen months Knox remained a prisoner, he recorded in his *History* only two incidents. The first was that 'merry fact' on their arrival at Nantes, when the 'great *Salve* was sung, and a glorious painted Lady' was brought in to be kissed and, amongst others, was presented to one of the Scottishmen then chained. He gently said, ''Trouble me not; such an idol is accursed; and therefore I will not touch it.'' The patron and the arduesyn (lieutenant of the galley), with two officers, having the chief charge of all such matters, said, ''Thou shalt handle it''; and so they violently thrust it to his face, and put it betwix his hands; who seeing the extremity, took the idol, and advisedly looking about, he cast it in the river, and said, ''Let our Lady now save herself: she is light enough; let her learn to swim.'' After that was no Scottish man urged with that idolatry.'

The other incident concerned the remarkable prophecy of his return to St Andrews to preach. 'Lying betwix Dundee and Saint Andrews, the second time the galleys returned to Scotland, the said John [Knox] being so extremely sick that few hoped his life, the said Master James [Balfour] willed him to look to the land, and asked if he knew it? Who answered, ''Yes, I know it well; for I see the steeple of that place, where God first in public opened my mouth to his glory, and I am fully persuaded, how weak that ever I now appear, that I shall not depart this life, till that my tongue shall glorify his godly name in the same place.'' '

Knox was released in 1549 and found his way to England, where he was appointed to be a licensed preacher in Berwick. From there he went to Newcastle, and then to London where he became one of King Edward VI's royal chaplains. During this period, he met Mrs Elizabeth Bowes and her daughter Marjory who later became his wife. He declined preferment, including the Bishopric of Rochester, but preached zealously every day of the week 'if the wicked carcass will permit'. With the accession of Mary Tudor in 1553, he fled with others of the Reformed faith to the Continent. He was eventually appointed as one of the preachers to the English congregation at Frankfurt-am-Main, but after six months a controversy over ceremonies forced him to withdraw to Geneva. There he became pastor to another English congregation, and was able to study at first hand the government of a 'perfect city' according to the word of God.

In 1555 he made a brief visit to

Scotland and, taking advantage of the Queen Regent's toleration, he addressed a *Letter* to her, praying her 'to study how that the true worshipping of God may be promoted, and the tyranny of ungodly men repressed'. But the time was not yet ripe for reformation, and he returned to his congregation at Geneva, this time with his wife and mother-in-law. He remained there for nearly four more years, though in 1557 he was invited to return to Scotland and had reached Dieppe on his homeward journey before going back to Geneva.

May 1559 found him once more in Scotland, and this time he had come to stay. He pressed on from Edinburgh to Perth and Dundee, to 'assist his brethren and to give confession of faith with them'. In Perth on 11 May he preached a sermon 'vehement against idolatry': a riot ensued, and the revolution had begun.

The Queen Regent had to rely on a small force of French troops to restore both the peace and her position. The 'Army of Christ Jesus his Evangel', on the other hand, was not sufficient by itself to decide the issue, and the Reformers looked to Protestant England for support and supplies. But the Reformed cause was strengthening and spreading. Knox preached in Perth on 11 May; in St Andrews on 11 June, fulfilling his earlier prophecy; and in St Giles, Edinburgh, on 29 June.

In July, the Lords of the Congregation appealed directly to England for aid. The Queen Regent, seeking the active support of France, began to fortify Leith. Stalemate ensued, but Knox by his preaching put fresh heart into the Protestant lords and inspired them to stand firm. Randolph, the English ambassador, reported, 'I assure you the voice of one man is able in one hour to put more life in us than five hundred trumpets continually blustering in our ears.' Eventually, help from England did arrive; the French were defeated; Mary of Guise died in Edinburgh Castle; and the Protestants were left in control of Scotland. In August 1560 the Scottish parliament abolished papal jurisdiction, forbade the celebration of the Mass, and now approved the Scots confession as a statement of the faith now to be acknowledged in Scotland. But the next step, to organise and endow the Reformed Church, was not taken, and parliament rejected the *Book of Discipline* which expressed so much of Knox's hopes and dreams for the future.

In December 1560, François II, King of France and husband of Mary Queen of Scots, died; and in August 1561, Queen Mary, not yet nineteen years old, returned to her own country. Knox recorded, 'The very face of heaven ... did manifestly speak what comfort was brought into this country with her, to wit, sorrow, dolour, darkness and all impiety. For in the memory of man, that day of the year was never seen a more dolorous face of the heaven than was at her arrival, which two days after did so continue ... The sun was not seen to shine two days before, nor two days after. That forewarning gave God unto us; but alas, the most part were blind.'

Scotland was now a nominally Protestant realm with a Catholic monarch. Some accommodation would have to be reached if peaceful government were to be achieved. But to Knox, all compromise was anathema. On the first Sunday following her landing, when Mary heard Mass in her own chapel at Holyrood, the 'gentlemen of Fife' provoked a riot and threatened the life of the officiating priest. It was Lord James Stewart (q.v.), the warrior of the Army of the Congregation, who barred the door against them and prevented bloodshed. But Knox saw in the queen's Mass the thin edge of a mighty wedge, and from his pulpit in St Giles he inveighed against it. To him, one Mass was more fearful than if 'ten thousand armed enemies were landed in any part of the realm, of purpose to suppress the whole religion'.

He was summoned to the first of his interviews with the queen, and found her to be of 'a proud mind, a crafty wit, and an indurate heart against God and his truth'. Maitland (q.v.) and the other Lords of the Congregation urged Knox to be more gentle with the queen, more politic and patient, and to remember her youth and her upbringing. When they argued that 'the Queen should have her religion free in her own chapel,' he was quick to retort that 'her liberty should be their thraldom ere it was long'. And when Maitland doubted whether the General Assembly of the Kirk could be held without the queen's knowledge and sanction, Knox was equally quick with his reply: 'Take from us the freedom of Assemblies, and take from us the Evangel.'

Knox feared Mary would become the magnetic centre of a Catholic revival, and he had begun to distrust the temporising Protestant lords who were her early advisers. When the question of Mary's marriage was being canvassed in the courts of Europe, Knox made his position clear. In a sermon before 'the most part of the nobility', he said, 'And now, my Lords, to put end to all, I hear of the queen's marriage: Dukes, brethren to Emperors, and Kings all strive for the best game. But this, my Lords, I will say … wheresoever the Nobility of Scotland professing the Lord Jesus, consents that an infidel (and all Papists are infidels) shall be head to your Sovereign, ye do so far as in ye lieth to banish Christ Jesus from this Realm; ye bring God's vengeance upon the country, a plague upon yourselves, and perchance ye shall do small comfort to your Sovereign.' There followed another interview with the queen, but neither side would give way to the other.

Mary's reign was, in fact, moving rapidly to its close. In 1565 she married Henry, Lord Darnley, a union which Knox saw as an open threat to 'true religion'; and 'in the audience of many' he asked God's mercy 'that he was not more vehement and upright in the suppression of that idol from the beginning'. Mary seized the opportunity of her settled marriage to assert herself against preachers and politicians alike. She confronted and scattered them at the 'Chaseabout Raid', and many of them had to go into exile. Knox himself went to the west where he wrote and revised much of his *History*.

But Mary soon discovered that her marriage had been a great mistake, and she gave her confidence to Rizzio. Darnley's resulting jealousy and distrust provoked a plot against the favourite, and he was killed at Holyrood. On the day after the murder, the exiled

Protestant Lords rode into Edinburgh. Mary had nowhere to turn; the Earl of Bothwell began to find that he was in favour with her. A plot was hatched, in which murder and marriage were mixed, and on 10 February 1567 Darnley was 'blown up' at Kirk o' Field. On 15 May 1567 Mary and Bothwell were married. Her hasty marriage, and the circumstances around it, alienated too many who would otherwise have supported the queen. On 15 June, one month after her marriage, she surrendered to the Protestant Lords at Carberry without a fight. On 24 July, she demitted her crown to her infant son. In December 1567 Parliament re-enacted the anti-papal legislation of 1560, and re-affirmed the Scots Confession.

Knox had little to do with these final days of stress and strain. His wife Marjory had died towards the end of 1560; his second marriage, to the seventeen-year-old daughter of Lord Ochiltree (q.v.), took place in 1564, and they had three daughters. During the days of turmoil, he was either in the west, or in England visiting his sons. But with the fall of Mary he returned, and preached at the coronation of the infant king. He preached at the opening of parliament in December 1567; and his funeral sermon of the Regent Moray is said to have moved 3,000 hearers to tears.

In the autumn of 1570 he had a slight stroke, and early the following year, as Edinburgh was held by the Marians, he retired to St Andrews where he taught and preached. But August 1572 saw him once more in Edinburgh, preaching in St Giles, though he was now so feeble that 'scarce can he stand' and his voice was so weak that he could be heard only by those immediately around him. On 9 November he inducted his successor in St Giles, but on Tuesday the 11th, he was 'stricken with a great host' (a severe fit of coughing). On the Saturday two friends called, and he caused a hogshead of wine to be broached for them.

But he was failing rapidly. About five o'clock on 24 November, he asked his wife to 'read where I first cast my anchor', and she read the seventeenth chapter of St John. About eleven o'clock he cried suddenly, 'Now it is come!' Those who were with him asked him for a sign: 'He lifted up his one hand, and thereafter incontinent rendered the spirit.' At his funeral, the Regent Morton is said to have spoken the words: 'Here lieth a man who neither feared nor flattered any flesh.'

LESLIE, GEORGE, 4th EARL of ROTHES
c. 1500–1558
LESLIE, NORMAN, MASTER of ROTHES
c. 1518–1554
LESLIE, ANDREW, 5th EARL of ROTHES
c. 1530–1611

George, fourth Earl, the second son of William the third Earl and Margaret, daughter of Sir Michael Balfour of Montquhannie, succeeded to the title on the death of his father in 1513. In 1529, he was made Sheriff of Fife, an appointment which was made hereditary and passed on to his arguably illegitimate eldest son Norman in December 1540.

Rothes attended the marriage of James V in Paris in 1536. He was made a Lord of Session in July 1541, and a Lord of Articles in November 1544. He was not involved in the murder of Cardinal Beaton (q.v.) on 29 May 1546, although his brother John and his sons Norman and William were deeply implicated. In June 1550, he was sent as ambassador to Denmark. In February 1558, he was one of eight commissioners sent to France to represent Scotland at the marriage of Queen Mary to the Dauphin François (q.v.). The fact that they did not send for the crown of Scotland caused much ill feeling and four of them, including Rothes, mysteriously died on the way home, supposedly poisoned by the Guises. Rothes died in Dieppe on 28 November.

In 1517, he contracted an alliance with, and may have married, the twice widowed Margaret Crichton, daughter of William, third Lord Crichton of Frendraught and Princess Margaret Stewart. By her, he had two sons, Norman and William, and a daughter. The marriage, if such it was, was dissolved in 1520. In 1525, he married Elizabeth Gray, daughter of Andrew, second Lord Gray, and widow of firstly John, fourth Lord Glamis, and then Alexander, third Earl of Huntly. She bore him no children and died in 1527. In 1528, he married Agnes, daughter of Sir John Somerville and widow of John, second Lord Fleming. By her he had three sons and four daughters including Andrew, later fifth Earl of Rothes. Agnes died in 1542, and the following year he married Isobel Lundy, daughter of Lundy of Lundy and widow of David, eighth Earl of Crawford, by whom he had no children. Ever since 1520, he had continued his relationship with his first wife, Margaret Crichton, who bore him another son and four more daughters between then and her death in 1545. He also had at least four illegitimate children.

Norman, Master of Rothes, was the eldest son of the fourth Earl by Margaret Crichton. Norman's legitimacy and that of his younger brother, William, was always in doubt. Although their twice widowed mother was nominated their father's 'sponsa affidata' in 1517 and bore him eight children, the earl does not appear to have married her canonically until 1542 and perhaps not even then. He even went so far as to marry and have seven children by another woman between 1528 and 1541. Nevertheless, on 7 December 1540, Norman became Sheriff of Fife, a hereditary office, on the resignation of his father.

He fought and was taken prisoner at Solway Moss on 24 November 1542 but was soon released with others after signing a bond to promote the interests of Henry VIII in Scotland. His antipathy towards Cardinal Beaton, Archbishop of St Andrews, probably originated then, but was exacerbated on 12 December 1543 by the restoration to Sir James Colville, at the cardinal's instance, of the lands of Wemyss Castle. The lands had been forfeited some years earlier by Sir James and bestowed on the Rothes family by James V.

Norman fought at the battle of Ancrum Moor on 12 February 1545. His arrival, with 300 spearmen from Fife, persuaded the Scots to risk the battle, which might not otherwise have taken place, and the English were defeated. Despite fighting the English, he was sporadically in contact with Henry VIII from 1544 onwards concerning a plot to murder Beaton, after which the conspirators were to take refuge in England. Henry was indecisive about the scheme, but the martyrdom of George Wishart (q.v.), on 1 March 1546 on the cardinal's orders, provided the final pretext. Men under Norman's command seized St Andrews Castle on 29 May but he took no personal part in the murder, the fatal blow being struck by his uncle, John Leslie.

After the murder, the conspirators remained in the castle and defended it against the besieging forces of Regent Arran (q.v.), eventually surrendering to the French on 31 July 1547. A condition of the surrender was that the lives of those in the castle should be spared, although the principal defenders were taken to France. Norman escaped in January 1550 and returned to Scotland. There he found that there was a search in progress for him so he fled to England via Denmark. He was given a pension by Edward VI, but on the accession of Mary Tudor in 1553, found he was a wanted man again, and returning to France, offered his services to Henri II (q.v.).

On 14 August 1554, he was involved in an action near the stronghold of Renti near Cambrai. Leading thirty Scots, he heroically charged sixty horsemen armed with culverins, unseating five of them before his lance broke. Desperately wounded, he made his way back to the king just as his horse dropped dead beneath him. He was carried into the royal tent and died fifteen days later. The French king was so impressed with his bravery and the manner of his death that he used his influence with Mary of Guise (q.v.), the regent of Scotland and mother of Mary Queen of Scots (soon to become his daughter-in-law), to effect the restoration of Cardinal Beaton's murderers. Norman was married to Isobel Lindsay, daughter of John, fourth Lord Lindsay of the Byres, but they had no children.

Andrew, fifth Earl, was the son of George, the fourth Earl, and Agnes Somerville. He inherited the title on the death of his father in 1558 but not the family estates because of the claim of his elder half-brother William, whose legitimacy was in contention. The dispute was submitted to Queen Mary who, in January 1566, decided in his favour on condition that he make over certain lands to William. His claim to succeed his father as Sheriff of Fife was opposed by Patrick, Lord Lindsay of the Byres (q.v.), and it was not until April 1575 that the Lindsays finally withdrew their objections.

Rothes was a prominent member of the Lords of the Congregation and a staunch adversary of Mary of Guise (q.v.). He was one of those who barred her march to St Andrews in June 1559 and he signed the ratification of the Treaty of Berwick the following year. After Queen Mary's return from France, he became a member of the Privy Council and, in September 1561, the queen stayed for a night in his house at Leslie. He was, however, opposed to Mary's marriage to Darnley in 1565, and supported the Earl of Moray (q.v.) on the 'Chaseabout Raid' in the autumn of that year, being forced to take refuge in England after the collapse of the campaign. In November, with others, he was summoned to appear in parliament the following February to hear himself 'decerned of the crime of lese majesty'. To preempt this, the plot against Rizzio was hatched and Rothes was one of those who signed the bond for the murder which took place in March 1566.

The next day, he returned to Scotland with Moray and took part in discussions as to the future government of the country. After Mary's escape to Dunbar, he broke with the other conspirators and thereafter was a steadfast supporter of the queen. There is no evidence that he was involved in the plot to murder Darnley, but he was one of the members of the assize, on 12 April 1567, which acquitted Bothwell of the crime. He was not at Carberry but was one of the lords who assembled at Hamilton after Mary's escape from Lochleven and fought for her at Langside on 13 May 1568. When Kirkcaldy of Grange (q.v.) decided to hold Edinburgh Castle for the queen, Rothes went to France to represent her cause there. In January 1571, he was reported 'to be in the Castle with the captain [Kirkcaldy]' but by August, had been won round to the king's party by Morton (q.v.).

In December the following year, he was acting as an intermediary between Morton, who was now Regent, and the defenders for the surrender of the castle. The negotiations were fruitless and the castle held out until 28 May 1573, when it fell to Morton's forces reinforced by 1,500 English troops with

cannon under Sir William Drury (q.v.). Rothes was involved in the fall of Morton in 1578, and in 1581 was a member of the assize which found him guilty of the murder of Darnley, despite having sat on a similar assize fourteen years earlier, which had found Bothwell innocent of the same crime. On 27 July 1588, he was appointed to the commission for executing laws against Jesuits and papists, and on 31 October 1593, he became a member of the commission for the trial of the Catholic lords for their connection with the 'Spanish Treason'. He died in 1611.

By his first wife, Lady Grizel Hamilton, daughter of Sir James Hamilton of Finnart, he had three sons including James, Master of Rothes, who predeceased him, and two daughters. By his second, Jean, daughter of Patrick, third Lord Ruthven (q.v.), he had two daughters. By his third, Janet, daughter of David Durie of Durie, he had three sons. He was succeeded by his grandson, John, son of James, Master of Rothes.

LESLIE, JOHN,
BISHOP of ROSS
c. 1527–1596

Born the illegitimate son of the rector of Kingussie and a laird's daughter, John Leslie studied at Aberdeen, Paris and Poitiers and became a skilled canonist and civilian lawyer. Already the holder of preferments in the church, he was priested in 1558 and became a major figure in the diocese of Aberdeen.

In the events of the onrush of the Reformation in Scotland, the death of

Mary of Guise and the return of Mary, Leslie played a substantial part. He disputed with John Knox, who tried to belittle him, and, on a mission to France, tried vainly to persuade the widowed queen to sail to Aberdeen and take her kingdom by force. When Mary did return, Leslie settled readily into the regime as a Canon Law Professor, a Judge of the Court of Session, a Privy Councillor and, in 1566, Bishop of Ross. He was thus in a central position for the stirring events of the final years of Mary's rule.

Leslie was at Holyrood on the night of Rizzio's murder; Darnley allowed him to leave. He attended the queen at Dunbar and, from that time, became one of her chief advisers. A friend to Bothwell, he later claimed to have opposed the marriage. Certainly he sat at the Council Board when Bothwell was condemned, but his strong attachment to Mary must be set against his fears about her matrimonial venture. Diocesan affairs after Carberry conveniently kept Leslie away from Mary's fall, imprisonment and escape. With the queen's detention in England, Leslie, as a lawyer-diplomat, came into his own. From then on, he was a familiar figure in the negotiations, the representations, and the intrigue which surrounded Mary's English life. The Bishop of Ross, no ecclesiastic now but a royal legate, was skilful, devious, patient, occasionally panicky, always loyal in his fashion to his queen.

After serving as Mary's chief commissioner at the conferences at York and London and later being arrested in England and losing his episcopal revenues in Scotland, Leslie settled into

John Leslie, Bishop of Ross, *artist unknown, 16th century (National Galleries of Scotland)*

the role of the queen's ambassador. While giving him no formal status, it enabled him to mastermind the queen's relations with Scotland, England and France. It was Leslie who was involved both in the early stages of Mary's proposed marriage to the Duke of Norfolk and also in the final episodes which led to Norfolk's execution. After several spells of imprisonment, he was allowed to leave England (having made his peace with Mary) for France in 1573. He acted for the queen at Rome and in Paris. Appointed suffragan bishop at Rouen in 1579, he was made Bishop of Coutances in 1591. He did not reside in his troubled diocese, but died at a monastery near Brussels in 1596. He had at least one daughter.

Leslie was not only a fine canon lawyer and a pertinacious diplomat, but also a skilful historian. In 1568–70 he wrote, in Scots, a *History of Scotland* (not published until the nineteenth century) and a fuller Latin account, published in Rome in 1578.

LINDSAY, DAVID,
10th EARL of CRAWFORD
1524–1574
LINSDAY, DAVID,
11th EARL of CRAWFORD
1547–1607

David, tenth Earl, the eldest son of Alexander, 'the wicked Master of Crawford' and his wife, Jean, daughter of Henry, third Lord Sinclair, inherited the title, not from his father but from his kinsman, David Lindsay of Edzell, the ninth Earl. The 'Master' had been found guilty, not only of the murder of a servant of Lord Glamis, but also of constructive parricide. His seizure and imprisonment of his father had led to the eighth Earl's untimely death, and the punishment for the crime was that the master and his heirs be attainted forever. However, the ninth Earl saw his role as that of life tenant, and accordingly adopted the tenth Earl as his heir in 1546, despite having sons of his own, and on his death in 1558, David Lindsay was allowed to inherit his grandfather's title and become tenth Earl.

Crawford was a faithful adherent to the queen's cause. At her marriage to Darnley, he was a cup bearer, and took part in the 'Chaseabout Raid'. After her imprisonment, he was one of those who met at Dumbarton in June 1567 to plan her escape, and when this was effected in the following year, joined in planning her defence. However, like the other northern lords, he was not able to reach Langside in time for the battle. After the defeat, he was denounced as a rebel, but on 5 May 1569, after swearing allegiance to the young king and Regent Moray, received a pardon.

He died in 1574, having acquired, like his father, a reputation for lawlessness and violence, and was buried in Dundee. He married Margaret, daughter of Cardinal Beaton, by whom he had five sons, and one daughter: David, eleventh Earl; Henry, thirteenth Earl; Sir John, of Ballinsho and Woodwray; Alexander, who was chamberlain to King James, and created Lord Spynie; Sir James of Pittodrie; and Helen, who married Sir David Lindsay of Edzell.

David, eleventh Earl, inherited the prodigality of his father and grandfather and was, if anything, even more lawless than they. He continued the hereditary feud with the Lord Chancellor, the eighth Lord Glamis, which had been partly the cause of the disinheritance of his grandfather and in 1578, was involved in an affray in Stirling, where both lords were in attendance on the king, and which resulted in the death of Glamis.

Although there was no conclusive evidence that Crawford had committed the murder, he was imprisoned in Edinburgh, but shortly afterwards permitted to return home on surety. On 3 November he was tried for the murder, and acquitted, although he was required to give surety not to molest the three-year-old ninth Lord Glamis. Soon after he went to France with the sixth Earl of Huntly, an equally lawless character who thirteen years later was to be responsible for the murder of 'the bonnie Earl of Moray'. He remained there for three years, not returning to Scotland until 1581. His support for James VI after the king's escape from the Ruthven Raid in 1582 resulted in considerable royal favour, and on the return of James Stewart, Earl of Arran to power, Crawford became one of his principal supporters. Following the trial of the Earl of Gowrie, he received from the king the barony and regality of Scone and the church lands of Abernethy.

He attended a banquet at Holyrood in May 1587, when a reconciliation between him and young Glamis was effected, but this was short-lived and their private feud continued. Having been converted to the Catholic faith, he joined Lord Claud Hamilton with Huntly and Errol in the plot for the Spanish invasion, and in 1589, he and Huntly took arms against the king, Crawford at the same time escalating his feud with Glamis. Their rebellion was short-lived, and Crawford submitted to the king in May 1589. On 21 May, he was convicted of treason, and confined to St Andrews, but was released the following September. Although after his release he went to France, he was again reconciled to the king, and appeared at meetings of the council in 1591, and continued to do so until his death in 1607.

The earl was married twice: first to Lilias, daughter of David, Lord Drummond, and secondly to Grizel, daughter of John fourth Earl of Atholl. His marriage to his first wife, which was brief, inspired a ballad. By his second wife, he had three sons. David, twelfth Earl, who surpassed even his predecessors in wickedness, was eventually confined in Edinburgh Castle at the instigation of his relatives, in order to protect the estates from forfeiture, and

died there in 1621. The other two sons, James and Claud, both died young. His daughter, Mary, eloped with Alexander Rynd, a servant, some say a public herald, and died a beggar. On the twelfth Earl's death the title and estate passed to his uncle, Sir Henry, son of the tenth Earl.

LINDSAY, PATRICK,
6th BARON LINDSAY
of the BYRES
1521–1589

The eldest son of John, fifth Lord Lindsay, and his wife Helen Stewart, daughter of John, second Earl of Atholl, Patrick was born in 1521 and succeeded his father in 1563.

He was one of the first of the Scottish nobility to join the Reformers openly. In 1559, he was among those who defended Perth against the Queen Regent, and was instrumental in the expulsion of the French garrison from the city after the Treaty of Cupar Muir. He further distinguished himself in Fife, under Kirkcaldy of Grange in 1560 (q.v.), slaying La Bastie, a French captain of repute, in single combat. His enthusiasm for the Reformed faith was such that he was a signatory not only to the bond to 'defend the liberty of the Evangel of Christ', but also to the *Book of Discipline*, and when Mary made known her intention of celebrating the Mass in her private chapel at Holyrood, he and his followers gathered to prevent her from doing so, but his purpose was foiled by her half-brother, Lord James Stewart (q.v.). Through Lord

James's mediation, Lindsay and the queen were eventually reconciled, and he was foremost in her support in the fourth Earl of Huntly's (q.v.) rebellion, playing a leading role at the battle of Corrichie.

Unlike the other Reformers, Lindsay was in favour of the queen's marriage to Darnley, to whom he was related by marriage, and accompanied the king in the 'Chaseabout Raid' against Moray. He was a zealous supporter of the plot to murder Rizzio and, with 150 men, occupied the palace of Holyrood while Darnley, Ruthven and others carried out the deed. Afterwards, he treated the queen with great brutality, threatening to 'cut her into collops' should she summon help. When Mary escaped to Dunbar, Lindsay, with others in the plot, fled to England, but returned to Scotland shortly before the murder of Darnley. There is, however, no suggestion that he was aware of, or took any part in, the plot to murder his kinsman, and he was one of the signatories of the bond to free the queen from Bothwell, and to punish Darnley's murderers.

At Carberry Hill, he besought the Lords to permit him to accept Bothwell's challenge to single-handed combat, because of his near relationship to Darnley, but the queen's personal intervention prevented the encounter. With the fourth Lord Ruthven, Lindsay was made joint guardian of the queen after her surrender, and together they conveyed her to Lochleven, where Lindsay compelled her, with much harshness, to abdicate in favour of the infant prince. According to one (admittedly partisan) account, Lindsay threatened to cut her throat if she refused to do so. At the prince's coronation, both Lindsay and Ruthven testified that her resignation was voluntary.

Subsequently, Lindsay was one of Regent Moray's staunchest supporters, and after Mary's escape he fought against her at the battle of Langside, and his timely reinforcement was instrumental in her defeat. When Moray attended the conference in York in 1568, Lindsay accompanied him, and later defended him against the accusation of implication in the murder of Darnley, made by the fourth Lord Herries (q.v.) at Westminster, to where the York conference had adjourned. At Moray's funeral, he assisted in carrying the coffin.

During the civil war, he was of the king's party, and rendered invaluable service, his forces slaying the commendator of Kilwinning, Gavin Hamilton, in 1571 and intercepting French gold, sent for the support of the queen, at Wemyss in May of that year. He was taken prisoner shortly afterwards, but purchased his freedom. In retaliation for a raid on his estate of the Byres, Lindsay took part in a skirmish with the enemy in Edinburgh and succeeded in capturing the fifth Lord Seton. Appointed Lieutenant of Leith during the absence of the regent at Stirling, he repulsed a powerful attack made against him on the last day of August 1571 and in 1572, he was elected Provost of Edinburgh by the king's party, while the siege of the castle was in progress. He promised Knox (q.v.), who was on his deathbed, that he would make no terms with the opposing party, but later tried to induce Morton (q.v.) to spare the life of his old comrade-in-arms Kirkcaldy of Grange. The effort was however a failure and Kirkcaldy was hanged.

Lindsay played little part during the remainder of Morton's regency, being no great supporter of his and, in 1578 was one of those who overthrew the regent. Together with Ruthven, he received the surrender of Stirling Castle on 1 April 1578, and was appointed one of the council responsible for administration until parliament could be convened. On Morton's return to power, Lindsay and Montrose, as representatives of the disaffected nobles, attended under protest the convention held at Stirling and were arrested. Both were soon free, and with the other dissenting lords, and a force numbering 7,000, marched on Stirling. They effected a compromise, by which Morton nominally returned to power, and Lindsay was appointed a member of the Privy Council. During the remainder of the regency, he was loyal to Morton, after whose fall he retired from public life.

Lindsay joined in the Ruthven Raid and, after the king's rescue, fled with the other conspirators to England. He returned in 1584, and was committed to Tantallon, but on the fall of James Stewart, Earl of Arran, in November, was released. He died in 1589. He married, in 1545, Euphemia, daughter of Sir Robert Douglas of Lochleven, a kinswoman and half-sister of Regent Moray. By this marriage he had a son and a daughter. The son, James, seventh Lord Lindsay, was born in 1554, and married Euphemia Leslie, daughter of Andrew, fifth Earl of Rothes (q.v.). Their daughter, Margaret, married, as his first wife, James, Master of Rothes, and died about 1594.

LIVINGSTON, WILLIAM, 6th BARON LIVINGSTON
c. 1528–1592

The second son of Alexander, fifth Lord Livingston, and Lady Agnes Douglas, daughter of John, second Earl of Morton, William the sixth Baron succeeded his father in 1553. Although a Protestant, he was throughout a strong supporter of Queen Mary, who often stayed at his castle at Callender. His sister was one of the 'four Maries' (q.v.) who had accompanied the queen to France when she was five years old.

After the queen married Darnley on 29 July 1565, he accompanied her on the 'Chaseabout Raid' in pursuit of Moray (q.v.). He was not involved in the plot against Rizzio (q.v.), but was in attendance on the queen at Holyrood when the murder occurred on 9 March 1566 and was one of the targets of the conspirators. With Atholl (q.v.) and Bothwell, he made his escape by climbing out of a window at the back of the palace.

In January 1567, when Mary travelled from Edinburgh to Glasgow to bring back her sick husband, she stayed a night at Callender. There is no evidence that Livingston was involved in the murder of Darnley although he was in Edinburgh when it happened. After the murder, he was in attendance on the queen at Seton where she went to recover from the shock. Livingston disapproved of the queen's marriage to Bothwell and was not with her when she surrendered at Carberry on 15 June

1567. However, he signed a bond to free her when she was imprisoned in Lochleven Castle and, after her escape, fought for her at Langside on 13 May 1568. He accompanied her on her flight from the battlefield, crossing the Solway and arriving at Workington in Cumberland on 18 May. On 24 May, he was charged to render up his castle at Callender.

Mary appointed Livingston one of her commissioners at her first trial in York at the end of 1568, and he was again in England as her agent in the summer of 1570. During the hostilities in Scotland he remained abroad, but was given leave by Morton (q.v.) to return on 13 June 1573, a fortnight after the fall of Edinburgh Castle.

In 1577, he was one of those who advised the eleven-year-old king to terminate Morton's regency and take the government into his own hands. When Morton retook possession of Stirling Castle and resumed custody of the king, on 5 May 1578, Livingston joined the lords who had assembled against him and marched on Stirling. A reconciliation, however, took place through the mediation of the English ambassador, and Morton remained regent, albeit with reduced powers.

Towards the end of his life, Livingston was thought to lean towards the Catholic religion but, on 6 March 1590, he was appointed to the commission for enforcing the laws against the Jesuits. In 1591, he walked in the procession at the coronation of Queen Anne of Denmark. He died the following year.

By his wife, Agnes Fleming, second daughter of the third Lord Fleming and sister of the fourth lord (q.v.), he had four sons and two daughters. His eldest son, Alexander, became the seventh Lord Livingston and the first Earl of Linlithgow.

MAITLAND, WILLIAM, of LETHINGTON 1525–1573

Eldest son of the noted sixteenth-century literary figure, Sir Richard Maitland, a Lord of Session and Keeper of the Privy Seal, by his wife, Mariota, daughter of Sir Thomas Cranstoun of Corbie, Maitland was educated at the University of St Andrews and abroad. His talents received early recognition from the Queen Regent, who employed him in her service from 1554, sending him as ambassador to Queen Mary Tudor early in 1557, and in March of that year, to France in connection with the Treaty of Cambrai. In 1559 he was appointed Secretary of State, but in October 1560, more for political reasons than through religious zeal, he resigned the office and joined the Lords of the Congregation. He also placed himself under the protection of Kirkcaldy of Grange (q.v.), stating that his outspokenness on religious matters had placed his life in danger. Fearful of the French threat to Scottish independence, he persuaded the fourth Earl of Huntly (q.v.) and other Catholic lords to withdraw their support from the Queen Regent. At the Convention of Estates in 1560, which formally abolished the supremacy of the papacy in Scotland, he delivered the inaugural address.

Maitland enjoyed the confidence of the Reformers, who recognised his diplomatic skills, and employed him in the negotiations with Elizabeth which led to the Treaty of Berwick in February 1560, and later that year was instrumental in persuading the Lords to agree to the Treaty of Edinburgh. He was one of those chosen to negotiate with Elizabeth on the proposed marriage between her and the third Earl of Arran (q.v.), although his knowledge of Arran's growing mental incapacity, and his private knowledge of Elizabeth's disinclination for the match, must have made him realise that its failure was inevitable.

On the announcement of Mary's return to Scotland in 1561, he was fearful for his future, on account of his known anglophile policies, and his previous relations with the Queen Regent. Mary's somewhat ambiguous letter of reassurance did nothing to allay his fears. However, by stressing the continued threat from France, not only to Scotland's independence but also to the Reformed religion, both in Scotland and England, he succeeded in obtaining the support of Elizabeth (real or feigned) for Mary's return, and her promise to enter into negotiations for an alliance between the two kingdoms, based on Mary's claims as heir presumptive.

On 1 September, shortly after the queen landed in Leith, he was sent as ambassador to England to announce her arrival formally, and on his return, was appointed Secretary, with responsibility for foreign policy, especially with regard to England. He continued to work for an accommodation between the two sovereigns, and believed that recognition as heir presumptive would satisfy Mary's ambitions and avert the

Said to be Sir William Maitland of Lethington, *Flemish School, mid-16th century (Lennoxlove)*

threat of a religious revolution in Scotland. However, his policies were threatened by the attempt of John Knox (q.v.) to establish a Protestant theocracy, which posed a direct threat to Mary and to her policy of religious tolerance. Ministers of the Reformed Church also attempted to interfere in matters of state. Maitland succeeded in thwarting these plans.

In May 1562, he went to England to arrange an interview between Elizabeth and Mary, but renewed hostilities between France and England led to the breakdown of negotiations, and he returned to Scotland with the unwelcome news that the meeting had been postponed until the following year. In 1563, Maitland was again dispatched to London, to press Mary's claims with parliament, but with little hope of success, and used this opportunity to discuss with the Spanish minister the plans to marry Mary to Don Carlos (q.v.). From there he went to France,

213

where, on 17 April, he offered to act as mediator between England and France, although there is no reason to suppose that Mary really desired to help Elizabeth. His real reason for going to France was to obtain the support of the Cardinal of Lorraine, Mary's uncle, for her marriage to Don Carlos. On his return from this mission, on 23 June, he spent three days in close conference with the queen, but by the end of the year, all hopes of success in the Spanish marriage had disappeared, along with the sanity of Don Carlos. Nonetheless, for his part in the negotiations, Mary rewarded him with the abbacy of Haddington.

The suggestion that Mary should marry, instead, the Earl of Leicester (q.v.), Elizabeth's favourite, did not meet with Maitland's approval any more than that of Mary, although he probably recognised that the offer was less than sincere. Mary's subsequent decision to marry Darnley was a serious blow to his hopes, but he gave tacit support to the marriage, recognising that it strengthened considerably Mary's claims to the English succession. He was sent to England to inform Elizabeth of Mary's desire to marry Darnley, and to seek her approval, but on learning that Mary was treating the matter as a *fait accompli*, returned precipitately to Scotland, fearing that Mary's duplicity would lead to an irreconcilable rupture with Elizabeth. Seeing that Mary was determined to marry Darnley, come what may, he made no attempt to oppose her.

Although officially still Secretary, Maitland had, to all intents and purposes, been superseded by Rizzio, but

although he was in Holyrood on the night of the murder, he took no part in the action. Despite being denounced by Bothwell, who hated and feared him (and was covetous of his estates), and by Darnley, as one of the conspirators, his usefulness in her negotiations with Elizabeth led Mary to restore him to favour after only a short absence from court.

Thereafter, he was deeply opposed to Darnley, and became one of the prime movers in the Craigmillar Bond designed to liquidate Darnley, although previously he had suggested to the queen that divorce should be considered as a means of ridding herself of the husband she despised and detested. On 6 January 1567, he married Mary Fleming (q.v.), one of the queen's 'Maries', an act which tied him the more firmly to the queen's interests. On hearing of the proposed marriage, Kirkcaldy of Grange is reported to have said: 'Maitland is as qualified to marry Mary Fleming as I am to be Pope.' Shortly after his marriage, he was with Bothwell when the latter proposed to Morton (q.v.) that Darnley should be murdered. Since he had supported the recall of Morton, on the grounds that means should be found to rid the queen of Darnley, his inclusion in the conspiracy was inevitable. Darnley's murder followed on 10 February.

Maitland was one of those who accompanied the queen to Seton after the murder, but was averse to her marriage to Bothwell, although he recognised that any interference would be to no avail. Despite fearing an attempt by Bothwell on his life, he accompanied the queen from Dunbar to Edinburgh, and was present at her marriage. He remained at court, ostensibly on good terms with Mary, but eventually matters with Bothwell came to such a pass that he escaped from Edinburgh and joined the fourth Earl of Atholl. With Atholl, he returned to Edinburgh, where he joined the Protestant lords, although his main purpose seems to have been to save the queen from the consequences of her disastrous marriage. At Carberry, Mary summoned Maitland, and proposed that she and Bothwell should be permitted to leave Scotland together, and although he appears to have considered this, he advised her that, should she separate from Bothwell, all might still be well.

He was present when the silver casket was opened on 21 June and, after the flight of Bothwell, seems to have devoted himself wholeheartedly to the queen's interests. At the opening of parliament in December of that year, he attempted to reconcile all parties to the rule of Regent Moray, in the conviction that the queen's interests would best be served by such a reconciliation. He was one of the commissioners of the York Conference and, as far as possible, tried to shield Mary, although it was not in his own interests to have any thorough enquiry into the murder of Darnley. Although Mary named him as one of the prime conspirators, he continued to be devoted to her cause, and despite Elizabeth's disapproval, revived the scheme for her marriage to Norfolk.

In July 1569, he made an attempt to gain the support of the Scottish parliament for the queen's divorce from Bothwell, but this failing, he retired again to Atholl. From there, he was enticed back to Stirling, where he was accused of the murder of Darnley. He was imprisoned in Edinburgh Castle, but on the death of the regent, was released in February 1570. After the election of Regent Lennox (q.v.), he again retired to Atholl, where he was acknowledged as head of the queen's party, despite increasing ill health. On April 1571, he arrived in Leith, and from there was carried up to Edinburgh Castle, where he joined Kirkcaldy, who was holding out for the queen. Despite waning support from France, he continued to hope for salvation, and inspired the beleaguered garrison to maintain their defences against increasing odds. In November 1572, he negotiated a truce with Regent Morton, but on learning that this would involve the betrayal of the Hamiltons and Gordons, refused to continue the negotiations. This refusal sealed his fate.

When the final assault on the castle began, Maitland was so weak that he had to be carried down to the vaults. The final assault began on 21 May 1573, and on May 29, the defenders surrendered, having previously failed to make terms. Kirkcaldy was hanged, but Maitland died before sentence on him could be carried out. Some said that he died by his own hand, others that he was poisoned. After his death, his body was treated with the utmost indignity. His last resting place is not known. Regarded by both Protestants and Catholics as a traitor, Maitland was in fact a patriot, the well-being of Scotland being the most important matter in his life.

He married first Jonet, daughter of William Menteith of Kerse, by whom he had at least one daughter, Marion, who married Robert Fawside of that Ilk. She had no children. By his second wife Mary, daughter of Malcolm, third Lord Fleming, he had two children: James, who married Agnes Maxwell, daughter of William, fifth Lord Herries; and Margaret, who married Robert Ker the Younger of Cessford, who was created Earl of Roxburghe in 1616.

BEATON, MARY
c. 1542–before 1599
FLEMING, MARY
1542–?
LIVINGSTON, MARY
c. 1540–after 1583
SETON, MARY
c. 1541–after 1615

Sadly, little information survives of the four Maries, and even the few portraits that exist are not contemporary and of dubious authenticity. It is known that they were all about the same age, sailed for France with Mary in August 1548, and were sent by Henri II (q.v.) to the Dominican convent at Poissy to continue their education, and in particular to learn French. In August 1561, they arrived back in Scotland together, on the same galley as the queen, three of her uncles, the chronicler Brantôme and the poet Châtelard. They all attracted the censure of John Knox (q.v.), which at times amounted to nothing less than slanderous lies. None of them was with Mary during the final days at Fotheringhay.

Mary Beaton was the daughter of Robert Beaton of Creich, in North Fife,

and his French wife. Her grandfather was Sir John Beaton, the hereditary keeper of Falkland Palace. The Beatons of Creich were a junior branch of the family from whose senior line came the three men who were to dominate the Catholic ecclesiastical scene in Scotland for nearly a century. Robert was a member of Queen Mary's household. A kinswoman, Elizabeth Beaton, had borne a daughter to James V. The daughter, Jean, married Archibald, fifth Earl of Argyll (q.v.) in 1554, but they were soon separated and Jean became a faithful confidant of the queen.

Mary Beaton was the most classically beautiful of the four Maries, but lacked the physical attraction of Mary Fleming or the vivacity of Mary Livingston. In 1566, she married Alexander Ogilvy of Boyne. He fought for the queen, was taken prisoner at Langside in May 1568 and fought for her again in 1571. It is not known when Mary died but it must have been before 1599 because, in that year, the widowed Alexander married the fifty-four-year-old twice-widowed Lady Jean Gordon, the first wife of the fourth Earl of Bothwell (q.v.).

Mary Fleming was a daughter of the third Lord Fleming and sister of both the fourth Lord (q.v.), who died in Paris in 1558, and the fifth Lord (q.v.), who so gallantly held Dumbarton Castle for Queen Mary from 1569 to 1571. Her sister Margaret was the second wife of the fourth Earl of Atholl (q.v.) and reputed to be endowed with powers of sorcery. Her mother, Johanna Stewart, an illegitimate daughter of James IV, went to France with her and later had a scandalous affair with Henri II.

Mary Fleming was the undoubted 'belle' of the four. At one court festivity, she was dressed in the queen's clothes and the English ambassador Randolph (q.v.) described her as 'contending with Venus in beauty, with Minerva in wit, and with Juno in wealth'. After the alarm caused by Châtelard's invasion of privacy, she shared the queen's bedchamber. She kept in touch with Queen Mary at Lochleven and later in England. The queen pleaded for her company in 1581.

In January 1568, after four years' courtship, Mary married the statesman William Maitland of Lethington (q.v.), a widower eighteen years her senior by whom she had two children. Although Maitland was far from being a constant supporter of his wife's royal mistress, he was one of the last, holding out for the Marian cause in Edinburgh Castle until its fall at the end of May 1573. He died a few days later and, within a month of his death, the Privy Council charged his widow 'to deliver up a chain of rubies with twelve marks [clusters] of diamonds and rubies, and a mark of two rubies, which had belonged to Queen Mary, to the Regent [Morton (q.v.)] for the King.' Mary subsequently married George Meldrum of Fyvie. Her children by Maitland were: James, who died without issue, and Margaret, who married Robert, first Earl of Roxburghe.

Mary Livingston was the daughter of Alexander, fifth Baron Livingston, and Agnes Douglas, daughter of John, second Earl of Morton. She was the sister of William, the sixth Baron (q.v.), one of Queen Mary's staunchest adherents. Her younger sister, Magdalen was also a maid-of-honour to the queen and, in January 1562, was married to Arthur Erskine of Blackgrange (q.v.), a younger brother of John, Earl of Mar, later regent of Scotland (q.v.).

Mary was the most vivacious of the quartet and enjoyed dancing, which she indulged in with energy, agility and enthusiasm. In March 1565, she married John Sempill of Beltries, called 'the Dancer', a younger son of Robert, third Lord Sempill. The wedding was celebrated with great splendour at the expense of the queen, who also made the couple a grant of lands which had belonged to the fourth Earl of Huntly (q.v.). On the restoration of the fifth Earl (q.v.), in April 1567, the grant was ratified by parliament. Sempill was in attendance on the queen when Rizzio was murdered, and assisted in her attempted escape from Lochleven. With Margaret Carwood, Mary helped the queen draw up her will before the birth of James VI and along with her sister Magdalen was among the legatees. Her husband died in 1579 and she survived him by several years.

Mary Seton was the daughter of the fourth Lord Seton and Marie Pieris, a French lady who had come to Scotland with Mary of Guise (q.v.) in 1538. His brother, the fifth Lord (q.v.), spent much time in France, and in 1561 returned to Scotland with his niece Mary and the queen, whose Master of the Household he became in 1563. He was a confirmed Catholic.

Mary was the meekest and most pious of the four. She was also the least interested in the pleasures of the court

217

and the most devoted to the service of her mistress, whom she was allowed to join at Lochleven in September 1567. She facilitated Queen Mary's escape on 2 May 1568 by impersonating her, and rejoined her at Bolton Castle a few months later. Despite several suitors she never married and remained with the queen till the autumn of 1583 when, due to ill health, she was allowed to retire and went to the convent of St Pierre aux Dames at Rheims, where the queen's aunt, Renée of Guise, was abbess. She was still there thirty-two years later. In England, she had been described as the finest dresser of women's hair in the country.

Mary of Guise, wife of James V and mother of Queen Mary, attributed to Corneille de Lyon, c. 1550 (National Galleries of Scotland)

MARY of GUISE-LORRAINE, QUEEN of SCOTS 1515–1560

The eldest child of Claude, Duke of Guise, second son of René II, Duke of Lorraine, and Antoinette de Bourbon, daughter of François de Bourbon, Count of Vendôme, she was born at Bar-le-Duc on 20 November 1515. Her father was one of the closest friends of King François I, and her mother a descendant of King Louis IX (St Louis). She was exceptionally tall, a characteristic which her daughter was to inherit. Her early education was at the Convent of the Poor Clares.

At fifteen she was presented at court, and three years later married the Grand Chamberlain of France, the twenty-three-year-old Louis, Duke of Longueville. On New Year's Day 1537, they both attended the marriage of the king's daughter, Madeleine, to James V, King of Scots. Six months later, her young husband died, leaving her pregnant with her second son, Louis, who was born in August but died in December. At the end of the year, the French king decided that she should marry the recently widowed James V, despite an ardent suit for her hand from Henry VIII, whose young wife, Jane Seymour, had died in October.

Leaving her elder son behind, Mary came to Scotland to marry James. She was forced to come by sea since Henry ungraciously refused her passage through England. Landing at Crail, she and James were married by Cardinal Beaton (q.v) at the Cathedral of St Andrews in June 1538. For two years, Mary was childless and it was not until the prospect of an heir was assured, in February 1540, that she was finally crowned. The child, James, died in infancy, as did another, Arthur, born in April 1541. In the summer of 1542, she again became pregnant, and went with the king on a pilgrimage to the Chapel of Our Lady of Loretto at Musselburgh. The child was born on 8 December shortly after the disaster of Solway Moss. Within a week, James was dead, leaving his wife a widow again, and his daughter, Mary, Queen of Scots.

Cardinal Beaton, as head of the Catholic and hence anti-English party, had a strong common interest with the Queen Dowager, with whom he was uncharitably (and probably falsely) alleged to be having an affair. Despite strenuous skullduggery on the part of the cardinal, they were unable to prevent the nomination as regent of James Hamilton, Earl of Arran (q.v.), heir presumptive to the throne, since this was required by the constitution. The two parties were, however, eventually reconciled. Despite the decision of parliament in 1543 to accept the offer of Henry VIII to marry the infant queen to his son, the Queen Dowager was determined on a French marriage, a policy which both Beaton and Arran regarded with disquiet, each seeing in this a threat to his own position. When in June 1544 a coalition of the Douglases and other nobles summoned by the Queen Dowager attempted to discharge Arran of his responsibilities, he and Beaton formed an alliance to overturn the decision and prevent the meeting of parliament. This unlikely alliance came to an end with the murder of Beaton in 1546, which left the Queen Dowager the leading Catholic figure in Scotland.

During the 'Rough Wooing' the Queen Dowager showed great firmness and courage in raising an army to protect the young queen, whom she removed for safety to Inchmahome on the Lake of Menteith. In 1548, she persuaded the nobles to agree to her daughter's immediate departure for France with a view to her eventual marriage to the dauphin, son of Henri II (q.v.). Arran cooperated with her in this, and was rewarded for his efforts by being made Duke of Châtelherault by the French king. With the aid of French troops, she eventually restored peace to Scotland, and was able to pay a visit to France in 1551 in support of her claim to act as regent during her daughter's minority, but it was not until 1554 that Châtelherault was finally ousted, and the Queen Dowager became Queen Regent.

Mary then proceeded to rule Scotland in a spirit of conciliation, in order to persuade the nobles to conclude the marriage of the young queen and the dauphin. Her ousting of Scots nobles from important offices at court in favour of French appointees, however, caused much resentment, and the growth of Protestantism weakened her position to the point where her feudal army refused to invade England in 1557. The signing of the First Bond of the five Lords of the Congregation in the same year was in effect a declaration of war against Catholicism and, in March 1559, the Queen Regent attempted to suppress the heresy, which led to open conflict with Knox (q.v.) and his followers. Their occupation of Perth, and destruction of the local monasteries there, was treated by Mary as open rebellion, which she suppressed with the aid of French troops. Hollow assurances of mutual religious tolerance followed, both sides secretly preparing for the renewal of the conflict. With the arrival of further French troops the Queen Regent, feeling insecure in Edinburgh, began to turn Leith into an impregnable fortress, while Châtelherault returned to Scotland to lend his support to the Lords of the Congregation.

Despite help from England, the Lords were unable to sustain the siege of Leith and in November were forced to evacuate Edinburgh. Following the Treaty of Berwick in February 1560, English troops were sent under the command of Lord Grey to join in the siege of Leith, upon which the Queen Dowager, whose health was failing, was given shelter in Edinburgh Castle, from where she could watch developments at Leith. Negotiations between Mary and the Lords about the reduction in the numbers of French troops in Scotland broke down when Mary imposed unacceptable conditions, including the renunciation of the treaty, and on 29 April, Mary put the castle in a state of defence. By now mortally ill, Mary continued to attempt to negotiate with the Lords, while also seeking further aid from France. On 8 June, she had a final audience with them, assuring them that at all times she had nothing but the good of the country at heart, and imploring them to acknowledge their duty to the young queen. She also besought them to rid Scotland of all foreign troops, both English and French.

On 11 June, she died, while the English and French ambassadors held preliminary discussions in Newcastle. It was agreed that she should be buried in France, but it was not until March 1561 that her body was removed to Fécamp

in Normandy, and she was finally buried in July in the church of the Convent of St Pierre aux Dames in Rheims, where her sister was abbess. Her fulllength monument in bronze was destroyed during the French Revolution. Both friends and foes alike bore testimony to the power of her strength of will and her ability; the venomous language in which Knox described her reflects the fears of the Protestants. Throckmorton (q.v.), on the other hand, spoke of his admiration of 'her queenly mind'. Her resolution ensured the sovereignty of her daughter whose interests were always uppermost in her mind.

MAXWELL, SIR JOHN, of TERREGLES, 4th BARON HERRIES
c. 1512–1583

The second son of Robert, fifth Baron Maxwell, by Janet Douglas, daughter of Sir William Douglas of Drumlanrig, he was educated at Sweetheart Abbey, Kirkcudbrightshire. In 1547, he married Agnes Herries, eldest daughter and coheiress of William, third Baron Herries. The marriage to Lady Herries, whose lands marched with his own, was not accomplished without difficulty. In order to achieve it, Maxwell had to plot against her guardian, Regent Arran (q.v.), who had intended that the lady should marry his own son, Lord John (q.v.). His right to represent his wife's peerage, according to the custom of the time, was not recognised until the baptism of the prince in 1566, when Maxwell first appeared as Lord Herries, and he sat in parliament under this title in the same year.

After the battle of Pinkie, Maxwell, in common with many other Border lords, was forced to swear allegiance to England and, having been thwarted in his marital designs by Arran, entered into a plot with Lennox (q.v.), promising support for Lennox's return to Scotland, with the assistance of Lord Wharton, the English commander. This alarmed Arran sufficiently for him to relent and agree to the marriage as an inducement to Maxwell to renege on his promise to Lennox, which Maxwell duly did, with the result that Lennox's raid in February 1548 failed. As a reprisal, the hostages given by Maxwell to Wharton were hanged.

For his early support of the Reformers, Maxwell was imprisoned in Edinburgh Castle by the Queen Regent in 1559. The following year, he was one of those who signed the Convention of Berwick; he also subscribed to the bond to rid Scotland of the French in April of that year, and was a signatory of the *Book of Discipline*. His espousal of the Reformed faith was never in doubt. Notwithstanding this, on the return of Queen Mary, he was one of her foremost supporters, which caused doubts at the time about his true religious allegiance, although he continued to be on terms of great friendship and mutual respect with Knox (q.v.) until 1563, when a disagreement about the Mass brought the relationship to an end. At the time of the queen's marriage, he attempted to mediate between her and Moray (q.v.), and when it became obvious that Moray's revolt had failed, he helped him to escape to England.

After the murder of Rizzio, Herries joined the queen following her escape from Edinburgh to Dunbar, and from that time on, was one of her most devoted followers. He was a member of the assize which acquitted Bothwell of the murder of Darnley, although he used a legal technicality as an excuse for doing so, rather than asserting his conviction of Bothwell's innocence. He was, in fact, no friend of Bothwell and, when the news of the impending marriage reached him, besought the queen on his knees not to proceed, but despite all, remained faithful to her, even after the disasters which resulted from the marriage.

When the queen was imprisoned at Lochleven, Herries initially declined to support Moray's regency but, eventually, in October 1567, submitted, although his support was purely nominal. Despite a remarkable speech in December, in which he advised Argyll (q.v.) and others to follow his example and give their support to the king, he continued to work for the queen's release and, immediately after her escape, once more joined her and was with her at Langside, where he commanded the horse.

When the queen realised that her cause was lost, she first sought refuge in the area controlled by Herries. However, despite his misgivings, she eventually decided to cast herself on the mercy of Elizabeth and, accompanied by the constant Herries, made the fateful crossing of the Solway from Dundrennan to Workington. She sent him as her ambassador to Elizabeth to seek an interview to explain her position, but the English queen refused either to meet Mary, or to permit her to leave

England until her name had been cleared. Herries, whether on his own initiative or at the queen's instigation, suggested a compromise, whereby the regent should still rule in Scotland but that he should do so under the direction of Elizabeth.

For this Herries was formally forfeited at a meeting of the Estates in August 1568, although proceedings were suspended pending the result of the proposed conference in England, at which Mary chose him to be one of her commissioners. On 1 December, he accused Regent Moray, and some of the other commissioners, of complicity in the murder of Darnley and, following Moray's return to Scotland in the spring of 1569, Herries joined the Hamiltons in an attempted revolt, for which he was imprisoned in Edinburgh Castle. Following this, he found it necessary to reassure Elizabeth that he had not double-crossed his mistress, while, at the same time, he attempted to assuage the not-unreasonable doubts which Moray harboured about his true loyalty, in an effort to gain his release.

Moray did not relent, however, and it was not until after his assassination that Herries regained his freedom, at the behest of Kirkcaldy (q.v.). Immediately on his release, he joined the queen's lords at Linlithgow, and was involved in their plan to assemble at Edinburgh in April, but their further plans were thwarted by Regent Morton (q.v.) who instigated a raid by the English on Maxwell lands in the Borders. Again Herries attempted to come to terms with Elizabeth, promising her his services, but at the same time, he pleaded for her aid in Mary's cause, making veiled threats that, should this be withheld, assistance would be sought from foreign princes, a reference to Elizabeth's arch-enemy, Philip of Spain (q.v.), with whom some of the Marian lords had secretly been plotting.

By August 1571, however, convinced that no help was likely to be forthcoming from England, and that the queen's cause was hopeless, he sought a reconciliation with Morton, an uneasy truce which was to last only until 1578 when, with his nephew, Lord Maxwell, Herries took part in the plot to remove Morton from the regency. With Morton's resignation effected, Herries became a Privy Councillor. The following September, Herries was one of those chosen by the king to ensure the peace of the realm, and in 1579 was appointed Warden of the West Marches, a position previously held by his nephew, and which he held only until August of that year.

The execution of Morton in June 1581 again quickened Herries' interest in Mary's cause, and he became one of the most strenuous supporters of the Duke of Lennox. After the Ruthven Raid of 1582, he made an unsuccessful attempt to mediate between the king and Lennox. This was his last public act. He died suddenly the following January at the lodgings of Will Fowler, having foregone the afternoon session of the Kirk on grounds of ill-health, preferring instead to 'go to see the boys bicker'.

By his wife Agnes, he had four sons and seven daughters. The sons were: Sir William, fifth Lord Herries; Sir Robert, of Spottes; Edward, Commendator of Dundrennan and Laird of Lamington; and John, of Newlaw. Their daughters were: Elizabeth, Lady Lochinvar; Margaret, Countess of Lothian; Agnes, Lady Amisfield; Mary, Lady Hay of Yester; Sarah, Lady Johnstone; Grizel, Lady Bombie; and Nicolas, Lady Lag.

MELVILLE, ANDREW
1545–1622

The youngest son of Richard Melville who was killed at the battle of Pinkie, Andrew was brought up by his eldest brother. After studying at St Andrews, he went to Paris in 1564. Here his teacher was Peter Ramus, the celebrated classical scholar and educator, whose methods and curricula Melville was to introduce to Scotland. He went on to Poitiers as a law student and then to Geneva. At this great Calvinist centre, Melville, already a committed Protestant, made friends with some of the new faith's most prominent leaders and apologists including Theodore Beza and Joseph Scaligor. He returned to Scotland in 1574 as a well-informed and ardent religious Reformer.

Melville's official task in his homeland was to be a university administrator and teacher. At Glasgow and, from 1580, at St Andrews, he overhauled the curriculum, bringing in the humanist practices of Ramus. Henceforward, Scottish higher education could hold its own with the best in Europe. But it was religion which increasingly claimed Melville's attention. Knox (q.v.) was dead; Protestantism was firmly rooted and the Reformers were in the ascendant. Under the regents, the state was on the side of the Protestants, although the

Andrew Melville, *late 18th-century engraving*

structure of the Reformed Church and its relations with secular power became matters of intense dispute. Episcopacy was not the sole, nor even the most important, issue but it came to symbolise many aspects of the conflict.

Melville was involved with the compilation of the *Second Book of Discipline*, approved in 1581 by the church and confirmed by the state in 1592. He worked for the regularisation of the system of kirk sessions and general assemblies, and the intervening stage of presbyteries, which was a significant element in the French and Genevan structures. James VI's assumption of authority led to continual conflict with Melville over the crown's ecclesiastical authority in general, and that of the bishops in particular. Charged with sedition in 1584, he was imprisoned and

223

then escaped to England, where he was welcomed by the leading Puritan preachers.

An uneasy truce with King James enabled Melville to return to Scotland in 1586, where he soon distinguished himself by the strength of his attack on Spain's growing hostility to England. By 1597 the religious balance had changed and Melville found the king's pro-episcopal policy difficult to withstand. In the same year he lost control of St Andrews University although he remained there as a divinity teacher.

Melville applauded the Union of the Crowns in 1603. Yet it meant disaster for him and the views he championed. Strengthened by a loyal and crown-dominated Church of England, James could give full vent to his dislike of Presbyterianism as the enemy of the monarchy. Melville, who had publicly criticised the royal theories when they had been enunciated in Scotland, now found himself in a weaker position. In London from 1606 he became embroiled in violent controversies and finished up in the Tower. In 1611 he was allowed to go abroad where he taught at Sedan until he died, still unmarried, in 1622.

Melville's last years were bitter with defeat. A fine scholar and a man of generous impulses, he had spent so long in urgent and tough dispute on behalf of his vision of the church. Yet in the long run Melville was the victor. It was his view of the future of the church, not that of King James, which was to prevail. Andrew Melville was the architect of Scots Presbyterianism.

MELVILLE, SIR JAMES, of HALHILL 1535–1617

James was the third son of Sir John Melville of Raith by his second wife, Helen Napier. His elder half-sister Janet was the mother of Sir William Kirkcaldy of Grange (q.v.), who was therefore his nephew despite being fifteen years older than him. When fourteen, he was appointed page at the French court to Mary Queen of Scots who was then seven. In 1552, he entered the service of the Constable of France, accompanying him in the field against the Holy Roman Emperor; five years later, he was wounded at the battle of St Quentin.

In 1559, Melville was introduced by the Constable to Henri II (q.v.), who sent him to Scotland to discover the real aims of Lord James Stewart (q.v.), whom Mary of Guise (q.v.) was accusing of wanting the Scottish crown for himself. The mission was one of the factors which led to the return of Mary Queen of Scots to Scotland in 1562.

On Melville's return to the Continent, he became attached to the court of the Elector Palatine, and acted as a marriage broker on the Elector's behalf. He recommended the marriage of the Elector's second son, Duke John Casimir to Queen Elizabeth, that of Archduke Charles of Austria to Mary Queen of Scots, and that of Charles IX of France (q.v.) to Elizabeth, daughter of the Emperor Maximilian II. None of these schemes was successful, although Charles IX eventually married Elizabeth of Austria in 1570.

Melville went back to Scotland in 1564 at Queen Mary's request and was appointed Privy Councillor and Gentleman of the Bedchamber. Mary used his diplomatic skills to discuss with Queen Elizabeth her proposed marriages first to the Earl of Leicester (q.v.) and then to Darnley. He foresaw the murder of Rizzio, which he vainly tried to prevent, and was in Holyrood on the night of the crime although he did not witness it.

In 1566, he was sent to Elizabeth to announce the birth of Prince James; it was to him that she made the famous remark: 'the Queen of Scots is lighter of a fair son and I am a barren stock'. He was not involved in the plot against Darnley, but after the murder made himself unpopular with Bothwell by trying to dissuade Mary from marrying him.

After Mary's incarceration in Lochleven Castle, the nobles sent him to offer the regency to Moray (q.v.) at Berwick. His brothers Sir Robert and Sir Andrew were in Edinburgh Castle while it was being held for the queen by their nephew Kirkcaldy. Melville, however, knew a loser when he saw one and did not take part in the dissension between her supporters and those of her son. Throughout James VI's minority, he was entrusted with the most delicate diplomatic missions but retired from court during the latter part of Morton's regency.

His advice was often sought by James VI after he started to rule in person, but he declined missions to England, Denmark and Spain. On the king's return from Denmark with his new queen, Melville was knighted and appointed Privy Councillor and Gentleman of the Bedchamber to Queen Anne. In 1603, however, when the king earnestly asked him to accompany him to London, Melville declined on account of his age and retired to his estate of Halhill. He made one visit to the king in London and was graciously received, but spent most of the rest of his life writing his memoirs. He died at Halhill on 13 November 1617.

By his wife, Christina Boswell, he had one son, James, who succeeded him, and two daughters.

MONTGOMERIE, HUGH, 3rd EARL of EGLINTON
c. 1531–1585

The eldest son of Hugh, second Earl, by his wife Mariota, daughter of George, third Lord Seton, he succeeded his father in 1546. Because of his marriage to Lady Janet Hamilton, daughter of Regent Arran (q.v.), he gave his political support to the regent, despite being a Catholic. In October 1559 he assembled his troops in support of the Lords of the Congregation.

Although in December 1559 he had declared against the French, by February of the following year he had fully endorsed the queen's cause and, after the death of François II (q.v.), attended the convention at Dunbar in December 1560, when he signed the bond on behalf of Queen Mary. In 1561, he was one the nobles who escorted Mary on her homeward journey. The vessel in which he was sailing was captured but released when it was realised that the queen was not aboard.

Eglinton was one of the most constant supporters of the queen, especially in her efforts to re-establish the Mass. At the banquet following her marriage, he was one of the nobles who waited on Darnley, and in the 'Chaseabout Raid', his forces formed part of the van. Knox (q.v.) reported that he was one of the nobles who assisted at the baptism of the young Prince James according to the rites of the Catholic Church.

He was not involved in the plot to murder Darnley and, although he was opposed to the marriage with Bothwell, he at first adopted a strictly neutral stance and, alone of the nobles who attended the Ainslie Tavern supper, managed to avoid signing the bond. Although he joined with the lords in their attempt to separate the queen from Bothwell, after her imprisonment in Lochleven, he took no further part in their actions. Following her escape, he joined the Hamiltons, and fought for her at Langside, making his escape after the battle. For failing to deliver up the castles of Eglinton and Ardrossan, and for conspiracy on behalf of the queen with the Hamiltons and others, he was declared guilty of treason at the parliament held in August 1568. For some time he continued to adhere to Mary's party but eventually, in May 1571, was forced to submit to Regent Lennox (q.v.). Notwithstanding this, he was confined to the castle of Doune until July, and with the Earls of Argyll (q.v.) and Cassillis (q.v.), bound himself to serve the king and Regent Lennox at Stirling in August. He was with the regent's party in Stirling on 3 September when the conspirators arrived, and Lennox was killed. During the raid, he was confined to his quarters under guard.

After the election of Regent Morton (q.v.) in November 1572, Eglinton endeavoured to secure religious tolerance for Catholics, but was careful to express abhorrence of the St Bartholomew's Eve Massacre. Following Morton's downfall in 1578, he subscribed to the measures taken for the safety of the king and the peace of the country but, on Morton's restoration to power, Eglinton was chosen a Lord of the Articles and appointed a Privy Councillor. In April 1579, he supported the order for the prosecution of the Hamiltons for the murders of Regents Moray (q.v.) and Lennox and was appointed one of the commissioners to put the order into effect, for which he received the thanks of the council. He was a member of the assize for the trial of Morton in 1581.

Although not directly involved in the Ruthven Raid, he was present at the convention at Holyrood on 18 October 1582 which approved it. He did not long survive this event and died on 3 June 1585. He married as his first wife Janet Hamilton, which marriage was dissolved by the Pope in 1562 on grounds of consanguinity. Janet, however, obtained a divorce from the Kirk on the grounds of the earl's adultery. They had no children. Shortly after the divorce, Eglinton married Margaret Drummond, daughter of Sir John Drummond of Innerpeffrey and widow of Sir Hugh Campbell of Loudon, by whom he had two sons and two daughters: Hugh, fourth Earl, who died without issue; Robert of Giffen, who died without male heirs; Margaret, who married the first Earl of Winton; and Agnes, who married Robert, Lord Sempill.

PHILIP II,
KING of SPAIN
1527–1598

Philip of Spain presided over the Spanish Empire at its zenith. He had four wives who among them managed to bear him only two sons. One was mad and the other, although sane, was in almost every other respect unsuitable to be his successor. A dapper, fair-haired, blue-eyed man of rather under medium height, he is remembered for the horrors of the Inquisition, the disaster of the armada, and for being king while the worst excesses of the Conquistadors were being perpetrated in America.

Born at Valladolid on 21 May 1527, the son of the Holy Roman Emperor Charles V and Isabella of Portugal, he was educated in Spain, and brought up by his father to have a profound sense of the high destiny to which he was born. He grew up grave, self-possessed and distrustful, and was a frenetic worker.

In 1543, he was married to his cousin Mary of Portugal, who died two years later but bore him a son, the ill-fated Don Carlos (q.v.), one of the candidates for the hand of Mary Queen of Scots. In 1554, his father arranged his marriage with Mary Tudor, Queen of England, to cement an alliance of Spain, the Netherlands and England against France. He thus became king of England, although he was never given the Crown Matrimonial, and the marriage was barren. Mary Tudor died in 1558.

In 1556, his father abdicated and he assumed responsibility for Spain's

Philip II of Spain,
(The Mansell Collection)

possessions in America, Italy, France and the Netherlands as well as Spain itself. It was a daunting legacy. France was bound to try to ruin a power which threatened her independence. However, the Spanish were victorious at St Quentin and Gravelines, and the French were forced to make the Peace of Cateau Cambrésis.

On 22 June 1559, he married Elisabeth de Valois, which gave Spain security from France for a generation, but she died childless in 1568. The accession of Elizabeth Tudor to the English throne in 1558 meant that, despite his later efforts to marry her and convert her to Catholicism, he had exchanged one enemy for another.

His fourth wife was another cousin, Anne of Austria, whom he married in 1570. She died in 1580, but not before supplying him with the son who was to succeed him as Philip III.

He was proud to play the champion of the old religion, but the atrocities

227

carried out by the Spanish Inquisition hardened the obstinacy of the Dutch, exasperated the English, and provoked a revolt of the Moriscoes (the Spanish Muslims). Nonetheless he was never troubled by self-doubt; in a message to the Pope he wrote: 'Rather than suffer the least damage to religion and the service of God, I would lose all my states and an hundred lives if I had them; for I do not propose nor desire to be the ruler of heretics.' This could have been his epitaph.

The worst disaster of his reign was caused by his decision in 1588 to send an 'invincible' armada under the Duke of Medina Sidonia, to assist in the proposed invasion of England by the Spanish army in the Netherlands. On board the 130 ships there were 7,000 sailors and more than 17,000 soldiers, so the armada was more like a floating army than a fighting fleet. In the English fleet, the sailors far outnumbered the soldiers, so it is not surprising that the Spaniards were outgunned and out-manoeuvred. Actions were fought off Plymouth, Portland, the Isle of Wight, in the Calais roads and off Gravelines. Medina Sidonia abandoned his original plan but, pursued by the English and with the wind in the south-west, had no choice but to run up the North Sea and return home round Scotland and Ireland. Many ships were wrecked on the coasts and their crews massacred by the local inhabitants. More were lost on the open sea. Less than half the ships that set out returned to Spain or Portugal, and in those death and sickness were appalling.

Philip died at his magnificent but gloomy palace, El Escorial, on 13 September 1598. Despite his many failures, Spain was still at the height of her power, and it was to be another half century before it became clear that the counter-Reformation would make no further conquests. He was a laborious, self-righteous man whose ability to engage in endless discussions, and write mountains of minutes, stifled his administration.

RANDOLPH, THOMAS
1523–1590

The son of Avery Randolph of Badlesmere, Kent, he entered Christ Church, Oxford at the time of its foundation, where, after a brief spell as a lawyer, he became head of a hall of residence. By then a convinced Protestant, he went into exile in Paris when Mary Tudor came to the throne. Here he met George Buchanan (q.v.), Kirkcaldy of Grange (q.v.) and other prominent Scots and gained a useful insight into Scottish affairs. Returning to England on Elizabeth's accession, Randolph entered the queen's service. He was friendly with the new Secretary of State, William Cecil (q.v.); both were, if anything, firmer Protestants than Elizabeth.

Randolph conveyed Arran (q.v.) from France, via England, to Scotland and then became Elizabeth's agent at Edinburgh. Mary Queen of Scots came to trust him, though he had earlier stirred up trouble for her mother, Mary of Guise (q.v.), when she had been regent, and he was quite open in his friendship with the Protestant lords. But Randolph was unable to prevent the queen's marriage to Darnley. Mary, resenting his opposition, accused him of complicity in the Chaseabout Raid and of writing a tract, *Mr Randolph's Phantasy* against her. Elizabeth recalled him to London mid-1566.

Randolph was absent from Scotland during the events which led to Mary's flight, but returned on four later occasions. An embassy in 1577 failed to help Regent Morton (q.v.), and one in 1580 was no more successful. Randolph fell out with the powerful Esmé Stewart, Duke of Lennox. A bungled attempt to seize James VI led to his flight to Berwick, his second sojourn there as a refugee. His final northern tour of duty was happier. It resulted in the treaty of 1586, which neutralised Scotland in England's coming war with Spain.

Scotland was Randolph's chief interest. He probably knew its people and problems better than any other Englishman. His lively and informative letters form a vital record of much of Mary's personal reign. But Randolph was not a top-class diplomat. He was sometimes outwitted by the Scots. More importantly, he was a stronger Protestant than he was an upholder of English policy and allowed his religious sympathies to influence his judgement. Randolph's admiration, in particular, for Buchanan, one of Mary's most trenchant critics, was strong; he even gave Buchanan help in the publication of his *History*, in which he libellously vilified Mary.

Randolph's diplomatic duties took him far afield. He undertook several missions to France and led a spectacular embassy to Russia, where he gained privileges from Tsar Ivan the Terrible for the English merchants of the Muscovy Company. The Hakluyt Society has published Randolph's account of his Muscovy travels, but he spent much time about the English court as an administrator. His position there was strengthened in 1571 by his marriage to Anne, sister of Francis Walsingham. He had become Postmaster General in 1566 and later added to this the office of Chancellor of the Exchequer, a post less important than it became in the eighteenth century. Randolph continued to hold these appointments until his death in London on 8 June 1590.

RUTHVEN, PATRICK,
3rd BARON RUTHVEN
c. 1520–1566
RUTHVEN, WILLIAM,
4th BARON RUTHVEN,
1st EARL of GOWRIE
c. 1541–1584

Patrick, third Baron, the eldest son of William, second Lord Ruthven and Janet, daughter of Patrick, Lord Haliburton, was educated at St Andrews University. He succeeded to the title on the death of his father in December 1552. Like his father, he was hereditary sheriff of Perth, and from 1553 until his death, he was annually elected Provost of the town.

In 1559 when the Queen Regent, Mary of Guise (q.v.), requested him to suppress the Reformation heresy among the inhabitants of Perth, Knox (q.v.) reported that Ruthven answered 'that he would make their bodies come to Her Grace and to prostrate themselves before her [but that to] cause them do against their conscience, he could not promise'. He took no action to prevent the sacking of the monasteries in the area on 11 May that year, and was diplomatically absent when the army of the Queen Regent approached. However, when she entered the town on 29 May and deposed him and the bailies from their offices, his patience was exhausted. He immediately joined Argyll (q.v.), Lord James Stewart (q.v.) and the other Lords of the Congregation. In February 1563, Maitland (q.v.) persuaded a reluctant Queen Mary to appoint Ruthven to the Privy Council. This was not popular, since he had acquired a reputation as 'a highly unsavoury character' because of his use of sorcery. He continued to be a staunch defender of Protestantism and, on 8 May 1564, Mary appointed him Sheriff-clerk of Perthshire.

His first wife was Jean, natural daughter of Archibald sixth Earl of Angus (q.v.), who was Darnley's grandfather. Although they were now divorced, his children by her were cousins of Darnley, whose marriage to Mary he felt obliged to support. During the Chaseabout Raid, Ruthven joined the forces of the queen, with a command in the rearguard of the battle.

The ascendancy of Rizzio, accompanied by the declining influence of Darnley and the friends and relatives who had supported the marriage, was viewed by Ruthven with deep resentment. He or Morton (q.v.) probably inspired George Douglas (q.v.) to propose to Darnley that he approach Ruthven 'to aid him against the villain David'. Ruthven, although so ill that he (in his own words) 'was scarcely able to walk twice the length of his chamber', promised to assist to the utmost of his power and formally told Morton of the request. Morton and Ruthven made the arrangements for seizing Rizzio and their names are the only ones known to have been on the bond signed by Darnley. Ruthven, in full armour, pallid and haggard from his illness, was the first of the conspirators to enter Mary's supper chamber after Darnley had taken his seat beside the queen. So appalling were his appearance and manner that the assembled company thought that he was 'raving through the vehemency of a fever'. After the murder, Ruthven, ill though he was, joined the other conspirators in deliberations as to the future government of the country. On Mary's escape to Dunbar, however, they all prudently fled to England, where Ruthven died at Newcastle on 13 June 1566. According to Calderwood, he 'made a Christian end, thanking God for the leisure granted to him to call for mercy'.

By his first wife, Jean Douglas, he had three sons and two daughters, including Patrick, Master of Ruthven and William, fourth Lord Ruthven and first Earl of Gowrie. By his second wife, Lady Jane Stewart, eldest daughter of the second Earl of Atholl, he had one son.

William, fourth Baron and first Earl of Gowrie, was the second son of Patrick, third Lord Ruthven. Like his father, he was implicated in Rizzio's murder and as a result of his forfeit for his part in the plot, his accession was at first only nominal, but through the mediation of the Lords of the Congregation, he, together with Morton (q.v.), was pardoned and permitted to return to Scotland towards the end of December that year.

There is no evidence that Ruthven was aware of the plot to murder Darnley, his cousin, nor was he implicated in the plot. He did not sign the Ainslie Tavern Bond, and his stance against the queen at Carberry may have been solely influenced by a desire to avenge the death of his kinsman. Initially appointed to have charge of the queen during her imprisonment at Lochleven, he was relieved of the duty after charges of partiality towards her had been made against him. His later harshness towards her when obtaining her consent to abdication was marked and, after her escape, he again opposed her and was present at her defeat at Langside.

As Provost of Perth, an office to which he was elected in 1567, he prevented Huntly (q.v.), a supporter of the queen, with a force of 1,000 men, from attending the parliament in 1568, and in July 1569, at the Convention of Perth, he voted against Mary's divorce from Bothwell. Later in the year he was rewarded by Moray for his services with the appointment of Lieutenant of Perth and Bailie and Justice of the king's lands of Scone. During the civil wars which followed, he continued to adhere to Mary's opponents, distinguishing himself in several engagements from the north to the Borders, and in 1571 was appointed Lord High Treasurer for life. He was a commissioner for the Pacification of Perth, and also negotiated with the English ambassador for the arrangements on the capture of Edinburgh Castle.

During the intrigues which led to Morton's resignation and, eventual execution, Ruthven played a leading role, being trusted by both factions, and in September 1578 was one of the eight noblemen entrusted with the reconciliation between them. In November he was appointed an Extraordinary Lord of Session. At the Convention of Dalkeith to discuss Morton's trial, Ruthven became ill and it was rumoured that he had been poisoned, but he recovered. After Morton's execution, he was rewarded for his efforts by being created Earl of Gowrie in August 1581. In October, he was given a grant of the lands and barony of Gowrie, which had previously belonged to the monastery of Scone.

His involvement in the dispute about who should bear the crown at the opening of parliament as next of kin to the crown led to the Ruthven Raid of 1582. Gowrie and other conspirators seized the king in Perth, and compelled him to go to Gowrie's seat of Ruthven Castle, where he was held in the custody of the nobles despite unsuccessful attempts to rescue him. It was thought that Gowrie played a part in the king's escape and when he appeared at St Andrews, he was permitted to enter the king's presence, receiving from him a formal pardon and being appointed a member of his new council. Full remission to him and his servants who had taken part in the raid was granted in December. He then, however, became involved in a plot to seize Stirling Castle and on 13 April 1584 was arrested at Dundee, where he purported to be taking ship into exile. He was taken to Edinburgh and then to Stirling to await his trial for high treason. Since there was no direct proof that he was involved in any plot to abduct the king, he was induced to make a confession and it was this that was the main evidence against him at his trial. Convicted of high treason, he was beheaded at Stirling on 2 May 1584, and his lands were forfeited.

After his execution it was discovered that Gowrie had in his possession the famous casket, in which the incriminating letters which played such a major part in Mary's downfall were discovered. It was probably entrusted to him by Morton. Attempts by Queen Elizabeth to gain possession of it were met initially by Gowrie's refusal to admit that he had it and then by saying that he could not hand it over without the king's permission. After his death, the letters disappeared totally; it is thought that they were given to the king, who in all probability destroyed them.

Gowrie married Dorothea Stewart, daughter of Henry, first Lord Methven, and Jane Stewart, his father's second wife. He had five sons and eight daughters. Two of the sons died in the mysterious Gowrie Conspiracy in 1600. In November that year, parliament pronounced sentence, declaring that the name of Ruthven be abolished for all time. Gowrie's last surviving son, Patrick Ruthven MD, died in the King's Bench prison in May 1652. Queen Mary's vengeance against the Ruthvens had continued until after the death of her grandson, Charles I.

SADLER, SIR RALPH
1507–1587

Born at Hackney, Sadler was the son of a nobleman's steward. He entered the service of Thomas Cromwell, Henry VIII's principal minister, and then that of the king. In 1537 he became the king's emissary to Margaret Tudor, the Queen Mother, who was at odds with her son James V and his pro-French advisers. Sadler succeeded in bringing about an understanding but was less successful, three years later, in persuading James to adopt an anti-church policy. Nonetheless, he retained Henry VIII's confidence, even after the fall of Cromwell, and became a Secretary of State.

With the death of James V, Sadler again became the royal envoy to Scotland. He was deeply involved in the negotiations for the betrothal of the infant Queen Mary to the Prince of Wales but, as before, found the influence of Cardinal Beaton (q.v.) and the French too strong. As Scottish hostility to England deepened, leading to war, Sadler found his life in danger in Edinburgh. He retreated under Douglas protection to Tantallon Castle and thence to the border, returning with the raiding English army.

On the accession of Edward VI and with Somerset as Protector, Sadler's fortunes advanced. He was a friend of Somerset and went with him to Scotland as treasurer of the army and fought with distinction at Pinkie. Somerset's fall from grace, however, weakened Sadler's position and, during the reign of Mary Tudor, he retired altogether from public life. Already a rich man, he settled into life in the country. With the accession of Elizabeth, Sadler returned to court. He formed a strong and lasting alliance with William Cecil (q.v.), the new queen's leading minister. Both were firm Protestants, skilful and careful administrators and strongly impressed with the need to secure English influence in Scottish affairs. Sadler was the diplomat, Cecil the maker of policy. It was Sadler who was entrusted by the minister with the most delicate commissions.

Sadler settled Anglo-Scottish border disputes in 1559 and went on to become Cecil's special commissioner to the Lords of the Congregation. The attempt to maintain England's position in the face of French military power made Sadler very busy in the complex events which led to the treaty of Edinburgh in July 1560. Thereafter, Sadler lived quietly in England until the return of Mary, holding only minor offices. He was by now a big landowner, lived in some state and spent generously. But he was the obvious expert to call on when Mary's affairs became dangerously embroiled with those of England.

He was one of the English commissioners at York and Westminster and had a hot-line to Cecil, regularly reporting to the Secretary of State on the evidence against Mary for complicity in her husband's murder. The casket letters made a significant impression on him. Then followed the long years of Mary's imprisonment. Sadler, by now advanced in years, was frequently consulted. He had already been called to arms during the rebellion of the northern earls. He was called up for duty again in 1584, when he was summoned to replace Lord Shrewsbury as Mary's keeper. Shrewsbury's reputation for over-familiarity with the captive queen, confirmed by his wife, Bess of Hardwicke, had led to his dismissal. Sadler, aged and prudent, was not likely to make the same mistake. His appointment was temporary, but a replacement was hard to find. He complained about the 'cold and miserable country' where he saw only 'woods and mountains'. The Elizabethans were not lovers of wild, romantic scenery and Sadler removed Mary to Tutbury.

Released from his wardership, Sadler was given one last Scottish chore to perform. It fell to him to explain to King James the circumstances of his mother's execution. It was no easy task, although James's wrath could not be sustained in the face of his need for English support. Sadler returned to die at his beloved country house, Standon, in 1587. His wife, Margaret Mitchell, widow of Ralph Barré, like her husband of no ancient lineage, bore him three sons and four daughters. Sadler spent most of his long life in the service of the English crown. For fifty years he was the acknowledged expert on Scottish affairs. Though never attaining the highest rank at court, and rarely a maker of English policy, he maintained a steady influence on the attitude of the Tudors to their northern neighbour.

SETON, GEORGE, 5th BARON SETON
c. 1530–1585

Eldest son of George, fourth Lord Seton, and his first wife, Elizabeth, daughter of John, Lord Hay of Yester,

*George Seton, 5th Baron
Seton, with his wife
Isabel Hamilton of
Sanquhar and their
family, Frans Pourbus the
Elder (National Galleries of
Scotland)*

Seton succeeded his father in 1550. His early education in France may have influenced his strong allegiance to the royal cause with which, throughout his life, he was strongly identified. Despite an early flirtation with the Reformed religion, according to Knox (q.v.), he remained a staunch Catholic, which may have been a factor in his adherence to Mary.

Appointed Provost of Edinburgh in 1557, in the same year he was one of the commissioners sent by the Scottish parliament to France to witness the marriage of Mary to the Dauphin. He accompanied the queen from France to Scotland in 1561, and on her arrival, was appointed a member of her Privy Council, and in 1563 became Master of the Royal Household. A quarrel with Maitland of Lethington (q.v.) in 1564 made it advisable for him to leave the country for a time, and accordingly he went to France, and was absent from the queen's marriage to Darnley, although they spent their honeymoon at his house of Seton, an indication that he still stood high in the queen's favour. He returned shortly afterwards, and was re-admitted to the queen's closest circle.

After the murder of Rizzio, Seton helped Mary to escape on the following night and accompanied her on her flight to Dunbar. He was one of the Catholic noblemen present at the christening of the young prince with the Earls of Eglinton (q.v.) and Atholl (q.v.). After the murder of Darnley, the queen again visited Seton House. Because of his earlier feud with Bothwell (they were commanded to keep the peace in 1561) he was not amongst those who were in favour of his marriage to Mary, but after the marriage, Seton remained faithful to the queen, and it was at Seton that she spent her last night with Bothwell before her surrender to the Lords at Carberry on 15 June 1567.

He was deeply implicated in the plot to free the queen from Lochleven and, after her escape, was waiting on the south shore of the Forth to receive her and to convey her to the safety of his own castle of Niddry before continuing to Hamilton. He was among the leaders at the battle of Langside, at which he was taken prisoner, and conveyed to Edinburgh. He was released in 1569, and following the assassination of Regent Moray (q.v.), was one of the signatories to the letter of May 1570 to Elizabeth, in support of the queen, and later made a half-hearted attempt to raise the people of Edinburgh to the queen's standard. Shortly afterwards, he was sent to seek assistance for the queen from the Duke of Alva, Spanish Viceroy in the Low Countries, where he succeeded in raising some money. While he was there, Mary wrote to the duke, praising Seton's efforts on her behalf and his fidelity to her cause.

He returned to Edinburgh in 1572, and after the fall of the castle, made his peace with Morton's (q.v.) government, and shortly afterwards was made a member of the Privy Council. This did not save him and his sons from excommunication by the Kirk, and soon thereafter, Seton again made his way to France. In July 1578, he was one of the nobles who opposed the reinstatement of Morton. For kidnapping Bowes, the English ambassador, in the same month, he was summoned by the council and on failing to appear, was put to the horn. The following year he was again summoned for having misappropriated the king's goods but, on 12 June, Seton and his eldest surviving son signed a bond, pledging their allegiance to the king and promising to cease communication with Lords John and Claud Hamilton (q.v.), against whom the old charges of the murder of Regents Moray and Lennox (q.v.) had been revived. After the final fall of Morton, in 1581, Seton was one of the lords who conveyed him to Dumbarton and, although Morton quite properly objected to his inclusion, sat as one of the judges at his trial and, with his sons, witnessed his death.

In 1583, James showed his confidence in Seton by appointing him as ambassador to France to negotiate the renewal of the treaty of friendship between the two countries, although in a letter to Mary, Seton assured her that his main reason for accepting the commission was to advance her cause. In March 1584, he wrote to Pope Gregory, informing him of the existence of a rebellion in Scotland and imploring his assistance.

Seton finally returned to Scotland in 1584, and died in January 1585. By his marriage to Isabel, daughter of Sir William Hamilton of Sanquhar, one of the Lords of Council, he had five sons and one daughter: George, who died young; Robert, who succeeded his father as sixth Lord Seton, and married Lady Margaret Montgomerie, daughter of Hugh, Earl of Eglinton; John, who was brought up at the court of Spain; Alexander, later Chancellor of Scotland and Earl of Dunfermline; and William of Kylesmure. His daughter Margaret married Lord Claud Hamilton, afterwards first Lord Paisley.

SINCLAIR, GEORGE, 4th EARL of CAITHNESS
c. 1520–1582

George, as the second but only surviving son of John, third Earl, by his wife, Elizabeth, daughter of William Sutherland of Duffus, succeeded in 1529, when his father was killed trying to suppress feudal warfare among his kinsmen at Somersdale. He showed early signs of the rapacity and aggression which were to be so much a part of his later career; in 1544, in the absence of Robert Stewart, Bishop of Caithness, abetted by his neighbour Donald Mackay, the earl seized the bishop's castles of Skibo and Strabister, and only the intervention of the fourth Earl of Huntly enabled the bishop to regain possession. For this, and other transgressions against his neighbours, the earl was forced to resign the earldom in favour of his son, John, in 1545. His continuing internecine warfare with his neighbour and erstwhile ally, Mackay, resulted in an act being passed against him in 1553, while his refusal to attend the Northern Progress of the Queen Regent, together with other misdemeanours, led to his imprisonment in Edinburgh Castle, from which he was released in 1556 after the payment of a large fine. Later that year, however, he obtained remission for this and other crimes. Notwithstanding his misbehaviour, he was appointed to the office of Justiciar of the land between Portinculter to the Pentland Firth, held by his forebears.

Caithness was among the Catholic lords who urged the return of Mary through Aberdeen, and late in 1561, she appointed him a member of the Privy Council. In 1563, during the Queen's Progress in the North, he was again committed to Edinburgh Castle for murder, but was soon released. He was in Edinburgh at the time of Rizzio's murder, but dreading the return to power of the Protestant Lords, fled three days later with Atholl and other Catholics.

His office of Hereditary Justiciar was confirmed in 1567, although before his appointment, he had promised to attend the Mass. He continued to be loyal to Mary, and was deeply implicated in the murder of Darnley, although this did not prevent him from acting as foreman of the jury in the travesty of a trial which acquitted Bothwell

of the murder. He also subscribed to the bond promoting the marriage of Bothwell and the queen and again showed his support for Mary in 1571 by signing the letter to Elizabeth asking for her intervention in the quarrel between Mary and the supporters of her son. By the end of the civil war in 1572, however, he had become reconciled to Regent Morton (q.v.).

In the main, Caithness concerned himself with the politics of the north, particularly that of his immediate neighbourhood. His feud with the earls of Sutherland (q.v.), whose lands he coveted, led to the murder of the tenth earl and his countess by his cousin Isabel Sinclair. After their deaths, he captured the fifteen-year-old eleventh Earl of Sutherland, and obtained his guardianship. He forced the young man to marry his daughter Barbara, who was then aged thirty-two, but eventually Sutherland escaped and the marriage was annulled. He continued his feud with the Mackays, and made an unprovoked attack on the Murrays, sacking Dornoch Cathedral in the process, and murdering three Murray hostages. His son, John, Master of Caithness, supported the Murrays in this feud and for this act of what Caithness viewed as filial treachery, he imprisoned him in 1571. The privations which the Master suffered at the hands of his gaolers, including being given salt beef to eat but denied anything to drink, led to his death in 1577.

The Earl of Caithness died in Edinburgh in 1582, and was buried in the Rosslyn Chapel. By his marriage to Elizabeth Graham, second daughter of William second Earl of Montrose (q.v.), he had three sons and five daughters. John, Master of Caithness, mentioned above, married in 1566 Jane Hepburn, only daughter of Patrick, third Earl of Bothwell, and their eldest son, George, succeeded his grandfather in 1582. The second son, William, of Mey, was strangled by his brother, the Master, and died before his father, leaving no legitimate heirs. The third son, George, also of Mey, was Chancellor of the Diocese of Caithness, and married, before 1582, Margaret, daughter of William, seventh Lord Forbes, and was ancestor, through their son, William, of the twelfth Earl of Caithness. The daughters were: Barbara, who married Alexander, eleventh Earl of Sutherland (q.v.); Elizabeth, married first to Alexander Sutherland of Duffus, and secondly to Hugh Mackay of Farr; Margaret, who married William Sutherland of Duffus; Barbara, who married Alexander Innes of Innes; and Agnes, who married, as his second wife, Andrew Earl of Erroll.

SINCLAIR, HENRY, of ROSLIN, BISHOP of ROSS
1508–1565
SINCLAIR, JOHN, of ROSLIN, BISHOP of BRECHIN
c. 1511–1566

Henry and John were the younger sons of Sir Oliver Sinclair of Roslin, and the nephews of Sir William Sinclair, second Earl of Caithness, who was killed at Flodden in 1513. Two more of their uncles were Sir David Sinclair of Sumburgh, Governor of Shetland, and John Sinclair, Bishop of Caithness. Their elder brother, another Sir Oliver, was the Scottish commander at the disastrous battle of Solway Moss. Henry and John were both lawyer-bishops – two of the last before the extinction of the species.

Henry Sinclair was born in 1508 and educated at St Andrews University. In 1537, having gained the special favour of James V, he became a Lord of Session and Rector of Glasgow. He added to these offices the abbacy of Kilwinning in 1541. Soon he was engaged in diplomacy in Flanders and France; then he was trying to reform the Court of Session, whose presidency he assumed in 1558. In 1560, the Pope sanctioned his election to the bishopric of Ross. As a judge-prelate, Henry joined Queen Mary's Privy Council in 1561, the only ecclesiastic among its members. In a lawless age, when religious passion prevailed, his concern was for the upholding of law. He restricted Mary to holding Mass within her own chapel, and censured Knox's (q.v.) followers for attacking it. Knox abused him with typical vehemence, but Henry would not convict him for sacrilege on poor evidence. The English mocked his religious ambiguity, yet thought him a good diplomat and jurist. He was ever the practical man of law and may have assisted his brother in composing a lawyer's handbook or *Practick*. He died in Paris after an unsuccessful operation for 'the stone', in 1565.

John Sinclair made his mark on Scottish history in the same year. He also was a churchman-lawyer – a Lord of Session and Dean of Restalrig. Knox thought that he might have turned Protestant but for Catholic pressure. He was certainly one of the Catholic party at Mary's court. It was in this capacity that he officiated at the marriage of the queen and Darnley at Holyrood on 29 June 1565. John's fee was the bishopric of Brechin. He died in 1566 after a brief episcopate.

STEWART, ANDREW, 2nd BARON OCHILTREE
c. 1520–c. 1597

The son of Andrew, third Lord Avandale and first Lord Ochiltree, by Margaret Hamilton, daughter of James, first Earl of Arran, he succeeded his father in 1548. In 1549, he received a grant of the lands of Pennymore, Ayrshire, and in 1557, the lands of Barloch-hill.

Ochiltree came to the relief of the Protestants at Perth in 1559, and subscribed to the contract between Queen Elizabeth and the Lords of the Congregation in May 1560. He went with Knox (q.v.) to Holyrood in 1563 to lend him support in his assertion that Mary Queen of Scots should not marry a papist.

He supported Moray (q.v.) on the Chaseabout Raid in the autumn of 1565 and on 1 December was declared lese-majesty. He supported the lords who conspired to murder Rizzio, and took an active part against the queen after Darnley was assassinated. He subscribed the acts of the assembly in July 1567 when the murder and popery met the same condemnation, and attended the infant king's coronation the same month.

At the battle of Langside, on 13 May 1568, he fought against the queen and was wounded by Lord Herries (q.v.). Consistently against Mary, he voted against her divorce from Bothwell in 1569. After the murder of Regent Moray, he was one of the nobles who carried the body from Holyrood to St Giles.

After Moray's death, Ochiltree largely ceased to take an active part in politics, although he was one of the new Privy Council chosen after Morton's (q.v.) return to power in July 1578. In the light of the fact, however, that Ochiltree's son, Captain James Stewart, later Earl of Arran, was one of Morton's accusers of the Darnley murder, the relationship cannot have been an easy one.

Towards the end of his life, Ochiltree was much preoccupied with two murders: the first, that of his own son by the fifth Earl of Bothwell in 1588, and the second, that of the 'bonnie' Earl of Moray by the sixth Earl (later first Marquis) of Huntly in 1592. Ochiltree pursued both culprits with great vigour but little effect. He died some time between December 1593 and March 1601.

By his wife Agnes, daughter of John Cunningham of Caprington, he had five sons and two daughters: Andrew, Master of Ochiltree, who died in 1578; Captain James of Bothwellmuir, afterwards Earl of Arran; Sir William of Monkton; Sir Henry of Nether Gogar; Robert of Wester Braco; Isabel, married to Thomas Kennedy of Bargeny; and Margaret, who was the second wife of John Knox (q.v.), and later married Andrew Ker of Fawdonside (q.v.).

Ochiltree was succeeded by his grandson, Andrew, who was a Gentleman of the Bedchamber to James VI, Governor of Edinburgh Castle, and in 1619 became Baron Castle Stewart in the peerage of Ireland.

STEWART, LORD JAMES, later EARL OF MAR, EARL of MORAY, REGENT of SCOTLAND 1531–1570

A natural son of James V, his mother was Lady Margaret Erskine, the younger daughter of John, fifth Baron Erskine. She had been a favourite mistress of the king and, consequently, had detested Mary of Guise (q.v.) whom he married in 1538. Her antipathy was extended to Queen Mary who, of course, would not have come to the throne had her son James been legitimate. She was married to Sir Robert Douglas of Lochleven.

James was made Commendator of St Andrews priory in 1538, and attended the university there from 1541 to 1544, but there is no evidence that he graduated. He accompanied the five-year-old Queen Mary to France in 1548, but was back in Scotland the following year, when he repelled a force of English raiders under Lord Clinton in Fife, and drove them back to their ships. The English lost 600 killed and wounded, and 100 prisoners. He was an early sympathiser with the Reformed Church, and in March 1557, with four others, signed a letter inviting John Knox (q.v.) to return to Scotland.

In December 1557 he was appointed to be one of eight commissioners to go

Lord James Stewart, Earl of Moray, Regent of Scotland, *School of Antonio Mor, mid-16th century (Lennoxlove)*

to France to represent Scotland at the marriage of Queen Mary to the Dauphin François (q.v.). The fact that they did not send for the crown of Scotland caused much ill feeling, and most of them, including James, were attacked by a sudden illness on the way home, supposedly poisoned by the Guises. Four of them died, but Lord James recovered although he suffered the after-effects for the rest of his life.

On the outbreak of the revolt against the Queen Dowager and Regent, Mary of Guise, in May 1559, he initially supported her and negotiated on her behalf but, on discovering that she was making agreements which she had no intention of keeping, he deserted her and became her implacable enemy until her death on 10 June 1560.

He was a signatory of the Treaty of Berwick in February 1560, leading the

239

provisional government after the death of the regent, and being seriously considered for the throne should Queen Mary stay in France. But Mary's husband, now François II, died, leaving her Queen Dowager of France, and it became clear that she would come back to Scotland. James was sent to France to negotiate the conditions for her return in the light of the views of the reformers. He made it clear that Mary would be free to worship privately in her own (Catholic) way, but that Scotland had now irreversibly become a Protestant country. Mary accepted, and returned on 19 August 1561. James was made a member of the new Privy Council on 6 September and, for the first three and a half years of her reign, was her right-hand man and was largely responsible for laying down the policy for governing the country.

On 7 February 1562 he was created Earl of Mar, and the following day he was married by John Knox (q.v.) to Agnes Keith, eldest daughter of William Earl Marischal (q.v.). In July he led an expedition against the thieves of Liddesdale, and compelled the fourth Earl of Bothwell, then a fugitive from justice, to leave the country. In August of the same year he accompanied Mary on an expedition against the over-mighty Catholic Highland chief of the Gordons, the fourth Earl of Huntly (q.v.). The campaign ended with Huntly's defeat and death at the battle of Corrichie. At the beginning of the campaign Mary announced that she had given James the lands and earldom of Moray, which had previously been held by Huntly. One by one his rivals were being eliminated, and after it became clear that the young

third Earl of Arran (q.v.) was insane, Moray (as he now was) had things more or less his own way until the arrival of Lord Darnley on the scene.

Moray was strongly against Queen Elizabeth's plan to foist the 'shopsoiled widower', the Earl of Leicester (q.v.), in marriage on his half-sister, and he was even more opposed to the match with Darnley. As he saw it, both his personal career, and his policy of reconciliation with England, were threatened. Following months of plotting before the wedding, which took place on 29 June 1565, he raised a futile rebellion (the Chaseabout Raid) immediately after it. The revolt was easily crushed by the queen's forces, and in October he was forced to take refuge in England, where he found that Elizabeth had no time for a loser.

From England he entered negotiations with Darnley and the lords involved in the Rizzio conspiracy. The plan was that Darnley would be given the 'crown matrimonial', enabling all his heirs to succeed and not just his children by Mary; Rizzio would be murdered; the queen would be detained; and pardons would be given to the leaders of the Chaseabout Raid, including Moray, who would resume power. The murder took place on 9 March 1566. Moray returned to Edinburgh the following day and, having persuaded Mary of his non-involvement, was reconciled to her. The murderers were still in possession of Holyrood, so Mary persuaded Darnley to detach himself from them and escape with her to Dunbar that night. The conspirators immediately took refuge in England.

Late in 1566 Moray became aware of

plots against Darnley. It is probable that he knew of the Kirk o' Field conspiracy, as he prudently left Edinburgh the afternoon before the murder – albeit to visit his sick wife. Equally prudently, he decided to take no part in Mary's deposition and went abroad, returning in time to give his half-sister a terrifying lecture, just after her abdication, in Lochleven Castle. He was formally installed regent on 22 August 1567. After Mary escaped from Lochleven, Moray led the army which defeated her forces at Langside on 13 May 1568.

Early in 1569 he went to York to take part in Mary's first trial. The proceedings were inconclusive: Moray and his adherents were not found to have proved their case; Mary was not found guilty; Elizabeth did not deliver judgement; and Moray returned to Scotland to resume his government.

In his short period as regent he did much to maintain law and order and secure the position of the Reformed Church. Although he made several attempts at reconciliation, he had many enemies among the supporters of Queen Mary, especially the Hamiltons. On 3 January 1570 James Hamilton of Bothwellhaugh (q.v.) hid himself in the house of his kinsman, Archbishop John Hamilton (q.v.), in Linlithgow. The regent was due to go past that afternoon. Bothwellhaugh had a gun which had to be ignited with a fuse and his target was a moving one, so his task was not easy. However, he made no mistake, and Moray fell. The regent was taken to a nearby house where he died late that night, urging those around him not to exact excessive vengeance.

By his wife Agnes he had no sons.

His elder daughter, Elizabeth married James Stewart, eldest son of Sir James Stewart of Doune. His son-in-law became the ultra-Protestant 'Bonnie Earl of Moray' and was murdered by the Catholic-leaning sixth Earl of Huntly at Donibristle on 7 February 1592.

STEWART, JOHN, 4th EARL of ATHOLL, CHANCELLOR of SCOTLAND
c. 1518–1579

The eldest son of John, third Earl of Atholl, and Grizel, daughter of Sir John Rattray of that ilk, John the fourth Earl succeeded his father in 1542. In 1554 he was an ally of Mary of Guise (q.v.) in her successful efforts to supplant the Duke of Chatêlherault (q.v.) as regent. He continued to back her in her contest with the Lords of the Congregation in 1559, and was one of only three lords to vote against the Confession of Faith at the parliament of 17 July that year. On 23 September 1559, however, he joined the fifth Earl of Argyll (q.v.) and Lord James Stewart (q.v.) in a perpetual league against the fourth Earl of Huntly (q.v.), whose power in the north was becoming unbridled. Although still a Catholic, his new support for the Protestant party was demonstrated by his adherence to the movement in favour of the marriage of Queen Elizabeth to Chatêlherault's son, the third Earl of Arran.

After Queen Mary's return in 1561, Atholl was appointed to her Privy Council and for a time worked harmoniously with Lord James, although he was always on more intimate terms with Maitland of Lethington (q.v.). He accompanied the queen and Lord James, whom Mary had elevated to the earldom of Moray, on the expedition to the north in August 1562, which ended with Huntly's defeat and death at Corrichie on 28 October.

With the demise of Huntly, the Scottish Catholic nobles now looked to Atholl for leadership. When in May 1565, Moray withdrew from court in disgust at Mary's proposed marriage to Darnley, Atholl superseded him as the queen's chief councillor. On the outbreak of the Chaseabout Raid after the marriage, he was named Lieutenant in the North and on 23 August, he was detached to counter the rebel Earl of Argyll. On 10 October, he was appointed to lead the rearguard of the force for the suppression of Moray, although the latter had crossed the border into England four days earlier, and the rebellion was over.

Atholl had no connection with the plot to murder Rizzio, and possibly did not even know of Darnley's grievances against Mary. On the evening of 9 March 1566, he was at supper in Holyrood with Bothwell and some other lords, including the fifth Earl of Huntly (q.v.), whose family was now reconciled with the queen. Alarmed by the uproar in the royal apartments and finding themselves surrounded by Morton's armed men, they escaped through a window at the back of the palace. Mary and Darnley escaped the following night, and made their way to Dunbar, where Atholl and the other loyal lords joined them. Atholl then helped to raise a force of 8,000 men and accompanied Mary at the head of it on

her triumphal return to Edinburgh.

It was with Atholl that Maitland sought refuge after the murder. Maitland was implicated in that he knew in advance of the conspiracy although he took no part in it. Atholl, who was probably not unhappy at Rizzio's removal, interceded with Mary on behalf of Maitland, who was duly allowed to return to court.

Atholl was also kept in the dark about the plot against Darnley with whom he was still on good terms. He had, however, witnessed the ascendancy of Bothwell with dismay and was so horrified by the king's assassination on 10 February 1567, and the queen's association with the principal murderer, that he immediately took up arms against her, and joined the Protestant lords. One of the leaders who accepted her surrender on 15 June 1567 at Carberry, he approved of her removal to Lochleven Castle.

He was one of those with Morton (q.v.) when the casket containing the alleged letters from Mary to Bothwell was opened and the contents were first read on 19 July 1567. He was present at the queen's abdication at Lochleven on 26 July, and at the coronation of the infant King James VI at Stirling on the 29th. He served as one of the Council of Regency until Moray returned from abroad to become regent.

Gradually, however, Atholl's sympathies moved back towards the queen, especially at the time of her escape from Lochleven on 2 May 1568. Although not supporting her openly, and not at the battle of Langside, he was secretly in close touch with Maitland with a view to her restoration. To this end, in 1569, he voted in support of her divorce from Bothwell. After Moray's assassination in 1570, with Maitland, Huntly and others, he joined the Hamiltons in a league against the king's party.

Atholl deplored the election of Lennox (q.v.) as regent in July 1570, and two years later tried to prevent the election of Morton to the same office. In 1574, proceedings were taken against him as a papist without any concrete results. In 1578, he joined the sixth Earl of Argyll, the brother of his old enemy, in a coalition to oust Morton. They were successful, and a council of regency was appointed, with Atholl as a member. On 29 March, he became Chancellor of Scotland.

But Morton was not yet finished. On 5 May 1578, he obtained entrance to Stirling Castle and resumed his custody of the eleven-year-old king. Atholl and Argyll marched on Stirling with 7,000 men. A reconciliation, however, took place through the intervention of Sir Robert Bowes the English ambassador. It was decided that Atholl and Argyll should be added to the new council which was to assist Morton in the government.

After a banquet to celebrate the reconciliation, at Stirling Castle, Atholl was seized with a violent illness, from which he died on 24 or 25 April 1579. It was suspected that Morton had poisoned him but this was never proved.

Atholl had two daughters by his first wife, Elizabeth Gordon, daughter of the fourth Earl of Huntly. By his second wife, Margaret, daughter of the third Lord Fleming, he had three daughters and a son, John, fifth Earl of Atholl, on whose death in 1595 the earldom reverted to the crown. Margaret was said to be a sorceress and, when the queen was in labour in June 1566, she endeavoured to transfer Mary's pains of childbirth onto Lady Reres, causing considerable discomfort to the latter and little or no relief to the former.

STEWART, LORD JOHN, COMMENDATOR of COLDINGHAM
c. 1532–1563

A natural son of James V by Elizabeth, daughter of John, Lord Carmichael, he was half-brother of Queen Mary and Lord James Stewart (q.v.). He was made Prior of Coldingham at the age of only three and in 1546, Mary of Guise (q.v.) bestowed on him the lands of Greigston.

In 1560, he renounced popery, and the following year, the recently returned Queen Mary committed the stronghold of Dunbar to his custody. In December 1561, he was involved with the fourth Earl of Bothwell (q.v.) to abduct one 'Alison Craik', who was thought to be the mistress of the third Earl of Arran (q.v.). This exercise was reported to have 'highly commoved all Godly hearts'. In January 1562, he married Jane Hepburn, sister of Bothwell, at Seton 'with good sport and many pastimes'.

He died at the end of 1563 while holding Justice Courts in Inverness, and is reputed to have asked God's forgiveness for his wickedness. Knox (q.v.) expressed the view that he had good reason to repent, especially as he had expressed the desirability of 'sticking

The Darnley Vengeance picture. Included are the Earl of Lennox, the Countess of Lennox, and the future King James VI, in front of the corpse of Darnley. This painting hangs in the Palace of Holyrood not far from the scene of Rizzio's murder. In the bottom left-hand corner may be seen a reproduction of the scene at Carberry. L. de Vogeleer, 16th century, oil on panel (Reproduced by Gracious permission of Her Majesty The Queen)

Knox in his pulpit rather than that he should trouble the Queen as he was doing'.

By Lady Jane Hepburn, he had two sons, Francis, later fifth Earl of Bothwell, and Hercules.

STEWART, MATTHEW, 4th EARL of LENNOX 1516–1571

Son of John, third Earl of Lennox and Elizabeth, eighth daughter of John Stewart, first Earl of Atholl, Matthew succeeded in 1526 after his father's murder by James Hamilton of Finnart, a natural son of the first Earl of Arran. This act, allied to the two families, opposing claims to be heirs to the throne of Scotland, further exacerbated the enmity between Lennox's family and the Hamiltons.

Lennox first sat in parliament in 1531, and the following year went to France where he was naturalised as a French subject in 1537. A grant to him and his heirs of the keepership of Dumbarton Castle in 1531 was to have an important effect on his future. On the death of James V in 1542, Lennox was induced by Cardinal Beaton (q.v.) to return to Scotland to assist in the overthrow of Regent Arran (q.v.). He was given hope of marrying the Queen Dowager and, on the grounds of Arran's alleged illegitimacy, being named heir presumptive to the infant queen. Landing at Dumbarton in 1543, he joined with the other lords in rescuing the Queen Dowager and her daughter from Edinburgh. Arran, thoroughly alarmed by his rival's success, had by now come to terms with Cardinal Beaton. Lennox, suspecting that the cardinal's true purpose was to use him for his own self-aggrandisement, immediately sought a new ally. Despite his citizenship of both France and Scotland, he immediately offered his services to Henry VIII, in

244

return for the king's agreement for him to marry Lady Margaret Douglas (q.v.), Henry's niece. The price for Henry's agreement to this proposal was Dumbarton Castle, a price which Lennox was initially not prepared to pay.

After an abortive attempt to reconcile him to Arran's governorship, Lennox decided in January 1544 to join the sixth Earl of Angus (q.v.) and the other lords of the English party, and marched with them on Edinburgh where they were routed by the much stronger forces of Arran. Following this débâcle, despite an agreement signed by both parties to obey the queen's rule, Lennox continued his negotiations with England. In March of the same year, he finally agreed to hand over to the king of England several of the strongest fortresses in Scotland, including Dumbarton, and to promote the marriage of the young queen to Prince Edward, Henry's son. In return Lennox was to marry the Lady Margaret and be appointed governor in place of Arran. The third Earl of Glencairn, for his part in this treacherous act, was rewarded with a pension of 1,000 crowns per annum. Moreover, Lennox agreed to become a Protestant and promote the Reformed faith in Scotland. As a final act of treachery, when signing the treaty for his marriage on 26 June in London, he agreed to give up to Henry what title he had to the Scottish throne, and to support Henry's claim to be overlord of Scotland. On 10 July 1544, Lennox received letters of naturalisation, and on the same day married Lady Margaret.

In her, he had made the ideal match. He was indolent and of mediocre intellect; she was the opposite, uniting in her personality the ambition and resolution of the Tudors with the cunning and courage of the Douglases. She set out to obtain for her house all that could be attained, and made the most of every political opportunity that presented itself. Immediately after the marriage, Henry forced Lennox to keep his side of the bargain, sending him on an expedition to the west of Scotland with the title of Lieutenant for the North of England and South of Scotland. Landing at Dumbarton on 10 August with a force of eighteen ships and about 600 men, he was first welcomed by the captain of the castle, Stirling of Glorat, but when Lennox claimed it for the English, the captain and garrison immediately took up arms, and Lennox and his retinue, in fear of their lives, were forced to flee. Passing down the Clyde, they were fired on by the fourth Earl of Argyll (q.v.) from Dunoon Castle, but landed and laid waste a large part of Bute before returning to Bristol, having achieved nothing by their expedition. A further expedition mounted from Dublin also ended in failure when it was discovered that Dumbarton was in the hands of Arran, Lennox's lands having been distributed to various nobles when he was formally declared a traitor by the Scottish parliament. In 1547, while Somerset routed the Scots at Pinkie Cleugh, Lennox ravaged the west of Scotland with Wharton, and obtained the submission of Annandale. He took part in a further invasion of Scotland the following year.

While Mary Tudor was on the throne of England, Lennox flourished, but with the accession of Elizabeth his fortunes changed. She refused to recognise his wife's rights to the succession to the Scottish and English crowns, and consequently their house at Temple Newsam in Yorkshire became the focus of Catholic intrigue in Britain. With the death of François II (q.v.), and the sudden availability of the young Queen Mary, their hopes became concentrated on their son, Henry Lord Darnley. By his marriage to the widowed queen of Scotland, who also claimed to be the rightful queen of England, both crowns might be secured for their descendants.

Lennox now sought to return to Scotland, the way having been prepared in 1559, but this so alarmed Elizabeth that she sent him to the Tower, and it was not until 1564 that his request was granted. That both Moray (q.v.) and Maitland (q.v.) 'were disposed to further rather than to hinder his coming' was a factor in his favour.

Lennox arrived in Scotland in September 1564, and shortly afterwards his attainder was repealed, a necessary preliminary before he could appear at court, which he did on 23 September. His lands were restored to him on 9 October, and on the 27th, he and Châtelherault were formally reconciled at Holyrood, although all were aware of the empty formality of the act. Shortly afterwards, Elizabeth permitted Darnley to go to Scotland, but on learning that Mary had determined to marry him, she summoned both Lennox and Darnley to return to England on 10 June 1565, a summons which both ignored.

Despite the marriage of his son to Mary, Lennox received no political appointments of importance. Although he was appointed lieutenant of the western counties in September, and commanded the vanguard of the army against Moray and the rebel lords in the Chaseabout Raid, he was a figurehead, resented by the nobles and despised by the queen. The absence of his wife, who alone could control both husband and son, but who had been detained by Elizabeth in England, was disastrous for both. Lennox was privy to the plot to murder Rizzio, and it is probable that it was his unwise counsel which led Darnley into the ways leading to his downfall and eventual death. When Darnley proposed to leave the kingdom, and desert Mary, it was Lennox who warned the queen of his intentions.

Following Darnley's murder, Lennox appealed to Mary to call a meeting of the council, so that the perpetrators of the murder might be apprehended. When this was refused, Lennox formally accused Bothwell of the crime on 24 March, with the demand that he be brought to trial. This could not be ignored but, at the trial, Lennox was unable to appear as Bothwell's accuser, since the accused had filled the city with his own supporters. Lennox deemed it wise to bring a force for his own protection but, when the queen learned that a force of almost 3,000 men was approaching the city, she forbade him to be accompanied by more than six. Fearing for his life, Lennox sought to send his servant, Robert Cunningham, as his substitute, but this was denied, and the result was the acquittal of Bothwell partially on the grounds that no accuser had appeared.

On 29 April, Lennox decided that a longer stay in Scotland was neither warranted nor safe, and returned to England, but after the queen's surrender at Carberry in June, and her imprisonment at Lochleven, he returned to Scotland in July. On the queen's escape, he joined the lords who opposed her at Langside and, in 1569, delivered a paper at the Westminster Conference which accused the queen of conspiracy against the life of his son. After the assassination of Moray in January 1570, Lennox was, on the recommendation of Elizabeth, chosen regent on 12 July. The appointment found favour in no quarter, and the queen's supporters declared, at the parliament held at Linlithgow on 10 August, that they would never acknowledge him as regent, while Kirkcaldy of Grange (q.v.) declared openly for the queen and resolved to hold Edinburgh Castle on her behalf.

The fifth Earl of Huntly (q.v.) assembled his forces and marched south, but was surprised and defeated by Lennox at Brechin on 18 August. Elizabeth mediated between the two parties, which agreed to a ceasefire for two months on 12 January 1571. This was broken in February by the Hamiltons at Paisley, but Lennox quickly defeated them, and when on 2 April one of Lennox's adherents, Captain Thomas Crawford, succeeded in capturing the well-nigh impregnable stronghold of Dumbarton, the power of the regent was established over the west of the country.

Lennox then turned his attention to the east. On 13 April Kirkcaldy published an act of defiance against the regent in Edinburgh, and Lennox, having arrived at Leith on 11 May with a large force, fortified an area of the Canongate on 14 May to enable him to hold a parliament within the city. After several acts of forfeiture had been pronounced, the parliament was adjourned, to be reconvened in Stirling. On 4 September the main party of the regent's supporters were surprised there by an armed force sent by Kirkcaldy from Edinburgh, and many of the nobility, including the regent, were taken prisoner. A rescue was effected by Mar (q.v.), but not before the regent had been stabbed in the back by Captain Calder. The mortally wounded Lennox rode back to the castle, where he died, but not before commending the care of the young king to the assembled nobles, and charging Mar with the task of carrying his last message to his wife. He was buried in the Chapel Royal of Stirling.

By Lady Margaret, Lennox had four sons and four daughters, of which only two sons survived infancy: Henry, Lord Darnley; and Charles, who succeeded only to the lordship of Darnley and the family estates, the earldom reverting to James VI. James, however, conferred the earldom of Lennox on Charles the following year although he had only four years to enjoy it. In that time, however, Charles married Elizabeth Cavendish, daughter of Bess of Hardwicke, by whom he had an only daughter, Arabella Stewart, who died in the Tower of London in 1615.

STEWART, ROBERT, BISHOP of CAITHNESS
c. 1517–1586

The second son of John, third Earl of Lennox, and his wife, Elizabeth

Stewart, daughter of John, first Earl of Atholl, Stewart was the brother of Regent Lennox (q.v.). He was created seventh Earl of Lennox in 1578 by James VI, his great-nephew. On the rise of his own nephew, Esmé Stewart, who became the king's favourite, Robert resigned the title in his favour in 1580, receiving the title of Earl of March instead.

Intended for the priesthood, he was Provost of Dumbarton College, and Canon of Canterbury, and was elected Bishop of Caithness in 1542. On being forfeited with his brother, he went abroad where he remained for twenty-two years. He was never ordained. On his return, he moved with the times and became Protestant, but nevertheless continued to bear the title of Bishop of Caithness, and to enjoy the revenues of the diocese. From his brother, Regent Lennox, he obtained the gift of the priory of St Andrews.

Described as a simple man, 'of lyttle action or accompte', he died at St Andrews in March 1586. In 1579, at the age of sixty-two, he married Elizabeth, daughter of John, fourth Earl of Atholl, widow of Hugh, Lord Fraser of Lovat, but she obtained a decree of nullity in May 1581, and there were no children.

STEWART, LORD ROBERT, later EARL of ORKNEY 1533–1593

A natural son of James V, by Euphemia, daughter of Alexander Elphinstone, first Lord Elphinstone, he was half-brother of Queen Mary, and Lord James Stewart (q.v.). In 1539, the king gave him the abbacy of Holyrood, and in 1552

he became a member of the Privy Council. He was one of the early members of the Lords of the Congregation and, in 1559, was present during the surprise attack of the French on the Canongate and, on their withdrawal, was one of the first to follow them in pursuit. He subscribed to the Treaty of Berwick in May 1560, and attended parliament later that year, which renounced papistry.

On the return of Queen Mary, he and his half-brother, Lord John (q.v.), placed themselves at the disposal of Lord James, and protected the Catholic priest after the celebration of Mary's first Mass, and conveyed him to his chamber.

He took no part in the murder of Darnley, but almost certainly had foreknowledge of the crime, since he warned the king of the mischief intended against him shortly after his arrival at Kirk o' Field.

In 1569, Lord Robert exchanged the temporalities of Holyrood for the temporal estates of the See of Orkney with Adam Bothwell, Bishop of Orkney. He was, however, soon at loggerheads with the Bishop who, in 1570, explained that Lord Robert had 'violently intruded himself on his whole living with bloodshed and hurt of his servants'.

In 1575, he was accused of treason, in offering the Isles of Orkney to the King of Denmark, and in August of that year was imprisoned, on the orders of Regent Morton (q.v.), in the Castle of Orkney, where he remained until Morton's resignation. Thereafter, he was one of the chief conspirers towards Morton's ruin, and in January 1581 joined those who conveyed the ex-regent to imprisonment in Dumbarton Castle.

On 21 October 1581, King James VI created him Earl of Orkney. He died in 1592. By his wife, Lady Janet Kennedy, eldest daughter of Gilbert, third Earl of Cassilis, he had five sons and four daughters, including Patrick, who succeeded him as the infamous second (Stewart) Earl of Orkney.

THROCKMORTON, SIR NICHOLAS 1515–1576

The fourth of eight sons of Sir George Throckmorton and Katherine, daughter of Lord Vaux, Nicholas's mother was an aunt of Catherine Parr, sixth wife of Henry VIII. Sir George gained the enmity of Thomas Cromwell, Henry's powerful minister, and so Nicholas's early rise became difficult. After Catherine Parr married the king, the Throckmorton interests revived. Nicholas, already a Protestant sympathiser, became a member of parliament and a court official. Under Protector Somerset, he began to become a man of influence.

He accompanied Somerset to Scotland in 1547 and was knighted. When the protector's power waned, he switched his allegiance to the new strong man of Edward VI's minority, Northumberland, to the extent of condoning the latter's abortive attempt to place Lady Jane Grey on the throne instead of Mary Tudor. The accession of Mary placed Throckmorton in a difficult position. He made his peace with the new queen, but was soon charged with complicity in Wyatt's rebellion in 1554. Acquitted by the jury (a rare happening in a treason trial), Throckmorton

Sir Nicholas Throckmorton, *artist unknown, inscribed c. 1562 (National Portrait Gallery)*

remained under a cloud of royal disapproval, as did the jury.

With the accession of Elizabeth, Throckmorton, who had been her friend in Mary's reign, came into his own. He was the associate of Cecil (q.v.), Dudley (Leicester) (q.v.) and one of the new breed of Protestant, nationalist politicians. Cecil indeed thought of him as a successor for the secretaryship. Yet he was not included in the queen's council. Though he warned Elizabeth against hasty religious change, he had the reputation for a 'too exuberant Protestantism'. Instead, Throckmorton became ambassador to Paris, which was a key diplomatic post as it involved Scottish as well as French affairs. It was Throckmorton's task to advise Cecil on French reactions to the Protestants' attacks on Mary of Guise (q.v.) in Scotland, especially at Leith. Good Protestant as he was, he favoured a strong English policy on Scotland, assuring Elizabeth, who was always

249

hesitant, that the French would not intervene. The result was the Treaty of Edinburgh, to which Throckmorton could not get Mary of Guise to agree.

The death of François II (q.v.) involved Throckmorton in the proposals for the remarriage of Mary and, more immediately, her return to Scotland. He met Lord James Stewart (q.v.) in Paris and forged a working relationship with him. He wanted Elizabeth to give Mary help to go to Edinburgh and was dismayed by her refusal. But at least Elizabeth did not block the return. By this time Throckmorton was Cecil's chief confidant in diplomatic affairs, but there were signs that the minister and the ambassador were not wholly at one.

With the Huguenots in open rebellion in France, Throckmorton espoused their cause. He was more bellicose and urgent on their behalf than Cecil could allow. By 1562, Throckmorton was probably drawing closer to Leicester, Cecil's rival at Court, and he became the proponent of a war policy on behalf of the Protestants. Eventually Throckmorton was replaced by Sir Thomas Smith, a more pacific diplomat but, unable to leave, he conducted a joint, if mutually hostile, embassy. Captured by Protestant rebels, he actually took part in the battle of Dreux. Peace came to the two parties at Troyes in 1564 although Throckmorton accused Smith of betraying England's cause and the two ambassadors actually drew daggers on each other during the negotiations.

England's attention then shifted to Scotland and the matter of Queen Mary's marriage. While Elizabeth mistrusted Throckmorton's excessive Protestant zeal and Cecil disliked his political ambitions, he was sent on a mission to Edinburgh to dissuade Mary from marrying Darnley and present a case for Leicester. He failed, and then presented a memorandum advocating a forceful response by England when the Darnley marriage took place. Cecil and the Privy Council were greatly impressed, but once again Elizabeth took no decisive action.

Throckmorton returned to Scotland during Mary's imprisonment at Lochleven. He was charged with conveying Elizabeth's displeasure at the queen's treatment and her alarm at the possibility of Mary's execution. Believing he could accomplish little, Throckmorton wanted to return home. Elizabeth agreed, and then changed her mind. She wished Throckmorton to secure the regency for Moray, as a guarantee of Mary's safety. To a degree he was successful and, as a firm Protestant, he was keen on the regency, believing that with Moray as regent, the lords would not kill the queen.

French affairs then took Throckmorton's attention. He was a fervent supporter of the Huguenot cause. But in Elizabeth's year of crisis, 1569, he allied with some unlikely supporters to favour the marriage of the Duke of Norfolk to the captive Mary. For this, he spent some time in custody and died in London, soon after his release, on 12 February 1571. He had earlier dined with Leicester although the rumour that Throckmorton was poisoned by his host is untrue. Leicester, who generally took a strongly Protestant stance, had become something of an ally, since both were resentful of Cecil's predominance.

Throckmorton was able, witty and

well-informed. His letters, especially to Cecil, are an historian's delight. But he lacked stability and often let his religious enthusiasm outrun his diplomatic discretion. So he never achieved the high office to which he felt entitled. He had married Anne, daughter of Sir Nicholas Carew, who bore him two sons and three daughters.

WALSINGHAM, SIR FRANCIS 1530–1590

The only son of William Walsingham, a lawyer and city official with estates in Kent, Francis lost his father at an early age. He was educated at King's College, Cambridge and at Gray's Inn, London. He was already a staunch Protestant and when Mary Tudor came to throne, he went abroad. He acquired an extensive knowledge of European laws, customs and people and began to construct the network of acquaintances that served him in good stead in later life. Back in England after Elizabeth's accession, he became a member of parliament. Although he held no official post, he came to be used by the government, especially Cecil (q.v.), in acquiring and assessing information from the Continent. This culminated, in 1569, in his unofficial, but very significant, role as the controller of the secret service. In this capacity he helped unravel the Ridolfi plot.

Walsingham married Anne, the daughter of Sir George Barnes and widow of Alexander Carleill, but she died in 1564 without bearing him any children, although she left him the custody of her son by her first marriage and considerable estates. In 1567 he married another widow, Ursula Worsley, who bore him two daughters, one of whom, Mary, died unmarried in 1580. The other, Frances, married successively Sir Philip Sidney; Robert Devereux, second Earl of Essex; and Richard de Burgh, Earl of Clanricarde.

By 1570 Walsingham was being entrusted with dealing with the French, both over the Huguenot rebels and Elizabeth's marriage negotiations. His skills as a diplomat and his strong Protestantism were clearly evident. Succeeding Cecil as Secretary of State, Walsingham inherited, and greatly enhanced, the system of informers and spies at home and abroad that state security seemed to require. Nonetheless, he was no cold-blooded realist, having a passionate devotion to the Protestant cause, and believing England to be its champion. He could be ruthless in pursuing these ideals in a way that the moderate Cecil and the temporising Elizabeth were not.

In Scottish affairs Walsingham's role, although generally subordinate to that of Cecil, was unambiguous. He upheld Regent Morton (q.v.) as the friend of England and Reform. He viewed James VI's assumption of personal rule with alarm and sought to strengthen the Douglas faction against the king's pro-French and pro-Catholic favourites. After James escaped from the Ruthven Raiders and reassembled his own advisers, Walsingham led an elaborate embassy to Edinburgh in 1583 to bring him to a better understanding with England. The embassy, in Walsingham's estimation, was unsuccessful, although the canny James was less under the influence of his mother, the French Catholics, or anyone else, than Walsingham believed. From then on, Walsingham advocated a sterner English policy. But, fearful of attempts to return Mary to the Scottish throne, he came to see that James must be conciliated and this is largely what led to the agreement of July 1585 and the League of Edinburgh a year later.

For Walsingham, the stern Puritan nationalist, the Catholic Mary Queen of Scots was the ultimate threat. Since 1570 he had been at the centre of the government's intelligence system. He did not handle the complex Ridolfi plot well; the Throckmorton plot, on the other hand, was thoroughly exposed. The Babington plot sealed Mary's fate, as it was intended to do. Henceforward Walsingham, though he had fallen out with his fellow-Puritan sympathiser, Leicester (q.v.), maintained pressure on Elizabeth to execute Mary. The Spanish Armada of 1588 was, in a sense, the vindication of Walsingham's policy.

He died on 6 April 1590. Cecil wrote to a mutual friend: '. . . though he hath gained a better estate, as I am fully persuaded, for his soul is in heaven, yet the Queen's Majesty and her realm and I and others, his particular friends, have had a great loss, both for the public use of his good and painful long services and for the private comfort I had by his mutual friendship!'

Walsingham was a key member of the council in the high noon of the reign of Elizabeth. He was never a dominating force like William Cecil, and he lacked the personal connections of Leicester. Indeed, he appeared almost colourless in the brilliant assembly of Elizabeth's

court. But his administrative and diplomatic skill and his devotion to the Protestant cause gave him power and prestige no less than his rivals.

WINYET, NINIAN
1518-1592

Ninian Winyet (or Winzet or Wingate) was born in Renfrew in 1518 and educated, under the name of William Windegate, at Glasgow University from 1537 to 1539, although he remained at the university as assistant to the rector until 1552. He was ordained in 1540 and became schoolmaster of the grammar school at Linlithgow. He was aware of the faults and abuses of the old Church, and put forward proposals for its reform. He was, however, a resolute opponent of the Reformation in the shape it assumed in Scotland, and annoyed the Reformers by acutely identifying the weaknesses and inconsistencies of their position.

He rose to prominence as a defender of the Catholic Church when Knox (q.v.) returned to Scotland in 1559 and, two years later, was ejected from his office of schoolmaster for refusing to sign the Protestant Confession of Faith. He went to Queen Mary's court and acted as her chaplain for a time. His three tracts, composed while he was there, were sensible and far-seeing, but too late. He again took on Knox, parodying the pamphlet that the Protestant leader tried so hard to live down. Winyet's *The last Blast of the Trumpet of God's word against the Usurped Authority of John Knox*, published in July 1562, was his own last blast for he was exiled two months later and went to Antwerp and later Paris from which cities he continued his polemical campaign against the Scottish Reformers.

From 1565 to 1570, Winyet was at Paris where he became Preceptor in Arts in the university, and in 1571 he visited Mary in England and entered her service. But his lines were now clearly laid on the Continent. He resided at Douai, a place of considerable learning and the centre for English Catholics preparing for the reconversion of their native land. He thus became part of the Counter-Reformation, and the Pope rewarded his work in 1577 by appointing him to the abbacy of Ratisbon (now Regensburg), a recently reconstructed Benedictine Monastery of Scottish foundation.

He did not forget his Scottish origins and used the educational methods of his native land in his Scoto-German establishment. He published further works including, in 1582, *Velitatio in Georgium Buchananum* (A Skirmish against George Buchanan). Winyet's writings (when not in Latin) were models of the old Scots prose.

This attractive, witty and sensible Scottish scholar ended his life in 1592 as a German abbot. It is a sad reflection on the collapse of Catholicism in Scotland.

WISHART, GEORGE
c. 1513–1546

Apart from the fact that he was born at Pittarrow, near Montrose, the early life of Wishart is unknown, although he is said to have studied at King's College, Aberdeen before becoming a school-

George Wishart, *studio of John Scougall, undated (Hunterian Art Gallery, University of Glasgow)*

master at Montrose. After being charged with heresy in 1538 by the Bishop of Brechin, John Hepburn, he fled to England, where a similar charge was made against him later in the same year by the Dean of Worcester. Despite recanting, he found it prudent to leave the country and went to study in Germany and Switzerland, returning to England in 1543 to become a member of Corpus Christi College, Cambridge.

In 1544 Wishart returned to resume his ministry in Scotland, preaching in Montrose and other eastern towns before being prohibited at Dundee in 1545. He then went to Ayrshire where the Reformed faith had been gaining many adherents. There he preached wherever he could, in the open air if no kirk were available to him, but he was always subject to persecution from the established Church, and moved continually from district to district.

Hearing that the plague was rife in Dundee, he returned there in August 1545, where he not only preached but also visited the plague-stricken poor, and remained until the epidemic was over. During this time, Cardinal Beaton (q.v.) made many attempts to have him killed, and Wishart actually prophesied his own early death at the cardinal's hands. Continuing to preach, he passed from Dundee to Lothian, delivering a sermon at Leith on 10 December, and reached Haddington shortly after Christmas. On his arrival in Lothian, he had been joined by his friend and disciple, Knox (q.v.), to whom Wishart complained that 'he wearied of the world'. His sermons at Haddington were poorly attended through the influence of Patrick Hepburn, third Earl of Bothwell who, on 19 January 1546, seized Wishart and delivered him to Edinburgh Castle, with the promise that he would not be given up to Cardinal Beaton against his will. Notwithstanding this, the governor of the castle surrendered him to Beaton who imprisoned him in his own castle of St Andrews.

There Wishart remained until his trial on 28 February before a convocation of bishops and other clergy. The trial was a travesty and its result a foregone conclusion. No temporal judge could be found to deliver the judgement, and he was condemned by the convocation to be burned as a heretic. Beaton was present with the bishops to witness the execution, which took place in front of the castle. Before his death, Wishart prophesied the impending death of the cardinal.

Wishart went bravely to his hideous death, prolonged because of the failure of the polks of gunpowder concealed in his gown to ignite since it was a damp day. His death fuelled the flames of the Reformation of Scotland which were to have such a far-reaching influence on the events of years to follow, and which changed the destiny of the nation.

CHRONOLOGY

1502	2 Apr	Treaty of Perpetual Peace
1503	8 Aug	James IV marries Henry VII's daughter, Margaret Tudor, at Holyrood
1509	21 Apr	Death of Henry VII of England, aged 52. Henry VIII becomes king, aged 17
	11 Jun	Henry VIII marries Catherine of Aragon
	24 Jun	Coronation of Henry VIII at Westminster
1512	10 Apr	Birth of James V at Linlithgow
	12 Jul	Renewal of the 'Auld Alliance'
1513	9 Sep	Battle of Flodden – Major Scottish defeat. James IV killed, aged 40. James V becomes King of Scots, aged 16 months
1515–24		Regency of the Duke of Albany
1516	18 Feb	Birth of 'Bloody' Mary Tudor at Greenwich
1520	30 Apr	'Cleansing of the Causeway'. Douglases eject Hamiltons from Edinburgh
	7 Jun	Field of the Cloth of Gold
1527	18 Aug	Treaty of Amiens
1528	29 Feb	Martyrdom of Patrick Hamilton at St Andrews
	May	James V starts to rule, aged 16
1529	3 Aug	Treaty of Cambrai
1533	7 Sep	Birth of Elizabeth Tudor at Greenwich
1537	1 Jan	James V marries Princess Madeleine of France
	7 Jun	Death of Queen Madeleine in Scotland, aged 16
	12 Oct	Birth of Edward Tudor Prince of Wales at Hampton Court
1538	18 May	James V marries Mary of Guise by proxy
1542	24 Aug	Battle of Hadden Rig – minor Scottish victory
	24 Nov	Battle of Solway Moss – major Scottish defeat
	8 Dec	Birth of Princess Mary at Linlithgow
	14 Dec	Death of James V at Falkland Palace. Mary becomes Queen of Scots, aged 6 days
1543	15 Mar	Parliament declares James Hamilton, Earl of Arran, Second Person in the Realm and Governor until the Queen's 'Perfect age' (12)
	1 July	Treaties of Greenwich. Marriage of Mary with Edward Tudor agreed. Mary to go to England when she reached the age of 10
	23 July	Cardinal Beaton removes Mary and her mother to Stirling
	25 Aug	Treaties of Greenwich ratified by Arran
	9 Sep	Coronation of Mary at Stirling
	11 Dec	Treaties of Greenwich repudiated by Scottish parliament

1544	19 Jan	François, future 1st husband of Mary, born at Fontainebleau
	6 May	Start of 'Rough Wooing'. English sack Edinburgh
1545	27 Feb	Battle of Ancrum – minor Scottish victory
	7 Dec	Birth of Henry Stewart, Lord Darnley in Yorkshire
1546	3 Jan	Martyrdom of George Wishart at St Andrews
	29 May	Assassination of Cardinal Beaton at St Andrews Castle. Murderers retain possession of the castle and defend it against Arran's forces
1547	28 Jan	Death of Henry VIII. Edward VI becomes King of England, aged 9. Earl of Hertford becomes Duke of Somerset and Protector
	31 Mar	Death of François I of France, aged 52; succession of Henri II, aged 28
	31 Jul	St Andrews Castle taken with French help. John Knox and others sent to the galleys
	9 Sep	Battle of Pinkie – major Scottish defeat. Mary moved to Inchmahome
1548	28 Feb	Mary transferred to Dumbarton Castle
	7 Jul	Treaty of Haddington
	13 Aug	Mary arrives in France, aged 5
1549	8 Feb	Earl of Arran becomes Duke of Châtelherault
1550	25 May	Treaty of Boulogne
1553	6 Jul	Death of Edward VI at St James's, aged 15
	10 Jul	Lady Jane Grey proclaimed Queen in London, aged 16
	19 Jul	Mary Tudor proclaimed Queen in London, aged 37
1554	12 Feb	Lady Jane Grey beheaded on Tower hill
	12 Apr	Mary of Guise succeeds Arran as Regent of Scotland
1557	3 Dec	First bond of the Lords of the Congregation
1558	24 Apr	Mary, aged 15, marries François Dauphin of France, aged 14, at Nôtre Dame
	17 Nov	Death of Mary Tudor. Accession of Queen Elizabeth
1559	2 Feb	John Knox returns to Scotland
	2 Apr	Treaty of Cateau-Cambrésis
	10 May	Mary of Guise summons Knox and others and outlaws them when they do not appear
	31 May	Perth bond
	18 Sep	Death of Henri II. Mary becomes Queen of France
1560	27 Feb	Treaty (Convention) of Berwick
	20 May	First Book of Discipline brought out by Knox and others
	11 Jun	Death of Mary of Guise
	6 Jul	Treaty of Edinburgh
	17 Aug	Confession of Faith. Church of Scotland reformed by parliament but not sanctioned by the queen
	6 Dec	Death of François II. Mary becomes Queen Dowager of France

	10 Dec	Dunbar bond
1561	18 Mar	Lord James Stewart, Mary's half-brother, leaves for France to negotiate her return
	15 Aug	Mary sails from Calais
	19 Aug	Mary arrives in Leith as Queen Regnant
	25 Aug	Mary's proclamation suppressing the Mass outside her own household
1562	30 Jan	Lord James Stewart created Earl of Moray
	7 Feb	Lord James Stewart created Earl of Mar
	15 Feb	Act of Council making provision for Reformed Church
	11 Aug	Mary starts her royal tour north
	11 Sep	Mary reaches Inverness Castle
	22 Sep	Mary arrives in Aberdeen
	28 Oct	Battle of Corrichie
	Sep	Ayr bond
1563	4 Jun	Acts of Parliament for repair of churches and for manses for ministers
1564	Dec	David Rizzio appointed secretary for Mary's French correspondence
1565	10 Feb	Darnley arrives in Scotland
	16 Feb	Mary meets Darnley at Wemyss Castle
	Apr	Moray's bond
	15 May	Darnley created Earl of Ross (betrothal present?)
	20 May	Moray's last attendance at council
	2 Jul	Elizabeth recalls Lennox and Darnley to England
	15 Jul	Mary's proclamation of no change in religion
	16 Jul	Mary and Darnley stay at Seton House
	22 Jul	Darnley created Duke of Albany. Wedding banns called
	24 Jul	Mary writes to the Pope protesting loyalty
	28 Jul	Darnley becomes King
	29 Jul	Mary and Darnley marry
	1 Aug	Moray summoned on pain of treason
	3 Aug	Lord George Gordon released
	6 Aug	Moray put to the horn
	14 Aug	Properties of Moray, Rothes and Kirkcaldy seized. Châtelherault and Argyll warned
	22 Aug	Rebels gather at Ayr. Mary orders a muster in Edinburgh
	26 Aug	Mary's army leaves for the west
	31 Aug	Rebels enter Edinburgh
	2 Sep	Rebels withdraw from Edinburgh
	6 Sep	Rebels in Dumfries
	7 Sep	Earl of Bothwell returns from France
	c. 19 Sep	Bothwell re-appointed Lieutenant of the Borders

	6 Oct	Moray crosses the border into England
	23 Oct	Moray received by Elizabeth
1566	24 Feb	Bothwell marries Lady Jean Gordon
	c. 20 Feb	Rizzio bond pledging support for his murder
	9 Mar	Murder of Rizzio at Holyrood
	11/12 Mar	Mary and Darnley escape to Dunbar
	15 Mar	Bothwell receives lands and lordship of Dunbar
	17 Mar	Rizzio's murderers and Knox leave Edinburgh
	18 Mar	Mary returns to Edinburgh at the head of 8,000 men
	28 Mar	Joseph Rizzio becomes Mary's French Secretary
	3 Jun	Mary makes her will
	19 Jun	Birth of Prince James at Edinburgh Castle
	30 Jun	Priory of North Berwick conferred on Bothwell
	28 Jul	Mary goes to Newhaven and Alloa
	c. 6 Oct	Mary leaves Edinburgh for Jedburgh, arriving by the 9th
	16 Oct	Mary visits Bothwell at Hermitage
	25 Oct	Mary 'thought to be dead' in Jedburgh
	20 Nov	Mary spends a fortnight at Craigmillar
	17 Dec	Baptism of Prince James at Stirling
	24 Dec	Darnley leaves Stirling for Glasgow
	23 Dec	Archbishop Hamilton reinstated
	24 Dec	Mary pardons Rizzio's murderers
1567	20 Jan	Mary travels to Glasgow to bring back Darnley
	Jan	Craigmillar bond pledging support of Darnley's murder
	1 Feb	Darnley arrives at Kirk o' Field
	10 Feb	2 a.m. Murder of Darnley
	10 Apr	Moray leaves for the Continent
	12 Apr	Trial of Bothwell
	19 Apr	Ainslie Tavern Bond supporting marriage of Mary to Bothwell
	24 Apr	Bothwell 'abducts' Mary to Dunbar
	1 May	Earl of Argyll's Bond to rescue Mary
	3 May	Lady Bothwell obtains a divorce (Protestant)
	7 May	Bothwell obtains an annulment (Catholic)
	11 May	Mary and Bothwell's banns proclaimed
	12 May	Bothwell created Duke of Orkney
	15 May	Mary marries Bothwell at Holyrood
	6 Jun	Confederate Lords' Bond to rescue Mary from her 'captivity'
	15 Jun	Confrontation at Carberry. Mary surrenders
	16 Jun	Mary taken to Lochleven
	19 Jul	Casket letters delivered to the Earl of Morton
	24 Jul	Mary miscarries twins at Lochleven
	26 Jul	Mary's enforced abdication
	29 Jul	Coronation of James VI at Stirling

	11 Aug	Moray returns and 'interviews' Mary at Lochleven
	22 Aug	Moray declared Regent
	Dec	Official establishment of Reformed Church – Parliament re-enacts legislation of 1560
1568	2 May	Mary escapes from Lochleven
	8 May	Hamilton bond for the restoration of Mary
	13 May	Battle of Langside
	16 May	Mary crosses the Solway into England
	12 Sep	Dumbarton bond supporting Mary
	4 Oct	Mary's first trial starts
1569	10 Jan	Conclusion and inconclusive findings of first trial
1570	23 Jan	Moray shot dead by Hamilton of Bothwellhaugh at Linlithgow
	12 Jul	Earl of Lennox appointed Regent
1571	7 Apr	Archbishop Hamilton hanged in his vestments
	3 Sep	Lennox killed in skirmish with Hamiltons and Gordons at Stirling. Earl of Mar becomes Regent
	10 Sep	Mar proclaims Morton lieutenant-general of the forces
1572	27 Apr	Treaty of Blois
	24 Aug	Massacre of St Bartholomew's Eve
	28 Oct	Death of Mar
	24 Nov	Earl of Morton elected Regent
		Death of John Knox
1573	23 Feb	Pacification of Perth
	28 May	Edinburgh Castle (held by the Marians) falls. Kirkcaldy of Grange hanged. Maitland dies of disease (or poison)
1578	8 Mar	Morton overthrown
	Apr	Second Book of Discipline brought out by Andrew Melville and others
	14 Apr	Death of Bothwell at Dragsholm
	12 Jun	Morton reinstated
1579	Jan	Unions of Arras and Utrecht
	25 Apr	Death of Atholl
1580	29 Dec	Final fall of Morton
1581	Apr	Second Book of Discipline approved by General Assembly
	2 Jun	Morton beheaded on 'The Maiden'
1586	5 Jul	League of Edinburgh
1587	8 Feb	Mary beheaded at Fotheringhay, aged 44
1588	29 Jul	Spanish Armada first sighted off Cornwall
1603	4 Mar	Death of Queen Elizabeth, aged 69
		Accession of James VI to English throne

APPENDIX 1

Treaties

1502 2 Apr TREATY of PERPETUAL PEACE – James IV of Scotland and Henry VII of England.
The first since 1328. Agreement to refrain from war, accompanied by a treaty whereby James IV was to marry Margaret Tudor. Renewed by Henry VIII in 1509.

1512 12 Jul RENEWAL of the 'AULD ALLIANCE' – James IV of Scotland and Louis XII of France.
Alliance whereby each country would assist the other in the event of a war against England, originally signed in October 1295. The 1512 renewal resulted in Scotland's defeat and James IV's death at Flodden.

1517 26 Aug TREATY of ROUEN – James V of Scotland (Regent Albany) and François I of France.
Treaty providing that France and Scotland should give mutual assistance in the event of hostile action by England against either and offering James certain hypothetical prospects of a French princess as a bride. Unratified.

1520 7 Jun FIELD of the CLOTH of GOLD (near Calais) – Henry VIII of England and François I of France.
Vain attempt of François to form an alliance with Henry against Emperor Charles V. The following year, Henry allied with Charles against François (Treaty of Bruges, 25 Aug 1521).

1527 18 Aug TREATY of AMIENS – Henry VIII of England and François I of France.
One of several (another was the Treaty of Westminster, 30 Apr 1527) negotiated by Cardinal Wolsey as part of a largely futile attempt to maintain England's influence on the balance of European power between France and the Hapsburgs.

1529 3 Aug TREATY of CAMBRAI (Paix des Dames) – François I of France and Emperor Charles V.
Agreement which ended most of the warfare between France and Hapsburgs until the death of François I in 1547. England agreed to the treaty but was not a signatory. It allowed Henry VIII, on the fall of Wolsey, to abandon an active European policy and concentrate on religious affairs at home.

1543 1 Jul TREATIES of GREENWICH – Mary of Scotland (Regent Arran) and Henry VIII of England.
Treaties providing for Anglo-Scottish peace, Queen Mary to be sent to England when she reached the age of ten, and her subsequent marriage to Edward, Prince of Wales. In the event of Edward's death, she would be returned to Scotland as a childless widow. The arrest and impounding by the English of some Scottish ships sailing to France, gave the Scots the pretext for repudiating the treaties before the end of the year.

1548 7 Jul TREATY of HADDINGTON – Mary of Scotland (Regent Arran) and Henri II of France.
Agreement that, in return for French military aid, the Scottish government would send Queen Mary to France where she would eventually be married to the dauphin. Regent Arran's governorship of Scotland during Mary's minority was to be guaranteed, he was to be given the dukedom of Châtelherault and the French were to withdraw any obstacles directed against his half-brother John becoming Archbishop of St Andrews.

1550 25 May TREATY of BOULOGNE – Edward VI of England (Protector Somerset) and Henri II of France.
Agreement involving, among other things, the sale of Boulogne back to France. The French, who had the upper hand, declined to support English policy towards Scotland.

1559 2 Apr TREATY of CATEAU-CAMBRÉSIS – Henri II of France and Philip II of Spain.
Major agreement marking the end of the long period of intermittent warfare in Europe between France and Spain mainly for control of Italy. It did not apply to the New World. The treaty did not diminish the importance of England or Scotland as allies or enemies of the two powers but it gave them breathing space in international relations.

1560 22 Feb CONVENTION of BERWICK – Mary of Scotland (Châtelherault, Lord James Stewart and Maitland) and Elizabeth of England.
The agreement between the Lords of the Congregation and the English to adopt a policy of mutual assistance against France – sometimes thought to be the beginning of the Anglo-Scottish cooperation which was to lead to the Union of the Crowns in 1603.

1560 6 Jul TREATY of EDINBURGH – Elizabeth of England and Charles IX of France (Catherine de Medici).
Marking the end of hostilities in the Scottish Reformation, it was an agreement whereby the French and English forces were to withdraw from Scotland. French fortifications were to be dismantled, foreigners were to be prohibited from holding office in the government and there were to be no

261

reprisals against any of the Reformers. The French government was to recognise Elizabeth as rightful Queen of England. Although Queen Mary ceased to quarter the English Arms with her own (thereby implicitly recognising Elizabeth's sovereignty), she declined to agree to a treaty made without her consent or that of her parliament.

1572 27 Apr TREATY of BLOIS – Charles IX of France and Elizabeth of England. Defensive alliance between the two countries, directed chiefly against Spanish power in the Low Countries.

1573 23 Feb PACIFICATION of PERTH – King's party and Queen's party.
The agreement between Regent Morton and the, until then, pro-Marian Gordon-Hamilton faction, which undertook to transfer their allegiance from Mary to Morton, disband their forces and return all prisoners and property they had taken. In return, all measures taken against them since Mary's abdication were to be revoked, their lands were to be restored and certain individuals, notably Archbishop John Hamilton (who had been executed nearly two years earlier) rehabilitated. The agreement allowed Morton to concentrate on the siege of Edinburgh Castle, which was the last bastion of Marian support.

1579 Jan UNIONS of ARRAS and UTRECHT – Low Countries.
The former was a pact among the Walloon, mostly Catholic, provinces in the south of the Low Countries, subsequently extended to Spain; the latter involved the Protestant-dominated Flemish provinces and those of the northern part of the Low Countries. Utrecht was to be a cornerstone of the subsequent Dutch Republic, although its territorial basis was smaller. It was to involve war against Spain, in which England became entangled.

1586 5 Jul LEAGUE OF EDINBURGH – James VI of Scotland and Elizabeth of England.
A renewal of the agreement of July 1585, negotiated by the Master of Gray and Walsingham, whereby James accepted an annual subsidy from Elizabeth and agreed to assist England if attacked. James could not secure Elizabeth's formal recognition of his right of succession; the pension was set at £4,000 p.a.

Appendix 2

Bonds

1557   3 Dec   FIRST BOND of the LORDS of the CONGREGATION – Argyll, Lorne, Glencairn, Morton, Erskine of Dun

1559   31 May   PERTH BOND, pledging to maintain the liberty of the 'whole Congregation' – Glencairn, Argyll, Lord James Stewart, etc.

1560   10 Dec   DUNBAR BOND, on behalf of the queen after the death of François II – Eglinton, etc.

1562   Sep   AYR BOND, for the defence of the Protestant religion – Glencairn, barons and gentlemen of the district

1565   MORAY's BOND, pledging support should the Darnley marriage take place

1566 *c.* 20 Feb   RIZZIO BOND, supporting the murder – Morton, Lindsay, G. Douglas, A. Douglas, P. Ruthven, W. Ruthven, Ochiltree, Boyd, Glencairn, Argyll, Rothes, Moray (2 Mar), Darnley, etc.

1567   Jan   CRAIGMILLAR BOND, supporting the murder of Darnley – Maitland, Bothwell, Argyll, Huntly, Balfour, Morton, etc.

19 Apr   AINSLIE TAVERN BOND, supporting the marriage of Bothwell to the queen – 8 bishops, 9 (10) earls, 7 (11) barons, including: Morton, Maitland, Argyll, Huntly, Cassilis, Sutherland, Glencairn, Rothes, Seton, Sinclair, Boyd, Herries, Bishop Gordon, etc.

1 May   ARGYLL BOND, to rescue the queen after her 'abduction' – Argyll, Morton, Atholl, Murray of Tullibardine, etc.

15 May   EDINBURGH CASTLE, to secure support of Sir James Balfour
-6 Jun

6 Jun   CONFEDERATE LORDS BOND, to rescue the queen from her 'captivity' – 12 earls, 14 lords led by Glencairn

1568   8 May   HAMILTON BOND, for the restoration of Queen Mary – 9 earls, 9 bishops, 17 lords, 14 commendators, *c.* 90 lairds (Argyll), etc.

12 Sep   DUMBARTON BOND, supporting Queen Mary – 7 earls, 8 bishops, 12 lords, 9 commendators, etc.

263

Appendix 3

Scotland's Military Potential in the Time of Queen Mary

In the later Middle Ages Scotland had an army ('the host') some 20,000 men strong to defend itself against the English. The men were required to serve for up to forty days and to supply their own equipment at their own expense. Successive kings and governors spent lavishly on military hardware, ships and fortifications. There was a strong desire to make the country as independent as possible from supplies or manufacturers from abroad.

By 1520 there was a gun foundry in Edinburgh Castle, a ship-building yard at Newhaven on the Forth, two miles to the north, and a dry-dock at Airth, further up the river. In the 1530s there was an armour mill at Holyrood and there were several craftsmen in the main Scottish towns capable of making and repairing a wide range of arms and armour. In the 1530s and 40s, major improvements were made to the defences of the royal castles at Edinburgh, Stirling, Blackness and Tantallon (which was temporarily in royal hands). The rest of the country was well covered with castles and towers of the nobles and lairds, some with significant new fortifications like the Hamilton strongholds of Cadzow and Craignethan and the archiepiscopal fortress of St Andrews.

The wars of the 1540s and 50s put an enormous strain on all these military resources. In an attempt to coerce the Scots into a marriage alliance between the young queen and Henry VIII's son, Edward, Prince of Wales, later Edward VI, the English in Scotland had dug themselves in, secure within the ditches, ramparts and bastions of sophisticated new artillery forts. Scottish arms alone were not enough to evict them so French money and forces were sought and given. This turned out to be a mixed blessing. The French soldiers were generally richer than, and unpopular with, most Scots who saw the danger of their country becoming a dependency of France. Their queen, absent since 1548, married the dauphin in 1558 and became queen of France the following year. In 1560, however, the death of her mother, Mary of Guise (q.v.), who had been regent, and renewed exertions by the English at the behest of a powerful, growing Scottish Protestant faction, abruptly brought the French involvement to an end. Mary's husband died in December 1560 and she returned in August 1561 to a country at peace as a result of the Treaty of Edinburgh between France and England. There were, however, still deep underlying tensions and divisions, the inevitable legacy of the wars with England and the Reformation. Nevertheless, Mary set herself the task of restoring stable government with a good measure of success.

On the military side, a change in the constitution of the host did not seem prudent. The mechanism for raising it was ancient and well-tried; innovations might be expensive and inefficient. In 1552 Mary of Guise had been asked by Henri II to raise a militia force to serve in France, but failed. Her attempts in 1556 to keep forces in the Borders were highly unpopular since they were to be paid for by taxation. It was not until eighty years later that, under Alexander Leslie, Scotland successfully created militia armies, thus funded, and able to remain in the field for years at a time.

Many Scots had been involved in the campaigns and sieges of the recent wars when they had often served alongside professional troops, sometimes French and sometimes English. The old leaders from the 1540s, like the Earls of Huntly (q.v.) and Lennox (q.v.) and the Duke of Châtelherault (q.v.), were still to the fore, but in the 1560s, it was the younger generation who were to leave their mark in military ventures. The main commanders were still drawn from the nobles and the lairds, like Mary's half-brother, Lord James Stewart (q.v.); the man who was to become her third husband, James, fourth Earl of Bothwell; and Sir William Kirkcaldy of Grange (q.v.).

Lord James had first shown his abilities as a leader in 1549 when, still in his teens, he thwarted an English invasion of Fife. In 1562 he commanded Mary's army at Corrichie, defeating the fourth Earl of Huntly and his sons, and six years later led the army of the Confederate Lords to victory over his half-sister at Langside.

The Earl of Bothwell had been entrusted by Mary of Guise with a body of French auxiliaries in 1559, and in 1562 he was given an appointment in the Scots Guards in France. Had the confrontation at Carberry in 1567 become a battle, he might well have won it. The French ambassador, Philibert du Croc, at least, was impressed by his preparations.

The young (third) Earl of Arran (q.v.) had shown early promise, having been appointed to command the Scots Guards in 1550, but it was not long after his return to Scotland in 1562 that he started showing signs of the mental disorder that kept him out of public affairs for the rest of his life.

The most outstanding commander of all was the Fife laird, Sir William Kirkcaldy of Grange. He had been one of those responsible for the murder of Cardinal Beaton (q.v.) in 1546 and, on the surrender of St Andrews Castle, was imprisoned at Mont St Michel in France. Escaping in January 1550, he entered English and then French service as a soldier. Returning home in 1557, he distinguished himself against the French at the siege of Leith. He led the horse of the Confederate Lords at Carberry in 1567 and played a decisive part in Mary's defeat at Langside a year later. It is ironic that it was Kirkcaldy who was to be the queen's last champion in Scotland, holding out in Edinburgh Castle for her until it was battered into submission by English guns in 1573.

The Scots remained committed to fighting mainly on foot in large formations of pikemen, a battle tactic that required able and experienced captains and well

Operating a hagbut, as shown in Emperor Maximilian's Zeughausbuch. *Weapons like these were carried by Scotland's first regular military unit. They were almost certainly used by both sides in the battle of Langside*

drilled and steadfast troops. Even then, they were not always successful. At Pinkie in 1547, for instance, the foot-soldiers broke and fled before coming to grips with the opposing pikes of the English. At Langside, however, both sides locked their pikes together and slogged it out for half an hour or more. Pikes were spears with very long shafts, by statute at least six ells (18 foot 6 inches) long, and were the standard weapon for all the Scottish foot, although many aspired to carrying other weapons as well.

Swords were increasingly available, both the single and two-handed varieties. The former had broad blades like those of the basket hilted swords used so effectively by the Highlanders in the Jacobite uprisings at the end of the seventeenth century and during the first half of the eighteenth. These hilts were already appearing in the mid sixteenth, and there is evidence that they were a Scottish invention, though the blades they were mounted with were invariably imported from Germany. Two-handed swords and the various long-shafted axes favoured by the Scots could not have been wielded successfully along with pikes but were of significance in local conflicts. Pike formations would have benefited enormously from an infusion of hand gunners as the Scots found out to their cost at Pinkie, where the English hand gunners played an important part in routing the Scottish host. Pistols were adopted enthusiastically by mercenaries and by the 1560s many Scots had armed themselves with them. Lord Home (q.v.) is said to have been felled at Langside by pistols flung at him after they had been discharged.

The Scots continued to prefer light armour, essentially jacks – jerkins reinforced with metal plates. When Mary and Darnley led their army against Moray and his associates in the Chaseabout Raid in 1565, the English ambassador commented on the fact that only Darnley wore a 'gylte corselet', that is, richly decorated plate armour; everyone else in the queen's army was clad in jacks after the fashion of their country. Protection for the head was provided by a simple iron helmet.

At Pinkie, the Scots had been notably lacking in horse, whereas a third of the English army was mounted; this played a major part in the result. In the ensuing wars the English and French relied greatly on their cavalry, and the Scots belatedly learned to make more use of it. The Borders had for long produced men skilled in mounted warfare, light-horse ideal for coping with the raids and counter-raids endemic to the area. According to a French report of 1558, Scotland had by then a potential 4,000 to 5,000 horse, as against 20,000 to 25,000 foot. The main weapon of these horsemen was the lance.

In the 1560s the Scots had the capability of raising a national army as large and as well armed as in previous years. Lessons had been learned in tactics and training from the recent wars, and there were captains of ability. This was, however, a state of affairs inherited by Mary, who took little action to enlarge, develop or modernise her forces. Indeed, there were no occasions in her short personal reign when the whole host was brought together; all too often, one faction was pitted against another.

What Mary did do was to build up the force of professionals involved in national security. By the 1560s the employment of wageours (mercenaries) was an established, albeit irregular practice, particularly for bodyguards, garrison duty or small special purpose forces. The majority of these wageours were Scottish and were probably more reliable as soldiers and better equipped than the average fencible man. There was a Royal Guard consisting of twelve footmen armed with halberds, to guard the sovereign. Soon after her arrival in Scotland, Mary formed a new force of seventy-five archers, possibly using the Scots Guard of the French kings as a model. Most bands of wageours, however, equipped themselves with hand guns (culverins or hagbuts), and were normally less than a hundred strong. By 1565, she also had a band of culveriners.

The keepers of the royal castles like Stirling and Dumbarton were responsible for making their own arrangements, providing payment for the porters, watchmen and other necessary staff from the profits of lands assigned for this purpose. The garrison of Dunbar was strengthened by professional gunners paid by the treasurer, and Inchkeith, in the Forth, housed a band of forty hagbutters under a captain and a lieutenant, at least until 1562, when its garrison was reduced in size.

Edinburgh Castle was the home for most of the royal guns and the base for the gunners, smiths and wrights employed to work them and service them. When she arrived in Scotland, Mary kept all fifteen gunners she found in post, and by the end of her reign had raised their number to twenty-four. She also appointed John Chisholm to be Comptroller of the Artillery. He deputised for the Master of the Artillery and did much to put the guns in order after a period of neglect. The inventory of the guns in the castle that he drew up in March 1567, lists fifty-nine pieces. Taking into account the guns in other royal fortresses at the time – Stirling, Dumbarton, Dunbar, Blackness and Inchkeith – the total must have been over a hundred pieces. Of these, only a quarter were large guns; in addition to defending the major fortresses, they might also be required for sieges elsewhere or on naval expeditions.

Chisholm went to some lengths to make new carriages for the guns, but he could not get new guns made. In 1515 a simple cupola furnace, requiring bellows to raise the temperature, had been installed in the foundry in Edinburgh Castle. An attempt at founding in 1558 had gone disastrously wrong with the metal left solid in the furnace, so a new one was installed. It was a reverberatory type, in which the fuel was burned in a chamber separate from the hearth. By vaulting the whole furnace, the heat was deflected, or reverberated, downwards to the metal in the hearth. A chimney created a draught and drew off the smoke. There is no evidence that the new furnace was ever put into production though the meltars (gunfounders) under the master, David Rowan, continued to be paid into the reign of James VI. Rowan had his own foundry in the town and may have made guns there for private individuals.

Well-served guns consumed prodigious quantities of powder and shot, and at least two sieges in living memory (Tantallon Castle in 1528, Glasgow Castle in 1544) had been aborted through lack of one or the other. Although there was a powder mill in Edinburgh Castle, the production of gunpowder probably stopped before Mary's return to Scotland. The techniques of casting the iron shot required by the larger guns remained beyond the Scots for some time to come.

Mary did not give any direct encouragement to arms and armour makers. Nevertheless, it is during her reign that the genesis of the Scottish firearms industry took place in Edinburgh. 'Dutch' makers of hand guns had worked for James IV in the castle, and some wrights and smiths readily turned their hand to repairing and making them in the years following. A demarcation dispute between blacksmiths and locksmiths was settled in 1569 when both groups were allowed to mend or make firearms. By the 1570s some of them had specialised to such an extent that they described themselves as dagmakers (pistolmakers, gunsmiths). In 1575 they claimed to be able to make fifty calivers a week.

Of less military significance was the manufacture in Edinburgh and Canongate of daggers, normally described as whingers. As early as 1551, there was official concern about an Englishman, Edward Berwick, exporting them to the old enemy. They made good gifts, like the one sent by Randolph (q.v.), the English agent in Edinburgh, to Elizabeth's secretary, Cecil (q.v.), in 1561, or the whingers 'bravelie and maist artificiallie made and embroiderit with gold' presented by Mary and her ladies to the French ambassador du Croc and his party during a masque at Holyrood in 1566. They may have been similar in style and quality to the finely etched and gilt dudgeon daggers, with their highly polished and inlaid hardwood (often ebony) handles, surviving from the early seventeenth century.

The major royal castles were still important military bases and strongholds in the 1560s although they had been largely superseded in the recent wars by new earthwork forts erected by the English and the French. These were some of the most sophisticated fortifications in Europe at the time. They had ramparts, ditches and pointed bastions arranged in such a way that every square inch of ground around the defences could be covered by flanking fire. Since they were built from earth and turf and were not of great height, they were a difficult target for the attackers' guns to blow away. The English forts, however, had been dismantled after the Treaty of Boulogne in 1550, and the important French work at Eyemouth, begun in 1557, was destroyed by agreement with the English in 1559, probably before it was completed. The impressive French fortifications of Leith, unbreached after a long siege by the English and the Scottish Lords of the Congregation, were dismantled in 1560. Work did continue in the 1560s on the French fort on Inchkeith. The coat-of-arms above its gateway bears the date 1564. There was no other attempt by Mary to build new fortifications or improve existing ones, and the only significant work in the reign of her son was the remodelling of the defences of Edinburgh Castle by Regent Morton (q.v.) after the siege of 1573. There was also no concern about maintaining ship-building yards or keeping a navy.

It is possible from all this to detect a definite shift in military policy in the 1560s. Until then, Scottish kings and governors had attempted to compete in the first division of European nations, particularly with England and France, both of which had immensely more wealth, manpower and natural resources. Scottish military equipment and fortifications did not lag noticeably behind the best in northern Europe, and the Scots were quick to adopt new tactics and ideas. This was very expensive, and the Scots were not destined to be serious participants in the arms race for long. Even quite modest enterprises, like the recapture of the towerhouse at Langholm in the summer of 1547, required all the guns that the governor (Regent Arran) could muster and the entire host for a total of twenty days' service. If the army were beaten in battle there were no reserves to call out to take up the struggle or limit the damage. In October 1557, Mary of Guise gathered an army at Kelso for an invasion of England but the reluctant soldiers drifted away rather than fight for a cause in which they did not believe.

Success by Arran in the 1540s in besieging some strongholds, and victories over the English at Hadden Rig in 1542 and Ancrum in 1545, could not hide the fact that Scotland was losing its military independence. The government had to seek French assistance in 1545, 1547 and 1548. Scotland's problem was not only lack of money. Political division and religious schism played important parts. With more imaginative leadership, better strategies and tactics might have been developed to suit Scotland's impoverished condition.

During the queen's personal reign, there does not seem to have been any question of re-building the country into a substantial military power; similarly in the long reign of her son. This was clearly caused by dynastic rather than financial considerations, with both Mary and James standing to inherit the throne of England and anxious not to antagonise their potential subjects south of the border.

After Mary's flight and imprisonment by Elizabeth, English military aid was sought by Scottish governments on several occasions. In 1568, rather than reactivate the gunfoundry in Edinburgh Castle, Regent Moray requested 20,000 pounds weight of metal to be cast with the English ordnance, probably at Houndsditch near the Tower of London. His wish was not granted, but in 1587 James VI was lent English guns for the siege of Lochmaben Castle, and in 1596–97 he sought others for use against Torthorwald Castle. In 1608 and 1615 the guns for the siege of Dunyvaig Castle in Islay were sent from Ireland.

On two occasions English armies were sent north to support the government of the young James. In 1570 a force under Sir William Drury (q.v.) helped ravage the lands of the Hamiltons, destroying Cadzow Castle and Kinneil House. Three years later, with most of the Scottish artillery held by the Marian party in Edinburgh Castle, Sir William returned with English guns to reduce the castle to submission. The fact that the English had nothing to fear from Scottish arms in some measure ensured James's acceptability as Elizabeth's successor. It was the lure of the English throne rather than financial considerations which, in the long run, reduced the independence and effectiveness of Scottish military power to a shadow of what it had been earlier in the century.

Appendix 4

The Costume and Jewellery of Mary Queen of Scots

After the murder of Lord Darnley, speculation was rife in the courts of western Europe concerning the relationship between Mary Queen of Scots and James Hepburn, the fourth Earl of Bothwell. Was it true that she was madly in love with her late husband's murderer? It was certainly true that her former friends were telling the most amazing, derogatory stories about her. Sir William Kirkcaldy of Grange (q.v.) was reported to have declared that he had personally heard her say that she did not care if she lost her kingdom by consorting with Bothwell, and was ready to part with France, England and Scotland, and follow the earl to the world's end in a white petticoat.

Whether Kirkcaldy was accurately reported, and whether Mary actually said this, are matters of some doubt, but the story certainly conjures up a vivid image, of this most elegant of queens casting aside her royal robes in favour of the garb of an ordinary woman. The notion was even more shocking in the sixteenth century than it would be in the twentieth, for, in those days, garments were a vital indication of status for a monarch. Without her velvets and her ermine Mary would no longer appear as a ruling sovereign but as a plain person like any one of her subjects.

From her earliest days Mary had been conscious of the importance of status symbols. At the age of eleven she insisted on having a cloth of gold gown embroidered with her monogram so that she could outshine the princesses at the French court. At an earlier royal wedding she had been annoyed to observe that, while she was in silk, they had been flaunting themselves in gold and silver damask. She felt it important that she, with the precedence due her as a queen, almost from birth, should eclipse them.

In her years as the fiancée of the Dauphin of France (q.v.) and then as his wife, Queen of France as well as Scotland, Mary assembled a magnificent wardrobe and a fabulous collection of jewels which was the envy of the western world. She was accustomed to lavish praise from poets and writers who extolled her creamy complexion, her beautiful hazel eyes, her dark auburn hair and her tall, dignified figure. When she landed at Leith on that gloomy August morning in 1561 she came not as a poor, downtrodden widow but as a proud, regal figure, full of personal self-confidence and her subjects were immediately impressed. At first, she was still in mourning for François II, but she had brought chests packed with layer upon layer of silks, satins and velvets, coffers crammed with priceless jewels and a retinue of attendants which included a French tailor. By December her husband had been dead for a year. She was able to put away her widow's weeds and dress as a queen should.

In February 1562, Mary instructed one of her French *valets-de-chambre* to draw up a detailed list of the principal garments in her wardrobe. This he did, and throughout her first years in Scotland he was careful to keep it up-to-date, noting when any gown was altered or given away. The last amendment to the list was made in May 1567, at about the time of her wedding to Bothwell. By then some garments had been passed on as gifts to the queen's ladies, but most of her finery was still intact. The sumptuous satin gowns, the embroidered petticoats, the bodices and the cloaks so minutely described in Servais de Condé's inventory, must have been those she wore in her first pleasant years in her native land, during the traumas of her marriage to Darnley, and throughout her fatal liaison with Bothwell.

When the queen rose in the morning, her ladies would help her to dress. Usually at courts a formal ritual was observed with, for example, an important member of the nobility handing the king his shirt and valuing this duty as a mark of his own importance. Whether Mary's ladies helped her strictly according to hierarchy is unknown; no documents record these aspects of court life in sixteenth-century Scotland. What is known, with reasonable certainty, from Mary's own inventory, the accounts of her Lord High Treasurer, and from other costume information of the period, is what she wore.

Some princesses of the period chose vests of linen or velvet, according to the season, embroidered with metal thread and trimmed with sequins. These sound distinctly uncomfortable if really worn next to the skin, and Mary certainly seems to have preferred a different selection of undergarments. She possessed, for example, pairs of taffeta-lined, satin brassières. The Victorian editor of the printed edition of the treasurer's accounts translates them as 'armour for the arms', but perhaps this interpretation arose rather from his modesty than from a knowledge of female costume. 'Brassières' were also listed among the clothing of Mary's mother, and there is no reason to suppose that they were any different from the modern garment of the same name.

Over her brassières, Mary may have worn chemises, which were like long blouses. These do not appear in her accounts, but this may be because such personal garments were made up by her own ladies rather than by her tailors. Margaret Carwood, her chamberwoman, received large supplies of linen, cambric and lawn from the royal wardrobe for unspecified purposes, along with fine sewing silk, and the reasonable assumption is that this was for the queen's nightclothes and undergarments. Stockings, however, were made by a tailor in woollen cloth or velvet.

Whether Mary and her ladies wore drawers is more difficult to say. Her mother-in-law, Catherine de Medici (q.v.), is credited with having introduced them into France from Italy at a time when English ladies allegedly wore only petticoats and hose under their skirts. It may well be that when Mary returned to her chilly northern kingdom, she was grateful to the mother-in-law she never liked for that new fashion, if for nothing else. One entry in the treasurer's accounts is for twenty-two ells of linen for 'shirts, mutches, socks and breeks', but, although she personally authorised that the materials be given for that purpose to Marie McCleod, there is nothing to indicate that the garments were being made up for the queen herself rather than for a member of her household. 'Shirts', 'socks', and 'breeks' certainly sound like masculine garments, but no man ever wore the kind of cap called a 'mutch' and it could be that the Scottish clerk who wrote out this entry was translating from the queen's French into Scottish words he understood – 'shirt' for 'chemise' and 'breeks' for 'drawers'.

Other garments are less mysterious. Mary usually wore a satin doublet lined with taffeta. This was presumably in place of a vest. Usually these doublets were white, though she did have one that was black, and in the autumn of 1565 there is mention of a tawny satin one. With the relatively plain doublet went a farthingale petticoat, stiffened with hoops of whalebone. The smallest hoop was near the waist, the largest at the hem, so the skirt which went over it appeared funnel-shaped. It took seven ells of taffeta to line a farthingale for the queen, at a cost of £2 per ell, and hoops of whalebone usually came to five shillings each.

Over the farthingale went a much grander petticoat, designed to be partly visible because the skirt of the gown which went over it was often open down the front to show a triangle of petticoat beneath. In the winter of 1562, Mary had many such petticoats. Eight were cloth of gold and five were cloth of silver, each trimmed with gold fringes, silver braid or coloured silk threads. A further fifteen were of rich fabric in crimson, black, orange, blue, yellow and white, again with elaborate trimmings. A blue petticoat in the Spanish mode had bands of gold and silver embroidery on it, and seven petticoats 'with no enrichment' were nevertheless decorated with fancy slashes and perforations. Some of the petticoats had matching sleeves, for these were not part of a gown but detachable. Often in a colour which contrasted with the gown itself, they were fixed into position with laces. In warm weather a complete fancy petticoat would be very hot, and in any season such garments were heavy. Ladies therefore often wore a petticoat of a thinnish, plain material, with a 'foreskirt' or triangular piece of rich, embroidered fabric tied round the waist like an apron. Underneath an open gown skirt, this gave the illusion of being a complete petticoat. Mary had sixteen such foreskirts, four of them cloth of gold, three cloth of silver and the others of heavily embroidered satin. Some of them matched her cloaks.

Most spectacular of all were the gowns themselves, fifty-nine of them in de Condé's inventory. They would have high or square necklines, long sleeves, tight bodices and full, long skirts. It took sixteen and a half ells of cloth to make a gown for the six-foot-tall queen: velvet for winter, satin for summer, with taffeta or frieze to line it, velvet to edge it, buckram to stiffen the bodice, silk to sew it up, fancy braid and silk flowers to trim it and precious stones to fasten on it. Often these gowns were quilted for additional warmth; sometimes they had long sheaths sewn into the lining for whalebone busks or stays.

Recollecting the portraits of Mary during her years of captivity, when she wore severe mourning clothes, most people have a sombre mental picture of her which is a sorry contrast to their image of Queen Elizabeth, swathed in her vivid satins and ablaze with jewels. In fact, had a meeting between the two monarchs ever taken place during their younger days, Mary might well have outshone her English cousin, for she was nine years younger, and her inventories record a wardrobe of equal splendour.

Two of Mary's fifty-nine gowns were cloth of gold, and three were cloth of silver, sewn with coloured silks and wire braid. Twenty-one were black, but this was not the dull black of mourning – this was black as a fashionable colour in its own right. Diane de Poitiers chose black and white as her personal colours and so did Queen Elizabeth. These were regal colours, it seems, endowed from time immemorial with almost mystical properties. The retinues and champions of these royal ladies adopted them as a sign of their allegiance. It comes as no surprise, then, to find a preponderance of black and white in Mary's wardrobe. A black velvet gown had great sleeves covered with embroidered bands of gold thread and cord, the rest of the garment sewn with waves of the cord. Another black velvet gown had fancy slashes with a silver fringe and braid and a third, Spanish-style, had the bodice slashed to show the scarlet lining and was edged with bands of gold chevrons. Ten gowns were white, nine were crimson, four were yellow, four blue, two were orange, two were soft grey, one was carnation pink and one was green.

Round her neck, the queen usually wore a ruff, the long, narrow strip of fine linen and lace which was starched and then wound round short rods to give it the characteristic figure-of-eight appearance. It was fastened in front with short strings which were usually concealed by being tucked into the neck of the gown. Cuffs were lace-trimmed too, and sometimes took the form of hand-ruffs. On her head, Mary wore fine lawn caps and headdresses. Her accounts mention linen caps in various styles, a high horned headdress, hoods and a coif of black jet. Her shoes were often velvet slippers lined with taffeta.

To go with her flamboyant gowns were eleven cloaks. Strangely, none of these was of wool or velvet. All were either silk or taffeta. Either her gowns and under-garments were so warm that nothing thicker was required, or these cloaks were intended for ceremonial purposes and there were other, plainer ones for walking and riding. Those on the list are certainly elaborate, embroidered all over, trimmed with gold buttons and bunches of ribbon, fringed and banded with expensive braid. Some outdoor garments do appear in the accounts: velvet hats, pairs of gloves, and masks costing £1 each. It was customary, for high-born ladies of the French court, never to be seen out of doors without a fancy mask, presumably in the interests of modesty. They were not intended as a disguise: everyone knew who the wearer was, from her place in any procession, her general bearing and the rest of her garments.

Some of Mary's clothes were intended for specific, ceremonial purposes. A royal mantle of violet-coloured velvet would be for state occasions, such as the opening of parliament. At the other end of the scale, the 'little chamber mantle made of black velvet' embroidered in silver was probably a short cape which she wore over her shoulders when she was sitting privately with friends in her apartments. A special section of the 1562 inventory is devoted to mourning garments, which consisted of a great royal mantle trimmed with ermine and lined with white taffeta. This was perhaps part of her royal white mourning (*Deuil Blanc*) which she wore as the widow of François II. With it were two black gowns.

On a more cheerful note, there were masquing clothes too. Mary shared the French court's enthusiasm for dressing up as some legendary figure and taking part in elaborate musical entertainments. The first gown on this part of the list was made up in red cloth in the Picardy style, with a foreskirt of yellow satin. The next two dresses were in the Spanish fashion, one of them, its colour unspecified, set with little balls of imitation silver, the other dotted with small green buttons. A red, white and blue satin robe was fringed with silver.

The characters in masques were usually goddesses or mythological monarchs, but on at least one occasion in daily life Mary dressed as a plain burgess's wife and, another time, even less conventionally, roamed the streets of Edinburgh incognito, dressed as a man, in company with her future husband Lord Darnley. These were amusing whims, examples of the occasional desires of royal personages to shed the trappings of their onerous position, and experience for a few hours what it was like to be one of their subjects. Thus would Marie Antoinette play at being a shepherdess more than two centuries later. For Mary, however, dressing up later became a far more serious matter. In June 1567, she escaped from Borthwick Castle in masculine disguise and, in May the following year, she fled from Lochleven in the clothes of a washerwoman.

Before the Bothwell marriage, however, clothes had no such dramatic uses. They could, of course, be given away as presents and between February 1562, when the main inventory was drawn up, and May 1567, Mary gave away fourteen of the fifty-nine gowns. In December 1566, for instance, her illegitimate half-sister, Jean, Countess of Argyll, became the recipient of the crimson damask gown embroidered in gold. This was obviously a valuable item, still in good condition. Mary Livingston, one of the Four Maries (q.v.), was not so fortunate. By the time she was presented with a long-sleeved, crimson gown, the pearls sewn on it had been cut off, and when Annabella, Lady Mar, fell heir to a crimson velvet gown, its wolfskin collar and cuffs had already been removed and attached to one of the queen's black velvet mantles instead.

The advent of Lord Darnley is reflected very clearly in the royal accounts. Presumably his fond mother, the Countess of Lennox (q.v.), had seen to it that he arrived in Scotland with clothes which would take the eye and forward his courtship of the queen but, of course, as soon as he was married, he began to appear in the Lord Treasurer's books as 'the King's Grace'. Eight days after the wedding, three gross of silver points, for holding up his hose, were supplied at a cost of £43

Portrait of a Lady called
Mary Queen of Scots,
artist unknown, c. 1560
(National Portrait Gallery)

4/- from the Royal Wardrobe, and a week after that, on the orders of King Henry and Queen Mary, their secretary David Rizzio obtained from the Wardrobe 55 ells of holland cloth for 'sarks' (shirts), six ells for ruffs, twelve ells for linen (night) caps and six ells for 'foot socks'.

The following week saw Darnley's master tailor collecting black velvet, black satin, black corded taffeta, black silk and one pound five ounces of silver pasments, the elaborate braid which would trim this splendid new outfit. Later in the month he received more black velvet and silver pasments, this time no less than a hundred ells, and a great hank of gold, some red crimson velvet and an ounce and a quarter of red crimson silk to decorate his halberd.

By this time, Darnley and Mary were making preparations for the Chaseabout Raid, when they pursued the Earl of Moray (q.v.) and the other rebels all round the south of Scotland. Darnley's splendid appearance as he rode at the queen's side in his gilded armour was noted by at least one observer, and the Treasurer's Accounts record payments for the chamois skins which made his doublet, the buffalo skin for his coat, the silver trimmings for his 'concealed armour' and even the hair which was used to pad out his trunk hose.

Back in Edinburgh at the end of the campaign, Darnley began to prepare for Christmas. In December, a new satin doublet trimmed with satin and lined with black taffeta was made up, with cloth hose to match, stuffed into an elegant shape with ten pounds of hair and eighteen ells of linen. Four more doublets followed in quick succession trimmed with twelve dozen buttons, there was a new serge cloak and coat, more hose and a fur of marten sable, purchased from Nicol Udwart, one of the Edinburgh merchants.

By the beginning of 1566, there was already trouble between the queen and her husband and, as their relationship worsened, royal gifts to King Henry dwindled and ceased, although Mary's increasing reliance on Bothwell is not reflected in the accounts at this stage. A year later, however, shortly after Darnley's death, one of the queen's cloth of silver cloaks and a cloth of silver petticoat were taken to become part of what must have become a very grand bed, possibly in anticipation of her re-marriage.

If Mary's clothing accounts provide fascinating sidelights into her personal and political life, so too do the inventories of her jewellery. Some of her treasures had come to her from her father. After his death in 1542 they had been held in trust for her by James Hamilton, Duke of Châtelherault (q.v.), the governor of Scotland. But, in the early summer of 1556 as she approached her fourteenth birthday, he sent his cousin, Sir James Hamilton, to France to deliver them to her. On 3 June Mary signed the list which acted as a receipt.

The first section of the inventory details thirty-one finger rings. Thirteen were set with diamonds, mainly table-cut, although one was faceted, and several had stones which were polished but uncut. Eleven more rings were set with rubies, four had emeralds and three had little sapphires. The second section of the list, headed 'other jewels', included buttons set with diamonds and pearls, gem-set points for fastening garments, and some interesting 'jewels' which would be worn as brooches or as pendants with jewelled collars. A black-enamelled cipher, set with five table diamonds, was probably in the form of the letters JR, for Jacobus Rex. There was a mermaid with diamonds in her tail and a mirror decorated with a Cupid and a great heart of rubies. There were a few smaller items and finally, there was James V's gold dagger, its agate haft set with emeralds, rubies, diamonds and a great unpolished sapphire. None of Mary's jewels was specified as having come from her mother. This is not surprising since Mary of Guise (q.v.) had sold or pawned almost all of her valuables to raise money for the defence of her daughter's throne against her rebellious Protestant subjects.

Most of her gems, however, had been given to her by her husband François II, his family, her Guise relatives and her friends in France. These included specially commissioned pieces like the Great Harry. Given to her by her father-in-law, Henri II (q.v.), this consisted of the letter H set with a ruby and a huge diamond. The French king had also presented her with a costly jewelled girdle from which was suspended a gem-set miniature of himself, and it was he who had provided her wedding-ring when she married his son, the dauphin, in Nôtre Dame Cathedral.

With gems such as these, it was hardly surprising that her collection was the envy of Europe. Even her uncle, the Cardinal of Lorraine, cast longing eyes on it and as she had been about to embark for Scotland he had interrupted his farewell speech to suggest that she should leave the jewels with him, for safety. Mary would have none of that, however. If he were willing to entrust her to the high seas, she replied ironically, then surely her valuables would be safe too. Before setting out she had given orders that a careful inventory was to be drawn up, and another list compiled during her first winter in Scotland tallies with it. There it is possible to read the details of the fabulous collection. The most superb pieces were the diamond and ruby necklaces with their matching collars, girdles, earrings, bracelets and finger rings. There were also sapphires and emeralds as well as turquoises, garnets, coral, lapis lazuli and the curious gold pomander beads which opened in the centre and contained little balls of perfumed musk.

There were sixteen great necklaces in all, listed in order of importance, beginning with one set with a pointed diamond, eight table diamonds and sixteen pearls, moving on to the ruby necklaces set with diamonds and pearls and including the great ropes of pearls for which Mary was famous. One had no fewer than 530 medium-sized pearls in it. There were thirteen jewelled girdles, encrusted with diamonds, rubies, pearls and semi-precious stones. One contained 206 great pearls and two were strung with pomander beads.

Collars, bracelets, hood ornaments and borders for necklines were *en suite* with the principal items, and then, of course, there were earrings and finger rings, many set with pearls, others with diamonds, rubies, emeralds and sapphires. Buttons were frequently set with gems too, and so were furs. It was the fashion for ladies to wear furs with animal heads made from some precious metal attached to them. Mary had a little marten head set with two pearls, and some small rubies and sapphires. It had four matching paws. There were also two ornamental ermines, one with a gold head enamelled white, the other with a jet head covered in gold.

James V's dagger features in the 1561 list, as do the mermaid and Cupid jewels along with an agate cameo which had also come from her father. Possibly the gold sheep enamelled white and the gold dog enamelled black and white were brooches or pendants to be worn, rather than curiosities to be kept in a cabinet. The gold perfumed apple would probably have been worn from her belt, as would have been the *Book of Hours* which was almost certainly a miniature volume. A gold apple containing a miniature of her father would also be meant for wearing. The three crystal nuts with gold figures in them and the agate nut showing 'Our Lady led by Joseph' were probably pendants, but the gold parrot and cage was more likely to be an ornament for display. Other items in that section of the list were gold plate and gold chafing (heating) dishes, cups, basins, flagons and vases.

Throughout her early years in Scotland Mary continued to add to her collection of jewels. On at least one occasion she managed to redeem an item which had belonged to her mother. Her accounts show that on 3 February 1562 she paid £1,000 to John Hume of Blackadder for a gold cross set with diamonds and rubies, 'quhilk lay in plege to him be the Quenis Grace Regent' (which had been pawned with him by the Queen Regent). Later, she paid £66 for four ounces of gold to set rubies for a collar and a pair of sleeves, and in January 1565, James Gray supplied her with pearls, which may have been Scottish – they were being harvested in the River Tay at the time. A list of 1566 refers to an emerald and a ruby and pearl pendant which she had bought 'recently'.

The 1566 list is of particular interest because it formed part of the will that she drew up as she waited in Edinburgh Castle for the birth of her son James. What she did was to annotate an existing inventory, indicating the bequests of her various jewels. If she died in childbirth, and the baby survived, everything was to go to the child. If they both died, the collection would be divided. The most valuable pieces, including the Great Harry, would go to the Scottish crown to become the property of future kings and queens in memory of herself and the alliance between Scotland and the House of Lorraine.

Apart from that major gift, there were dozens of lesser bequests to her French and Scottish relatives. Her uncle, the cardinal, would have to be content with the fine emerald ring which she had recently bought. Other relatives in France would receive rings too. Her father-in-law, the Earl of Lennox (q.v.), was to have an enamelled diamond ring and his wife would have a faceted diamond ring. She intended her half-brother, Lord Moray, to have a ring with a pointed diamond. His wife would receive a set of filigree gold beads and there were small bequests to their children. Her faithful supporter, the Earl of Bothwell, was to have a table diamond set in a black enamelled ring, and his wife, the countess, would be given a coif set with rubies, garnets and pearls and a fine pair of detachable sleeves.

Although Mary and Darnley were on far from friendly terms, he was not overlooked. Twenty-five items were left to him, mostly minor, such as jewelled buttons and points, but she also left him a diamond ring enamelled in red. 'It was with this that I was married', she wrote, 'I leave it to the King, who gave it to me'. In similar manner, a jewel containing ten rubies and a pearl, that the murdered David Rizzio had given to her, was left to his brother Joseph. Her ladies, equerries, Captain of the Guard and other members of her inner household were remembered too.

As it happened, both Mary and the infant prince survived. When she surrendered at Carberry and was taken to Lochleven castle, many of her possessions were left behind at Holyrood and, despite her repeated pleas, never restored to her. That she did retain at least one pair of pearl earrings, we learn from her account of her escape from the island fortress. When her accomplices knew that everything was ready for her secret departure, they sent a servant to her with one of the earrings, telling her that it had been found in another room. This being the pre-arranged signal, Mary hurried away to disguise herself in an old red kirtle.

The very day before, six rows of Mary's beautiful pearls, strung like a rosary, were being displayed before Queen Elizabeth in London, along with individual pearls the size of grapes. The Earl of Moray had appropriated all Mary's jewels he could lay his hands on, given some to his wife, and was selling others. Catherine de Medici was interested in the famous black pearls, but Elizabeth outbid her and they became part of the English royal collection. The other gems were dispersed and most of them have vanished with the passage of the centuries. The rosary she wore at her execution is carefully preserved in Arundel Castle, the Royal Museum of Scotland has a short string of the gold filigree beads, her signet ring is in the British Museum and a beautiful sapphire ring is on display at Lennoxlove (Lethington), tantalising reminders of the magnificent jewellery once worn by Scotland's tragic queen.

Appendix 5

Royal Revenge

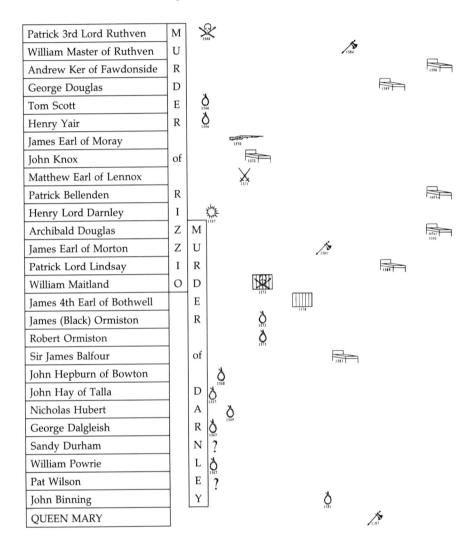

Patrick 3rd Lord Ruthven	M		
William Master of Ruthven	U		
Andrew Ker of Fawdonside	R		
George Douglas	D		
Tom Scott	E		
Henry Yair	R		
James Earl of Moray			
John Knox	of		
Matthew Earl of Lennox			
Patrick Bellenden	R		
Henry Lord Darnley	I		
Archibald Douglas	Z	M	
James Earl of Morton	Z	U	
Patrick Lord Lindsay	I	R	
William Maitland	O	D	
James 4th Earl of Bothwell		E	
James (Black) Ormiston		R	
Robert Ormiston			
Sir James Balfour		of	
John Hepburn of Bowton			
John Hay of Talla		D	
Nicholas Hubert		A	
George Dalgleish		R	
Sandy Durham		N	
William Powrie		L	
Pat Wilson		E	
John Binning		Y	
QUEEN MARY			

⚔	Died of Disease	🪓	Beheaded	▰	Assassinated
✕	Killed in Battle	▥	Died in Prison	🛏	Died Peacefully
⚵	Hanged and Quartered	💥	Blown up	?	Disappeared

The foregoing table endeavours to show what became of most of the major, and
some of the minor, characters involved in the Rizzio and Darnley murders. For a
variety of reasons, the list is incomplete, and in some cases, of dubious accuracy.
For instance, the records of criminal trials for the period around 1573 are lost, so
it is impossible to be absolutely certain that both the Ormistons met their deaths
that year. It is also difficult to ascertain whether (if they were executed) they were
beheaded or hanged and quartered, although in the light of their social status, the
latter seems more likely.

'Drawing' (disembowelling), in addition to hanging and quartering, was much
less common in Scotland, than it was in England, where the practice was probably
inherited from the Normans. Generally the Scots adopted a more civilised attitude
towards the disposal of their unwanted citizens. The practice of quartering was,
of course, enthusiastically carried out, as was the distribution of fragments of the
late offenders to distant population centres. In the days before the establishment
of a police force, it was thought that the glimpse of a dismembered head or leg,
over the gates of a town, would encourage a visiting potential wrong-doer to
moderate his behaviour.

Normally, unlike in England, it was no part of the scheme of things in Scotland,
to prolong the condemned person's suffering unduly. It is true that after the
assassination of James I in 1437, his murderers were treated with extreme savagery
and tortured to death – a process that took several days. But the punishments were
orchestrated by his widow, Johanna Beaufort, who was of course English, and this
was an isolated incident.

The main exceptions to the general rule of shortening, or at least not officiously
prolonging suffering, were manifested in the procedures adopted towards convicted heretics and witches. They were almost always sentenced to be burned at
the stake, an event that could last several hours, although well-wishers sometimes
helped shorten the agony by giving the victim polks of gunpowder to be concealed
about the person. This was by no means always effective especially in wet weather
(as in the cases of Patrick Hamilton and George Wishart). These events, however,
were pseudo-religious phenomena, by no means peculiar to Scotland. Witchcraft
in particular, from time immemorial, has been treated with the utmost illogical
barbarity, probably born of ignorance and fear. There are reports of a suspected
witch being burnt in Switzerland as recently as 1927.

In any case, the total number of sentences of death, passed for all offences, during
Mary Stewart's six years of personal rule in Scotland, were a mere fraction of the
number passed in England in the five years under Mary Tudor. It is, however,
important to view the subject in perspective – the total amount of blood shed and
human suffering experienced in all the judicial executions in Scotland and England,
aggregated together over the second half of the sixteenth century, was probably
roughly equivalent to the goings-on during any one of many bad afternoons in
Moscow's Lubianka Prison in the 1960s and 70s. Official figures have been sought,
but are so far not forthcoming.

As regards Rizzio's and Darnley's murders, several inferences may be made
from the table – for instance, it suggests that retribution was likely to come
sooner, and with more certainty, to those who contributed towards the murder of
the king than to those involved in the killing of the royal favourite. The sample is,
of course, statistically too small for firm conclusions to be drawn but it is surprising how few of those involved, are known to have lived longer than Mary herself.
Despite the fact that she died before she was forty-five, only five out of the
twenty-seven of them definitely survived her – and only two of the regicides out
of sixteen. It would be difficult, perhaps impossible, to compare detection and
conviction rates for the sixteenth century with those of the twentieth. The table
does, however, indicate that, in the time of Queen Mary, to a much greater degree
than today, those who lived violently had a high chance of dying similarly. The
list which follows makes no claim to be complete but does shed a certain amount
of light on the subsequent careers (if any) of some of those involved in either or
both of the two murders.

ASSASSINS

BALFOUR, SIR JAMES, of PITTENDREICH (c. 1525–83)
See main biographies.

BINNING, JOHN (?-1581)
Servant of Archibald Douglas, Parson of Glasgow, he was with his master at Kirk
o' Field on the night of Darnley's murder. He was not brought to justice until
1581, but was then tried, found guilty and hanged and quartered the same year.

BELLENDEN, SIR PATRICK, of STENNES and EVIE (c. 1535–1607)
Patrick was the son of Thomas Bellenden and brother of John Bellenden, both
Justice-clerks. Through his relationship to Adam Bothwell, Bishop of Orkney, his
first cousin, he acquired Evie and Stennes and became Sheriff of Orkney, but also
held office in Edinburgh as Clerk of the Coquet.

In March 1566, he was involved in Rizzio's murder but received remission in
December of the same year. He was married to Katherine Kennedy, lived to a
great age and was probably the last survivor of the murderers. He died in the
Canongate in 1607, heavily in debt; the only item specifically mentioned in his
inventory of goods was 'ane brewing cauldron – £40'.

DALGLEISH, GEORGE (?-1567)
Dalgleish was the tailor to the fourth Earl of Bothwell. He was imprisoned in Edinburgh Castle and made confessions under torture about the Darnley murder. It
was he who produced the silver casket but his interrogators asked him no questions about it, concentrating instead on the events on the night of the murder. He
was hanged and quartered.

DOUGLAS, ARCHIBALD, PARSON of GLASGOW (?-1600+)
Younger brother of William Douglas of Whittinghame and grandson of the second
Earl of Morton, he was an ecclesiastical careerist who held various benefices. He
was Parson of Douglas, Parson of Glasgow, Subdean of Orkney and Parson of
Newlands. He became an extraordinary Lord of Session in 1565 and an ordinary
Lord in 1568. After the Rizzio murder, Douglas was forfeited but had remission in
December 1566. He was present at Darnley's murder, and carelessly 'tint his mwlis'
(lost his slippers) at the scene of the crime.

   After the murder, he was a supporter of the queen. When he was restored to the
Parsonage of Glasgow in 1571, after forfeiture, the Kirk made difficulties about
admitting him. He was however accepted on the grounds that there was no
question of him serving as a minister, and that half the Lords of Session had to be
nominal or titular clerics. Escheated in 1581 for his part in the Darnley murder, he
was restored again in 1586 and became ambassador to England. He married, after
1573, as her third husband, Jane Hepburn, sister of the Earl of Bothwell, widow
of Lord John Stewart (q.v.).

DOUGLAS, GEORGE, BISHOP of MORAY (c. 1530-1589)
See main biographies.

DOUGLAS, JAMES, 4th EARL of MORTON (c. 1516-81)
See main biographies.

DURHAM, SANDY, Master of the Prince's wardrobe (?-?)
Styled 'young Sandy', he was Alexander Durham, the younger, the elder
Alexander being the Argenter of the Royal household. He was a deviser of the plot
to kill Darnley; a party to the scheme, but not an active murderer. He is reported
as having been in the Tolbooth in September 1567 but it is not known what happened to him thereafter.

HAY, JOHN, the Younger, of TALLA (?-1567)
The eldest son of John Hay, the elder, of Talla, he was a cousin of the Hays of
Yester. He became involved in the conspiracy against Darnley on 7 February 1567.
He was escheated for the murder, to which he confessed, and hanged and quar-
tered in September 1567.

HEPBURN, JOHN, of BOWTON or BOLTON (?-1568)
An adherent and cousin of Bothwell, he was approached on 6 February 1566
with a proposal to assassinate Darnley. He at first objected but later agreed to
take part in the conspiracy and supervised the laying of the gunpowder at Kirk
o'Field. He was tried for murder, confessed and was hanged and quartered in
January 1568.

HUBERT, NICHOLAS (French Paris or Joachim), Valet (?-1569)

A Frenchman, formerly in the service of Bothwell, Hubert was a *valet de chambre* of Queen Mary by the time of Darnley's murder. He was a somewhat reluctant accomplice, but had the key to the queen's room at Kirk o' Field and helped fill it with gunpowder.

After Carberry, he fled with Bothwell to Norway, but was enticed back to Scotland and arrived in Leith in June 1569. Under torture, he gave much evidence of the events on and before the night of the murder, and was sentenced to death. Queen Elizabeth pled for a stay of execution since it was desired to interrogate him in London, but her plea arrived too late and he was hanged and quartered later that year.

KER, ANDREW, of FAWDONSIDE (?-1598)

A signatory to the Book of Discipline in 1561, he was escheated for taking part in the 'Chaseabout Raid' in 1565. Ker played a major part in Rizzio's murder in March 1566, during which he restrained the pregnant queen by placing his loaded pistol against her stomach.

He was put to the horn but had remission in December of the same year. He signed bonds to support the infant king and Regent Moray in 1569 and later. In 1574, he contracted to marry Margaret Stewart, daughter of the second Lord Ochiltree and widow of John Knox.

KNOX, JOHN (*c.* 1512–72)
See main biographies.

LENNOX, MATTHEW, 4th EARL of, (1516–71)
See main biographies.

LINDSAY of the BYRES, PATRICK LORD (1521–89)
See main biographies.

MAITLAND, WILLIAM, of LETHINGTON (1525–73)
See main biographies.

ORMISTON, SIR JAMES, of THAT ILK ('BLACK') (?-1573)
ORMISTON, ROBERT ('HOB') (?-1573)

Black Ormiston was bailiff to the fourth Earl of Bothwell (q.v.). In December 1560, he was a member of a group which detached itself from the supporters of Châtelherault (q.v.), who formed the provisional government, between the death of Mary of Guise (q.v.) and Queen Mary's return from France.

Ormiston and his uncle, Robert (Hob), were drawn into the plot against Darnley by Bothwell. They were active participators in the king's murder on 10 February 1567. James was knighted by the queen shortly afterwards and was probably with her at Carberry in June of the same year. After Mary was taken to Lochleven, he stayed with his uncle, at the Laird of Whithaugh's house in Liddesdale where Andrew Ker of Fawdonside (q.v.) was temporarily being held prisoner. Both of them were reported to have visited Mary in Carlisle after the battle of Langside in May 1568. He was in the queen's party, and excluded from the pacification of 1572.

In 1573, they were both apprehended, tried and found guilty of the murder. Sir James made a long confession to John Brand, the Minister of the Canongate, making certain statements which could be construed as implicating the queen. They were both executed in December of that year.

POWRIE, WILLIAM (?-1567)
An adherent of Bothwell, he obtained lint (fuse) from a soldier whose name he did not know and candles from a lady in the Cowgate a few hours before the explosion at Kirk o' Field. He also helped with the transportation of gunpowder from Holyrood to Darnley's lodging. He was unwise enough to warn a friend not to be found on the streets that night. This last piece of evidence, in particular, was used at his trial at which he was found guilty. He had the distinction of being the first to be hanged and quartered for Darnley's murder in July 1567.

RUTHVEN, PATRICK, third LORD (c. 1520-66)
RUTHVEN, WILLIAM, MASTER of (c. 1541-84)
See main biographies.

SCOTT, TOM, Under-Sheriff of Perth (?-1566)
An adherent of the third Lord Ruthven (q.v.), who was Hereditary Sheriff and elected Provost of Perth, Scott was one of the murderers of Rizzio. His official position of Under-Sheriff, made his crime of 'warding the Queen within Holyrood Palace' all the more reprehensible in the eyes of the court. He was hanged and quartered in August the same year.

STEWART, JAMES, EARL of MORAY (1531-70)
See main biographies.

WILSON, PAT (?-?)
An adherent of Bothwell, he helped with the transportation of the gunpowder to Kirk o' Field before Darnley's murder. After the murder, he disappeared and was never brought to justice.

YAIR, HENRY (?-1566)
Yair was once a priest but later became a retainer of the third Lord Ruthven (q.v.). He was at Holyrood on the night of Rizzio's assassination. He murdered the Dominican priest, Father Adam Black, formerly private chaplain to Mary of Guise, who was under the protection of Queen Mary, later the same night. Tried for being accessary to the Rizzio murder, he was escheated in August 1566 and hanged and quartered the same month.

Appendix 6

Royal Succession

THE SCOTTISH ROYAL SUCCESSION

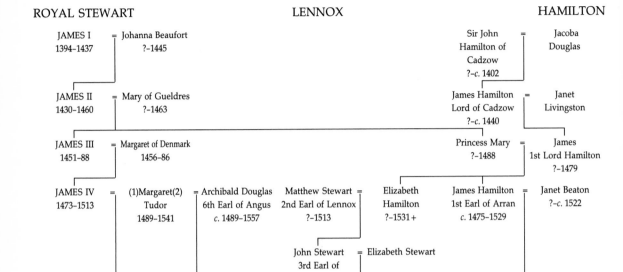

ROYAL STEWART   LENNOX   HAMILTON

JAMES I 1394–1437 = Johanna Beaufort ?–1445 — Sir John Hamilton of Cadzow ?–*c.* 1402 = Jacoba Douglas

JAMES II 1430–1460 = Mary of Gueldres ?–1463 — James Hamilton Lord of Cadzow ?–*c.* 1440 = Janet Livingston

JAMES III 1451–88 = Margaret of Denmark 1456–86 — Princess Mary ?–1488 = James 1st Lord Hamilton ?–1479

JAMES IV 1473–1513 = (1)Margaret(2) Tudor 1489–1541 = Archibald Douglas 6th Earl of Angus *c.* 1489–1557 — Matthew Stewart = Elizabeth Hamilton 2nd Earl of Lennox ?–1531+ ?–1513 — James Hamilton 1st Earl of Arran *c.* 1475–1529 = Janet Beaton ?–*c.* 1522

John Stewart 3rd Earl of Lennox ?–1526 = Elizabeth Stewart

JAMES V 1512–42 = Mary of Guise 1515–60 — Margaret Douglas[2] 1515–78 = Matthew Stewart 4th Earl of Lennox 1516–71 — James Hamilton[1] 2nd Earl of Arran *c.* 1515–75 = Margaret Douglas ?–1579+

MARY QUEEN of SCOTS 1542–87 = HENRY STEWART, LORD DARNLEY KING of SCOTS 1545–67 — James Hamilton 3rd Earl of Arran *c.* 1537–1609 — John Hamilton 1st Marquess of Hamilton *c.* 1539–1604 — Claud Hamilton 1st Baron Paisley *c.* 1544–1622

JAMES VI 1566–1625

1. James Hamilton, second Earl of Arran, and Matthew Stewart, fourth Earl of Lennox were both descended from James II through his daughter Princess Mary, who married James first Lord Hamilton. Arran was Mary's grandson, through his father the first Earl of Arran; Lennox was the grandson of her daughter Elizabeth. On the face of it, Arran had the better claim to the throne in the event of the royal Stewart line failing.

There was however a complicated suggestion that Arran's father had not been properly divorced from his first (or possibly second) wife by the time he married Arran's mother. If true, this would not only have rendered Arran illegitimate but eliminated him from the Scottish line of succession. Nonetheless, he was generally accepted (except by the Lennox faction) to be heir presumptive until the birth of Queen Mary's son.

2. Lennox's wife, Margaret Douglas, was the daughter of Henry VIII's sister, Margaret Tudor, who was also Queen Mary's grandmother. Darnley therefore, like Queen Mary, was descended from the English as well as the Scottish royal families. Both had a claim to both thrones – it is easy to see that the dynastic attraction of a marriage between them was hard to resist.

THE FRENCH ROYAL SUCCESSION

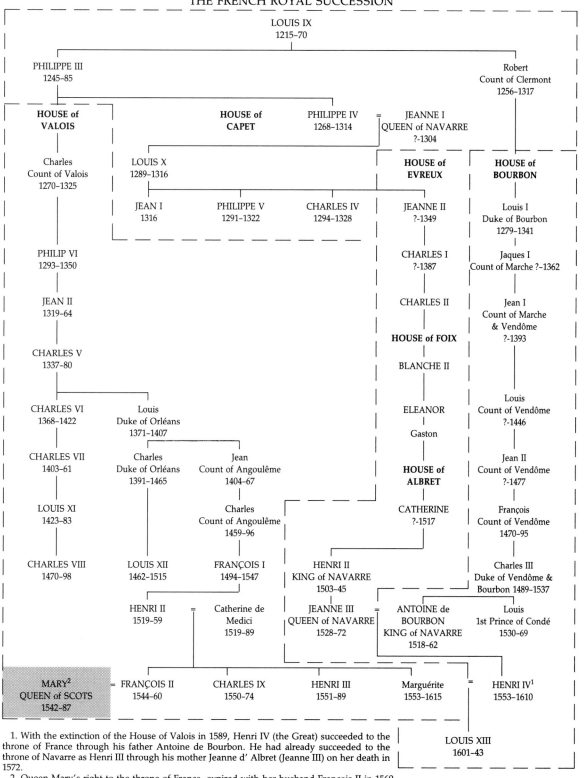

LOUIS IX
1215–70

PHILIPPE III
1245–85

Robert
Count of Clermont
1256–1317

HOUSE of VALOIS

HOUSE of CAPET

PHILIPPE IV
1268–1314 = JEANNE I
QUEEN of NAVARRE
?–1304

Charles
Count of Valois
1270–1325

LOUIS X
1289–1316

HOUSE of EVREUX

HOUSE of BOURBON

JEAN I
1316

PHILIPPE V
1291–1322

CHARLES IV
1294–1328

JEANNE II
?–1349

Louis I
Duke of Bourbon
1279–1341

PHILIP VI
1293–1350

CHARLES I
?–1387

Jaques I
Count of Marche ?–1362

JEAN II
1319–64

CHARLES II

Jean I
Count of Marche
& Vendôme
?–1393

CHARLES V
1337–80

HOUSE of FOIX

BLANCHE II

CHARLES VI
1368–1422

Louis
Duke of Orléans
1371–1407

ELEANOR

Louis
Count of Vendôme
?–1446

Gaston

CHARLES VII
1403–61

Charles
Duke of Orléans
1391–1465

Jean
Count of Angoulême
1404–67

HOUSE of ALBRET

Jean II
Count of Vendôme
?–1477

LOUIS XI
1423–83

Charles
Count of Angoulême
1459–96

CATHERINE
?–1517

François
Count of Vendôme
1470–95

CHARLES VIII
1470–98

LOUIS XII
1462–1515

FRANÇOIS I
1494–1547

HENRI II
KING of NAVARRE
1503–45

Charles III
Duke of Vendôme &
Bourbon 1489–1537

HENRI II
1519–59 = Catherine de
Medici
1519–89

JEANNE III
QUEEN of NAVARRE
1528–72 = ANTOINE de
BOURBON
KING of NAVARRE
1518–62

Louis
1st Prince of Condé
1530–69

MARY[2]
QUEEN of SCOTS
1542–87 = FRANÇOIS II
1544–60

CHARLES IX
1550–74

HENRI III
1551–89

Marguérite
1553–1615 = HENRI IV[1]
1553–1610

LOUIS XIII
1601–43

1. With the extinction of the House of Valois in 1589, Henri IV (the Great) succeeded to the throne of France through his father Antoine de Bourbon. He had already succeeded to the throne of Navarre as Henri III through his mother Jeanne d' Albret (Jeanne III) on her death in 1572.

2. Queen Mary's right to the throne of France, expired with her husband François II in 1560.

THE ENGLISH ROYAL SUCCESSION

TUDOR   **STEWART**

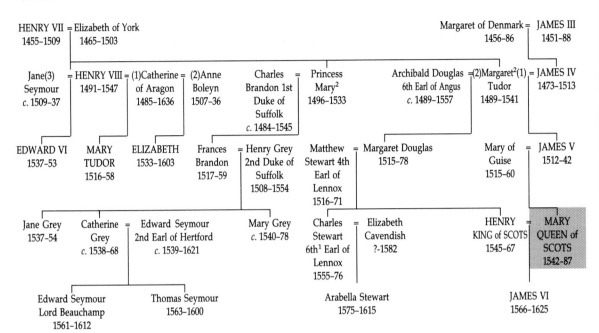

HENRY VII = Elizabeth of York   Margaret of Denmark = JAMES III
1455–1509   1465–1503   1456–86   1451–88

Jane(3) = HENRY VIII = (1)Catherine = (2)Anne   Charles = Princess   Archibald Douglas =(2)Margaret[2](1) = JAMES IV
Seymour   1491–1547   of Aragon   Boleyn   Brandon 1st Mary[2]   6th Earl of Angus   Tudor   1473–1513
c. 1509–37   1485–1636   1507–36   Duke of   1496–1533   c. 1489–1557   1489–1541
                                               Suffolk
                                               c. 1484–1545

EDWARD VI   MARY   ELIZABETH   Frances = Henry Grey   Matthew = Margaret Douglas   Mary of = JAMES V
1537–53   TUDOR   1533–1603   Brandon 2nd Duke of Stewart 4th 1515–78   Guise   1512–42
            1516–58   1517–59 Suffolk   Earl of   1515–60
                                           1508–1554   Lennox
                                                        1516–71

Jane Grey Catherine = Edward Seymour   Mary Grey   Charles = Elizabeth   HENRY = MARY
1537–54   Grey   2nd Earl of Hertford c. 1540–78 Stewart Cavendish   KING of SCOTS QUEEN of
           c. 1538–68 c. 1539–1621   6th[1] Earl of ?–1582   1545–67   SCOTS
                                                      Lennox   1542–87
                                                      1555–76

Edward Seymour   Thomas Seymour   Arabella Stewart   JAMES VI
Lord Beauchamp   1563–1600   1575–1615   1566–1625
1561–1612

1. On the death of Regent Lennox in September 1571, his title reverted to the crown, so James VI himself became the fifth Earl. In April 1572, however, James conveyed the title to his uncle Charles, who became the sixth Earl.

2. Despite their positions on the table, the descendants of Henry VIII's sister Margaret (born 1489), were closer in the line of succession to the English throne than those of her younger sister Mary (born 1496). The Stewarts (Margaret's descendants) were therefore the senior line.

Appendix 7

Sixteenth-Century Popes

ELECTED			BORN	DIED
1492 11 Aug	ALEXANDER VI	Roderigo Borgia	1431	18 Aug 1503
1503 22 Sep	PIUS III	Francesco Todeschini de Piccolomini	1439	18 Oct 1503
1503 Oct/Nov	JULIUS II	Giuliano della Rovere	1443	Jan/Mar 1513
1513 11 Mar	LEO X	Giovanni de Medici	1475	1 Dec 1521
1522	ADRIAN VI	Adrian of Utrecht	1459	14 Sep 1523
1523	CLEMENT VII	Giulio de Medici	1478	Sep 1534
1534 Oct	PAUL III	Alexander Farnese	1468	10 Nov 1549
1550	JULIUS III	Gian Maria del Monte	1487	23 Mar 1555
1555 9 Apr	MARCELLUS II	Marcellus Cervini	1501	30 Apr 1555
1555	PAUL IV	Gian Pietro Carafa	1476	18 Aug 1559
1559 26 Dec	PIUS IV	Govanni Angelo de Medici	1499	9 Dec 1565
1566 7 Jan	PIUS V	Michael Ghislieri	1504	1 May 1572
	Beatified by Clement X in 1572			
	Canonised by Clement XI in 1712			
1572 13 May	GREGORY XIII	Hugo Buoncompagni	1502	10 Apr 1585
1585 24 Apr	SIXTUS V	Felice Peretti	1521	27 Aug 1590
1590 15 Oct	URBAN VII	Giambattista Castagna	1521	27 Oct 1590
1590 Nov/Dec	GREGORY XIV	Nicholas Sfondrato	1535	16 Oct 1591
1591 29 Oct	INNOCENT IX	Gianntonio Facchinetti	1519	30 Dec 1591
1592 30 Jan	CLEMENT VIII	Ippolyto Aldobrandini	1536	3 Mar 1605
1605 1 Apr	LEO XI	Alessandro de Medici	1535	27 Apr 1605
1605 16 May	PAUL V	Camillo Borghese	1550	28 Jan 1621

GLOSSARY

ARGENTER. Financial agent, or officer having charge of money belonging to the sovereign. Argent = Silver.

ARQUEBUS (HARQUEBUS). The early type of portable gun, varying in size and supported by a hook or eye on a tripod, trestle or forked rest. The name (in German, 'hook gun') became generic for any portable firearm in the 16th century.

BAILIARY. Area under the jurisdiction of a bailie, an official who formerly operated in many rural districts, though latterly only in burghs.

CALIVER. A light kind of arquebus, fired without a rest for the weapon.

CARL. A man of the common people, particularly a husbandman; a villain; a fellow.

CATHOLIC. The word 'Catholic' is sometimes used for convenience to distinguish between the Unreformed and Reformed Church.

CHAMBERLAIN. Chief financial officer of the Scottish crown until the fifteenth century, when many of his functions went to the comptroller and the treasurer.

CLERK REGISTER. Officer responsible for the custody of the Scottish national archives, state and official papers.

COIF. A close fitting cap, covering the top, back and sides of the head, worn by both sexes, usually in conjunction with other headgear.

COLLEGE OF JUSTICE. Organisation formed when the Court of Session (q.v.) was endowed in 1532, now the collective name for the judges of the supreme civil court in Scotland. 'Senators of the College of Justice' are the Judges of the Court of Session.

COLLEGIATE CHURCH. Institution staffed by a body corporate (college) of priests, endowed for the conduct of divine service with special dignity and with the special duty of the saying of masses for the souls of the founder and his family.

COMMENDATOR. A person, not necessarily a member of a religious order, who nonetheless receives the revenues of an abbey, priory or other benefice.

COMMISSARY COURTS. Before and after the Reformation, much of the ecclesiastical jurisdiction in matrimonial and testamentary cases was vested in a Commissary Court in Edinburgh, and a number of subsidiary commissary courts throughout the country.

COMMISSIONER. A representative sent to the Scottish parliament or General Assembly, for example, from a shire or presbytery. The king's (or queen's) commissioner, or Lord High Commissioner, still takes the sovereign's place in parliament or assembly.

COMPTROLLER.   One of the two financial officers set up by James I to share with the treasurer, most of the functions previously exercised by the chamberlain.

CONGREGATION, LORDS of the.   The nobles and lairds who supported the reforming cause from 1558 onwards. The original signatories to their bond were: the Earls of Morton, Glencairn and Argyll, Lord Lorne (Argyll's son) and Erskine of Dun.

CONSTABLE.   See MARISCHAL.

COQUET.   Seal of the customs office in any royal burgh.

COURT OF SESSION.   The central civil court, which took shape in James IV's reign (See COLLEGE OF JUSTICE).

CROWN.   Usually the French gold écu or 'crown of the sun'. 1 crown ≈ 36/- Scots.

CULVERIN.   Originally a hand-gun, later a large cannon, very long in proportion to its bore (Colubrinus ≡ of the nature of a snake).

DECREET.   Decree or decision of a court.

DILIGENCE.   Collective term for processes whereby decreets of court for the enforcing of a payment or the recovery of a debt were made effective.

ELL or EL.   Unit of length, varying in different countries. 1 English ell = 45 inches; 1 Scottish ell = 37.2 inches.

ESCHEAT.   Confiscate in favour of the crown.

FENCIBLE.   A soldier, liable for service only in his home area for defensive duties.

FORFEIT.   Confiscate (usually heritable property as a penalty for treason).

GETT.   Bastard (originally any child; from 'get' or 'beget').

GOLDEN ROSE.   Ornament blessed by the Pope on the Fourth Sunday in Lent, sent as a mark of special favour to some individual or community. William the Lion, James III and Queen Mary all received it.

GREAT SEAL.   The king's principal seal, used to authenticate Crown Charters and Letters Patent. First known in 1094 and still in use.

HALBERD.   A combined spear and battle-axe.

HOAST (HOST, WHOAST etc.).   Coughing or a cough.

HORNING.   Legal process of technical outlawry (by blasts of the horn by the messenger), whereby the property of the offender could be confiscated by the crown, and (sometimes) made available to the creditors.

ISLES, LORDSHIP of the. Organisation of the Western Isles which took shape in the fourteenth century, but did not become official until the fifteenth and was annexed by the crown in 1493.

JUSTICE CLERK. Originally the clerk of the central criminal court, but later a judge, and more recently the second-in-command of the High Court of Justiciary.

JUSTICE DEPUTE. A deputy of the Justice General.

JUSTICE GENERAL. The chief judge of the High Court of Justiciary, an office now combined with that of Lord President of the Court of Session.

LAIRD. Landowner without a title of nobility.

LEGATE (LEGATUS) a LATERE. A prelate given special powers by the Pope – literally 'from the Pope's side'. The title was sometimes conferred on Scottish archbishops.

LIVRE. 2.25 livres ≈ 1 crown (q.v.).

LORD (KING'S) ADVOCATE. Crown Prosecutor; the principal law officer of the crown in Scotland.

LORD OF SESSION. A judge of the Court of Session (q.v.).

LORDS OF THE ARTICLES. A committee of parliament consisting of members drawn from all estates and the officers of state, which prepared business for the full house.

LYON KING OF ARMS. Chief officer of arms of Scotland, the official in control of Scottish heraldry and state ceremonial.

MARISCHAL. Officer with high military functions, hereditary in the Keith family from the time of Robert I. On the death of the tenth Earl Marischal in 1778, the comparable title of constable largely absorbed it and has been vested in the Hay family with the Earls and Countesses of Erroll ever since.

MERK. Two-thirds of a £ Scots (13/4d).

POLK or POCK. Bag or pouch. Sometimes an indeterminate unit of volumetric measurement.

POUND SCOTS. £5 Scots ≈ £1 Sterling.

PRECENTOR. Chantor; the canon or member of the chapter responsible for the music; the leader of the singing in churches without organs.

PRECEPT. Writ commanding an officer to take legal action.

PRIVY COUNCIL. The official body consisting of high officers of state and others, presided over by the chancellor. Subject to parliamentary ratification, it exercised judicial, legislative and executive power.

PRIVY SEAL. Dating from the time of Alexander III, it was used for precepts, commanding the keeper of the Great Seal to prepare and authenticate charters, and for various gifts of pensions, appointments to offices, presentations to benefices etc. Discontinued 1898.

RECTOR. University official, nowadays elected by the students.

REGENT. 1. Ruler on behalf of an infant or incapacitated monarch.
  2. University teacher, who conducts a class of students throughout their entire academic curriculum, as distinct from a professor who teaches only one subject.

REMISSION. Pardon.

SASINES, GENERAL REGISTER OF. Finally organised in 1617, the record of all transactions in heritable property in Scotland.

SILVER CASKET. Fifteenth century parcel gilt (jewellery) box given by the Dauphin to Queen Mary on their marriage. Alleged to have contained incriminating letters from her to Bothwell. Originals have vanished and only copies (probably forged or concocted) exist.

STEWARD (STEWART). The office of Steward of the Scottish Kings dates back to the twelfth century. It became hereditary in the family of Fitzalan of Breton origin, whose surname in due course became Stewart. The Stewart dynasty ruled Scotland (and later Britain) from 1371 to 1714.

STICK. Stab (usually to death).

SUPERINTENDENT. Diocesan overseer immediately after the Reformation, with the administrative, but not the sacramental, powers of a bishop.

TEINDS. Tithes (literally: tenths).

THIRDS OF BENEFICES. From January 1562, all holders of benefices had to remit one third of their revenues to the crown, which used this mainly for its own needs and partly to pay stipends to the reformed clergy. The system operated until early in the seventeenth century.

WRITERS TO THE SIGNET. The Signet Seal was the personal royal seal, which dates from the fourteenth century and was applied by the monarch to authenticate documents in which he was specially interested. It came to be appropriated to the use of the Court of Session. The solicitors who practised there, and by whom Signet writs were prepared, were incorporated as a Society of Writers to the Signet.

Bibliography

'Mary, Queen of Scots has been far too much written about by non-historians.' These daunting words were written by A.L. Rowse in his introduction to Professor Gordon Donaldson's short but penetrating *Mary Queen of Scots* (English Universities Press, 1974). It is true that more than 400 books have been written on the subject from many different viewpoints. Of those written before the Second World War, most are highly indigestible – almost unreadable to the modern reader. There are however at least eight exceptions.

In 1840, Alexandre Dumas published his *Marie Stuart*, drawing much from Brantôme and other contemporary writers. An English translation by Douglas Munro was published in 1975 by Blackie and Son. The historical accuracy is as questionable as his spelling of the queen's name but the book merits attention if only for the excellent translation and the superb prose.

Three books published around the turn of the century, David Hay Fleming's *The Life of Queen Mary from her Birth to her Flight into England* (Hodder and Stoughton, 1897), Andrew Lang's *The Mystery of Mary Stuart* (Longmans, Green and Co, 1901) and T.F. Henderson's *Life of Mary* (Hutchinson, 1905) advance opposing views on the authenticity of the casket letters. Intriguingly, in the 1911 reprint of his book, Andrew Lang indicates in an author's note that he had entirely changed his views as to the authenticity of at least one of the letters, partially as a result of reading T.F. Henderson's work.

Between the wars, General Mahon in *The Tragedy of Kirk o' Field* (Cambridge University Press, 1930) suggested that the gunpowder plot was directed by Darnley against Mary instead of the other way round. In the later 1930s, three books all entitled simply *Mary Queen of Scots* came out, Eric Linklater's slender offering (Dennis Dobson, 1933), distinguished by his superb use of the English language, Marjorie Bowen's compelling but contentious work (Bodley Head, 1934) and Stefan Zweig's account (Ebenezer Baylis and Son Ltd, 1935) notable for its deep psychological insight. Robert Gore-Brown's book *Lord Bothwell* (Collins, 1937) took

General Mahon's theories a stage further, suggesting that there were not two but three groups of conspirators at Kirk o' Field although this postulation does not have much support today.

After the Second World War, Maurice Lee's *James Stewart, Earl of Moray* (Columbia University Press, 1953) gave an interesting insight on the period as seen through the eyes of Mary's half-brother. Dr Armstrong Davison's *Casket Letters* (Vision Press, 1965) was an argument for Mary's innocence, and as a qualified medical practitioner, he was able to shed much light on ailments and diseases prevalent at the time. George Malcolm Thomson, in *The Crime of Mary Stuart* (Hutchinson, 1967), carried out an interesting exercise in retrospective investigative journalism, and came to the conclusion that if Mary had no complicity in the plot to blow up her husband, her conduct at the time is inexplicable.

Then came the book on Mary by which all others are judged, Lady Antonia Fraser's *Mary, Queen of Scots* (Weidenfeld and Nicholson, 1969). This massive and scholarly work of over a quarter of a million words is the best full-length study of Mary so far. Meanwhile Professor Donaldson had been hard at work producing several learned books about the period. *Scotland: James V–VII* (Oliver and Boyd, 1965) and *Scottish Kings* (Batsford, 1967) and of course *Mary, Queen of Scots* (already referred to) give a good background to the period and are easily digestible by the non-historian. His *The Scottish Reformation* (Cambridge University Press, 1960), *The First Trial of Mary Queen of Scots* (Batsford, 1969) and *All the Queen's Men* (Batsford, 1983) are somewhat heavier but nonetheless required reading for serious students of Queen Mary.

In 1974, Donaldson wrote what is possibly the best book for those trying to understand how Scotland has evolved into the country it is today: *Scotland: The Shaping of a Nation* (David and Charles – revised and extended 1980). A very close runner-up, if not its equal was, Professor Smout's *A History of the Scottish People 1560–1830* (Collins, 1969), although it dealt with a more limited period.

The quatercentenary of Mary's death, 1988, heralded something of a publishing boom. Dr Rosalind Marshall's beautifully illustrated and well written *Queen of Scots* (HMSO, 1986) does much to capture the imagination although, sadly, it has no index. David and Judy Steel's *Mary Stuart's Scotland* (Weidenfeld and Nicholson, 1987) is likewise lavishly illustrated but covers no new ground. Margaret H. B. Sanderson's *Mary Stewart's People* (James Thin, 1987) is diligently researched and paints a fascinating picture of what it was like to live in the time of Queen Mary.

The Scottish National Portrait Gallery brought out two excellent little books in 1987 in connection with exhibitions that were being mounted that year. *The Queen's World* by Dr David Caldwell and Dr Rosalind Marshall is illustrated with tapestries, furniture, jewellery, pictures and other artefacts that Mary would have recognised. The rather more substantial *The Queen's Image* by Helen Smailes and Dr Duncan Thomson (the curator of the gallery) contains paintings, woodcuts, lithographs, coins and drawings, contemporary and later, depicting Mary and the more dramatic incidents of her life.

David Breeze's *A Queen's Progress* (HMSO, 1987) is also beautifully illustrated and seeks (successfully) to draw attention to the importance of the architectural settings in which she lived. The following year, Jenny Wormald, in her provocative (in the best sense of the word) *Mary Queen of Scots – A Study in Failure* (George Philip, 1988) amazingly suggests, among other things, that Mary was 'someone born to supreme power who was wholly unable to cope with its responsibilities'. She is, however, humble enough to say that she does not expect every historian to agree with her and the book, clearly one of interpretation rather than description, commands respect. Later that year, *Mary Stewart – Queen in Three Kingdoms* (Blackwell, 1988) appeared; an interesting group of essays by eminent historians. Contributors include Professor Ian B. Cowan and Dr Michael Lynch, who also edited the collection.

This bibliography would not be complete without allusion to several invaluable reference books. The classic *Jamieson's Dictionary of the Scottish Language* (Alexander Gardener of Paisley, 1912) has to a degree been superseded by the scholarly *The Concise Scots Dictionary*, edited by Mairi Robinson (Aberdeen University Press, 1985). Gordon Donaldson and Robert S. Morpeth brought out *Who's Who in Scottish History* (Basil Blackwell, 1973) and *A Dictionary of Scottish History* (John Donald, 1977) which are both invaluable works. Finally, *Lines of Succession* by Jiří Louda and Michael MacLagan (Orbis Publishing, 1981), apart from being a joy to read because of the superb heraldic artistry, is an invaluable reference book for anyone seeking to understand the inter-relationship of the various European royal families.

It is hoped that this bibliography will prompt the reader to seek more, whether it be the recent books, which are readily available, or the yellowed volumes and papers on dusty shelves in libraries and private collections. It may just be that someone reading these words will one day uncover a document which will further clarify our understanding of Queen Mary and the part she played in one of the most fascinating stories in history.

O Lord God,

Give them according to their deeds,

and according to the wickedness of their endeavours;

give them according to the work of their hands,

render to them their deserts.

Attrib: Bourgoin, Fotheringhay, 1587

INDEX

298

INDEX of PLACES, Illustrations in bold

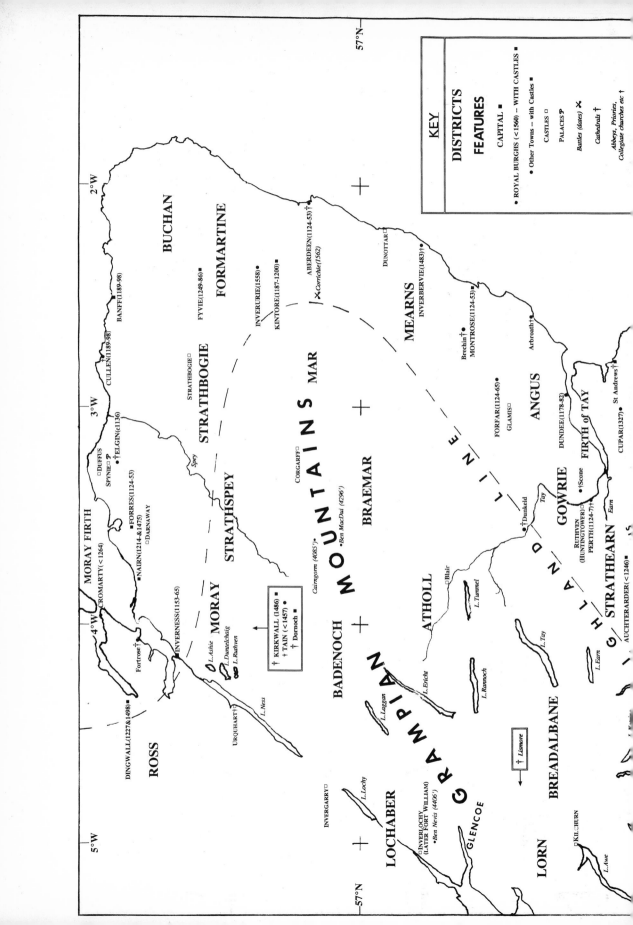